Digital Diversities

Digital Diversities: Social Media and Intercultural Experience

Edited by

Garry Robson and Małgorzata Zachara

With a Preface by Zygmunt Bauman

CAMBRIDGE
SCHOLARS
PUBLISHING

Digital Diversities: Social Media and Intercultural Experience,
Edited by Garry Robson and Malgorzata Zachara

This book first published 2014

Cambridge Scholars Publishing

12 Back Chapman Street, Newcastle upon Tyne, NE6 2XX, UK

British Library Cataloguing in Publication Data
A catalogue record for this book is available from the British Library

ISBN (10): 1-4438-6129-4, ISBN (13): 978-1-4438-6129-8

TABLE OF CONTENTS

Acknowledgements viii

Preface ix
Zygmunt Bauman

Introduction 1
Garry Robson and Malgorzata Zachara

Part I: The Digitalization of the Self and its Discontents

Chapter One 12
"You Are Forced to Be Who You Are": Embodiment and Social Media in Intercultural Experience
Garry Robson

Chapter Two 35
Mindful Rejection of Digital Technology at the User Level: Cognitive Determinants and Social Consequences
C.M. Olavarria

Chapter Three 54
In Quest of (Posthuman) Togetherness: Digital Communication and Affective Disconnection
Marek Wojtaszek

Part II: New Negotiations of Mobility, Place and Intercultural Experience

Chapter Four 74
Meaningful Connections: Digital Media, Social Networks and the Experience of Space and Place
Agnieszka Stasiewicz-Bienkowska

Chapter Five 91
Every Minute of Every Day: Mobilities, Multiculture and Time
Yasmin Gunaratnam and Les Back

Part III: 'Digital Natives' and Cosmopolitanism in 'Real' and 'Virtual' Worlds

Chapter Six 120
Negotiating Cultural Difference in the Digital Communication Era:
A Qualitative Pilot Study of Technology and Student Experience
David J Gunkel

Chapter Seven.. 144
Going Native: The Real Problem in Theorising the Communicative
Interaction of Digital Natives
Ann Gunkel

Chapter Eight... 164
Digital Natives, Facebook and Becoming a Global Citizen:
The Possibility of Using Facebook to Help Students Become
Ready for a Globalized World
Anne L. Bizub

Chapter Nine.. 182
Cosmopolitanism Online and Offline: Social Media and Polish
Students in Europe
Jolanta Szymkowska-Bartyzel

Chapter Ten 199
The Difference That Makes No Difference: How the Internet Evens
Cultures by Ignoring Them
Ciro Marcondes Filho

Part IV: Shaping Political Identities and Narratives through Social Media

Chapter Eleven 212
Private Voices of Public Diplomacy: How Digital Technology Shapes
the Image of States and Societies
Malgorzata Zachara

Chapter Twelve 230
Discursive Crossings and the Emergence of a Multiple Political Self in Social Media
Jasmin Siri

Chapter Thirteen 246
Unification of Discourses of Social Media during the *Gezi* Resistance
Irem Inceoglu

Chapter Fourteen 256
Narrating Digital Shoah Memory on YouTube
Alina Bothe

Part V: Digitalising Human Fundamentals across Cultures

Chapter Fifteen 274
Friendship in a Digital Age: Aristotelian and Narrative Perspectives
Douglas Ponton

Chapter Sixteen 296
E-Obituary and *E-Nekrolog* as Emergent Online Genres: A Contrastive Study
Magdalena Sczczyrbak

Contributors 314

Index 316

ACKNOWLEDGEMENTS

The editors would like to express their gratitude to The Polish National Science Centre (NCN), which sponsored the research project from which this book is derived with a grant from its *Harmonia* programme. Thanks are due Jola Szymkowska-Bartyzel, Ann Gunkel, David Gunkel and Agnieszka Stasiewicz-Bienkowska for their ideas, committed support and invaluable assistance in the completion of this book. We are also very grateful to Fred Dervin for his encouragement and guidance and, at Cambridge Scholars Publishing, Caroline Koulikourdi and Amanda Millar for their assistance in the commissioning and production of this work.

PREFACE

ZYGMUNT BAUMAN

We – each one of us – live now, intermittently though quite often simultaneously, in two universes: online and offline. The second of the two is frequently dubbed "the real world," though the question whether such a label fits it better than it does the first turns more debatable by the day.

The two universes differ sharply – by the worldview they inspire, the skills they require and the behavioural code they patch together and promote. Their differences can be, and indeed are, negotiated – but hardly reconciled. It is left to every person immersed in both of those universes (and that means to all and each of us) to resolve the clashes between them and draw the boundaries of the applicability of each one of the two mutually contradictory codes. But the experience derived from one universe cannot but affect the way the other universe is viewed, evaluated and moved through. There tends to be a constant and always heavy border traffic between the two universes.

One way of narrating the story of the modern era (a way whose pertinence and relevance was made particularly salient by the enthusiastic reception and spectacular, lightning-speed career of informatics technology) is to present it as a chronicle of a war declared on all and any discomfort, inconvenience or displeasure, and of the promise to fight such a war through to the final victory. In that story, the massive migration of souls in not the bodies from the offline world to the newly discovered online lands can be seen as the latest and most decisive among departures and developments; after all, that battle currently has been waged on the field of inter-human relations - a territory heretofore most resistant and defiant to all attempts to flatten and smooth its bumpy roads and straighten its twisted passages, as is aimed at the cleansing that territory of the traps and ambushes with which it has been thus far notoriously been spattered. If won, the battle currently waged may render childishly easy the awkward and unwieldy tasks of tying and breaking human bonds, having liberated them first from the incapacitating burden of long-term commitments and non-negotiable obligations.

The modern war on inconvenience, discomfort, unwelcome surprises and all in all on the haunting feeling of uncertainty deriving from the unpredictable caprices of the natural and social world, was started in earnest under the impact of the shock caused by the triple catastrophe (an earthquake followed by fire followed by tsunami) that in 1755 destroyed Lisbon, then one of the richest, most admired and proudest centres of European civilization. That shock prompted the need to take nature as well as human history under a new, this time human and guided by Reason, management. Two and a half centuries later Jonathan Franzen suggested in his rightly praised commencement speech at Kenyon College[1] that the "ultimate goal of technology, the telos of techneis to replace a natural world that's indifferent to our wishes – a world of hurricanes and hardships and breakable hearts, a world of resistance – with a world so responsive to our wishes as to be, effectively, a mere extension of the self." "Our technology has become extremely adept at creating products that correspond to our fantasy ideal of erotic relationship, in which the beloved object asks for nothing and gives everything, instantly, and makes us feel all-powerful, and doesn't throw terrible scenes when it's replaced by an even sexier object and is consigned to a drawer." In other words: are old dreams now coming true, are words becoming flesh? Is the centuries-long war on life discomforts about to be won? Well, the jury (if there is a jury competent to pronounce verdicts) must be still out. Because there is a price-tag attached to each successive spoil of war, gains and losses need to be counted - but reason suggests that the balance of gains and losses ought to be calculated *retrospectively*; the time for competent retrospection (let alone for ultimate evaluation) has however not yet arrived.

Alain Finkielkraut, a writer/philosopher newly elected to join the small exquisite company of the "Immortals" of Academie Française, speaks of the "malediction" of the Internet.[2] "No doubt, it (the Internet) offers tremendous services (...) Researchers, academics, are delighted – they don't have to go to libraries, the journalists can fill their files on invited guests much faster, etc. I however believe that in the universe of

---

[1] Quoted after the *New York Times* of 28 May 2011.

[2] Quoted after "TAISEZ-VOUS !" – Alain Finkielkraut, "l'homme qui ne sait pas comment ne pas réagir," *Le Monde* of 10th April 2014 : "Bien entendu ça rend énormément de services (...). Les chercheurs, les universitaires sont ravis, ils ne sont pas obligés d'aller en bibliothèque, les journalistes aussi peuvent constituer leurs dossiers beaucoup plus vite quand ils invitent des gens, etc. Mais je crois, moi, que dans cet univers de la communication, tout peut être dit (...). C'est quand même un monde sans foi ni loi. Il est interdit d'interdire, on le voit sur Internet (...)."

communication everything can be said (...) All the same, it is a world with no faith and no law. It is prohibited to prohibit, as seen on the Internet." The Internet: blessing and curse rolled into one and rendered inseparable...

The Internet's blessings are many and varied. In addition to the ones Finkielkraut has mentioned by name, let me name as the first and foremost the promise to put paid to one of the most awesome banes of our liquid-modern, thoroughly individualized society afflicted by the endemic frailty of inter-human bonds: the fear of loneliness, of abandonment, of exclusion. On Facebook, one needs never more feel alone or dropped, discarded, eliminated – abandoned to stew in one's own juice having one's [illegible] companion. There is always twenty four hours a day and seven days a week, someone somewhere ready to receive a message and even respond to it or at least acknowledge its reception. On Twitter, one never needs to feel excluded from where things happen and the action is: there are no gatekeepers guarding and most of the time barring to most people the entry to the public stage. One does not need to rely on the sparsely apportioned grace and benevolence of TV or radio producers and/or newspapers or glossy magazines editors. The gate to the public stage seems to stay, invitingly and temptingly, wide open, supplemented with a counter of visits and "likes" – that privately owned equivalent of TV ratings, bestsellers tables or the tables of box-office returns. Thanks to the Internet, everyone has been given the chance of the proverbial 15 minutes of fame - and the occasion to hope for a public celebrity status. Both appear easy and near-to-hand as they never did in the past. And the attraction of becoming a celebrity is to have a name and likeness turning more worthy in our world made to the measure of a vanity fair than one's achievement.

These, no doubt, are blessings. Or at least they are deemed, and for good reasons, to be blessings by millions of people sagging and groaning under the burden of abasement and humiliation visited upon them by social degradation or exclusion - or the fear of their coming. Such a gain is huge enough to outweigh the possible losses brought by the constantly growing number of hours spent online by the constantly growing numbers of the Earth's inhabitants. And let's note that in most cases Internet users and addicts are blissfully unaware of what things and qualities they are in danger of losing or what has been lost already - as they had little or no chance of experiencing them personally and coming to value them; the younger generations of the present were born into a world already split (and since times for them immemorial) into its online and offline domains. But what are those losses - recorded or anticipated?

To start with, there are losses afflicting (or suspected to afflict) our mental faculties; first of all, the qualities/capacities thought indispensable to set a site needed by reason and rationality to be deployed and come into their own: attention, concentration, patience - and their durability. When connection to the Internet takes as long as a minute, many of us feel angry about how slow our computer is. We are becoming used to expecting immediate effects. We desire a world to be more and more like instant coffee: just mix powder into water and drink your coffee... We are losing patience, but great accomplishments require great patience. One needs to stand up to the obstacles encountered, the odds one did not anticipate though they confuse one's plans or arrest their fulfilment. Much research has been devoted to this issue, and most results show the attention span, ability to prolonged concentration - and altogether the perseverance, endurance and fortitude, those defining marks of patience - all falling, and rapidly. Academic teachers note that their students find it increasingly difficult to read an article (let alone a book) from the beginning to end. An argument demanding consistent attention over more than a few minutes tends to be abandoned well before its conclusion is reached. "Multitasking" tends nowadays to be the widely preferred strategy in the use of the web with its ever more numerous apps and gadgets, vying for a moment of (even if passing) attention; given the enormity of opportunities, fixing attention to one single screen at a time feels as if a reprehensible waste of priceless time.

There are of course indirect yet collateral casualties of such a run of affairs, not yet counted in full and needing more research to evaluate. Among the best scrutinized while also potentially most harmful damages caused by the wilting and accelerated scattering of attention are however the decay and gradual decrepitude of the willingness to listen and of comprehension powers as well as the determination to "go to the heart of the matter" (in the online world, we are expected to "surf" on visually or audibly conveyed information; the metaphor of swimming would suggest something resented for being more time-consuming as well as calling for deeper immersion and more engagement - like "swimming") - which in turn leads to a steady decline in the skills of dialogue, a form of communication vital in the offline world. Closely related to the trends just described is the potential harm to memory, now increasingly transferred and entrusted to servers rather than stored in brains. As the process of thinking (and creative thinking in particular) relies on connections emerging between brain cells, it cannot but suffer from storing information in servers instead. As John Steinbeck is reputed to have said well before the servers were built in Mojave deserts and cloud Internet invented: ideas are like rabbits; you get a couple, learn how to handle them and pretty soon you have a dozen. We may add: indeed, unless that handling consists in depositing them in warehouses to prevent burdening your brain.

Next to consider is the likely impact on the nature of human bonds. Tying and breaking bonds online is immensely easier and less risky than it is offline. Tying them there does not entail long term obligations, let alone the "till death do us part, for better or worse" style commitments, it does not require so much of the protracted, toilsome and conscientious labour that offline bonds demand; in case all that proves too complex and onerous and the odds are felt overwhelming, it is easy to withdraw and abandon the effort. Breaking bonds, on the other hand, can be done with pressing some keys and desisting to touch some others, and calls for no awkward negotiation of settlement neither incurs the risk of Franzen's "terrible scenes" to be thrown. Selecting and reselecting a network of friends and keeping it as long as the heart desires is an achievement attained with little skill, yet less effort, and virtually (yes, virtually) without risk. As the French sociologist Jean-Claude Kaufmann[3] comments, it all feels so safe as long as one can log on with one click and log off with another; touching icons on screen one can feel, however counterfactually, in complete control of the social contacts and one's own position they imply. No wonder that having tested and compared the two kinds of bonds, many internauts, perhaps their large and growing majority, prefer the online variety to its offline alternative. Though quite a few others think that those who do it, do it to the friendship's (not to mention love's) and their own detriment... According to those others the true (difficult, alas, and risky, calling for constant care and all too often sacrifice) love is the prime whistle-blower signalling the falsehood of the pretences on which many of us sometimes try to perch our self-esteem while laboriously avoiding testing it in field action. What the electronically sterilized and whitewashed version of love truly offers is not "looking forward in the same direction" as Antoine de Saint-Exupéry famously phrased it, but bets-hedging in the effort of defending one's own self-esteem against the hazards for which the genuine article is notorious.

One more, perhaps the most contentious among the issues cropping up in the debate about the blessings and curses of the world-wide web. Universal, easy and convenient exposure to the world events in "real time," coupled with opening similarly universal, and an equally easy, undisturbed entry to the public stage has been welcomed by numerous observers as a genuine turning point in the brief though eventful and

[3] See his *Sex & Amour* (Armand Colin 2010).

stormy history of modern democracy. Contrary to quite widespread expectations that the Internet will be a great step forward in the history of democracy, involving all of us in shaping the world which we share and replacing the inherited "pyramid of power" with a "lateral" politics– evidence accumulates that the Internet may serve as well the perpetuation and reinforcement of conflicts and antagonisms while preventing an effective polylogue with a chance of armistice and eventual agreement. Paradoxically, the danger arises from the inclination of most internauts to make the online world a conflict-free zone; though not through negotiating the conflict-generating issues and the conflicts being resolved to mutual satisfaction - but thanks to the removal of the conflicts haunting the offline world from their sight and worry...

Numerous researches have shown that Internet-dedicated users can and do spend a great part of their time or even their whole online life encountering solely like-minded people. The Internet creates an improved version of a "gated community": unlike its offline equivalent it does not charge the occupiers with an exorbitant rent and does not need armed guards or a sophisticated CCTV network; a simple "delete" key would suffice. The attraction of all and any – online as offline – gated community is that one lives there in the company of strictly pre-selected people, "people like you," like-minded people – free from the intrusion of strangers whose presence might require the awkward negotiation of a mode of cohabitation and present a challenge to your self-assurance that your mode of life is the only proper one, one bound to be shared by everybody within your sight and reach. They are mirror reflections of yourself and you are a mirror reflection of them, therefore by living there you are not taking the risk of falling out with your neighbour, of arguing or fighting about political, ideological or indeed any other kind of issues. A comfort zone indeed, sound-insulated from the hubbub of the diversified and variegated, quarrelsome crowds roaming city streets and workplaces... The snag is that in such an artificially yet artfully disinfected, sanitized online environment one can hardly develop immunity against the toxins of the controversy endemic to the offline universe; or learn the art of stripping them of their morbid and eventually murderous potential. And because one has failed to learn it, the divisions and contentions carried by strangers in city streets appear yet more threatening - and perhaps incurable. Divisions born online are equipped with a self-propelling and self-exacerbating capacity...

Admittedly, the above inventory of actual and potential virtues and vices of splitting the Lebenswelt ("lived world") into online and offline universes is far from complete. It is obviously too early to evaluate the summary effects of a watershed-like shift in the human condition and cultural history. For now, the assets of the Internet and digital informatics as a whole seem to bear a considerable admixture of liabilities - though such an impression could only reflect the usual birth-pangs of new forms of life and the juvenal afflictions accompanying their maturation. For all that can be asserted at the moment with any measure of confidence, one of the least prepossessing sequels is that of the higher scores reached by the online universe on the scale of comfort, convenience, risk avoidance and freedom from trouble taking their toll – and by design or by default prompting a tendency to transplant the worldviews and behavioural codes made to the measure of online life-sphere upon its offline alternative, to which they could be applied only at the cost of much social and ethical damage.

One way or another, the consequences of the online/offline split of the Lebenswelt need to be closely monitored. The studies collected in this book combine into a timely attempt to fulfil that task.

INTRODUCTION

GARRY ROBSON AND MALGORZATA ZACHARA

The scholarly analysis of ubiquitous computing and the rise of a global digital infrastructure is beginning to come of age. These relatively recent but utterly transformative developments, or perhaps more accurately their profound socio-cultural, social-psychological and philosophical ramifications, are now coming under sustained scrutiny from a range of perspectives as the trickle of critical studies that began to emerge in the early- to mid-2000s becomes a torrent. This volume adds to that torrent with an innovative multidisciplinary focus on interconnections between the two key themes of social media and intercultural experience, thereby drawing together in a range of integrated analyses two of the central processes of contemporary globalization: digitalization and global mobility.

As far as the latter is concerned we have been keen to explore the extent to which the use of social media may enhance (or indeed inhibit, as a number of chapters argue) the development of open and reflexive interactions, where personal experiences and understandings of culture are concerned, in globalized settings. This emphasis on the performative and fluid potential of such encounters connects with the broader debate on post-'culturalist' interculturalism – in which an emphasis on process, active negotiation and dynamic cultural syncretism replaces the reifying and culturally essentialising thinking of earlier phases of interculturalism and, indeed, of multiculturalism itself. Examples of this kind of stance include Paul Gilroy's critique of official multiculturalism and endorsement of the improvised "conviviality" that characterizes everyday interactions in diverse settings,[1] Simon Fanshawe and Danny Sriskandarajah's emphatic rejection of multi- and "traditional" interculturalism in favour of a sense of dynamic, post-multicultural agency,[2] and studies of interpersonal and inter-group relations in unprecedentedly diverse or liminal social contexts

[1] Paul Gilroy, *After Empire: Melancholia or Convivial Culture*, London and New York: Routledge, 2004.

[2] Simon Fanshawe and Danny Sriskandarajah, *You Can't Put Me In a Box: Super Diversity and the End of Identity Politics*, London: IPPR, 2010.

such as those by, respectively, Stephen Vertovec[3] and Fred Dervin and Mari Korpela.[4]

Five of our chapters (those of Ann Gunkel, David Gunkel, Garry Robson, Agnieszka Stasiewicz-Bieńkowska and Malgorzata Zachara) originate in a specific research project into social media usage among international student sojourners, the details of which are set out by David Gunkel. The rest do not, but all, in one way or another, probe interconnections between digital experience, culture and identity. The three chapters in the first section, *The Digitalisation of the Self and Its Discontents*, appear at first blush to converge quite clearly on a discussion of the role played by social media in "enframing" or "interpellating" young users into experientially reduced subject positions, as the trend towards the production of "avatar selves" influences, contends with, ruptures or replaces longer established modes of embodied self-understanding and presentation and communication. Garry Robson offers a discussion of issues relating to absence and presence in intercultural encounters, and in particular of the ways in which the limitations of disembodied interaction, posthuman ideology and the corporatization of the Internet intersect as forces tending to "reduce" the subjectivity of many users. Christian Olavarria is similarly preoccupied with what he sees as the deleterious consequences of disembodied, asynchronous forms of interaction in social and work contexts; he argues, after Jacques Ellul, that for many of us conformity to the requirements of heavily technologized social systems is unavoidable, and that those who might want to disconnect from or "mindfully reject" this close-to-mandatory membership of the global hive face an uphill struggle, to say the least. Marek Wojtaszek offers a similarly trenchant analysis of the "life-degrading" and narcissistically conformist aspects of digital technology immersion and the threat it poses to the capacity for mindful solitude, and to some extent supports the arguments of Robson and Olavarria. However, Wojtaszek's insistence on at least the potential for life-enhancement inherent in *techne* ends by taking him in a different direction altogether: where Robson and Olavarria variously probe questions of self-reduction, psychological dysfunction, distorted communication and the undermining of embodied experience, Wojtaszek concludes, via his philosophically framed discussion of the concept of the "interface," that a new ontology for the posthuman age will become possible only if we become *more* closely and

[3] Stephen Vertovec, 'Super-diversity and its Implications', *Ethnic and Racial Studies*, 30/6, 2007.

[4] Fred Dervin and Mari Korpela, *Cocoon Communities: Togetherness in the 21st Century,* Newcastle-Uopn-Tyne: Cambridge Scholars Publishing, 2013.

profoundly engaged in virtual processes. Thus does Wojtaszek take that ongoing, Heidegger-inspired argument for the shift from epistemology to being which is also at the centre of Robson's argument, and arrives at very different conclusions. Where the essence of social experience is to be found, for Robson and Olavarria, in embodiment and the direct phenomenological experience of face-to face encounters with others, Wojtaszek argues that a transition to a new kind of being, aided by digital, synthetic technologies, might emerge: an "immanent environment wherein to be and to know are no longer hierarchically juxtaposed but essentially co-expressive."

The next section, *New Negotiations of Mobility, Place and Intercultural Experience*, focuses on relationships between technology and mobility at a less philosophical level, with two papers focused on the practical experiences of global mobility; both chapters here argue that considerations of space and place, and in fact the ways in which the former is converted into the latter by those on the move, must be afforded a central analytical role. Agnieszka Stasiewicz-Bienkowska bases her analysis on a conception of place as being "constructed" out of social interactions and networks of social relations. Place is understood and experienced, from her perspective, through movement and interaction and, crucially, the effort each individual must make to turn mere space into meaningful place. Social media, rather than undermining this effort, facilitate it in a number of important ways. First of all there is the potential of Facebook, Skype and the rest to aid sojourners in their attempt to manage feelings of vulnerability and dislocation early in their stay; as a set of tools and practices with which to convert the vulnerabilities and insecurities of depersonalized space into places which can be experienced as safe, solid and restful. In this respect Stasiewicz-Bienkowska attributes far more positive potential to social media than Filho, Robson or Szymkowska-Bartyzel; the process of shaping a place to meet individual social-psychological needs is a prerequisite of the new global mobility, and is almost unimaginable as a general phenomenon without new media and digitalized connections. Ultimately, however, it is argued that a fully satisfying conversion of space into place is best achieved through embodied interaction with others who are culturally situated in and "know" places in three dimensions, explored here through a discussion of the phenomenon of couchsurfing, an interesting example of the merging of off- and online experience.

The significance of digital photography and self-representation in the creation of a stable and manageable experience of place - both for posters of pictures and their followers on social media - is at the centre of

Stasiewicz-Bienkowska's discussion; the visual plays a key role in the apprehension and rendering of place. It is likely that this centrality of the visual is increasing, and the recent emergence of an exponentially expanding and globalised realm of digitalised image making, and its manifold and as yet poorly understood ramifications, is something with which all of those attempting to make analytical sense of globalization must contend In the next chapter Yasmin Gunaratnam and Les Back consider the role of the visual and the immediacy of social media in a dual context: of the ever-shifting patterns of urban multiculture in the inner London borough of Newham, and the experimental "real time" ethnographic methods that they have been developing in order to meet the challenge of studying complex experiences of place, time and intercultural experience, linking "movements through life as well as migrations across space." Starting from the contention that the smartphone has profoundly transformed the contemporary experience of migration and mobility, they go on to suggest that it is also affording new possibilities to re-imagine ethnographic observation and the generation, analysis and communication of research. More than this, the smartphone and social media may also offer the potential to re-think the relationship between not just participants and researchers but also the public circulation of findings and knowledge.

In seeking to extend the spatio-temporal and conceptual boundaries of research in globalized, intercultural urban settings, Gunaratnam and Back focus their attention on a number of the core themes of this volume: the problem of the "real"; the emergence of off/online as a merged and increasingly significant realm of presentation management and social interaction; embodied experience and place; and the extent to which social media may enhance or degrade intercultural communication and understanding. And they present a critique of the techno-determinist view that sees the ubiquitous users of digital technology and social media as somehow enjoying privileged access to and understanding of the unfolding "now" of social experience in the age of globalisation.

Opening the section *"Digital Natives" and Cosmopolitanism in the "Real" and "Virtual" Worlds*, David Gunkel brings to the fore some key themes in the study of student experience, and the need for much more research into them, in the framework at hand. He sets out the details of the research project from which five of the chapters in the book are derived (see above); in doing so he discusses important issues relating to the roles played by digital and social media in intercultural student experience, noting that our understanding of these relationships and processes is much in need of development.

Ann Gunkel takes up this proposition in a chapter which asks some fundamental questions about some of our underlying suppositions about digital experience, the students comprising the research sample described in the previous chapter and the conceptual frames of reference they draw on in reflecting upon their experience. By way of problematizing the widely used and by now naturalized term "digital natives," she examines the problem of the "real" and its supposed counterpart "virtuality," asking why so few young users of social media seem to have a problem with treating these two notions as distinct and largely exclusive of one another. This gives rise to some of the central questions in the study of ubiquitous computing: what are the ramifications of the emergence of a fused sphere of offline/online experience and interaction?; what effects does one have upon the other; can or should we continue to consider embodied, face-to-face interactions as "realer" than those that take place remotely?; what are the implications for these kinds of questions for the attempt to better understand, and perhaps promote among the young, meaningful intercultural communication and understanding in the age of globalization? The chapter concludes, pointedly, by questioning the widely prevailing view that "digital natives" enjoy some kind of privileged understanding of the new digital landscape: "It is genuinely fascinating to report from our data that so-called digital natives make frequent use of social practices of digital communication which they simultaneously suspect, according those practices less authenticity and even less reality. It is really interesting that in the context of our research, our so-called native informants know just as little about the territory as we do."

Moving on from these theoretical issues in online communication and discussions of the real, we come to some more empirical discussions of the ways in which social media may frame and influence efforts at experiencing or encouraging intercultural communication. Though it is argued in a number of the chapters that the creation of digitally mediated social "cocoons" (after Dervin and Korpela – see the chapter by Robson) or "bubbles" may actually *decrease* the likelihood of open intercultural encounters among sojourning international students, (an argument made also by Filho, Szymkowska-Bartyzel and, to a lesser extent Stasiewicz-Bienkowska), it is clear that social media have a role to play in fostering the kind of cosmopolitan perspectives that underpin positive intercultural relations - both in education and in the broader sphere of cultural diplomacy. Though it is now commonplace to question the easy (or, perhaps, early) assumption that the apparent openness and cultural heterogeneity of the Internet is somehow linked to the emergence of new forms of cultural openness, the extent to which homophily and social separation occur on sites such as Facebook can remain striking. Examining examples of practice with students in the USA, Anne Bizub offers a strong argument for the potential effectiveness of using Facebook to challenge homophily and draw young people away from small-world thinking towards the kind of cosmopolitan awareness that can make them more "world ready." Again, the notion of "mindfulness" makes an appearance, this time in terms of the cultivation of the mindful openness engendered among groups encountering, for the first time and via social media, not only classroom challenges to stereotypical thinking but "other" people (in South Africa and Egypt) themselves. Bizub argues that educators have been slower on the uptake than might have been expected in utilizing the kinds of social media favoured by students in the attempt to build global perspectives in a society which, despite its apparent diversity, appears also not to be characterized by high levels of intercultural curiosity at the global scale.

In this regard the comparison with Europe offered by Jolanta Szymkowska-Bartyzel's chapter is instructive. Her assessment of the effectiveness of the Erasmus educational exchange programme, with a particular focus on the participation of Polish students, in building a pan-European cosmopolitan student culture, and the role played by social media as part of this, suggests that the differences between Europe and the USA may be considerable. What comes across most strongly here is the existence of a sphere of grounded cosmopolitan experience, with students of various nationalities relatively comfortable with moving between geographical and cultural spaces. This is not to suggest that exchange programme "culture shock" has become a thing of the past; far from it. But the familiarity with Europe on the one hand, and the use of social media and digitalised cultural consumption on the other, minimizes experiences of strangeness and isolation that for many would once have been the norm. Szymkowska-Bartyzel's study suggests that the cocoon/bubble phenomenon is as characteristic of the Erasmus experience as it is of sojourning student experience more generally. E-nearness allows students to manage homesickness in a new way and social media allow protective social spheres to be formed and maintained, but they also lead to increasingly mediated experiences of new situations and enable the avoidance of deeply immersive (and often challenging) experiences of otherness.

Ciro Marcondes Filho concludes this section with a study that combines its two main elements, being a philosophical discussion of places, the people in them and their encountering by sojourning students, in both the world before social media and now. For him, travelling abroad for extended periods in the pre-digital age was a rite of passage through which the young person faced the existential difficulty resulting from their separation from home and sense of dislocation and moved towards the self-actualisation and maturity that comes from having the grounds of one's prior experience cut away. This experience of "disturbing loneliness" and disorientation was staged in places - strange places, with strange others dwelling in them. His discussion of the effects of social media on these processes and the international sojourns of his Brazilian students echoes, to some extent, some of the other contributions in this volume; his insistence that the self-protective, ghettoizing "bubbles" enabled by social media and the gadgets that deliver them tend to prevent people from engaging fully in deeply intercultural experience: if an encounter with the metaphysical "face" of the other is lacking, the experience of place risks becoming depersonalized and superficial. Culture shock - in its potentially creative sense - is minimized and the existential grounds of immature selfhood are not challenged or remade.

New and emerging strategies of political communication and elaborations of political identities are, broadly speaking, the theme of *Shaping Political Identities and Narratives through Social Media.* Malgorzata Zachara argues that the use of social media, albeit at a less concrete level than those examined by Bizub and Szymkowska-Bartyzel, has played a major role in building new global perspectives on difference and intercultural understanding. Like Jasmin Siri in the following chapter she is interested in the ways in which social media have transformed the public communications of politicians and political organizations and supported the development of novel forms of civic activism, while noting that beyond the formal routes of political discourse, in the sphere of public diplomacy, digital-cultural representational practices (such as marketing-derived place and nation branding) across geopolitical boundaries have done much to facilitate common experiences and understandings between members of different cultural and national groups. Thus have emerged, Zachara argues, new modes of group identification and reconfigured ways of initiating and developing individual interactions.

Next is Jasmin Siri's analysis of "multiple political selves" in the German context. Contrasting Facebook homophily with the more fluid heterophily of Twitter - these constituting the primary platforms on which new modes of political communication and identification have emerged in recent years - Siri suggests that different social media are used to create varieties of "desired political self." Every medium frames and produces specific aesthetics and political narrations, leading to the emergence of a "multiplicity of political selves" constructed through specific channels of communication. This analysis leads Siri to promulgate nothing less than the emergence of a new *political public,* characterized as a "diverse and multi-contextual non-place."

This conception of a social media-driven and disembodied realm of political communication receives further elaboration - and complication - in the chapter by Irem Inceoglu, in which she argues that Twitter was at the centre of a very concrete example of civic activism and cross-cultural coalition building in Istanbul's 2013 Gezi Resistance. Inceoglu's primary focus, like Siri's, is on the way in which social media platforms can underpin and channel the creation of new political public spaces. What is especially important in the case under discussion here is that these spaces make clearly visible the various identity positions often excluded from or marginalized in the formal politics of the public sphere and largely estranged from one another in the normal course of events. This social media-led emergence of a new awareness of diversity and its value represents, to return to Zachara's argument about digital-cultural diplomacy, the creation of novel forms of intercultural communication and identification *within* the framework of a nation state.

As is well known, new media offer plentiful contexts for the restaging of both old hatreds, and attempts on the part of people of good will to overcome them. For an example of intercultural communication at its most intense we have Alina Bothe's analysis of the "commentary culture" that has developed around Holocaust survivors' testimonies on Youtube. Focusing on testimonies both benign and hateful, Bothe sets out an account of the modes of interaction involved, the temporal peculiarities and lags which characterise this form of communication, and the relationship between the online and offline worlds. She notes that those posters aiming hateful messages at survivors tend overwhelmingly to choose anonymity, a reflection perhaps not only of potential legal consequences but of the kind of unrestrained spitefulness that becomes possible when interlocutors do not, literally, see eye-to-eye. Olavarria and Robson also refer to this effect, acknowledging the ease with which online contexts can produce not meaningful intercultural cultural communication but its opposite.

In the final section*, Digitalising Human Fundamentals Across Cultures,* Douglas Ponton takes us back to probably the most crucial question of all in the attempt to understand the complex and thorny question of online/embodied selves and the nature of the relation between these spheres: what is real? As we have seen, some of our authors argue that we should continue to position the embodied and face-to-face at the top of a hierarchy of interaction, others that this hierarchy should, or perhaps will, be collapsed or redefined. Ponton examines the contention, made by a number of the subjects in his study, that virtual friendships may be as real as face-to-face ones. From a linguistic perspective he examines online discussions and experiences of virtual friendship and builds a corpus of the terms and concepts used on selected websites. He concludes, though he himself is broadly sceptical as regards the extent to which the online experience of friendship can be fully equated with the embodied variety, that when a poster under consideration talks of the pain and joy associated with real and virtual friendships being identical, "she is making an ontological statement. There is no such thing as 'virtual' pain."

Talking as we are of fundamentals, matters of death and remembrance arise in Magdalena Szczyrbak's comparative study of Polish and American online obituary sites. This comparison highlights two important aspects of the shifting to online contexts of much older, customary forms of expression. Firstly, the ways in which these older genres evolve to accommodate changes in the "socio-rhetorical" setting in which they are made - there is an echo here of Siri's discussion of the ways in which the structures and conventions of different online platforms are producing distinctive and novel rhetorical styles and perspectives in the political sphere. Secondly, such sites not only express societal approaches to death and remembrance but continue to convey culturally specific values, attitudes and emotions in a more general sense. In the midst of digitalized life we are in death; and "death notices or obituaries, in whatever shape and form, will continue to exist as long as people attach much importance to death and feel the need to share their grief and relate to other human beings."

PART I:

THE DIGITALIZATION OF THE SELF AND ITS DISCONTENTS

CHAPTER ONE

"YOU ARE FORCED TO BE WHO YOU ARE": EMBODIMENT AND SOCIAL MEDIA IN INTERCULTURAL EXPERIENCE

GARRY ROBSON

> In the face-to-face situation the other is fully real. This reality is part of the overall reality of everyday life, and as such is massive and compelling. To be sure, another may be real to me without my having encountered him face-to-face… Nevertheless, he becomes real to me in the fullest sense of the word only when I meet him face-to-face. Indeed, it may be argued that the other in the face-to-face situation is more real to me than I myself.
> —Peter Berger and Thomas Luckmann, *The Social Construction of Reality*

> It may very well be that one gets different types of relationships through social media than face-to-face (and again, this would need to be demonstrated empirically rather than just asserted), but this whole formation of hierarchy of relationships by medium is getting old and tiresome. There is no reason to assume a priori that face-to-face interactions are more authentic or deeper than digital ones.
> *—thecrankysociologists.com*

Introduction

This chapter takes as its starting point the clear preference, among respondents in the research at hand, for face-to-face over online communication. There is little doubt that social media enable the sojourning students in our cohort to psychologically "anchor" themselves at home through daily contact with family and friends, and also that it can facilitate the development and maintenance of a highly meaningful "cocoon community"[1] within which to live for the duration of the sojourn -

---

[1] See Fred Dervin and Mari Korpela, *Cocoon Communities: Togetherness in the 21st Century,* Newcastle-Upon-Tyne: Cambridge Scholars Publishing.

however disassociated from the surrounding cultural reality that cocoon may be. But the repeated appeal to "reality" seems also to point in other directions, to hint at a desire for un- or less-mediated experience at, apparently, two levels: the first is connected to a sense that communicating with others in the cocoon is facilitated by digital technology but also reduced and simplified in ways which compare unfavourably with direct, embodied experience, and that something may be being lost in the latter as a consequence; the second, with a feeling that living in the cocoon, and remaining at the centre of a gadget-anchored "youniverse,"[2] actually inhibits the risky and demanding project of opening oneself to the cultural Other in a meaningful and potentially transformative sense - the sense which many of our respondents left home somehow wanting to experience. After presenting, in brief, salient aspects of the research that support this interpretation, the bulk of the chapter attempts to start unpicking, and theoretically framing, the apparent disjuncture between the observations and preferences of this particular sample of mostly twenty-something "digital natives" (see below) and the claim now frequently being advanced by certain social theorists, technophiles and futurologists that the "hierarchy" of social interactions which privileges face-to-face is archaic, and dissolving; and more than this, that the shift to disembodied, remote interaction somehow presages a brighter future for humanity.

Embodied and Disembodied Interactions: The Preference for *Reality*

For the purposes of this piece I analysed the interviews from a "grounded theorising"[3] approach, working to identify emergent categories and concepts in the data for subsequent analysis. This beginning point of analysis yielded three main categories for further investigation. Two of these seem relatively uncomplicated at the theoretical level, and will be introduced only briefly; the third is denser and less clear, and therefore is at the centre of analysis here. These categories are, respectively, *Anchoring Cocoon Community* and a more imprecise cluster of themes connected to the sense of *Reduction,* or simplification, or contraction, in

[2] http://www.urbandictionary.com/define.php?term=youniverse

[3] Meaning here, in a general sense, the data-led generation of concepts to be investigated in this chapter rather than a full scale *Grounded Theory* approach to the project as a whole. For an account of the distinction between these two things see Martin Hammersley and Paul Atkinson, *Ethnography: Principles in Practice*, London and New York: Routledge, Third Edition 2007, 159.

face-to-face social experience occasioned by routine social media interactions. As can be seen in David Gunkel's report on the NCN research project from which this chapter is derived, many respondents had at least some reservations about the "knock on" effects of social media, and Facebook in particular, on their embodied social lives; almost all voiced a preference for face-to-face interactions given the choice. This, of course, is not to imply a rejection of social media per se; the psychological and emotional continuity provided by the ability to "anchor" oneself at home - or wherever there are significant others - is widely seen by most as an obvious gain, and helps support users in their orientation to the new place.[4] One effect of this is that many individuals remain significantly focused on home and home culture, while simultaneously participating in the creation of a social media-enabled collective, especially on the Polish side of the study. It is clear that these two processes are closely intertwined, if not continuous: anchoring is arguably a core, psychologically stabilising element in the creation of the kind of flexible, short term, unbinding but very meaningful collectives identified, as we have seen, by Fred Dervin and Mari Korpela as "Cocoon Communities."[5] Largely independent of the surrounding cultural reality - in the Polish case, almost by necessity for reasons of deficits in language and cultural expertise - such groups enjoy a mobile, rolling and supportive field of social support and leisure activity existing, on the whole, on its own terms. The extent to which this 21st century phenomenon of collective sojourning in culturally opaque settings is enabled and framed by social media cannot, if our data is anything to go by, be overestimated. Thus are the undoubted benefits of routine social media use for most of our respondents; it allows individuals to both expose themselves to much that is new while significantly staying the same:

> I actually expected my micro culture group to be left [at home]... I predicted I would leave it, come here and form a new one. But I'm glad that didn't happen because that micro culture is me, what I can demonstrate as being me. I use the same clothes as I did [at home]… I kind of expected to be immersed in the high culture [in Krakow], smoking pot for weeks but, of course, nothing…I expected to come here and be

[4] For a full discussion of the dynamics of this process see Agnieszka Stasiewicz-Bienkowska's chapter in this volume.

[5] This finding is also congruent with those presented in this volume by Ciro Marcondes Filho, who writes of his Brazilian students' tendency to wish to dwell in a social media-framed "bubble" when travelling or sojourning abroad, and Jolanta Szymkowska - Bartyzel in her chapter on students in the Erasmus exchange programme.

> extremely open to new experiences, open a gate and absorb all of it and go back as a new person, but it just didn't happen. My modes of being are pretty much the same as they were back home.

But beyond the surface of convenience and social ease made possible by social media, many respondents express a sort of unease about what I call "Reduction," the contracted and simplified nature of online communication in relation to face-to-face (and, in fact, its impact on face-to-face meetings themselves):

> I think that having a real social life is so much more satisfying than doing it through the Internet. Through the Internet everything is based on image, and the spontaneity is gone. And it's so much more fun to have a real social life, with real people. And actually having to get to know them or even, like, sit down and have a conversation and they tell you something that surprises you. And Facebook just gives it all away.

In addition to the reductive, shorthand way of approaching a new person through Facebook, of gaining an initial understanding of them, there is the problem of the slowed down, calculative, cognitive deliberation involved in chatting online; the unpredictable, improvised nature of embodied communicative encounters is missing:

> I don't really like chatting on Facebook; I prefer a normal conversation with someone. And the reason is because you don't have the trips and tumbles of normal conversation. You can sit down and think what you want to say, read it; I can just sit for a couple of minutes, think about it.

The version of the self, or the avatar, displayed on social media is reduced, calculated, unreal:

> On Facebook you can plan everything, even if you're just chatting with someone. When someone asks you a question, you don't have to respond straight away, you can just plan your answer. And that's much harder in real conversation…That's why I think eye-to-eye contact is much realer, because you're forced to be who you are, and you don't have time to make up the image that you want to convey to others.

This idea of Facebook as a barrier to real and open interaction with others is highly suggestive, but may represent only the beginning point of a critique of social media, and their relation to intercultural experience, as it emerges from our data. Observations of a still more profound kind were made by another respondent: following a discussion of his habit of sending pictures and messages home on Facebook every day, he drew a distinction between this kind of comfortable and undemanding activity, of acting as a sort of cultural ambassador for eastern European culture through his continual framing and presentation of it for home consumption (an essentially self-centred activity, as he admitted) to being forced to confront cultural difference in a much more demanding way:

> I learnt all sorts of things about the way my brain works and the way I think that I didn't know before. I learnt how irrational I was. How irrational everyone is. We think of ourselves as rational people but we are not. I have a better relationship with who I am and where I'm going in life than I had a few years ago. And that, I think, has greatly accelerated here...here you're sort of forced to change. And seeing things I haven't seen before. I've been forced into situations, situations where I've been powerless. Especially in terms of having legal rights, having the ability to speak and be understood. That puts you in a position... Like it's humbling to be that powerless. It gives you a different perspective on things.

This humbling feeling of powerlessness, disturbing though it may be, is clearly understood as a potential benefit in terms of long term self-development and actualization; to be thrown upon the mercy of little-understood others in an opaque foreign land, to be no longer anchored in superficial communication with home and the easeful pleasures of the cocoon. A direct, phenomenological experience of the confrontation with the mystery of the cultural other; *this* is intercultural experience at its most profound. And it is exactly the kind of experience, of unsettling otherness and of social risk, that the ubiquitous use of social media tends to shield sojourning students from. Facebook and its ilk, by keeping the preoccupation with the simplified self and with the remote control of communication at the centre of daily experience, tend to constrain rather than enable the coming together of people in unmediated intercultural interaction.

The majority of our respondents seem to recognize this simplification and delimitation of "real" experience by social media, and it explains the preference for face-to-face communication. This insistence on defining face-to-face as *real* remains strong and is of the utmost significance: what is at stake here, in a world increasingly saturated by digitalized mediation, is a desire to experience others in the kinds of direct ways that humans have for millennia. While social theorists and ideologues of one stripe or another have now spent decades "deconstructing" the subject, or the very idea of a coherent and integrated self at all, it still forms the basis for intersubjective communication, and as I will suggest "culture" itself, in the world beyond the often toxic derogations of humanity issuing from the academy and the ever more strident attempts to undermine what most of us think of as human beings emerging from the forces of corporate digitalization and their supporters in the commentariat.[6]

Technophilia and its Discontents

The last few years have seen the emergence of a new and troubling strain of research and literature which calls into question the utopian enthusiasm of the 1980s and 1990s for the possibilities of digitally mediated social relations and open ended technological innovation. One of the anchor points of this enthusiasm for the transformation of life in the Web 2.0 world as we entered the 21st century was Marc Prensky's contention that a generation of "Digital Natives" would lead the way in generating novel and liberating forms of social organization, cultural innovation and educational experience.[7] This generation would, in short, do some things very differently than they had been done before; they would represent a step change in the relationship between humans and technology, being creatively empowered by their immersion and know-how in the new technological landscape.

Recent developments in patterns of young people's actual use of social media have problematized this enthusiasm. Serious questions have been asked about the assertions of Prensky and other technophiles who support (and sometimes market) the idea of the Digital Native - or terminological variations thereof [8] -, which turns out to be an overly generalized and

---

[6] For examples see the gung-ho enthusiasm for the Internetisation of everything in Clay Shirkey, *Here Comes Everybody: How Change Happens When People Come Together*, London: Penguin, 2009; or the simplistic boosterism for digitalization-as-globalisation to be found in Thomas Friedman, *The World is Flat: Globalization in the 21st Century*, London: Penguin, 2007 (especially chapter 12).

[7] Prenksy, M., "Digital natives, digital immigrants," *On the Horizon*, Vol. 9 No. 5, 1-6, 2001. For a more recent elaboration of Prensky's thinking see *From Digital Natives to Digital Wisdom: Hopeful Essays for 21st Century Learning*, Thousand Oaks, CA: Corwin, 2012.

[8] Significant examples include John Palfrey and Urs Gasser, *Born Digital: Understanding the First Generation of Digital Natives,* New York: Basic Books, 2008; Siemens, George, "Connectivism: Learning theory for the digital age" *International Journal of Instructional Technology and Distance Learning* 2:1, 2005; Don Tapscott, *Growing Up Digital: Rise of the Net Generation*, New York: McGraw-Hill, 2000; and Vim Veen and Ben Vrakking, *Homo Zappiens: Growing up in a Digital Age*, London and New York: Continuum, 2006.

empirically questionable concept.[9] These doubts revolve not so much around the educational benefits or disbenefits of digital nativism in the educational sphere as on more fundamental matters concerning online emotional disinhibition, narcissism, addiction, depression, distraction and affective disconnection from the face-to-face world of embodied others in general.

Examples abound of this more recent and less sanguine view of culture and mediated social relations in the computer-in-the-pocket era, and the list grows monthly. Prominent among them are, for example, Nicholas Carr's *The Shallows: What the Internet is Doing to Our Brains* (2010), the extensive sales of which would seem to indicate a growing public concern with the emerging downsides of life online; Andrew Keen's *Digital Vertigo: How Today's Online Social Revolution Is Dividing, Diminishing, and Disorienting Us* (2012), which as its title suggests covers similar terrain; Jaron Lanier's *You Are Not A Gadget,* in which the early prophet of virtual reality bemoans the culturally corrosive effects of Web 2.0 (2011); or Evgeny Morozov's, *To Save Everything Click Here: The Folly of Technological Solutionism* (2013), which in many important respects echoes Lanier's arguments. Even Ethan Zuckerman - an advocate of the potential benefits for globalized humankind of the digitalization of social organization and connectivity - is forced to concede in his *Rewire: Digital Cosmopolitans in the Age of Connection* that under current conditions homophily and small-world thinking prevail on Facebook and that the potential of social media to open up and transform the planet for the better still seems some way from being realized.

But perhaps the most striking example of this shift in tone in the analysis of the expansion of life online and its consequences has been in the work of Sherry Turkle. Her journey from prophet of the potentially liberated and digitally enhanced self (*The Second Self*, 1984) to writer of one of the most powerful jeremiads about the unintended and potentially catastrophic consequences of dissociative Internet addiction in the age of ubiquitous computing (*Alone Together*, 2011) traces a trajectory through which the broader shift can be seen.

Many of the writers asking questions about what has "gone wrong" with the promise of digitalization may now be located in an older strain of techno-sceptic analysis which examines the consequences to selves and

---

9 Neil Selwyn, "Digital natives: myth or reality?," presentation to CILIP (Chartered Institute of Library and Information Professionals), London seminar series, London, 10th March 2009.http://pl.scribd.com/doc/9775892/Digital-Native

communities of man, as Thoreau had it, becoming the tool of his tools.[10] In this connection we might cite Lewis Mumford's account of the ways in which commercialized "megatechnics," with its open ended expansion, built in obsolescences and manipulation of consumers' desires, works against the interests of human comfort and satisfaction;[11] Jacques Ellul's comprehensive theory of technological modernity's tendency to sacralise innovation and products, the forced adaptation of people to successive technological improvements and the downgrading of the humanities in technocratic systems[12] (an argument later taken up in the work of Neil Postman[13]); and Martin Heidegger's work on the human cost, the cost to *being*,[14]of being all but unavoidably enframed - we might, after Louis Althusser,[15] say "interpellated" as subjects - in increasingly totalising technological systems.

Intersubjectivity, Intercorporeality and Culture

The study in hand is concerned with how "cultural difference" is negotiated via social media. Let us now, therefore, identify a working definition of what is meant by "culture" - a word, as Raymond Williams[16] so famously noted, which is one of the three most complex in the English language. For current purposes I propose a definition of culture as intersubjective process, which accords with Edward Sapir's suggestion that the

---

[10] Henry David Thoreau, *Walden*, Princeton, NJ: Princeton University Press, 1971 [1854]: "But Lo! Men have become the tools of their tools," 37.

[11] Lewis Mumford. *The Myth of the Machine Vol. II: The Pentagon of Power*, New York: Harcourt Brace Jovanovich, 1970.

[12] Jacques Ellul. *The Technological Society,* New York: Knopf, 1964.

[13] Neil Postman. *Technopoly: The Surrendering of Culture to Technology,* New York: Alfred Knopf, 1992.

[14] Martin Heidegger, *The Question Concerning Technology,* New York & London: Garland Publishing Inc., 1977 [1954]. See also Jan Harris and Peter Taylor, *Digital Matters: The Culture and Theory of the Matrix*, London and New York: Routledge, 2005, for an admirably clear and useful presentation of Heidegger's thinking on technology and totalisation, and a discussion of connections between his thinking and Ellul's.

[15] Louis Althusser, *Essays on Ideology*, London and New York: Verso, 1984

[16] In *Keywords: A Vocabulary of Culture and Society*. New York: Oxford University Press, 1976.

> …true locus of culture is in the interactions of specific individuals and, on the subjective side, in the meanings which each one of these individuals may unconsciously abstract for himself from his participation in these interactions[17].

Such face-to-face interactions, it has long been assumed by analysts from a range of perspectives, require on the part of the subject the presence of embodied others; such an assumption lies, for example, at the starting point of the long history of the symbolic interactionist understanding of the "interaction order" central to social experience. In the words of Charles Horton Cooley, an influence on George Herbert Mead and therefore on the development of the "interactionist" tradition of analysis,[18] his "looking glass self" is a conception comprised of three elements:

> …the imagination of our appearance to the other person; the imagination of his judgment of that appearance, and some sort of self-feeling, such as pride or mortification…The thing that moves us to pride or shame is …the imagined effect of this reflection upon another's mind.[19]

This sense of co-presence in the formation of a coherent self, of meaningful social interactions and ultimately, of the interaction order upon which cultural processes are based hinges, to repeat, on the physical presence of actual others. This sense is based upon an understanding of human subjects as corporeal beings. The "return" of the body and the concept of embodiment in sociology, social and cultural theory, anthropology and social psychology in recent decades reflects a growing awareness of the need to reconceptualise the nature of the self, and the self in social interaction, and to move beyond the formerly prevailing, reductive models of personhood and subjectivity that the social sciences and humanities inherited from the Enlightenment.

The strain of thinking which has sought to develop this more holistic conception of self and agency, and counter the effects of the installation of the Cartesian model of the modern person as an autonomous cognitive

---

[17] Edward Sapir. *Selected Writings in Language, Culture and Personality*, Berkeley: University of California Press,
1961 [1949], 151.

[18] See Dennis Waskul and Phillip Vannini (Eds), *Symbolic Interaction and the Sociology of the Body,* Aldershot: Ashgate, 2006, for a number of interesting elaborations on these ideas.

[19] Charles Horton Cooley, *Human Nature and the Social Order,* New York: Schocken, 1964 [1902], 184.

ego, is too long and complex to be properly discussed here.[20] But a short list of central contributions to the process should include important benchmarks such as Heidegger's promotion of being over epistemology as the central focus of his philosophy;[21] Maurice Merleau-Ponty's phenomenological account of the corporeal sources of self-identity and action;[22] the work of Peter Berger and Thomas Luckmann, substantially inspired by the interactionism of Mead, on the "social construction of reality"; Charles Taylor's repeated attempts to move beyond the "monological" conception of subjectivity and emphasise the importance of connectedness-to-background in social interaction;[23] Pierre Bourdieu's justifiably influential account of the embodiment of the habitus;[24] and the more recent work of those, such as Thomas Csordas, who have sought to set out the character and dimensions of "intersubjectivity as intercorporeality."[25]

---

[20] For comprehensive discussions of this matter see George Lakoff and Mark Johnson, *Philosophy in the Flesh: The Embodied Mind and its Challenge to Western Thought,* New York: Basic Books, 1999; Thomas Csordas (Ed), *Embodiment and Experience: The Existential Ground of Culture and Self,* Cambridge, UK: Cambridge University Press, 1994; and Nicholas Crossley, *Embodiment and Reflexivity in Contemporary Sociology,* Maidenhead: Open University Press, 2006. For influential accounts of the "arrival" of the body in social theory see Chris Shilling, *The Body and Social Theory*, London: Sage, 1993 and Bryan Turner, *The Body and Society,* London: Basil Blackwell, 1984. These issues are discussed in the context of ubiquitous computing in Paul Dourish, *Where the Action Is: The Foundations of Embodied Interaction,* Cambridge, MA: MIT Press, 2004 and Hubert L. Dreyfus, *On the Internet,* Abingdon and New York: Routledge, 2001.

[21] Martin Heidegger, *Being and Time*, trans. by Joan Stambaugh, Albany: State University of New York Press, 1996 [1927].

[22] Maurice Merleau-Ponty, *The Phenomenology of Perception*. London: Routledge, English translation 1962 [1945].

[23] See Charles Taylor, "To follow a rule," in Craig Calhoun, Edward LiPuma and Moishe Postine (Eds) *Bourdieu: Critical Perspectives,* Cambridge, UK: Polity Press, 1993, and "Engaged agency and background in Heidegger," in Charles B. Guignon (Ed) *The Cambridge Companion to Heidegger*. Cambridge, UK: Cambridge University Press, 1993.

[24] Pierre Bourdieu, *Outline of a Theory of Practice*, Cambridge, UK: Cambridge University Press, 1977. For arguably the most fascinating and useful grounding of Bourdieu's theory of habitus/embodiment in a concrete situation see Loic Wacquant, *Body and Soul: Notebooks of an Apprentice Boxer*, New York: Routledge, 2004.

[25] Thomas Csordas, "Intersubjectivity as intercorporeality," *Subjectivity*, 22, 2008, 110–121.

Following on from these insights, and in contrast to the "death of the subject" argument about the impossibility of a coherent post-Cartesian self (see below), recent research by those such as Christian Kogler[26] has more positively, and usefully, advanced our understanding of the intersubjective grounds of self-consciousness and self-identity as they relate to a complex and non-reductive notion of agency. Drawing on the heuristic framework provided, again, by Mead, Kogler analyses the ways in which, if we accept the idea that self-consciousness emerges from intersubjective perspective-taking and dialogue, a socially embedded and symbolically mediated notion of self-identity - one which is able to preserve the core features of human agency - becomes viable. His argument revolves around recognizing the extent to which *the Other's irreducible agency is constitutive of the self's capacity to establish an identity*, now understood as a socially situated, narrative self-interpreting process. Self-identity reveals itself in this account to be an open but coherent dynamic, a socially situated yet agent-driven phenomenon, and ethically indebted to the Other as providing the gift of selfhood.

Kogler's approach offers new insights into how selves are formed and maintained - we will refrain here from saying "constructed"[27] - as active processes in embodied, everyday interactions. This seems an eminently sensible, practical and hopeful way of thinking about the subject which does not resort to the reductive simplifications of those who would have the fullness and unpredictability of phenomenological experience equated with the dissociated and purely cognitive practice of contact with others from behind the controlled safety of a screen.

---

[26] Hans Herbert Kögler, "Agency and the Other: On the intersubjective roots of self-identity," *New Ideas in Psychology,* 30:1, 2012, 47–64.

[27] For an analysis of the shortcomings of the ubiquitous claim that all of significance in the human world is somehow ideologically "constructed" see Ian Hacking, *The Social Construction of What?* Cambridge, MA: Harvard University Press, 1999, and Paul Boghossian, *Fear of Knowledge: Against Relativism and Constructivism*, Oxford: Clarendon Press, 2006.

"Being There," Post-humanism and Assimilation to the Hive

Google's appointment in December 2012[28] of "hard" Artificial Intelligence guru and futurologist Ray Kurzweil as "head of engineering" clarified and made more explicit than ever the disembodying, post-humanist trend in Silicon Valley ideology. Kurzweil's suggestion that it will become possible to create consciousness in an artificial being is well known to his regular readers; his claim that we will be "uploading our brains" to computers by mid-century - in part, at least, to cheat death and achieve a kind of virtual immortality[29] - now entered the popular media and gained widespread prominence.[30] It is true that his narrative is striking, and not without a certain comedic charm: his prediction that "software based humans" will "live out on the Web, projecting bodies whenever they need or want them, including holographically projected bodies, foglet-projected bodies and physical bodies comprising nanobot swarms"[31] is of course beyond parody. But his assimilation into the Google hive is actually rather disconcerting; the increasing convergence of ideas drawn from tech-utopianism, futurology and post-humanist social theory, and their operationalization by globally powerful and "visionary" corporations convinced that they hold the keys to the future, represent forces that

[28] Stephen Levy, 'How Ray Kurzweill Will Help Google Make the Ultimate AI Brain', *wired.com,* 25.04.2013, http://www.wired.com/business/2013/04/kurzweil-google-ai/

[29] At the risk of being accused of "bioconservatism," I would suggest that Kurzweil's dream of tech-immortality for the information-processing self is the fullest expression of the arrogant and wildly immature utopianism of much post-humanist thinking. For it is the very transience and finitude of our enfleshed human being, so much derided by Kurzweil et al., that frames the spiritual, emotional and ethical depth of human experience. For an account of the significance of the fleetingness of life and the "blessings of finitude" see Leon Kass, *Life, Liberty and the Defence of Dignity: The Challenge for Bioethics*, New York: Encounter Books, 2004; Roger Scruton, *The Uses of Pessimism and the Danger of False Hope*, London: Atlantic Books, 2012, and Gilbert Meilaender, "Transitional humanity," *The New Atlantis*, Spring 2011, http://www.thenewatlantis.com/publications/transitional-humanity.

[30] Woolaston, Victoria. "We'll be uploading our entire MINDS to computers by 2045 and our bodies will be replaced by machines within 90 years, Google expert claims," *Daily Mail*, 19.06.2013, http://www.dailymail.co.uk/sciencetech/article-2344398/Google-futurist-claims-uploading-entire-MINDS-computers-2045-bodies-replaced-machines-90-years.html.

[31] Ray Kurzweil, *The Singularity is Near.* New York: Viking, 2005, 325.

should unsettle all of those who cherish our human being as it is and has been. For beneath this ostensibly hopeful and utopian vision of the post-human future lies a core of fantastically reductive and anti-human nihilism, in which the human being as we now experience it is viewed as a transitory and dispensable condition from which we must now move on.

This deeply troubling view of the person has not, of course, arisen out of the blue in the last fifteen years. Prominent among the intellectual streams which have nourished it are those other "posts," - structuralism and modernism - which in the 1970s began in earnest their long and corrosive work of deconstructing - one might say degrading and excessively relativizing - much thinking about personhood.[32] The move from a concern to deal with the problem of "Descartes' error"[33] has in many quarters led not to an attempt to find a human solution to the problem of the subject as reductively over-rationalised - an area inviting constructive research and reflection on how we might re-embody the subject and integrate the role of reason into a more holistic conception of the person - but to a rejection of both humanism in particular and the human (represented by the idea of a stable, coherent and integrated self) in general.

There is something of a paradox in play here, however, which has bequeathed to contemporary post-human, tech-utopian thinking a kind of double deficit. For while much of the work of the previous "posts" was about dismantling the rationalist Cartesian ego as part of the claim that we

[32] For overviews of this process in the American context see Roger Kimball, *Tenured Radicals: How Politics has Corrupted Our Education*, New York: Harper Collins, 1990, Christopher Lasch, *Revolt of the Elites and the Betrayal of Democracy*, New York: W.W. Norton, 1996, and Paul R. Gross and Norman Levitt, *Higher Superstition: The Academic Left and its Quarrels with Science*, Baltimore: John Hopkins University Press, 1997; for an argument that the attack on the subject is characterized - ironically enough - by the excessive individualism of postmodernist authors see Bob McKinley, "Postmodernism certainly is not science, but could it be religion?" *CSAS Bulletin*, *36*(1), 16-18, 2000; for critiques of the postmodernist technique of linguistic obfuscation and "theoretical" incoherence in the attack on science and objectivity see Noretta Koertge (Ed), *A House Built on Sand: Exposing Postmodernist Myths About Science,* Oxford: Oxford University Press, 2000 and, famously, Alan Sokal and Jean Bricmont, *Intellectual Impostures*, London: Profile Books, 2003; and for an account of the cultic elitism of many intellectuals in this sphere see Roger Scruton, "Whatever happened to reason?," *City Journal*, Spring 1999, http://www.city-journal.org/html/9_2_urbanities_what_ever.html.

[33] Antonio Damasio. *Descartes' Error: Emotion, Reason and the Human Brain,* New York: Avon Books, 1999.

can have no coherent self at all, many post-humanists rely on highly questionable notions, drawn from Cartesian/Enlightenment thinking, of barely embodied persons as little more than information-processing machines analogous to the computer itself. For example, to take one example among many, in Katherine Hayles' influential 1999 book *How We Became Posthuman*, it is asserted that our bodies are essentially prostheses - material supports for the immaterial mental processes which are our most salient feature - and that consciousness is an epiphenomenon reducible to information-processing activities in the brain. These ideas saturate, or saturated, the AI movement for long enough, and loom large in the thinking of Kurzweil - and Google. Thus do our bodies become meaningless and replaceable props or hindrances rather than integral to our selves, and the latter become little more than ever-enhanceable information processors. The Cartesian brain on a stick body, or perhaps nestled comfortably inside a nano-probe, returns.

This twofold weakening and reduction of the idea of the subject-this downgrading of the bases of our common humanity- has thus been deeply sedimented in the intellectual culture of our times and frames recent and emerging thinking on human experience and interaction in the age of digitalization and ubiquitous computing. It is little wonder, then, that the corporate forces running global digitalization and their supporters in the commentariat want to collapse the "hierarchical" boundary between embodied agents - dare we call them *real people*? - engaged in actual phenomenological activity in the world and the reduced self-representations of avatar selves interacting with one another remotely, from behind their gadgets.

The problem with this view, when it is applied to thinking about social media "friendship," is clearly set out by Roger Scruton :

> What we are witnessing is a change in the *attention* that mediates and gives rise to friendship. In the once normal conditions of human contact, people became friends by being in each other's presence, understanding all the many subtle signals, verbal and bodily, whereby another testifies to his character, emotions, and intentions, and building affection and trust in tandem. Attention was fixed on the other — on his face, words, and gestures. And his nature as an embodied person was the focus of the friendly feelings that he inspired. People building friendship in this way are strongly aware that they appear to the other as the other appears to them. The other's face is a mirror in which they see their own. Precisely because attention is fixed on the other there is an opportunity for self-knowledge and self-discovery, for that expanding freedom in the presence of the other which is one of the joys of human life. The object of friendly feelings looks back at you, and freely responds to your free activity, amplifying

> both your awareness and his own. As traditionally conceived, friendship was ruled by the maxim "know thyself."[34]

This idea of the "mirroring," of the co-creation of meaningful communication through proximate co-presence that we have already seen in the prescient work of Cooley can also be found in the writing of that wisest of early moderns, Michel de Montaigne.[35] In a suggestive article that links Montaigne's thinking to contemporary research in neuroscience, specifically with that being conducted into "mirror neurons" and the capacity for empathy, Saul Frampton suggests that:

> For Montaigne, as for ourselves, the language of emotion is couched in a language of spatial intimacy: we feel 'close to', 'attached to' and 'touched' by others - as Montaigne shows in his essay 'Of Friendship', dedicated to the memory of his close friend Etienne de La Boétie…For Montaigne, human proximity is at the heart of morality. Piety is easily faked: 'Its essence is abstract and hidden; its forms easy and ceremonial.' But 'to hold pleasant and reasonable conversation with oneself and one's family . . . this is rarer and more difficult to achieve'. What is interesting is how this link between moral urgency and proximity - so blindingly true - is also something that seems to be hard-wired within us.[36]

---

[34] Roger Scruton, 'Hiding behind the screen', *The New Atlantis*, Summer 2010, http://www.thenewatlantis.com/publications/hiding-behind-the-screen.

[35] It is worth noting that Montaigne, so often seen as a precursor of the *philosophes* of the Enlightenment in his scepticism and continual probing of self-identity, differed from post-Cartesian thinking in at least one vital respect: thought was not a product of the immaterial mind. For Judith Allen, Montaigne's technique of "essayistic theorizing" expresses his reliance "on experience, on feelings and on the linkage of mind and body," *Virginia Woolf and the Politics of Language*, Edinburgh: Edinburgh University Press, 2010, p.22. In similar vein, Dalia Judovitz suggests that "Montaigne circumscribes and designates the limits of the body. Rather than merely writing about it, Montaigne urges us to listen to and read the body, in order to understand the worldly limitations that define it through habits, customs, sickness, and pleasure. The body, as the object of our observation that we consider to be most private, personal, and intimate, is also that part of ourselves which bears extensively the imprint of our society and culture." *The Culture of the Body: Genealogies of Modernity*, Ann Arbor, MI: University of Michigan Press, 2001, 22.

[36] "Hardwired". This leads us into interesting new territory. Whether or not those working in the humanities and social sciences require or desire the validation of contemporary neuroscience in their efforts to better understand the social shortcomings of digitalization, recent research in that field appears to be supporting the ideas long ago advanced by Cooley, Merleau Ponty and others interested in the phenomenology of social experience. The discovery of mirror

There is no space here to examine the character of this "hardwiring," but it is clear that recent emergence of "neurosociology" is timely. One of the most urgent issues for research in this field must be into the consequences for patterns of face-to-face interaction of continual immersion in virtual spaces. Among these are questions of the apparent increase in narcissistic personality traits[37] among young heavy social media users and, more specifically, the "online disinhibition effect," in which the very absence of eye contact and embodied communication is held to be responsible for the triggering of deeply anti-social attitudes and behaviours.[38] These pathological, or potentially pathological, examples of symbiotic relationships between evolving technology and the deeper

---

neurons, in particular, seems to shed new light on just how central face-to-face experience is to deep human connection (as opposed to "connectivity") and the building of the capacity for empathy. See Christian Keysel, *The Empathetic Brain*, Social Brain Press, 2011 for a clear and enlivening account of the science, and Susan Greenfield, *ID: The Quest for Meaning in the 21st Century*, London: Hodder and Stoughton, 2008, which asks important questions about the challenges we face as a consequence of our lives being increasingly reduced to two dimensions as we meld ever more closely with our screens.

37 One of the most comprehensive discussions of this to date has been in Jean Twenge and Keith Campbell, *The Narcissism Epidemic: Living in the Age of Entitlement,* New York: Free Press, 2010. They do not make the simplistic claim that ubiquitous social media use among the young is necessarily the prime driver of increasing narcissism, but that digitalization may be acting as an accelerant of established processes of "entitlement" and self-regard rooted in the therapeutic turn, broadly conceived, in American culture since the 1960s and the widespread expression of this in popular culture. For the background to this idea see Christopher Lasch, *The Culture of Narcissism: American Life in an Age of Diminishing Expectations.* New York: W.W. Norton, 1979, and, for an update,
Christine Rosen, "The overpraised American: Christopher Lasch's The Culture of Narcissism Revisited," *Hoover Institution Policy Review* no. 133, 01.10.2005, http://www.hoover.org/publications/policy-review/article/8093 See also Elias Aboujaoude, *Virtually You: The Dangerous Powers of the E-Personality.* New York: W.W. Norton, 2011, and Christopher Carpenter, "Narcissism on Facebook: self-promotional and anti-social behavior", *Personality and Individual Differences,* 52:4, 2012, 482–486

38 See, for example, Noam Lapidot-Lefler, and Barak Azy, "Effects of anonymity, invisibility, and lack of eye-contact on Toxic
Online Disinhibition," *Computers in Human Behavior,* 28:2, 2012, 434–443, John Suler, "The Online Disinhibition Effect,"
Cyberpsychology & Behavior: The Impact of the Internet, Multimedia and Virtual Reality on Behavior and Society, 7:3, 2004, 321-6.

strains of asocial self-centredness to which they give shape and increasing potency are now of central concern.

The latest, and perhaps so far most dramatic example of this symbiosis has come with Touch ID, the authentication mechanism launched by Apple in 2013.[39] No longer, writes Norman Lewis,[40] "will our digital identity be made up of numerous usernames and passwords scattered across numerous platforms, applications and services. Touch ID could constitute a unified personal profile," thereby homogenising the offline and the online:

> The importance of what Apple is attempting cannot be understated. It is trying to change the meaning and content of digital identity, and transform mobile computing and telephony forever. And it does this by placing the self-absorption of contemporary culture at the heart of its strategy, and provides, at the very least, the appearance of a more secure 'youniverse'... It is not clear if anyone, Steve Jobs included, grasped the human drivers behind digital technology adoption, particularly among the younger generations. It was not technology that led to compulsive public self-expression and the need for constant affirmation, but fundamental shifts in the constitution of childhood in Western society. The changing nature of childhood informed the development of online chat rooms, blogging and then social networking though services like Facebook. Apple has had an uncanny ability to seize upon these shifts in user behaviour and design and take advantage of them. In the process, Apple has helped shape the world and our expectations.

---

[39] Seamus Byrne, "Apple Touch awaits iCloud keychain for its revolutionary moment," cnet.com.au, 16.09.2013, http://www.cnet.com.au/apple-touch-id-awaits-icloud-keychain-for-its-revolutionary-moment-339345456.htm.

[40] Norman Lewis, "Apple: master of the youniverse," spiked-online.co.uk, 19.09.2013, http://www.spiked-online.com/newsite/article/apple_master_of_the_youniverse/14052#.UnOLoHDmNCp 31 A concept which would seem to be increasingly relevant to our current situation; *enframing* describes the process whereby humans come both to relate to the world around them and become orientated, in terms of their subject positions, to it. The enframing capacity of technology involves the getting of things, humans included, into a "manageable framework in which they can be calculated and manipulated." See Michael Inwood, *A Heidegger Dictionary*, Oxford: Blackwell, 1999, 100. Recent work in surveillance as "social sorting," in which digitalization is seen to lead to an ever finer categorization (and manipulation) of individuals on the basis of endemic corporate dataveillance, validates and extends this insight. See David Lyon, *Surveillance as Social Sorting: Privacy, Risk and Automated Discrimination*, London: Taylor and Francis, 2002, and Zygmunt Bauman and David Lyon, *Liquid Surveillance: A Conversation*, Cambridge, UK: Polity Press, 2013.

Thus is a new kind of turbo-powered self-centredness being cemented into everyday reality? It appears that we may be on the threshold of a new level of human assimilation into an increasingly totalizing infrastructure of digitalized communication and, especially among the young, of what Heidegger calls *enframing*. What will be the personal consequences of this assimilation? And what is to become of open, outward-directed, empathetic and embodied communication with others, especially the culturally mysterious or ill-understood Other, in this context? These are key questions for the study of the socio-cultural consequences of digitalisation-as-globalisation, and they require urgent and concentrated attention.

Conclusion

Social media play a central role in the daily lives of sojourning international students in two main ways: 1) by "anchoring" them at home and helping them to maintain continuity of self, that is to say by enabling them to be exposed to new experiences whilst, on the whole, staying much the same; 2) by facilitating and framing loose and flexible "cocoons" within which to dwell comfortably with others for the duration of their stay in a way which is largely independent, in a cultural sense, of what surrounds them offline. In this way social media function in a twofold, and to some extent paradoxical, way: they make long sojourns in culturally opaque societies tolerable, or pleasurable, while shielding individuals from direct, problematic and risky exposure to intensive intercultural experience. Despite this, another important finding is that many of the students in our study recognize and state a preference for "real" interaction with others, facilitated perhaps by social media but not determined or overly transformed by them. At the same they seem poised, almost despite themselves, for assimilation into an ever expanding and deeply integrative digital communications infrastructure at the global scale. Their (our) predicament, in this sense, can be viewed as but the latest in a long line of technological development, of the extension of *techne*, whereby individuals become enframed as exploitable subjects and all but forced to adapt, as Ellul has it, to succeeding waves of innovation. This tension lies at the heart of growing unease about the unintended and largely unplanned consequences of global digitalisation, as the threats posed to customary modes of human being become clearer and more unsettling. Multiple, intersecting forces have brought us to this situation. Among them are the new media corporations which have successfully combined the global marketization of gadget fetishism with a rhetoric of personal empowerment and optimal dataveillance of consumers, and now seek to re-fashion thc world on the basis of tech-utopianism and post-human ideology; preceding waves of intellectual debunking which fed into the emergence of this post-humanism and so relativized and devalued older conceptions of humanity and healthy personhood that a body- and self-less future now seems attractive, at least to the driven ideologues of Silicon Valley and the acolytes of "visionaries" such as Ray Kurzweil; and deep cultural changes, gaining force in and since the 1960s, which have shaped the "therapeutic turn" in public culture and have triggered, in the West, an exponential increase in self-centeredness - with social media and the tools that deliver them now locked into an ever-expanding symbiotic relationship with these forces.

Bibliography

Aboujaoude, Elias. *Virtually You: The Dangerous Powers of the E-Personality*. New York: W.W. Norton, 2011

Allen, Judith. *Virginia Woolf and the Politics of Language*, Edinburgh: Edinburgh University Press, 2010

Althusser, Louis. *Essays on Ideology*, London and New York: Verso, 1984

Bauman, Zygmunt and Lyon, David. *Liquid Surveillance: A Conversation*, Cambridge, UK: Polity Press, 2013

Berger, Peter and Luckmann, Thomas. *The Social Construction of Reality: A Treatise in the Sociology of Knowledge*, Garden City, New York: Anchor Books, 1966

Boghossian, Paul. *Fear of Knowledge: Against Relativism and Constructivism*, Oxford: Clarendon Press, 2006

Bourdieu, Pierre. *Outline of a Theory of Practice*, Cambridge, UK: Cambridge University Press, 1977

Byrne, Seamus. "Apple Touch awaits iCloud keychain for its revolutionary moment," *cnet.com.au*, 16.09.2013, http://www.cnet.com.au/apple-touch-id-awaits-icloud-keychain-for-its-revolutionary-moment-339345456.htm

Carpenter, Christopher. "Narcissism on Facebook: self-promotional and anti-social behavior," *Personality and Individual Differences,* 52:4, pp. 482–486, 2012

Carr, Nicholas. *The Shallows: How the Internet is Changing the Way We Think, Read and Remember*, London: Atlantic Books, 2011

Cooley, Charles Horton. *Human Nature and the Social Order*. New York: Schocken, 1964 [1902]

Crossley, Nicholas. *Embodiment and Reflexivity in Contemporary Society.* Maidenhead: Open University Press, 2006

Csordas, T., "Intersubjectivity as intercorporeality," *Subjectivity*, 22, 2008, pp.110–121)

Csordas, Thomas (Ed). *Embodiment and Experience: The Existential Ground of Culture and Self.* Cambridge: Cambridge University Press, 1994

Damasio, Antonio. *Descartes' Error: Emotion, Reason and the Human Brain,* New York: Avon Books, 1995

Dervin, Fred. and Korpela, Mari. *Cocoon Communities: Togetherness in the 21st Century,* Newcastle-Upon-Tyne: Cambridge Scholars Publishing, 2013

Dourish, Paul. *Where the Action is: The Foundation of Embodied Interaction*, Cambridge, MA: MIT Press, 2004

Dreyfus, Hubert L. "Heidegger on the Connection between Nihilism, Art, Technology, and Politics," in Charles Guignon (Ed) *The Cambridge Companion to Heidegger*, Cambridge UK: Cambridge University Press, 1993

Dreyfus, Hubert L. *On The Internet.* Abingdon and New York: Routledge, 2001

Frampton, Saul. "Montesquieu and the macaques," *The Guardian*, 22.02.2011, http://www.theguardian.com/books/2011/jan/22/montaigne-macaques-saul-frampton

Franks, David H. *Neurosociology: The Nexus Between Neuroscience and Social Psychology*, New York: Springer, 2010

Friedman, Thomas, *The World is Flat: Globalization in the 21st Century*, London: Penguin, 2007

Greenfield, Susan. *ID: The Quest for Meaning in the 21st Century*, London: Hodder and Stoughton, 2008

Gross, Paul R., and Levitt, Norman. *Higher Superstition: The Academic Left and its Quarrels with Science*, Baltimore: John Hopkins University Press, 1997

Hacking, Ian. *The Social Construction of What?* Cambridge, MA: Harvard University Press, 1999

Hammersley, Martin and Atkinson, Paul. *Ethnography: Principles in Practice*, London and New York: Routledge, Third Edition 2007

Harris, Jan and Taylor, Paul. *Digital Matters: The Culture and Theory of the Matrix.* New York: Routledge, 2005

Hayles, Katherine. *How We Became Posthuman: Virtual Bodies in Cybernetics, Literature and Informatics*, Chicago, IL: University of Chicago Press, 1999

Inwood, Michael. *A Heidegger Dictionary*, Oxford: Blackwell, 1999

Judovitz, Dalia. *The Culture of the Body: Genealogies of Modernity*, Ann Arbor, MI: University of Michigan Press, 2001

Kass, Leon. *Life, Liberty and the Defence of Dignity: The Challenge for Bioethics*, New York: Encounter Books, 2004

Kimball, Roger. *Tenured Radicals: How Politics has Corrupted Our Education*, New York: Harper Collins, 1990

Kögler, Hans Herbert. "Agency and the Other: On the intersubjective roots of self-identity," *New Ideas in Psychology* 30:1, pp. 47–64, 2012

Keen, Andrew. *Digital Vertigo: How Today's Online Social Revolution Is Dividing, Diminishing, and Disorienting Us*. London: Macmillan, 2012

Keysel, Christian. *The Empathetic Brain.* Social Brain Press, 2011

Koertge, Noretta (Ed). *A House Built on Sand: Exposing Postmodernist Myths about Science,* Oxford: Oxford University Press, 2000

Kurzweil, Ray. *The Singularity is Near.* New York: Viking, 2005

Lakoff, George "Neural Social Science," in David D. Franks and Jonathan H. Turner (Eds) *Handbook of Neurosociology*. New York: Springer, 2011

Lakoff, George and Johnson, Mark. *Philosophy in the Flesh: The Embodied Mind and its Challenge to Western Thought*. NYC: Basic Books, 1999

Lanier, Jaron. *You Are Not a Gadget.* New York: Penguin, 2011

Lapidot-Lefler, Noam, and Azy Barak. "Effects of anonymity, invisibility, and lack of eye-contact on Toxic Online Disinhibition,", *Computers in Human Behavior,* 28 (2), 434–443, 2012

Lasch, Christopher. *Revolt of the Elites and the Betrayal of Democracy*, New York: W.W. Norton, 1996

—. *The Culture of Narcissism: American Life in an Age of Diminishing Expectations.* New York: W.W. Norton, 1979

Levy, Stephen. "How Ray Kurzweill Will Help Google Make the Ultimate AI Brain," *wired.com,* 25.04.2013, http://www.wired.com/business/2013/04/kurzweil-google-ai/

Lewis, Norman. "Apple: master of the 'youniverse'," *Spiked-Online*, 21/10/2013, http://www.spiked-online.com/newsite/article/apple_ master _of_the_youniverse/14052#.Ul6nH9JT7gE

Lyon, David. *Surveillance as Social Sorting: Privacy, Risk and Automated Discrimination*, London: Taylor and Francis, 2002

Meilaender, Gilbert. "Transitional humanity," *The New Atlantis*, Spring 2011, http://www.thenewatlantis.com/publications/transitional-humanity

Merleau-Ponty, Maurice. *The Phenomenology of Perception*. London: Routledge, English translation 1962 [1945]

Palfrey, John, and Urs Gasser, *Born Digital: Understanding the First Generation of Digital Natives,* Basic Books, 2008

Prensky, Mark. "Digital natives, digital immigrants," *On the Horizon*, Vol. 9 No. 5, pp. 1-6, 2001

—. *From Digital Natives to Digital Wisdom: Hopeful Essays for 21st Century Learning.* Thousand Oaks, CA: Corwin, 2012

Postman, Neil. *Technopoly: The Surrendering of Culture to Technology,* New York: Alfred Knopf, 1992

Rosen, Christine. "The overpraised American: Christopher Lasch's The Culture of Narcissism Revisited," *Hoover Institution Policy Review* no. 133, 01.10.2005, http://www.hoover.org/publications/policy-review/article/8093

Sapir, Edward. *Selected Writings in Language, Culture and Personality*, Berkeley: University of California Press, 1949

Scruton, Roger. *The Uses of Pessimism and the Danger of False Hope,* London: Atlantic Books, 2012

—. "Brain Drain: Neuroscience wants to be the answer to everything. It isn't.," *The Spectator*, 17.03.2012, http://www.spectator.co.uk/features/7714533/brain-drain/

—. "Hiding behind the screen," *The New Atlantis*, Summer 2010, http://www.thenewatlantis.com/publications/hiding-behind-the-screen

Selwyn, Neil. "Digital natives: myth or reality?," presentation to CILIP (Chartered Institute of Library and Information Professionals), London seminar series, London, 10th March 2009

Shilling, Chris. *The Body and Social Theory.* London: Sage, 1993

Shirkey, Clay. *Here Comes Everybody: How Change Happens When People Come Together*, London: Penguin, 2009

Siemens, George, "Connectivism: Learning theory for the digital age" *International Journal of Instructional Technology and Distance Learning* 2:1, 2005

Suler, John. "The Online Disinhibition Effect," *Cyberpsychology & Behavior: The Impact of the Internet, Multimedia and Virtual Reality on Behavior and Society,* 7 (3), 321–6, 2004

Tapscott, Don. *Growing Up Digital: Rise of the Net Generation*, New York: McGraw-Hill, 2000

Taylor, Charles. “To follow a rule,” in Craig Calhoun, Edward LiPuma and Moishe Postine (Eds) *Bourdieu: Critical Perspectives,* Cambridge, UK: Polity Press, 1993

—. “Engaged agency and background in Heidegger,” in Charles B. Guignon (Ed) *The Cambridge Companion to Heidegger*. Cambridge, UK: Cambridge University Press, 1993

Thoreau, David Henry. *Walden*, Princeton, NJ : Princeton University Press, 1971 [1854]

Turkle, Sherry. *Alone Together: Why We Expect More from Technology and Less From Each Other,* New York: Basic Books, 2011

—. *The Second Self: Computers and the Human Spirit,* New York: Simon and Schster, 1984

Turner, Bryan, *The Body and Society,* London: Basil Blackwell, 1984

Twenge, Jean and Campbell, Keith. *The Narcissism Epidemic: Living in the Age of Entitlement,* New York: Free Press, 2010

Veen, Vim and Vrakking, Ben. *Homo Zappiens: Growing up in a Digital Age*, London and New York: Continuum, 2006

Wacquant, Loic. *Body and Soul: Notebooks of an Apprentice Boxer*, New York: Routledge, 2004.

Waskul, Dennis and Vannini, Phillip (Eds). *Symbolic Interaction and the Sociology of the Body,* Aldershot: Ashgate, 2006

Williams, Raymond. *Keywords: A Vocabulary of Culture and Society.* New York: Oxford University Press, 1976

Woolaston, Victoria. “We’ll be uploading our entire MINDS to computers by 2045 and our bodies will be replaced by machines within 90 years, Google expert claims,” *Daily Mail*, 19.06.2013, http://www.dailymail.co.uk/sciencetech/article-2344398/Google-futurist-claims-uploading-entire-MINDS-computers-2045-bodies-replaced-machines-90-years.html

Zuckerman, E. (2013), *Rewire: Digital Cosmopolitans in the Age of Connection*

CHAPTER TWO

MINDFUL REJECTION OF DIGITAL TECHNOLOGY AT THE USER LEVEL: COGNITIVE DETERMINANTS AND SOCIAL CONSEQUENCES

C.M. OLAVARRIA

Introduction

Emerging research on the harmful effects of digital technologies on user well-being necessitates inclusion of the term "Mindful Rejection." Future discourse on digital technology abstention will be influenced by choice at the user level, and increasingly informed by both subjective and well-documented physical and cognitive ramifications, some of which include addiction, attention deficit disorder, memory loss, NPD (Narcissistic Personality Disorder), relationship difficulties, and identity crises. The rise of digital technology fads such as the "digital detox" show that cognitive determinants of digital technology overuse may one day lead toward mindful rejection rather than temporary resistance. Mindful rejection is impossible to discuss without considering consequences such as social and professional exclusion.

Historical Perspective

There are an abundance of thinkers and epochs in history with endless examples of the paradoxes of technology, when inventions and machines collide with unintended consequences.[1] The point when human civilization

[1] David Glen Mick and Susan Fournier. "Paradoxes of Technology : Consumer Cognizance, Emotions, and Coping Strategies." *Journal of Consumer Research*, 25 (1998) (2): 123–143.

first became cognizant of the negative effects of its innovations on their collective and individual behaviour became more and more manifest once innovations of comfort and luxury surpassed those of utility and need, and technologies of amusement and distraction supplanted those of purposeful function.[2] The lines between the two having blurred consistently over the centuries as justifications imposed by market forces and mass culture render the necessary distinction almost extinct. Yet there are always dissenting voices, attentive and eloquent in their ability to expose hard truths to the overwhelming herds that attempt to marginalize and discredit their accurate and often disturbing critiques of technology. The champion dissenter of the enlightenment period was Rousseau[3] who observed: "The more ingenious our apparatus, the coarser and more unskilful are our senses. We surround ourselves with tools and fail to use those with which nature has provided every one of us."[4]

Over two centuries after Rousseau, it was Heidegger who claimed, "Everywhere we remain unfree and chained to technology, whether we passionately affirm or deny it. But we are delivered over to it in the worst possible way when we regard it as something neutral."[5] He also warned of the "frenziedness of technology" which would "entrench itself everywhere." Neil Postman labelled the proliferating entrenchment of technology and the collectively passive unquestioning adoption of every emerging technology regardless of utility as a Faustian bargain.[6] At its basic core, the German legend is the source of the colloquialism "Make a deal with the devil." However, Postman's technological analogy in Faustian terms is not without intriguing metaphor. It infers the dehumanizing effects of modern technology on society and the individual, the devolution toward cyborg attributes, which renders both "soulless" as in the case of Faust sacrificing his soul to the devil in exchange for delimited wealth and power. The wealth produced by persistent technological innovation and the illusory power appropriated to both producers and consumers are mere temporary indulgences. The pretence is terrific efficiency across all areas

---

[2] Neil Postman, *Building a Bridge to the 18th Century: How the Past Can Improve Our Future*. (New York: Vintage Books, 2000), 49-51.

[3] His first published work "Discourse on the Arts and Sciences" offered a biting critique of scientific progress at the time.

[4] Rousseau, Jean-Jacques. *Emile* (First published 1762. Auckland: The Floating Press, 2009), 271.

[5] Heidegger, Martin. *The Question Concerning Technology* (New York & London: Garland Publishing Inc., 1977), 9.

[6] "Technology is no substitute for Human Values." Neil Postman interview with Alan Gregg. TVO Ontario, 2000.

of modern life, though often to distract and amuse until the toll collector rings announcing the final cost to their customary bemusement. Payment is never complete but recurring, and the deficits only measured once sufficient and alarming losses are finally realized. The losses always of less concern to the producers than consumers of technology, though hardly acknowledged by either and often denied.

At present, first world societies and its enthralled inhabitants are entitled and afforded through cheap labour, a limitless supply of digital gadgetry to absorb, however not without the aforementioned social and cognitive penalties that will sooner or later extract and exact a price on both the individual and the collective.[7] More simply Postman claimed: "Whatever technology giveth, it also taketh away."[8] Yet decades before Postman, it was Marshall McLuhan who wrote that our technological innovations end up "numbing" whatever human attribute they were intended to "amplify."[9] Nicholas Carr proffers a more contemporary yet similar assessment, "Every tool imposes limitations even as it opens possibilities. The more we use it, the more we mold ourselves to its form and function."[10]

One of the first human sacrifices and perhaps the most consequential is individual autonomy. Any measurable loss of autonomy, whether recognized or not by the individual, equates on some level to a consent of violations against one's whole being by surrounding social and cultural forces. With a loss of autonomy comes a loss of choice. However another paradox of technology then becomes apparent. If one part of the history of technology "can be told as the story of how human beings gave themselves more choices,"[11] then one might question how autonomy is sacrificed in the face of technology? In a technological society Jacques Ellul observed that human autonomy is antithetical to technology's desire toward social permeation. It is inevitable and necessary that technology will prevail over the human being for "there can be no human autonomy in the face of

---

[7] Bowers, C.A. "The Paradox of Technology: What's Gained and Lost?" NEA Higher Education Journal (1998): 111–120.

[8] Neil Postman, "Informing Ourselves to Death." (Lecture: German Informatics Society, October 11, 1990) Stuttgart, Germany.

[9] Marshall McLuhan, *Understanding Media: The Extensions of Man* (Corte Madera, CA: Gingko Press, 2003), 63-70.

[10] Nicholas Carr, *The Shallows: What the Internet is Doing to Our Brains* (New York: W.W. Norton & Company, 2010), 209.

[11] Douglas Rushkoff, Program or Be Programmed: Ten Commandments for a Digital Age (New York: OR Books, 2010), 51-54.

technical autonomy."[12] Digital technology, in line with the demands of mass consumption[13] may appear to always offer more choices on the surface, yet "our pursuit of choice has the effect of making us less engaged, more obsessive, less free and more controlled."[14] The only choice then becomes that the user must make a choice and is forbidden from rejecting all of the above. The choice of rejection becomes "inadmissible" by society and the individual must integrate all aspects of himself "in the drive toward technicization…making it impossible for him to escape this collective phenomena."[15]

With the abundance of continually emerging empirical research on the social and cognitive consequences of the present "digital age" and the hastened pace toward incessant technological innovation and integration, a re-examination of individual autonomy becomes increasingly significant. Is it impossible for individuals to choose to "escape" or reject digital technologies? If they are aware or mindful of the social and cognitive effects of certain technologies on their personal well being, will that sufficiently incentivize rejection? A closer evaluation of present research on cognitive effects may provide better insight.

While every choice we make, no matter how minor it's perceived requires thought and attention, there are consequences to endure for choosing not to choose what society collectively deems "necessary" in the realm of digital technology. Mindful rejecters of any technology, no matter its perceived value, must anticipate expectant fallout. As the continual digitization of everything permeates social life, accelerates perceived efficiency in the professional workplace, and technological solutionism is ceaselessly championed and propagated by its producers and profiteers,[16] [17] then the obvious yet comprehensive consequences of social exclusion and professional exclusion become practically impossible to elude. The cost-benefit analysis of rejecting the technological consequences for another set of resultant consequences could perhaps be quantified, but the popular assumption of the moment is the remedy of temporary abstention rather than outright rejection. If the pull of digital technology is far greater

---

[12] Jacques Ellul, *The Technological Society* (Toronto: Vintage Books, 1964), 138.

[13] Barry Schwartz, *The Paradox of Choice: Why More is Less* (New York: Harper Collins. 2004), 221.

[14] Rushkoff, Program or be Programmed, 52.

[15] Ellul, The Technological Society, 139.

[16] Ellul, The Technological Society, 319.

[17] Evgeny Morozov, To Save Everything Click Here: The Folly of Technological Solutionism (New York: Public Affairs, 2013).

than our ability to resist it,[18] then the advocated solution is to "disconnect and recharge" the self, or take a "digital detox" retreat.[19] The former alludes to humans as pieces of technology in service to machines and to function like machines. The latter implies that digital technologies poison the user and require detoxification. Solutions to technological solutionism have given rise to an entirely novel and exploitative self-help industry, not unlike tobacco companies shilling "help" products to tobacco addicts. When addictive and excessive behaviour becomes disruptive to well being, the marketplace of solutions produces various strategies for coping that often come with great financial costs and excessive promises. This has given rise in recent years to technological solutionism's "solution industry." Health professionals are cashing in on the problems of addiction, compulsivity, inattention, self-absorption and unhealthy dependence on digital gadgets with books, and in-out patient clinical treatment. Popular coping mechanisms include the digital detox, the digital diet, and the digital detox retreat where people pay for a holiday that requires they "disconnect" for the duration of their visit. Businesses are seizing the opportunity to offer "digital free" zones to customers, much like no smoking areas of decades past. The assumption for this cunning self-help industry is antithetical to genuine and authentic help, for the profits ahead require inescapable dependence of the individual on digital technology. The remedy then is often prescribed in the form of a substitute for the problem, originating from its very source.[20]

Mindful Rejection and Passive Resistance

Sufficient research has been geared toward resistance to new technology and means of greater inclusion and breaking the digital divide. Less focus has been given to the user's choice to reject new technology in the face of socio-cultural pressure based on their ability to individually assess its

---

[18] Sherry Turkle, Alone Together: Why We Expect More from Technology and Less from Each Other (New York: Basic Books, 2011) 152-154.

[19] Many of these advocates, including respected academics, shamelessly feel the need to preface their warnings and advice by revealing their unbridled adoration for the technologies they critique in order to win the ears of technology's fanatics, whom they hope to influence.

[20] The popular linking "news" website *Huffington Post* created a phone application called "GPS For the Soul." A "killer app for better living" which claims to monitor stress levels upon touching the screen. It is available for free on their self-help and "well being" section that is inundated with advice on how to live better with digital technologies by temporarily disengaging them.

worthiness to their overall well being. This implies mindfulness and courage for the individual to "escape" the forces of a technological society that Ellul deemed "impossible." Whether rejection or "escape" is possible, depends on the user's desire or ability to endure resultant social consequences that will be examined last.

Firstly, the distinction between resistance and rejection is important. Resistance implies that something is being forced upon the subject or "user"; that the user is suffering for their refusal toward inevitable submission. Motives for resistance are often socio-economic,[21] where users are victims of social conditions of techno-inaccessibility and psychological, as in the dated label of "cyberphobia" or the more encompassing but often misused term "technophobia." Both labels often assume and feature the prejudices of older generations and their "fear" of the new and unknown. According to Murthy and Mani, factors that serve as motives for rejection include technological complexity, technology fatigue, level of flexibility, altering user-base, switching cost and loss aversion.[22] All these factors differ from mindful rejection by inferring culpability on the technology's utility originating from the consumer's desires[23] and not the technology's effects on the user's physical or psychological well-being. In other words the user would engage the technology if it were less complex, more flexible, and more affordable. These are not psycho-cognitive determinants for rejection, such as addiction and dependence, attention deficit, memory loss or identity crisis. The user could be cognitive of a given technology's utilitarian deficiencies from experience or referral, thus resulting in an intended consumer's passive resistance, and likely instigating the search for a preferable alternative.[24] Passive resistance becomes a temporary consumer position based on the external factors of a consumerist society.[25] Mindful rejection assumes that an individual or "user" has embraced a given digital technology for an indeterminate period of time or considered becoming a "user" at some point. The user or potential user, through mindful

---

[21] Neil Selwyn. "Apart from technology: Understanding people's non-use of information and communication technologies in everyday life." *Technology in Society*, 25 (2003), 99-116.

[22] Suhir, Rama Murthy and Mono Mani. "Discerning Rejection of Technology." *SAGE Open* (2013) 3 (2) (April 23).

[23] The authors originate these factors based on how "social, economic, and environmental concerns influence individuals."

[24] Okada, E. M. "Trade-ins, mental accounting, and product replacement decisions." *Journal of Consumer Research*, 27 (2001), 433-447.

[25] Zygmunt Bauman, *Consuming Life* (Cambridge: Polity Press, 2007) 52-53.

assessment then determines that the technology has negatively affected them or others sufficiently enough to discontinue or reject that technology *a priori*. This assessment can be informed from both subjective experience of the user and the objective research conclusions of academic and health professionals of negative consequences on other users. The determinants of mindful rejection of import here are psycho-cognitive in nature. Four significant general areas of psycho-cognitive determinants briefly worth addressing are: i) Addiction and Dependence ii) Attention and Focus iii) Memory and Retention iv) Identity, Narcissism and Relationships.

Cognitive Determinants of Mindful Rejection

Addiction and Dependence

Internet addiction and gaming addiction are burgeoning areas of addiction research in psychology and psychiatry with the DSM-5[26] now including Internet addiction as a recognized and diagnosable behavioural problem. There are numerous behaviour factors that may contribute to Internet addiction including: escape or avoidance behaviour, operant and Pavlovian conditioning, impulsivity (lack of control), or any number of obsessive preoccupations related to the Internet.[27] Like most addictions, this compulsive behaviour triggers cravings or withdrawals that lead the subject back to the desired source. Various studies conclude that Internet addiction "seems to be associated with depression, anxiety, social phobia, loneliness, low self-esteem, hostility, substance use, harmful alcohol use, as well as lower frustration discomfort and higher impulsivity levels."[28]

A study of adolescent Taiwanese in 2006 identified the psychological needs and motivations underlying video game addiction within seven themes:[29] (1) entertainment and leisure, (2) emotional coping (diversions from loneliness, isolation and boredom, releasing stress, relaxation, discharging anger and frustration), (3) escaping from reality, (4) satisfying interpersonal and social needs (making friends, strengthening friendships, and generating a sense of belonging and recognition), (5) the need for

---

[26] American Psychiatric Association's Diagnostic and Statistical Manual of Mental Disorders.

[27] Khazaal, Yasser, Constantina Xirossavidou, Riaz Khan, Yves Edel, Fadi Zebouni, and Daniele Zullino. "Cognitive-Behavioral Treatments for 'Internet Addiction'" *The Open Addiction Journal* 5 (2012): 30–35.

[28] Khazaal, "Cognitive-Behavioral Treatments," 30-35.

[29] Wan Chin-sheng and Chiou Wen-bin. "Why Are Adolescents Addicted to Online Gaming?" *Cyber-Psychology and Behavior* 9 (2006), (6): 762–766.

achievement, (6) the need for excitement and challenge, and (7) the need for power (the sense of superiority, the desire for control, and facilitation of self-confidence).

Internet multi-player gaming, virtual world gaming, social media and digital technology use in general has been rising steadily among adolescents. In the United States 8-18 year-olds devote an average of 7 hours and 38 minutes (7:38) to using entertainment media across a typical day (more than 53 hours a week). And because they spend so much of that time "media multitasking" (using more than one medium at a time), they actually manage to pack a total of 10 hours and 45 minutes (10:45) worth of media content into those 7½ hours.[30] These figures don't account for texting which is estimated to be an additional hour and a half or talking on their cell phones, an additional half hour.[31] With the increase in smart phone use, the Internet becomes accessible from anywhere. Phone Internet use doubled from 2009-2013 to 63% among adult cell phone users in the United States.[32] Like any addiction, compulsive use of digital technologies can have detrimental consequences on individual well-being and relationships with family and friends.

Attention and Focus

Media Multitasking has been celebrated in work environments as moving between multiple tasks for greater efficiency presumably allowing the worker to accomplish more. It has now been shown to produce unexpected results between heavy media multi-taskers (HMMs) and light media multi-taskers (LMMs).[33] Multitasking involves the user to assume a state of focus on one task, then "switch gears, reassess the environment and

---

[30] Kaiser Family Foundation. *Generation M2: Media in the Lives of 8-18 Year Olds.* Study of Media and Health, Washington, DC: www.kff.org/entmedia/mh012010pkg.cfm, 2010.

[31] Tamar Lewin. "If Your Kids Are Awake, They're Probably Online." *New York Times.* January 20, 2010.

[32] Maeve Duggan and Aaron Smith. "Cell Internet Use 2013," Pew Internet Project: http://pewinternet.org/~/media//Files/Reports/2013/PIP_CellInternetUse2013.pdf, September 6, 2013.

[33] Lin, Lin. "Breadth-biased Versus Focused Cognitive Control in Media Multitasking Behaviors." *Proceedings of the National Academy of Sciences of the United States of America* (2009) 106 (37) (September 15): 15521–2. doi:10.1073/pnas.0908642106.

resume focus" on another task.[34] This back and forth results in switch costs[35] and it turns out that HMMs, forced to pay attention to a larger scope of information are less adept at switching tasks than LMMs. A new working definition of multitasking may be "the ability for one to engage multiple tasks with the likelihood for quality deficiencies increasing in proportion to the number of tasks engaged." Multimedia in learning environments strains our cognitive abilities that divide attention and retract focus, which subsequently compromise understanding and weaken comprehension.[36] Just like juggling multiple tasks impairs effectiveness and outcome quality depending on one's level of cognitive inhibition, simultaneous message presentations exact a toll on our attention, impeding our ability for retention.[37] While a portion of the messages are lost in the clutter of over stimulus, the amount of textual, auditory and visual messages incorporated into content will continue to increase. Will the plasticity of the brain adapt and adjust to continual exposure to increased stimuli, or will more information result in increased losses of retention through decreased focus? The greater our attention is spread and taxed across multiple stimuli, the less ability we have to focus in on what we deem important, or even determine accurately what that is. The Internet by design is "an interruption system" geared for "dividing attention."[38] Digital technologies are developed by companies to deliver that attention dividing interruption system with increased facility. The stimuli-attention cycle then becomes self-perpetuating. As single function digital technologies become obsolete, they are incorporated in multi-function devices with endless tools to distract, push and pull, demand and command the user to obey its service. That self-perpetuating cycle derives from shifting from a hyper stimulus environment to a quiet and more reflective state. Digital technologies condition the user to demand more stimuli,[39] triggering physical engagement with a device and "continual

---

[34] Maggie Jackson, Distracted: The Erosion of Attention and the Coming Dark Age (New York: Prometheus Books, 2008) 79.

[35] Jackson, *Distracted*, 80.

[36] Steven C. Rockwell and Loy A. Singleton, "The Effect of the Modality of Presentation of Streaming Multimedia on Information Acquisition," *Media Psychology*, 9 (2007): 179-91.

[37] Lori Bergman, Tom Grimes, and Deborah Potter, "How Attention Partitions Itself during Simultaneous Message Presentations," *Human Communication Research*, 31, no. 3 (July 2005): 311-36.

[38] Carr, *The Shallows*, 131.

[39] Torkel Klingberg, The Overflowing Brain: Information Overload and the Limits of Working Memory (Oxford: Oxford University Press, 2009) 166.

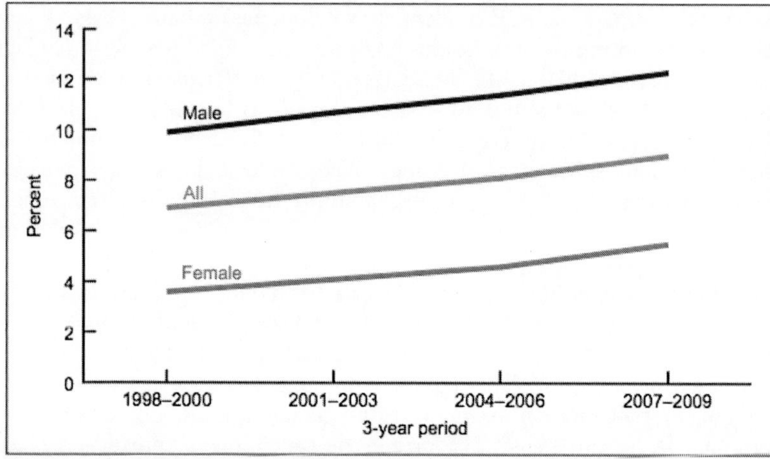

Figure 1: From NHCS - Vol. 70 - August, 2011

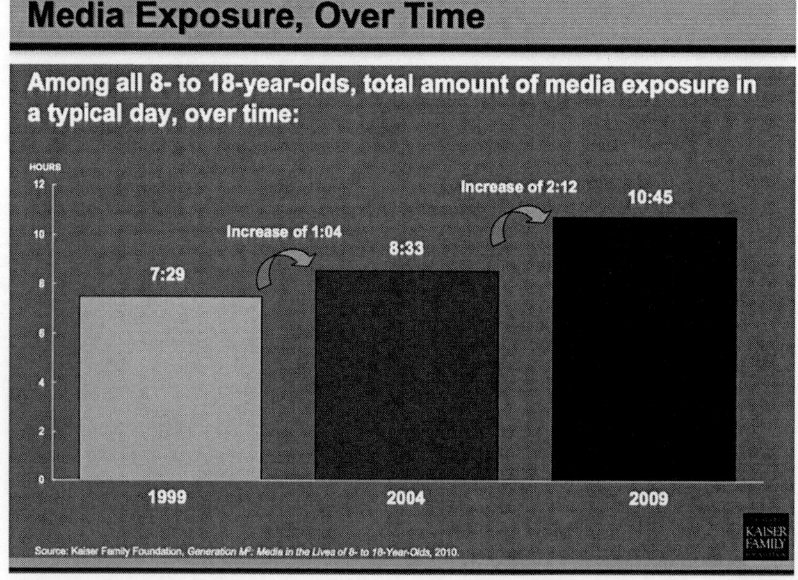

Figure 2: Includes Television, Movies, Digital Music Players, Cell Phones, and Internet Use

partial attention" (CPA) to multiple digital content.[40] Alerts are programmed, pings are triggered, refresh cycles set to high frequency and personal data is proffered thoughtlessly in exchange for the promise of more stimuli. The demand increases when the user's device is prompted by another user attempting to connect with them. The sound, signal or command prompt equates to the promise of human contact, or the symbiotic attention collective of more than one being. In the company of digital technology, we are prone to offer less continual partial attention (CPA) to our physical environment, as we get lost in the endless distractions of simulated partial connectedness. Devices serve the user by bestowing them attention through extracting their attention. The mere presence of smart phones while in the company of others can exact a toll on information retention and have a negative impact on social experiences.[41] The massive rise in diagnoses of Attention Deficit Disorder (ADD) and Attention Deficit Hyperactivity Disorder (ADHD), particularly in young people directly correlates to the equally massive adoption and use of digital technologies during the same period.[42]

Memory and Retention

We have come to rely on digital technologies, particularly the Internet for its vast swaths of easily accessible information. There are obvious consequences to memory and our increasingly compromised ability to retain long-term memories.[43] The reflexive reaction to forgetting a piece of information today is to "Google it." A popular term for those with inquiries, often followed by the lauded phrase "Google knows everything." "We should not assume that Google, with its focus on delivering what we want — or think we want — will deliver what we actually need."[44] In assuming that Google would obey its sinister slogan

---

[40] CPA is a phrase coined by Linda Stone, founder of "The Attention Project."

[41] Andrew K. Przybylski and Netta Weinstein. "Can You Connect with Me Now? How the Presence of Mobile Communication Technology Influences Face-to-face Conversation Quality." *Journal of Social and Personal Relationships* 30 (2012) (3) (July 19): 237–246.

[42] Kaiser Family Foundation. *Generation M2: Media in the Lives of 8-18 Year Olds.* Study of Media and Health, Washington, DC: www.kff.org/entmedia/mh012010pkg.cfm, 2010.

[43] Carr, *The Shallows*, 33.

[44] Vaidhyanathan Siva, *The Googlization of Everything* (Berkeley, CA: University of California Press, 2011) 202.

and "not be evil," "we made a grand mistake over the past few years"[45] by outsourcing human knowledge to a private corporation that inevitably must operate like a corporation.[46] We come to rely on Google and an endless offering of apps and artificial memory devices to store a great deal of what we are more than capable of storing in our brains. The search for all information, no matter how rudimentary, is encouraged with technological aides in learning environments at an early age. Outsourcing to devices what was once the function of working memory in the prefrontal cortex, before being stored as long-term memories in the hippocampus, deprives us of the cognitive exercises required to strengthen and develop these important regions of the brain.[47] [48] There is of course an obvious correlation between explicit memory and conscious attention. Memory making, "is all about the rich, carefully cultivated connections that thinkers since Aristotle have understood as the roots of knowledge. Attention, you might say, is the nectar of memory."[49] Fast and easy access to information that can easily be remembered by the brain becomes a habitual short cut to immediate gratification via digital technology, conditioned through slothful acquiescence. As flitting through digital content and multitasking spreads our attention thin, the overload of stimuli hinders our ability to retain long-term memories. The more we rely on technology to serve as memory tools, the more vulnerable we are in their absence. Resilience becomes reliance and memory development devolves into memory dependence. The brain may adapt to new technologies, but while new neural pathways are strengthened, others are weakened. Estimating the value of information retention or memory deprivation through those neural exchanges becomes a necessary process for the mindful rejecter.

Identity, Narcissism and Relationships

Adolescent identity development occurs in two spheres that have a reciprocal relationship. The online or digital sphere is built upon a framework that is biased toward spatial dislocation and asynchronous

---

[45] Vaidhyanathan, *The Googlization*, 202.

[46] With contempt and disregard to any forces that undermine its incessant pursuit of profits, power and control.

[47] Carr, *The Shallows*, 119-121.

[48] Jackson, *Distracted*, 220.

[49] Jackson, *Distracted*, 220.

communication.[50] For previous generations identity development and social interaction occurred in real time in the physical world. Today youth manage their online selves (digital self, e-personality, virtual self, or second self) through constantly connected digital devices. Their online self-representations are carefully crafted, packaged and presented to impress upon others a version of their "best self" and the pressures to live up to that altered self-image require greater energy for enhanced expectations. Online identities and relationships creep into offline lives and the associations between true self and digital self become affective and dissociative, often leaving users susceptible to both toxic and benign "online disinhibition effect."[51]

People are opting for less vulnerable methods of communication such as texting and messaging where social risk can be managed and words can be chosen carefully and responses crafted with sufficient time to convey the desired impression that satisfies the needs of self-awareness.[52] The desire to embrace the promised stimuli of a greater quantity of shallow friendships in SNS through by offering CPA in order to satisfy "Simulated Partial Connectedness" (SPC), taxes people's ability to foster deeper, meaningful real world relationships.

The construct of SNS encourages shallow relationships, superficial "friendships" and the attention rewards of unhinged exhibitionism disguised as "sharing." Not all users are susceptible to this programmable behaviour, but SNS by nature are "fertile ground for narcissists to self-regulate."[53] According to Elias Aboujaoude, narcissists are self-worshippers who want others to worship them as well and their grandiosity for self leaves them regarding others with inferiority.[54] SNS provide an outlet for people with low self-esteem to exhibit compensatory narcissism. These less daring, more conservative individuals also find the safety of the "digital wall" useful for amorous narcissistic behaviour such as indulging hedonistic desires and sexual fantasies often through creating exaggeratedly appealing yet false self-representations.[55] This self-indulgent promiscuous

[50] Ruskoff, Program, 30-37.

[51] John Suler. "The Online Disinhibition Effect." Cyberpsychology & Behavior : the Impact of the Internet, Multimedia and Virtual Reality on Behavior and Society 7 (2004) (3) (June): 321–6.

[52] Turkle, Alone Together, 187-190.

[53] Laura E. Buffardi and Keith W. Campbell. "Narcissism and Social Networking Web Sites," PSPB 34 (2008): (10), 1304.

[54] Elias Aboujaoude, Virtually You: The Dangerous Powers of the E-personality (New York, NY: WW Norton, 2011) 68.

[55] Aboujaoude, Virtually You, 29.

behaviour can have negative effects on real world relationships. Likewise, SNS can also delay the healing process of an emotional break up. The urge for surveillance of an ex-partner online stunts emotional recovery and personal growth.[56] Other consequences of narcissistic SNS use include jealousy and envy, which can leave users feeling inferior, depressed or even suspicious contempt for those "friends" who broadcast perceivably inflated and false representations with self-gratifying frequency.[57]

As digital technologies aid in satisfying our every need and want and encourage desire for fulfilment with increasing speeds, users grow less patient and more impulsive, fostering a greater likelihood of entitlement.[58] Web sites auto-customize themselves to user preferences. Advertisements target users based on a history of their online behaviour, logging and collecting endless data to profile their consumptive habits. Recommendations are made in the narrow window of patterns and practices that constitute the user's digital self, leaving them trapped and less exposed to new ideas, content or people that may be of interest to them. The so-called "limitless reach" of the Internet is collapsing in on users, making a once infinite medium shrink based on their increasingly limited patterns. This customization to user habits or digital individuation will likely exacerbate entitlement as efficient accuracy of automation becomes expectant, while further insulating them from varied exposure to an "Internet of possibilities" rather than the symbolic reductionist categorization from constant surveillance.

Consequences of Mindful Rejection

The choice to reject a particular digital technology in today's ever-connected world becomes increasingly impermissible as Ellul predicted decades ago. Mindful rejection comes with explicit and implicit consequences, that will leave the user questioning their decision before long. Rejecting use of a smart phone means less accessibility to others and greater isolation from others while being mobile, with email, IM, and SNS activity nonexistent. For SNS users who one day choose to reject broadcast

---

[56] Tara C. Marshall. "Facebook Surveillance of Former Romantic Partners: Associations with Post breakup Recovery and Personal Growth." Cyberpsychology, Behavior, and Social Networking 15 (2012) (10): 521-6.

[57] Hui Tzu, Grace Chou, and Nicholas Edge. "'They Are Happier and Having Better Lives Than I Am': The Impact of Using Facebook on Perceptions of Others' Lives." Cyberpsychology, Behavior, and Social Networking 15 (2012) (2): 117–121.

[58] Aboujaoude, Virtually You, 70-71.

and participation and go so far as to delete their alternative self, or digital self-representation, the result will be immediate social exclusion. Events that are officially posted to SNS and plans that are made through this medium disappear. Participants assume that everyone in their social circle has access to this information. For those no longer in the loop, the likelihood of others reaching out to them via alternative methods of communication may initially be possible, however over time this will decrease as others grow tired of having to make the "extra effort" for a single individual. The mindful rejecter then becomes isolated by choice and this test of patience with solitude and social exclusion will determine whether they return to a digital technology, or just how soon, as it is an inherently human desire to feel connected to others regardless of how slight that connection is in reality.

For adolescents and young adults, the need to belong is a desire that trumps all but the basic necessities for survival.[59] The idea of voluntary social exclusion seems absurd, as self-defeating behaviour increases for those who feel rejected or excluded. Social exclusion can cause anxiety, stress, low self-esteem and even aggressive behaviour.[60] The longer one remains "disconnected" from SNS and ICTs, the greater the effort required by that user to keep in touch with others through conventional means which others have long abandoned (or never used) and will have little patience for with special circumstantial utilization.[61]

As corporations rush to adopt every new technology perceived to increase efficiency, productivity and profit, employees must conform to the popular practice of their industry. These requisite digital tools end up efficiently controlling employees. Work becomes mobile. The day is never done, meetings are never finished, reports can be doctored from the dinner table, follow-up calls made behind the wheel of a car in the slog of evening traffic. Expectations increase for the connected worker so that disconnecting is impermissible. Mindful rejection of any digital technology in corporate western culture would leave the non-user

---

59 W.L. Gardner, C. L. Pickett, and M. B. Brewer. "Social Exclusion and Selective Memory: How the Need to Belong Influences Memory for Social Events." Personality and Social Psychology Bulletin 26 (2000) (4) (April 1): 486–496.

60 Twenge, Jean M., Kathleen R. Catanese, and Roy F. Baumeister. "Social Exclusion and the Deconstructed State: Time Perception, Meaninglessness, Lethargy, Lack of Emotion, and Self-awareness." Journal of Personality and Social Psychology 85 (2003) (3) (September): 409–23.

61 Correspondence by post, telephone, unannounced in-person visits: all now seem too direct and personal for those who prefer the illusory control of ICT and CMC and the safe emotional distance they provide.

incapable of fulfilling basic job requirements. Professional exclusion becomes common for those who reject SNS, such as LinkedIn, where users can self-promote and increase their labour stock through inflated impressions and nurtured connections. Employers in journalism, media, communications, and IT industries increasingly require their workers to be avid users of social media. These become prerequisites for hiring. The twitter user with the most followers may trump equally qualified candidates for their ability to broadcast multiple times daily in one hundred and forty characters or less. Employees become walking digital billboards for their employers, advertising their position, status and sheer adoration for the work that they do through the broadcasts they perform. Mindful rejection of SNS and other digital technologies automatically disqualifies a person from employment consideration in certain fields.

Conclusion

The concept of mindful rejection of digital technologies at the user level may be pervasive in a mindful society. As an abstract idea, it is unlikely that users en masse will respond to emerging research on the cognitive effects of digital technologies and reject a way of life they have become accustomed to, or be willing to endure the serious consequences of social and professional exclusion. The possibility for further research to quantify the consequences on various individuals for rejecting a particular technology in varying conditions would be a worthwhile undertaking.

For new and emerging technologies that are collectively and passively adopted by society, it is not enough to just ask questions. It is necessary to ask the right questions. At the dawn of this digital age Neil Postman asked important questions[62] that many of us ignore today as we sift through hundreds of thousands of apps for download, each one promising to compensate some deficit in our lives so that a new app becomes necessary to counteract the problem created by the former, and on into perpetuity.

The most important questions regarding our use or misuse of digital technologies will continue to be answered by advances in neuroscience

---

[62] [1] What is the problem to which this technology is the solution? [2] Whose problem is it? [3] Which people and what institutions might be most seriously harmed by a technological solution? [4] What new problems might be created because we have solved this problem? [5] What sort of people and institutions might acquire special economic and political power because of technological change? [6] What changes in language are being enforced by new technologies, and what is being gained and lost by such changes?

and neuropsychology and asked by those willing to endure the tide of forces of opposition: digital corporations and their billions of consumers. Engrossed by the awe and wonderment of digital products designed to distract our focus from the hidden tolls, we consume the promises of techno-profits as truth and elevate them to an iconic status once reserved for kings and princes. Mindful rejection may or may not be useful today or in the future, and it may be blind optimism to imagine it ought to be. Perhaps we're collectively beyond the point of individual user rejection, and it is sufficient enough to just be mindful of the cognitive deficits new technologies activate. No password required.

Bibliography

Aboujaoude, Elias. Virtually You: The Dangerous Powers of the E-personality, New York, NY: WW Norton, 2011.

Bauman, Zygmunt. Consuming Life. Cambridge: Polity Press, 2007.

Bergman, Lori, Tom Grimes and Deborah Potter, "How Attention Partitions Itself during Simultaneous Message Presentations," Human Communication Research 31 (2005): (3), 311-36.

Bowers, C.A. "The Paradox of Technology: What's Gained and Lost?" *NEA Higher Education Journal* (1995): 111–120.

Buffardi, Laura E, and Keith W. Campbell. "Narcissism and Social Networking Web Sites," *PSPB* 34 (2008): (10) 1303-1314.

Carpenter, Christopher J. "Narcissism on Facebook: Self-promotional and Anti-social Behavior." *Personality and Individual Differences* 52 (2012) (4) (March): 482–486.

Carr, Nicholas. *The Shallows: What the Internet is Doing to Our Brains.* New York: W.W. Norton & Company, 2010.

Chin-sheng, Wan and Wen-bin Chiou. "Why Are Adolescents Addicted to Online Gaming ?" *Cyber-Psychology and Behavior* 9 (2006), (6): 762–766.

Damrosch, Leo. *Jean-Jacques Rousseau: Restless Genius.* New York: Mariner Books, 2007.

Duggan, Maeve and Aaron Smith. "Cell Internet Use 2013," Pew Internet Project: http://pewinternet.org/~/media//Files/Reports/2013/PIP_CellInternetUse2013.pdf September 2013.

Ellul, Jacques. *The Technological Society.* Toronto: Vintage Books, 1964.

Evgeny Morozov. *To Save Everything Click Here*: *The Folly of Technological Solutionism*. New York: Public Affairs, 2013.

Foundation, Kaiser Family. *Generation M2: Media in the Lives of 8-18 Year Olds.* Study of Media and Health, Washington, DC: www.kff.org/entmedia/mh012010pkg.cfm, 2010.

Gardner, W. L., C. L. Pickett, and M. B. Brewer. "Social Exclusion and Selective Memory: How the Need to Belong Influences Memory for Social Events." *Personality and Social Psychology Bulletin* 26 (2000) (4) (April 1): 486–496.

Glen, David and Susan Fournier. "Paradoxes of Technology: Consumer Cognizance, Emotions, and Coping Strategies." *Journal of Consumer Research*, 25 (2013) (2): 123–143.

Heidegger, Martin. *The Question Concerning Technology*. New York & London: Garland Publishing Inc., 1977.

Jackson, Maggie. *Distracted: The Erosion of Attention and the Coming Dark Age*. New York: Prometheus Books, 2008.

Khazaal, Yasser, Constantina Xirossavidou, Riaz Khan, Yves Edel, Fadi Zebouni, and Daniele Zullino. 2012. "Cognitive-Behavioral Treatments for 'Internet Addiction'", *The Open Addiction Journal* 5 (2012): 30–35.

Klingberg, Torkel. *The Overflowing Brain: Information Overload and the Limits of Working Memory*. Oxford: Oxford University Press, 2009.

Lewin, Tamar. "If Your Kids Are Awake, They're Probably Online." *New York Times.* January 20, 2010.

Lin, Lin. "Breadth-biased Versus Focused Cognitive Control in Media Multitasking Behaviors." *Proceedings of the National Academy of Sciences of the United States of America* (2009) 106 (37) (September 15): 15521–2.

Marshall, Tara C. "Facebook Surveillance of Former Romantic Partners: Associations with Postbreakup Recovery and Personal Growth." *Cyberpsychology, Behavior, and Social Networking* 15 (2012) (10): 521-6.

McLuhan, Marshall. *Understanding Media: The Extensions of Man.* Corte Madera, CA: Gingko Press, 2003.

Okada, E. M. "Trade-ins, mental accounting, and product replacement decisions." *Journal of Consumer Research* 27 (2001): 433-447.

Postman, Neil. *Building a Bridge to the 18th Century: How the Past Can Improve Our Future*. New York: Vintage Books, 2000.

Przybylski, A. K., and N. Weinstein. "Can You Connect with Me Now? How the Presence of Mobile Communication Technology Influences Face-to-face Conversation Quality." *Journal of Social and Personal Relationships* 30 (2012) (3) (July 19): 237–246.

Rama Murthy, S., and M. Mani. "Discerning Rejection of Technology." *SAGE Open* 3 (2) (April 23). 2013. doi:10.1177/2158244013485248.

Rockwell, Steven C. and Loy A. Singleton, "The Effect of the Modality of Presentation of Streaming Multimedia on Information Acquisition," *Media Psychology*, 9 (2007): 179-91.

Rousseau, Jean-Jacques. *Emile*. First published 1762. Auckland: The Floating Press, 2009.

Rushkoff, Douglas. *Program or Be Programmed: Ten Commandments for a Digital Age.* New York: OR Books, 2010.

Schwartz, Barry. *The Paradox of Choice: Why More is Less.* New York: Harper Collins, 2004.

Selwyn, N. "Apart from technology: Understanding people's non-use of information and communication technologies in everyday life." *Technology in Society*, 25, (2003) 99-116.

Siva, Vaidhyanathan. *The Googlization of Everything*. Berkeley, CA: University of California Press, 2011.

Suler, John. 2004. "The Online Disinhibition Effect." *Cyberpsychology & Behavior : the Impact of the Internet, Multimedia and Virtual Reality on Behavior and Society* 7 (3) (June): 321–6.

Turkle, Sherry. *Alone Together: Why We Expect More from Technology and Less From Each Other.* New York: Basic Books, 2011.

Twenge, Jean M., Kathleen R. Catanese, and Roy F. Baumeister. "Social Exclusion and the Deconstructed State: Time Perception, Meaninglessness, Lethargy, Lack of Emotion, and Self-awareness." *Journal of Personality and Social Psychology* 85 (2003) (3) (September): 409–23.

Tzu, Hui, Grace Chou, and Nicholas Edge. "'They Are Happier and Having Better Lives Than I Am': The Impact of Using Facebook on Perceptions of Others' Lives." *Cyberpsychology , Behavior , and Social Networking* 15 (2012) (2): 117–121.

CHAPTER THREE

IN QUEST OF (POSTHUMAN) TOGETHERNESS: DIGITAL COMMUNICATION AND AFFECTIVE DISCONNECTION

MAREK WOJTASZEK

> Intercessors are fundamental. Creation's all about intercessors. Without them nothing happens … I need my intercessors to express myself and they'd never express themselves without me: you are always working in a group, even when you seem to be on your own.
> —Gilles Deleuze, *Negotiations*

> Our world is the world of "technic," that is the world in which cosmos, nature, gods, and complete systems in all its intimate articulation, exposes itself as "technic": the world of an ecotechnè. The ecotechnè operates through technical apparatuses, which permeates and plugs every part of ourselves. What is being made here is actually our bodies, that it gives birth to and plugs into this system. Thus created, our bodies become even more visible, more proliferating, more polymorph, more saturated, more contracted in "masses" and "zones," more than they ever were.
> —Jean-Luc Nancy, *Corpus*

Introduction

Let me commence with a critical observation that digitality and digitally supported media of communication—the Internet, in particular—appears to be amid the few technologies ever built by humans that they do not really comprehend. What began as a formal structure of relations guided by a mathematical logic of man-made symbols reserved for communication purposes in the military has developed into a ubiquitous and unendingly enfolded and multifaceted sphere of social experimentation of an anarchic nature unparalleled in Western history. The expansion of digital information and communication technologies has advanced at an unprecedented speed and represents opportunities for social and cultural breakthroughs. How we interact with others and how we perceive and view ourselves is more than ever before affected and driven by the technologies of virtual, real-time teleconnectivity and digital communication. Given the insinuation of digital forms of communication into practically every domain of civilisational activity as well as the — globally unquestioned — digital direction of human progression, it is worth lingering a moment on their contribution to the general state of a human being and her/his relation with other beings. Enforcing solitude by technologically projecting the sense of social union and connectedness, digital technologies cause human beings to unlearn how to experience and know themselves in their singularity, which in turn demands a capacity for solitude. It is in this sense that I will read humanity's infatuation with, and conformist adaptation to, digital technologies as a symptom of humanity's narcissistic proclivities on the one hand and its different vulnerabilities and flight from its complexity into a technologically fabricated (illusion of) simplicity, an unproblematic togetherness, on the other. I am especially interested in exploring further the potentials of digital technologies vis-à-vis the conspicuously human condition of solitude, i.e. being by oneself, being alone. I will side and simultaneously concur with Félix Guattari in his lamentation with regard to computerization,

> Why have the immense processual potentials brought forth by the revolutions in information processing, telematics, robotics, office automation, biotechnology and so on up to now led only to a monstrous reinforcement of earlier systems of alienation, an oppressive mass-mediated culture and an infantilising politics of consensus?[1]

Understanding the ambiguous being and cultural character of technology in general, and digital technology in particular, as both life-enhancing and life-degrading and its essentially contingent nature of actualisation, I distance myself from the prevailing paradigm of alienation and — by limiting my investigation to the question of the increasing sensibilisation (i.e. aestheticisation) of new digital technologies—I look at how the sensible digital interfaces, i.e. machinic liminal territories, *par excellence*, contribute to the reconstruction of the human *capacity* for solitude.

---

[1] Félix Guattari, "Regimes, Pathways, Subjects," in *Zone 6: Incorporations*, ed. J. Crary and S. Kwinter (New York: Urzone, 1992), 29.

The Challenge of Solitude

As an immediate consequence of the intensive digitisation of information-based societies, an increasingly discomforting sense of solitude as a cultural malaise has emerged to become one of the most pressing social issues and ethical challenges in the contemporary digital era. It is logical to infer that if the sense of solitude is growing, then social relations are effectively dissociating, thereby on the one hand engendering novel configurations of humanity to emerge and necessitating an analysis of the technology-driven process of social transformation on the other. As the original etymological pedigree of the term technology asserts, in its nature, *techne* reveals a praxis whose objective consists in the maximisation of the efficiency of life. In extending life's forces and potentials, technology inevitably involves a vital transformation of life. As much as it can equally be considered to result in human spatial enclosure in the virtual world and temporal entrapment in the present which in turn instantiate corporeal senility (in spite of the imperative of action, mobility and growth) and docility (against the prevalent aura of irruptive creativity and dissent), and stimulates larger cultural digital addiction,[2] I propose to venture into the sensible *interspatium*, the point of encounter of technology and humanity, and investigate its potential of disalienation and reconstructing of the inherently human *capacity* for solitude.

In our culture saturated with mobile digital ICTs, human beings are not solely conscious and controlling producers and users of these devices but remain under their enormous influence massively succumbing to the promises they create, adapting to their interfaces; and undergoing a transformation of their sensible capacities, which reveals humans' certain retardation at the level of sensation. It is interesting to inquire whether social (technologically mediated) networks — by virtue of real time existence and the capability of continuous communication — successfully eliminate one of humanity's primordial fears, loneliness. Or, quite to the

[2] I follow here Elias Aboujaoude's observation that we are all addicted to digitally sustained virtuality: *Virtually You. The Dangerous Powers of the E-Personality* (New York: W. W. Norton & Company, 2012). Even though this is not always and not necessarily a clinical situation, our contemporary culture (especially in its public and professional spheres) fosters our functional and practical addictive reliance and socio-psychological dependence on *(technologies of)* the virtual. In what follows I am interested in exploring further that which is oftentimes placed in parentheses, i.e. the techno-sensible point of encounter between the human and investigate what role it plays in the development of humans' affective bond with machines.

contrary, they work to generate and sustain it? Does an individual interaction with a digital medium result in the user's further alienation, which would follow the presumption that the more technology there is, the more distance? Or, perhaps, given that ICTs are making our social existence exclusively relative to (human and technological) others, that which they effectively eradicate is rather solitude, our characteristically human capacity for being alone? Or, yet alternatively, as I contend, do they — precisely due to the unique (sensible, mobile) character of the communication interface — create conditions for the emergence of a new sensation and understanding of solitude and thus can they contribute to disalienation? It is critical to explore whether digital technology, taking away our privacy and concentration, expropriates us of our ability to be by ourselves as well. I will investigate whether — given that contemporary digital communication technologies tend to appeal more directly to the senses, and require the user's more sensibly intensive participation and interaction with them — the digital ICTs help humans rediscover new affective ways of relating to themselves, technologies, and other human beings, thus moving beyond the humanist spectre of alienation altogether.

In subjecting ourselves to digital technologies, we tend to grow accustomed and develop a certain ease with them, thereby becoming habituated to their promises of functionality and assistance, remaining impervious to the affective and sensible transformational potential they carry and exert upon our embodied selves. In the context of solitude, the contemporary terror of anonymity is more than obvious. As Lionel Trilling rightly remarks, if the property that anchored and determined the self, in Romanticism, was sincerity, and in modernism it was authenticity,[3] then in postmodernism it is visibility. In the present culture of obscenity saturated with simulacra and shrouded in perverse scopophilia, we live exclusively in relation to others, and what disappears from our lives is solitude. As Guattari observes, "With capitalism nothing is secret at least in principle and according to the code; this is why capitalism is 'democratic' and can 'publicise' itself."[4] Losing touch with the present and our intimate self, yet paradoxically remaining narcotically enchained to its digital transcription, we find the prospect of being alone, by ourselves, so unsettling and disturbing that we easily succumb to the technology enabling a constant stream of mediated contact, virtual, notional, or simulated, which keeps us

[3] Lionel Trilling, *Sincerity and Authenticity* (Harvard University Press, 1972).
[4] Gilles Deleuze and Félix Guattari, "Capitalism: A Very Special Delirium," in *Chaosophy*, ed. Sylvère Lotringer (New York: Semiotext(e), 2008), 37.

wired in to the electronic hive.[5] Interestingly, though, contact, or at least two-way contact, seems increasingly beside the point altogether. The social-cultural priority is simply to become known, to turn oneself into a celebrity. The sense of self as well as the sense of one's worth relies heavily upon measurable visible notoriety, frequency and active participation in the digital world. The calculable (thus comparable and competitive) number of Facebook friends, blog readers, or Goggle hits generated by one's name undoubtedly testify to the dominant logic of public presence and belief in its promise to overcome the paralyzing fear of solitary insignificance. Visibility guarantees not only recognition and popularity; it becomes the superficial ground for self-esteem, all the while becoming a substitute for veritable connections. It is noteworthy that just a few decades ago it was all too easy to lapse into loneliness whereas now it is impossible, and culturally suspicious, to be single, alone, on one's own. Capitalism-fuelled hyper-individualism, albeit predicated upon the illusion of uniqueness, favours and appreciates experimentation and difference within the systemically demarcated and acceptable limits of (re)cognition.

Taking into consideration, however, the contemporary digital carnival of self-exposition or the narcissistic exhibitionism these days on the one hand, and the various forms and channels of collecting and control of the digital data by commercial companies and states on the other, I argue that our culture has not yet recognised the wider pedagogical need for developing a capacity of privacy. Our control over our own business has become illusory. Autonomy is certainly on the wane. From school through work to extended family, everyone can easily become a (digital) object of someone else's (sensible) interest. We are living in a more and more incestuous and promiscuous (digital) world. When everyone's a friend, is anything private? How does it affect my sense of proximity and togetherness? Does this mean that everyone has, thanks to Facebook, become all of a sudden more sympathetic and friendly? Certainly not, however, their relations may have indeed turned far more intense; it is nothing uncommon that you "become friends" with your parents, superior, ex-partner, the best friend in real life. In a recent publication, two leading global thinkers in technology and foreign affairs: Eric Schmidt (executive

---

[5] Symptomatic, and only apparently contradictive to this thesis, is the Western social-cultural trend of being a single. As a cultural simulacrum, the single is a social derivative and a cultural response, and *not* an original conscious and ethical solitary enterprise, supported by one's critically auto-reflexive decision. Attempting to realise the impossible of self-proclaimed autarky and self-satisfaction, it symptomatically reveals imaginative deficiency, despondency, and morose desperation; an affectively intense yearning for closeness.

chairman of Google) and Jared Cohen (director of Google Ideas and Senior Fellow at the Council on Foreign Affairs), emphasise that due to digital technologies we have less and less privacy, which effectively makes us unlearn how to live unconnected to (technological and human) others, how to be sole, (re)connected to oneself.[6] Thus viewed, digital communication fosters formal and technical teleconnectivity leading to connected isolation. Digitally sustained virtuality no doubt has opened novel and unprecedented potentials and opportunities before us to broaden and intensify our social interrelations, to reach a wider public, to decrease the level of fear and anxiety, to develop personally and professionally. Importantly, digitally-based virtuality is a great experiment made on our psyche, whereby humanity encounters a new type of machine, not entirely inanimate.

Digital communication has substantially altered the logic and mechanism of our experiencing as well as its organization; it has been immaterially mediated, deterritorialised beyond the material presence in a given territory, purged of both hierarchy and a solid centre of identity. Most importantly, however, digital media have de-linearised our thought heretofore woven by means of materially and territorially present objectivity. The itinerary of our progressive evolution shows a movement away from the linear syntax of thought towards its hyper-textual endless ramification. Contemporary intellectual technologies, it is worth adding, legitimise the progress of a spirit who remains totally independent in its figural associations of its material embodied location, i.e. a progress as a descent into a dream, a techno-logically assisted dream. To put it otherwise, and somewhat paradoxically, digital ICTs lure and seduce us by singing a lullaby of virtuality, a land of wonder, a return to paradise, an effective and successful reconstruction of the Tower of Babel. To partake in it, one shall put one's (presumably limited) sensibility to sleep so as to connect in the virtual life; an unrestrained, collectively orgiastic, *mind-ful* sensorial experimentation is promised. (Where) has solitude gone?

---

[6] It is significant that they prophesy that in the course of future cohabitation and co-determination of the physical and virtual civilizations users will radically renegotiate the social contract. This, most importantly, will happen by users relinquishing the things they value, such as privacy or security. Eric Schmidt and Jared Cohen, *The New Digital Age. Reshaping the Future of People, Nations and Business* (New York: Alfred A. Knopf, 2013), 253-257.

The Synthetics of Loneliness

These days younger generations, especially those raised surrounded by relatively easily accessible digital (synthetic) media technologies of various functions and applications, appear to have neither any interest in, nor need for, solitude; they can barely define it, let alone explain why it may be worth having at all.[7] Looking at the character, specificity, and globally unquestionable direction of the development of digital technologies (of various kinds and forms, ICTs being an important part of the business) and their consequences, there is no denying that the dominant optics remain enchained, to ironically cite Jean Baudrillard, to the mourning of representation and an obvious incapacity to effectively deal with, and go beyond, the representational matrix. Overwhelmed by the ubiquitous visibility and audibility of the tele-present being-in-becoming, Western culture aesthetically grows more and more hooked on the presently experienced, yet materially absent, being in its phantasmatic, simulative, informational, immaterial doublings, which increasingly evacuate the materially present being out of the living present, catapulting it into the electronically charged eternal realm of virtuality. The social-cultural abundance and ubiquity of synthetic (digital) media and their unprecedented modes of aesthetic communication effectively contribute, on the one hand, to the dispossession of the subject of their representational capacity and, quite paradoxically, to the expropriation of the subject of their subjectivity (as a source of representation) on the other. A fluid, protean, interchangeable collective subjectivity is digitally imposed onto the alienated and dematerialised subject, a collective intelligence of virtual communities, intellectually automated by the techno-logical operation of immaterial mediation of sensible experience. Unplugged, unconnected, we

---

[7] I consider this to be a symptom of a larger cultural predicament. I do not allude merely to the digital media of social communication such as the Internet which require some elementary knowledge about the use of indispensable technological apparatuses. It is of special import to note that the process of digital media infiltration commences far earlier when little children are exposed to various synthetic machines, for instance, "intelligent" and intuitive toys equipped with better and better AI capabilities. It is acknowledged that interaction with digital and synthetic technologies intensifies (sensible) contact and that virtual communication makes children experience their lives faster than their psycho-physical maturity permits, thus they develop faster. This inadvertently causes them to abandon sooner the phase where unique sensible capacities are explored and singularly learnt, which is an exercise in solitude. See Elias Aboujaoude, *Virtually You: The Dangerous Powers of the E-Personality* (New York: W. W. Norton & Company, 2012).

no longer imagine being, we are incapable of constructing our sens(e/a)tion of self, our identity. Solitariness emerges as our social-cultural predicament. The perceiving subject is expropriated of their capacity/power of representation. Little by little, we are becoming emptied of our unique and autonomous faculties of sensibility and conceptual thinking, not only of our capability to reason and judge but also, most crucially, our bodily singular power of sensible experiencing crumbles under the cargo of techno-logised, automatised functionalization. Connected with communication technologies, we are gradually becoming disabused of exercising our capacity to think for ourselves in the machinic process of interacting with technological apparatuses of (human-to-human, human-to-robot) communication. We stop thinking our own objects of thought thanks to our own mental representations, and in consequence, we begin unlearning to communicate them to others in our own representations, as an effect of our psycho-somatic labour. The digital media phantasmatise (i.e. synthetise) the sphere of objectivity, otherness for us; they double it digitally in simulating (purely mathematical) models. We lose more and more the illusion of control over our interfaces, let alone over "our" machines. The more we indulge ourselves in our techno-bio-logical romance with machines, and bask in their functionality, marvelling at our *human* technical genius, the more digital machines emancipate themselves from human jurisdiction. Little by little, the will becomes proper to machines; thanks to their own machinic computations, they regain their autonomy—this being an immediate consequence of the machinic elimination of material representations. Material imagination, whose job is to incorporate the idea/concept into the matter of its representation, is well over. The double, simulacrum, comes to prevail. The relationship between the subject and object of desire becomes purely phantasmatic, which necessitates constant titillation. Immanent narcissism, continuous masturbation effectuates disaffection, dispassion, *désamour*, and depression, leading to general apathy; a hedonistic trance of phantom satisfaction, whose essence dwells in metonymical hyper-link. And yet, accompanying the advanced development of digital media and channels of communication is the attempt to deny the sensible aura of loneliness by synthetically securing the (phantasmatic) tele-presence of others. Lionel Trilling in his text "The Situation of the American Intellectual at the Present Time," written as early as 1952, made a poignant observation of "the modern fear of being cut off from the social group even for a moment."[8] One can symptomatologically read the growth of digital,

[8] Lionel Trilling, "The Situation of the American Intellectual at the Present Time,"

synthetic, media of communication as a human attempt to eradicate the dread by devising ways of eternal (i.e. real-time) (tele)connectivity. This is, admittedly, far from saying that the fear of alienation has been successfully put to sleep. In point of fact, the more we invest in the digital repudiation of solitude, the more incapable we become of sensing it and learning how to constructively handle this conspicuously and inherently human condition. Given that the social-cultural feeling of loneliness is increasing proportionally, it seems, to the growth of digital means of communication, it is logical to infer that it is not the awareness of the lack of company that determines solitude (as we now obviously suffer from the digital and synthetic surplus thereof), but rather a singular and sensible mourning over this lack. Digital technologies of connectivity work to palliate this negative feeling and strengthen humans in their struggle against solitude.

Having evacuated the propensity for introspection, the Internet has made us disbelieve in the solitary mind; we hail networked intelligence, enduring real-time connectivity. David Brooks, the New York Times columnist, aptly captures this index of the social-scientific zeitgeist: cognitive scientists tell us that "our decision-making is powerfully influenced by social context;" neuroscientists, that we have "permeable minds" that function in part through a process of "deep imitation;" psychologists, that "we are organised by our attachments;" sociologists, that our behaviour is affected by "the power of social networks."[9] This inevitably endorses the thesis about the psychic reality being socially determined through and through.

Nevertheless, the digital world is gradually becoming more and more sensitive to the issue of its own boundless exposure and vulnerability and so generates various instruments of self-protection, thus contributing to the reconstruction of the sense of privacy and the reconfiguration of the sensation of solitude. In the digital era with its invasive imperative of customisation and personalization — aptly illustrated by the (in)famous Google algorithm, curiously named *AdSense*, which collects the data we type into the browser and consequently displays in the subsequent webpages we view respective advertisements — we have access to more and more tools which can be used to protect our private data from flowing out of our accounts. Amongst the most popular are: free browser

---

in *The Moral Obligation to Be Intelligent: Selected Essays* (Evanston, IL.: Northwestern University Press, 2008), 285.

[9] David Brooks, "The Social Animal," *New York Times*, September 11, 2008, accessed October 24, 2013,
http://www.nytimes.com/2008/09/12/opinion/12brooks.html?_r=0.

extensions such as Abine, DisconnectMe, Ghostery, or Privacyfic.com, which preclude tracking and allow one to have control over anything that is published online. Google Mail offers the additional option to activate SSL cyphering; Google Chrome makes it possible to surf online using the function "incognito" whereas the Internet Explorer browser is equipped with the function InPrivate. There are also other mail services such as SendEmail or AnoneMail which allow one to send e-mails entirely anonymously (it is impossible to track down the sender unless they sign). It is also possible to use the Internet via Virtual Private Network which connects our computer with servers in other countries and only then, via those servers, with concrete websites. The visited webpage, instead of "seeing" our computer's IP address, registers the server's address. Consequently, the tracking system is incapable of matching the website activity with our computer. Is this sufficient to rescue *some* private space from digital voracity?

I, therefore, on the one hand consider solitude as a social-cultural symptom, an outcome of a digital technological process of mediation which has created the general aura of social fragmentation and individual alienation (along with its traditional feelings of loss, lonesomeness, seclusion, estrangement and isolation). On the other hand, however, in intensifying sensible contact between humans and machines, solitude has contributed to the (re)emergence of singularity as a composition of novel capacities and tendencies, triggering a process of the construction of the communication ecology of being sole, being on one's own.

Admittedly, to be oneself is tantamount to being sole, on one's own, which necessitates the capability of being unique, of affirming one's hecceity, one's proper difference irreducible to (social) semblance, dialectical speculation or narcissistic individuality. Importantly, it is on a par with one's belonging to a group. Subjectivation emerges as one's ontological lifetime project and one's ethological accountability to oneself and (animate and inanimate) others. Rather than reveal the putatively dirty little secrets (we are presumed to have always already had), which only titillates the phallic desire and thus binds us into its perverse political economy, we in the course of our growing become secrets, folding in and out, immanently romancing with exuberant life, paradoxically — yet fortuitously and gratuitously — divesting, dispersing and vanishing into life. That which we call "privacy" is simultaneously created and expressed as our own solitude, our own capacity of being who we are, sole and alone.

Techno-humanity: The Gift of Affect

In a parallel fashion, the new digital interfaces are becoming more and more sensible, making use of various apparatuses: hapticity (e.g. touch screens, wearable technology), orality (e.g. voice recognition devices, voice-initiated writing), visibility (e.g. holographic projection, facial recognition), aurality (e.g. audio-books), mobility (e.g. gesture technology) and imitating human bodies (e.g. synthetic prosthetics). Undeniably, intelligence and sensibility have undergone a total mutation as a result of new computer technology, which has increasingly insinuated itself into the motivating forces of sensibility, acts, and thinking. A major shift in perception and experience takes place which paves the way to the resingularisation of existence. I argue that it is the realm of sensibility that is involved most profoundly in the ongoing process of cognitive reformatting; we see aesthetic thought inserted at a juncture. The sensible (affective) forces that enter this interstitial assemblage belong to various realms of nature: they are electronic, semiotic, machinic, and psychic. In the course of constructing this assemblage they test their collaborative potentials and endurability, eventually becoming compatible. It is the immanent — generative and distributive — principle of connectivity that underlies and stimulates this heterogeneous and transversal field of emergent being. Consequently, the gradual insinuation of the electronic into the organic as well as the intensive artificialisation of the (heretofore human) sphere of the living irreversibly transforms the relationship between sensibility and consciousness. It is no longer a (humanistic) consciousness of the technological progress of humanity; its genetic substance becomes thoroughly recreated with technical apparatuses infiltrating its proper structure and ineluctably becoming incorporated into its organic scaffold. Clearly, it is inadequate to view technology as a mere prosthetic extension of the body to correct or enhance its functioning. There is far more revolutionary a transition taking place derailing the dominance of anthropocentric consciousness, i.e. the immanent process of the sensible reorganisation of affective qualities and capabilities guided by reciprocity. As Brian Massumi puts it,

> The extension, whether off-world or not, is no longer a colonisation but a symbiosis. The body is opening itself to qualitative change, a modification of its very definition, by reopening its *relation* to things.[10]

[10] Brian Massumi, *Parables for the Virtual. Movement, Affect, Sensation* (Durham and London: Duke University Press, 2002), 116, original emphasis.

The problem, to paraphrase Gilles Deleuze and Félix Guattari, is *not* that we are too much mediated, but rather, we have not been mediated enough[11] so as to affirm, acclaim and ethologically assess the full potential of the digital.

In adopting a critical and realist-materialist approach to technology, which eschews both the polarisation of technophobic and technophilic discourses and the prevailing phenomenological and pragmatist nomenclature of functionalism, along with their humanist and anthropocentric assumptions, in the concluding part I will focus on the very nature of the interface, the in-between communication territory as a space of sensible (haptic, textual, oral, aural) alliances between the human and the machine. Harnessed as a heuristic instrument, the interface disavows the mediating function of the medium and thus opens up a novel terrain of exploration of sensible encounters between humans and technology. Working synaesthetically and encouraging multisensory immersion, the interface annuls primacy and the distancing quasi-security of vision along with its representational mode of cognition and enables a reflexive remodelling of one's cognitive apparatus. By concentrating upon the in-between sphere, I emphasise the immanent continuum of our every sensible doing, be it feeling, communicating or otherwise relating. It is the concept of the interface that best grasps and renders the genesis of singularity (i.e. machinic solitude), acknowledging its sens(e)ible emergence. As Gilles Deleuze asseverates,

> Concepts cannot be distinguished from a way of perceiving things: a concept forces us to see things differently. It would be nothing if it did not give us a new perception of it ... Concepts are also inseparable from

[11] In their introductory chapter to *A Thousand Plateaus,* titled "Rhizome," Deleuze and Guattari, enlisting the main characteristics of the concept of rhizome, critique the various traditions of thought predicated upon linearity. Significantly, reviewing linguistic models, they expose their conceptual limitations: "Our criticism of these linguistic models is not that they are too abstract but, on the contrary, that they are not abstract enough, that they do not reach the abstract machine that connects a language to the semantic and pragmatic contents of statements, to collective assemblages of enunciation, to a whole micropolitics of the social field" Deleuze and Guattari (New York 1987, 7). Inspired by this observation and viewing it as an adequate one to the dominant epistemological and methodological framework of the socio-cultural analyses of digital technologies, I am motivated to propose a non-dichotomous approach. By engaging with the concept of the interface, in the following I will attempt to explore the disalienating potential of new digital ICTs from the vantage point of the in-between (affective) space of the human and the machine.

> affects, from new manners of seeing or perceiving they provoke in us, an entire pathos.[12]

This inevitably necessitates a transposition of the question of the territory of the interface from the epistemological level of meaning onto the ethical ground of event (and emergence).[13]

From the vantage point of solitude the humanity's project of virtuality accentuates the properly sensible texture of the digital, offering a more democratic and inclusive use of its potential and a way out of its technocratic governance limited to abstract expert knowledge. The territory of the interface accounts for the techno-sensible, spatial (machinic) process of emergence of the capacity of solitude and maps emerging singular modes of techno-intimate existence, and thus contributes to the broader social-cultural pedagogical project of developing the cognition and literacy of new digital technologies of communication. Aden Evens in his exposition of digital ontology stresses the participation of the digital in the virtual and, secondly, emphasizing the creativity of the digital, maps the territories of their overlap.[14] Significantly, the cases of, for instance, the interrupt or glitch open the

---

[12] Gilles Deleuze, *Two Regimes of Madness. Texts and Interviews 1975-1995* (New York: Semiotext(e), 2006), 238.

[13] This is also observed and well-explicated in the recent work by Viktor Mayer-Schönberger and Kenneth Cukier, *Big Data. A Revolution That Will Transform How We Live, Work and Think* (London: John Murray, 2013). One of their main arguments is that the sphere of the digital calls for a radical rethinking of our traditional modes of knowing which were theorised and evolved within the Western intellectual context. Rather than pursue and explain the causes behind everything, the challenge of the (digital) world of big data and its technological handling is to account for and learn how to effectively harness its simulative (and simulacral) character at the level of origin, that is ontology. Technically enhanced humanity can crunch and process an amount of information which is beyond the comprehensive capabilities of a human being. Novel techno-scientific insights are, consequently, being made about *the what* in lieu of *the why*. This can equally be understood as a shift away from, and critique of, the domination of epistemology over ontology and a reopening of the realm of being. See Manuel DeLanda, *Philosophy and Simulation. The Emergence of Synthetic Reason* (London and New York: Continuum, 2011) for diverse accounts of how this transition away from knowledge to being — aided by digital, synthetic, technologies — is accomplished, thus leading to an immanent environment wherein to be and to know are no longer hierarchically juxtaposed but essentially co-expressive.

[14] Aden Evens, "Digital Ontology and Example," in *The Force of the Virtual. Deleuze, Science, and Philosophy*, ed. Peter Gaffney (Minneapolis and London: University of Minnesota Press, 2010), 147-168.

digital onto the virtual. I will add that sensible digital interfaces continue the project of the virtualisation of the digital, thus making the digital reopen and reach beyond itself to avail itself to human and material ends. Evens writes, "Anywhere the digital meets the human, anywhere these two worlds touch, there must be a fold."[15]

Sensible Interface: From Function to Manner

Prior to establishing an actual communicating connection, there is a more intensive interplay at work, i.e. a production of sensibility, rather than a mere receptivity. The encounter folds the digital onto the sensible thus constructing an interface communication between them which is in essence of an aesthetic nature. Aesthetic perception — here strictly conceived of as the realm of sensibility — is directly involved in this transformation. In a regular, everyday operational (i.e. functional) contact with the digital device consciousness works to take over and make sensibility subservient to its commands. This is premised upon an assumption that for there to be an interface at all, that is, for the connective sphere to emerge and function properly, one must minimise the potentially distracting and destructing powers sensibility wields. Sensibility stands for the faculty that enables human beings to interpret (i.e. perceive and recognise) *all sorts* of signs. In technical accounts of digital communication this faculty is either considered useless and left totally unaddressed or believed to be detrimental to the functional operability of the system and thus excluded entirely from both the practical and theoretical frameworks. Put differently, its status and being is reminiscent of the Kantian legacy, expressed in his doctrine of the (human) faculties.[16] Assigning each of them a particular role in the knowledge building process, Kant allocated to them a legitimate zone of operation, thus in effect circumscribing their unique epistemic powers. The faculties were subject to hierarchical ordering and regulated by common sense. Sensibility, albeit indispensable in the course of knowing, was reduced to mere receptivity and placed at the bottom of the epistemic ladder. Clearly, to be able to become cognizant of, and account for, the emerging singular machinic sensible territory, we have to move beyond the classical conception of empiricism as a philosophy of the origins of our knowledge which assumes that beneath

---

[15] Evens, "Digital Ontology and Example," 158.

[16] For an exposition of Kant's doctrine of the faculties and its epistemological implications, see Gilles Deleuze, *Kant's Critical Philosophy. The Doctrine of the Faculties* (London and New York: Continuum, 2008).

the impressions of sense experience, there is nothing more to be discovered and known. The impressions of sense experience are the ultimate foundation of all knowledge. Deleuze reopens that which at least since Kant has remained foreclosed and speaks of the *synthetic emergence* of sense experience as we (humans) know it, thus accounting for the genesis of sensibility itself. In doing so, Deleuze deepens Kant's transcendental aesthetic by evading or eliminating Kant's limitative assumptions. In *Difference and Repetition*, Deleuze writes,

> Kant defines the passive self in terms of simple receptivity, thereby assuming sensations already formed, then merely relating these to the a priori forms of their representation which are determined as space and time. In this manner, not only does he unify the passive self by ruling out the possibility of composing space step by step, not only does he deprive this passive self of all power of synthesis (synthesis being reserved for activity), but moreover he cuts the Aesthetic into two parts: the objective element of sensation guaranteed by space and the subjective element which is incarnate in pleasure and pain.[17]

In contradistinction to Kant, Deleuze sets off to account for sensation itself, the vital, affective sphere of intensive genesis. Crucially, he proceeds by discovering and affirming the self's *active* synthetic capacities. From a mere recipient of impulses, sensibility becomes the authentic source of creation, i.e. syntheticization. Reconstructing the emergence of the *sensibility* of sense permits Deleuze to conclude that an infinite number of different sensibilities or forms of receptivity are virtually possible.

Interestingly enough, sensation is that which animates the sensible, yet remains oddly static. As Deleuze and Guattari put it, "Sensation is pure contemplation . . . Contemplating is creating, the mystery of passive creation, sensation."[18] It may well offer a creative antidote for the contemporary dromological culture with its peculiar terror of action and saturated with so much talking and so little authentic conversation, animated by unrestrained digital communication and yet suffering from obvious affective dis-connection. One recalls Hannah Arendt's appeal for solitude as necessary for silent interpretation which nurtures and fosters thoughtfulness, thus preparing individuals for political action.[19] Our world

---

[17] Gilles Deleuze, *Difference and Repetition*, trans. Paul Patton (New York: Columbia University Press, 1994), 98.

[18] Gilles Deleuze and Félix Guattari, *What is Philosophy?*, trans. G. Burchell and H. Tomlinson (London and New York: Verso, 1994), 212.

[19] See especially Hannah Arendt, "Reflections on Little Rock," *Dissent* 6, no. 1 (1959).

needs more than anything else to rediscover the sensible capacity for solitude, of being on one's own, to relearn how to sensibly inter-relate to one's own singular being. Deleuze and Guattari lamented that "*we lack resistance to the present*,"[20] and yet we need it most, we need to regain intimacy, recreate our connection with the present, with our singular selves, which synthetic sensible digital interfaces can help us achieve. As points of intensive sensible encounters between humans and machines, the territories of interfaces *s(t)imulate* their interaction and interchange and the intensive intra-action, i.e. yield reconfiguration (and simultaneous reinterpretation) of affective attachments and the emergence of a singular being, capable of solitude yet retaining ecological relations with her/his environment. The corset of functionalism loosens up, liberating the cramped sensible-technical singular, flows as the events of becoming which co-found the interface and let it express its potential. It is the interface from which each singular subject extracts the manners that correspond to their point of view; *functionalism makes room for mannerism*. Instigating manners and infinite techno-sensible variations, the interface endowed with the digital software emerges as a most vibrant laboratory of novel machinic sensibilities stimulating the process of a sensible reinterpretation of solitude and of a rediscovery of the nexus of tendencies and capacities which originate through a machinic encounter of bodies and technologies, thereby contributing to a resingularisation of experience.

Inspired by Deleuze's work, I applaud mannerism as a singular project of developing new digital media sensible literacy, as an enterprise of solitude as singularity which can effectively lead us out of the present performative impasse and representational digital enclosure of today. The solution to mourning is not metonymical, lack-driven, substitution, but rather sensible labour consisting in the reconfiguration of our relations with otherness, i.e. the manneristic art of weaving It actualises itself through making machinic connections, interfacing with the virtual, opening oneself up to the novel sensible territories the digital technologies effectuate. In Deleuze's view, territory is above all a site of passage, the place where a rhizomatic assemblage conjoins and conjugates the forces of all the constituting elements; it is a space of the most intensive experimentation which concatenates milieus and rhythms.[21] The territory of the sensible machinic *interspatium* triggers a generation of new

---

[20] Gilles Deleuze and Félix Guattari, *What is Philosophy?*, 108, original emphasis.

[21] Gilles Deleuze and Félix Guattari, *A Thousand Plateaus. Capitalism and Schizophrenia*, trans. Brian Massumi (Minneapolis and London: University of Minnesota Press, 1987), 314-316.

relations as sensible events; the digital undoubtedly cofounds the virtual. Consequently, the sens(e/a)tion of togetherness is affirmed and attained at the level of sensibility in a mannerist assemblage of the communicating interfaces. In the course of development of the first global civilization and the gradual process of the syntheticisation which, via interfaces, reconnects singularity and society, new collective individuations emerge, for which we need an adequate conceptual apparatus.

Coda

It is our aesthetic and ecological responsibility to learn and teach the next generations how to be alone, i.e. how to be capable of solitude, how to existentially exercise its potential in a mutually resonant and productive manner with (human and technological) others, otherwise the generations to come will learn only how to feel and be lonely. The question of singularity has become key to imagining and developing a sustainable ecology of co-existence with technological and human others, which the contemporary social-cultural escalation of nationalisms, digital technocratism, and neotribalism clearly demonstrate. Awakened from the techno-logical dream of totalisation and fulfilment, communication must be reclaimed as a gratuitous act of generosity, reciprocal learning between humans and machines and their mutual enriching. Let me conclude by quoting a poem by Emily Dickinson, which I read as an affirmative appeal to rediscover through intercessors one's affective communicational capacity in solitude:

There is a solitude of space
A solitude of sea
A solitude of death, but these
Society shall be
Compared with that profounder site
That polar privacy
A soul admitted to itself—
Finite infinity.
(Dickinson 1998, poem no. 1696)

Bibliography

Aboujaoude, Elias. *Virtually You: The Dangerous Powers of the E-Personality*. New York: W. W. Norton & Company, 2012.

Arendt, Hannah. "Reflections on Little Rock." *Dissent* 6, no. 1 (1959): 45-56.

Baudrillard, Jean. *Simulacra and Simulation.* Translated by Sheila Faria Glaser. University of Michigan Press, 1994.

Braidotti, Rosi. *The Posthuman*. Cambridge: Polity Press, 2013.

Brooks, David. "The Social Animal." September 11, 2008. Accessed October 24, 2013. http://www.nytimes.com/2008/09/12/opinion/12brooks.html?_r=0.

Cukier, Kenneth and Victor Mayer-Schoenberger. *Big Data. A Revolution That Will Transform How We Live, Work, and Think*. London: John Murray (Publishers), 2013.

Deleuze, Gilles. *Kant's Critical Philosophy. The Doctrine of the Faculties.* London & New York: Continuum, 2008.

—. *Two Regimes of Madness. Texts and Interviews 1975-1995*. New York: Semiotext(e), 2006.

—. *Difference and Repetition*. Translated by Paul Patton. New York: Columbia University Press, 1994.

Deleuze, Gilles, and Claire Parnet. *Dialogues II*. Translated by H. Tomlinson and B. Habberjam. London and New York: Continuum, 2006.

Deleuze, Gilles and Félix Guattari. "Capitalism: A Very Special Delirium." In *Chaosophy*, edited by Sylvère Lotringer, 35-52. New York: Semiotext(e), 2008.

Deleuze, Gilles, and Félix Guattari. *A Thousand Plateaus. Capitalism and Schizophrenia.* Translated by Brian Massumi. Minneapolis and London: University of Minnesota Press, 1987.

Deleuze, Gilles. *What is Philosophy?* Translated by G. Burchell and H. Tomlinson. London & New York: Verso, 1994.

Evens, Aden. "Digital Ontology and Example." In *The Force of the Virtual. Deleuze, Science, and Philosophy*, edited by Peter Gaffney, 147-168. Minneapolis and London: University of Minnesota Press, 2010.

Franklin, Ralph, W., ed. *The Poems of Emily Dickinson*. Harvard University Press, 1998.

Genosko, Gary, ed. *The Guattari Reader*. Oxford: Blackwell Publishers Ltd, 1996.

Guattari, Félix. *The Machinic Unconscious*. New York: Semiotext(e), 2010.

—. *Chaosmosis. An Ethico-aesthetic Paradigm*. Bloomington and Indianapolis: Indiana University Press, 1995.

—. "Regimes, Pathways, Subjects." In *Zone 6: Incorporations*, edited by J. Crary and S. Kwinter. New York: Urzone, 1992.

Massumi, Brian. *Parables for the Virtual. Movement, Affect, Sensation*. Durham and London: Duke University Press, 2002.

Nancy, Jean-Luc. *Corpus*. Translated by Richard A. Rand. New York: Fordham University Press, 2008.

Schmidt, Eric and Jared Cohen. *The New Digital Age: Reshaping the Future of People, Nations and Business*. New York: Alfred A. Knopf, 2013.

Trilling, Lionel. "The Situation of the American Intellectual at the Present Time." In *The Moral Obligation to Be Intelligent: Selected Essays*, 275-291. Evanston, IL.: Northwestern University Press, 2008.

—. *Sincerity and Authenticity*. Harvard University Press, 1972.

PART II:

NEW NEGOTIATIONS OF MOBILITY, PLACE AND INTERCULTURAL EXPERIENCE

CHAPTER FOUR

MEANINGFUL CONNECTIONS: DIGITAL MEDIA, SOCIAL NETWORKS AND THE EXPERIENCE OF SPACE AND PLACE

AGNIESZKA STASIEWICZ-BIEŃKOWSKA

Theoretical Framework and Research Questions

When in August 2013 in an interview for the Polish magazine "Wysokie Obcasy" the traveller Jürgen Horn was invited to talk about his strategies of coping with a life of constant mobility, he pointed at his laptop as the source of his sense of belonging:

> When I switch on my computer, I feel that I am at home. And it doesn't matter what kind of pictures surround me, what kind of carpet covers the floor and what language the neighbours speak. So perhaps our home is online.[1]

By providing its users with revolutionary possibilities of communication and quickly accessible sources of information, cyberspace is often believed to endow them with the power of emotional and intellectual bi- or even multi-location which, although physically impossible, is to some extent achieved through maintaining instantaneous and real-time relationships with people, places and institutions in two or more different, and often distant, locations.[2] Resultantly, the use of digital media has the potential to enable the "cyberspace citizens" to "feel at home wherever

---

[1] Mike Powell and Jürgen Horn, "Żyć jak krab," interview with Łukasz Długowski, *Wysokie Obcasy*, August 24, 2013, 36. Translation from the Polish by A. Stasiewicz-Bieńkowska.

[2] See e.g. Wendy O'Brien, "There's No Place Like Home," in *Home in Motion: The Shifting Grammars of Self & Stranger*, ed. Pedro E. Marcelino (Oxford: Inter-Disciplinary.Net, 2011), 4.

they go and welcome wherever they arrive,"[3] offering new understandings of the processes of negotiating foreign space and transforming it into place.

As emphasised by Phil Hubbard and Rob Kitchin in their discussion on the contemporary development of spatial theories, over the last decades space and place have become "totemic concepts" in various disciplines, and they comprise a multiplicity of meanings that are characterised by a profound ambiguity.[4] Many scholars claim these notions to be highly complex and multifarious social constructs whose shifting meanings within the ever-changing world constantly demand new interpretations.[5] For the cultural geographer Yi-Fu Tuan space is a category that is "blurred," undifferentiated and evoking a sense of "out there." Perceived as untrodden and pathless, space is often associated with openness, mobility, freedom and venture, but it can also signify peril.[6] Place, on the other hand, connotes comfort, tranquillity, order, attachment and pause, along with a feeling of belonging and home.[7]

According to Tuan, a sense of place is established through the differentiation, familiarisation and reflection upon space. He further claims that the "[f]ear of space often goes with fear of solitude. To be in the company of human beings [...] has the effect of curtailing space [...]."[8] This perspective corresponds with Doreen B. Massey's understanding of place as constructed out of social interactions and experiences "articulated together at a particular locus."[9] Massey diverges, however, from Tuan's understanding of place as a bounded or constricted area,[10] viewing place as

---

[3] Zygmunt Bauman, *Globalization: The Human Consequences* (Polity, 2013), Kindle edition, Loc 828.

[4] Phil Hubbard, Rob Kitchin, "Introduction: Why key thinkers?," in *Key Thinkers of Space and Place*, ed. Phil Hubbard and Rob Kitchin (SAGE, 2010), 1-16 [quotation: page 2].

[5] For a critical guide to a selection of contemporary theorists of notions of space and place see *Key Thinkers of Space and Place*, ed. Phil Hubbard and Rob Kitchin (SAGE, 2010).

[6] Yi-Fu Tuan, *Space and Place: The Perspective of Experience* (London, Minneapolis: University of Minnesota Press, 2011), Kindle edition, Loc 291, 796, 812, 844.

[7] Tuan, *Space and Place*, Loc 473, 849, 885. Cf. the categories of "near" and "far away" in Bauman, *Globalization*, Loc 231, 236, 241.

[8] Tuan, *Space and Place*, Loc 932.

[9] Doreen B. Massey, "Power-geometry and a Progressive Sense of Place," in *Mapping the Futures: Local Cultures, Global Change*, ed. John Bird et al. (London: Routledge 1993), 66.

[10] See Tuan, *Space and Place*, Loc 849.

"open and porous networks of social relations."[11] Such a conceptualisation allows the notion of place that embraces communication and social networks as its crucial components, and that recognises its ties to the "outside" rather than rejects them.[12]

Informed by Tuan's and Massey's theorising of space and place, and based on the analysis of data gathered from qualitative interviews with fourteen young adults studying and living outside their country of origin,[13] the goal of this chapter is to examine the influence of new information and communication technologies (ICT), particularly digital social media, on the process of negotiating unfamiliar space through the development and maintenance of social networks. What is the significance of space and place in the process of adapting to a host location in the experience of international students? In what ways, if any, does the participation in digital social media communities facilitate the familiarisation of unknown space? Last but not least, how does it provide assistance in the process of transforming space into place, and thus—of creating a sense of belonging?

Space and Place That Matter

In the light of contemporary changes in mobility and communication technologies the significance of the attachment to (the idea of) place is sometimes problematised and challenged.[14] However, the analysis of the interviews conducted within this project clearly suggests that the respondents held the idea of place at the very heart of their foreign study experience. The transformation of the unknown space of a new location into a known and secure place was presented as vital to the successful negotiation of a foreign culture and environment.[15] "Knowing how to get

---

[11] Doreen B. Massey, *Space, Place, and Gender* (Minneapolis, MN, USA: University of Minnesota Press, 1999), 121. Here Massey follows N. Thrift, "The geography of international economic disorder," in *Uneven Re-Development: Cities and Regions in Transition*, ed. D. Massey and J. Allen (London: Hodder & Stoughton, Open University, 1988).

[12] Massey, *Space, Place, and Gender*, 169.

[13] The data have been gathered within the frames of the project "Negotiating Cultural Differences in the Digital Communication Era," financed by the Polish National Science Centre (HARMONIA). See the chapter by David Gunkel for full details.

[14] See e.g. Peter F. Smith, *The Dynamics of Urbanism* (London and New York: Routledge, 2013), 188.

[15] This process was occasionally claimed to be of more importance for the developing of a sense of belonging than the amount of time spent in the host

places without taking a map or [...] knowing basic directions" was described as crucial to "living somewhere,"[16] that is feeling at home at a certain place,[17] and acquiring the subjective right to renounce the "lesser" status of a tourist.[18]

The centrality of spatial experiences to developing a sense of belonging (or the lack thereof) emerged particularly clearly in the discussions on the differences between the host location (be it a country, a city or even a continent) and the location of origin. When requested to identify the most gratifying, most distressing and most unexpected aspects of "here," and to compare these aspects to their home area,[19] most respondents raised the issues concerning different patterns of spatial mobility. Yi-Fu Tuan claims that space is understood through movement;[20] traversing space makes it differentiated, individualised, known. Thus, those participants who had found the possibilities of moving through the foreign space manifold and relatively effortless expressed deep satisfaction and a sense of comfort within their new environment:

> [I like] lifestyle of walking around, public transportation. [...] I like that I don't have to own a car [...], buy petroleum and worry about the parking lot. The public transport in all European cities is fantastic, you can get anywhere by short amount of time, it is very inexpensive, very efficient.[21]

---

country; female participant, aged 21 (interview excerpt: Kraków, 25 November, 2012).

[16] Female participant, aged 21 (interview excerpt: Kraków, 25 November 2012). Cf. Anita Lundberg, Agnieszka Stasiewicz-Bieńkowska and Anna Enhörning Singhateh, "Border Crossing Networks: Virtual Makes It Real," in *Innovative Research in a Changing and Challenging World*, ed. Si Fan et al. (Launceston: Australian Multicultural Interaction Institute, 2012), 87-90.

[17] Here "living" acquires the Heideggerian meaning of "dwelling," that is being at home in a certain place; see Norman McIntyre, "Introduction," in *Multiple Dwelling and Tourism: Negotiating Place, Home, and Identity*, ed. Norman McIntyre, Daniel Williams, and Kevin McHugh (Wallingford, Oxfordshire, GBR: CABI Publishing, 2006), 7.

[18] See e.g. female participant, aged 21 (interview excerpt: Kraków, 25 November, 2012); male participant, aged 24 (interview excerpt: Kraków, 5 January, 2013).

[19] In the conducted interviews the category of "here" was used to avoid employing such terms as "host city," "host country" etc. in order not to suggest or limit the scope of the considered area. Similarly, the interviewers avoided the term "home" until it was employed by the respondents themselves.

[20] Tuan, *Space and Place*, Loc 199, 211, 812.

[21] Male participant, aged 36 (interview excerpt: Kraków, 9 January 2013). Cf. Female participant, aged 23 (interview excerpt Kraków, 20 December 2012); male

Analogically, all interviewees for whom mobility in a foreign space had proved problematic communicated bewilderment, frustration and a sense of constriction. The unfamiliar patterns of transportation, experienced as deteriorated mobility conditions, impeded their exploration of space and were considered as seriously limiting their opportunities for integration within the new environment:

> I thought that if I wanted to go to another town I would just need to take a bus and go. But then I realized that […] unless I have a car I won't be able […] to do many, many other things. And this really freaked me out […].Yeah, I would say this was the most irritating thing I did not anticipate. […] most other things I could deal with pretty easily.[22]

When the formerly unfamiliar space is eventually negotiated into becoming a place, it can inspire, as theorised by Tuan, a sense of safety, permanence and pause.[23] This imagining resonates in one of the interviews where a female participant recognises her host city as her new home. Having repeatedly emphasised her effectively acquired spatial knowledge and routines, the respondent identifies the city as her base—that is a place from which to venture into the exploration of "out there," and to contentedly come back to after experiencing the mobility and change signified by the unknown[24]:

> […] every time I go away, I come back. Always come back […]. You go away, then you come back. And then I'm ready to leave again. And come back.[25]

New Social Networks and the Construction of Place

While, according to Tuan, space evokes a sense of freedom, openness, excitement and multiple possibilities, it can also be seen as exposing

---

participant, aged 27 (interview excerpt: Kraków, 3 December 2012), female participant, aged 23 (interview excerpt: Kraków, 18 December 2012).

[22] Male participant, aged 23 (interview excerpt: Chicago, 18 March 2013). Cf. e.g. male participant, aged 23 (interview excerpt: Chicago, 19 April 2013); male participant, aged 28 (interview excerpt: Chicago, 19 April 2013).

[23] Tuan, *Space and Place*, Loc 71, 117, 122.

[24] For the meanings of space, see Tuan, *Space and Place*, Loc 71, 117, 122.

[25] Female participant, aged 21 (interview excerpt: Kraków, 25 November 2012).

human vulnerability, arousing disquiet or even posing a threat.[26] However, the employment of digital media, particularly social media, in the process of negotiating space demonstrates the potential for reducing these negative aspects and enhancing the positive ones, accelerating the transformation of space into place(s). As the analysis of the assembled data shows, this is primarily accomplished by maintaining the connection to the previous social networks and creating new ones that would be difficult or even impossible to establish in the pre-digital world. This perspective reverberates Tuan's identification of the anxiety invoked by space with the angst of loneliness and isolation,[27] as well as corresponds with Massey's argument of the impact of communication and social interactions on creating a sense of place.

The project participants frequently acknowledged the digital media's role in creating and maintaining social relations during their stay in the host country. They identified Facebook as an important platform for making social arrangements and reflecting on social events;[28] in addition, one respondent reported an "unintended social exclusion" due to the lack of a Facebook account.[29] Such tools as Facebook and Google Translate were also stated to effectively aid communication across the language barriers.[30]

From among the examples provided by the interviewees, the efficacy of developing social networks in the previously unknown locations and the significance of this process for producing meaning of space is most vividly illustrated by the cases of VKontakte and Couchsurfing. VKontakte, more commonly known as VK (Russian: ВКонтакте) advertises itself as the leading European social network with more than one hundred million members.[31] As the medium is particularly popular in Russia and the

---

[26] Tuan, *Space and Place*, Loc 117, 844, 849. Cf. the account of stress and fear evoked by the new environment; male participant, aged 32 (interview excerpt: Chicago, 25 March 2013).

[27] Tuan, *Space and Place*, Loc 932.

[28] Male participant, aged 26 (interview excerpt: Kraków, 12 January 2013); male participant, aged 21 (interview excerpt: Kraków, 18 December 2012).

[29] Male participant, aged 36 (interview excerpt: Kraków, 9 January 2013).

[30] Two respondents brought up the advantages of a computer-mediated, typed conversation when a person with a limited knowledge of English was involved; a slower pace, the deliberate character of the digital exchange, as well as the digital possibilities of instant translation were reported to greatly contribute to mutual understanding; female participant, aged 21 (interview excerpt: Kraków, 25 November, 2012); male participant, aged 21 (interview excerpt: Kraków, 1 December 2012).

[31] "About VK," VK, accessed September 15, 2013, http://vk.com/about.

Ukraine, one of the respondents employed it to contact the residents of the locations he intended to visit, offering them English conversation. In exchange, he hoped to learn more about the local areas.[32]

In a similar context another respondent brought up his experiences with the global digital community of Couchsurfing,[33] a cyberplace specifically designed for facilitating international mobility and spatial exploration. Couchsurfing serves as a forum and a communication platform for six million travellers and potential hosts in over one hundred thousand cities all over the world.[34] Couchsurfing's mission, as stated on their website, is to promote intercultural experiences and understanding, and to encourage its members to form "meaningful connections with the people and places they encounter."[35] The expected outcome of Couchsurfing-facilitated communication is the meeting of a host and a traveller in a non-virtual reality, the host offering gratuitous accommodation, company and/or guidance in their area of residence. Such arrangements open the possibilities of exploring new spaces to a greater number of digital media users as, apart from reducing expenses, they also diminish potential difficulties stemming from the unfamiliarity of the visited milieu.

The Couchsurfing procedure begins with a user creating a profile, that is constructing a virtual place where they present their homes and daily routines to prospective guests. Through the profile the traveller becomes pre-acquainted with the host's home and persona, and eventually establishes a virtual contact. This way, the process of making an unknown space distinctive and of creating social networks within it is set in motion, beginning the transformation of space into place(s) as theorised by both Massey and Tuan. Due to the mediation of digital media this process can be commenced before the traveller engages with the space bodily.

After the visit the host and the traveller contribute to the construction of each other's virtual places by leaving comments and references. Helping the visitor to get to know the new area is considered the primary condition for receiving positive feedback. As an experienced host declared, "I always get that I showed them the city, that they liked that [...]."[36]

---

[32] Male participant, aged 27 (interview excerpt: Kraków, 3 December).
[33] Male participant, aged 24 (interview excerpt: Kraków, 5 January 2013).
[34] "About us," Couchsurfing, accessed September 3, 2013, https://www.couchsurfing.org/n/about.
[35] "Our Values," Couchsurfing, accessed September 3, 2013, https://www.couchsurfing.org/n/values.
[36] Male participant, aged 24 (interview excerpt: Kraków, 5 January 2013).

The perspective and the guidance of a local person was reported to greatly contribute to the successful appropriation of the foreign space (particularly during a short-term visit) and the development of a sense of place:

> […] you get to know the city so much better if you stay with them [local people met on the Couchsurfing website] and they show you… You don't rely on a tourist guide, you just rely on information from people […]. And it's great—you can sorta… *really* get to know the place in a much different way [emphasis original].[37]

In this context the tourist becomes the Other, someone on the outside, whose supposedly shallow understanding of the visited space provides a point of reference *against* which to define an effectively acquired sense of place and belonging. Linking Tuan's emphasis on the significance of the insider's view[38] with Jay Appleton's association of home with the sense of realness,[39] the guidance of a local host is presented as ensuring the authenticity and the exclusiveness of the place experience unavailable to "ordinary" tourists:

> I *really* try to show them [emphasis mine], that's why I take them to local spots because I know most people wouldn't go there. I often take them into the university building just to show them the view because they get much better pictures than they would if they stayed down there. It's really the only way you can get up here.[40]

Providing its participants with a local host/guide who is willing to share, both metaphorically and literally, their own *place* within the unknown space by both receiving a guest at home and introducing them into the area, the digital community of Couchsurfing aims to offer travellers an opportunity to make a short-cut in the cognitive journey from space to place.[41] Furthermore, the Couchsurfing philosophy encourages its members to "domesticate" new spaces by accepting responsibility for their condition and development.[42] The emotional connection between a

---

[37] Male participant, aged 24 (interview excerpt: Kraków, 5 January 2013).
[38] Tuan, *Space and Place*, Loc 303.
[39] Here I follow McIntyre, "Introduction," 7.
[40] Male participant, aged 24 (interview excerpt: Kraków, 5 January 2013).
[41] Cf. Tuan, *Space and Place*, Loc 303.
[42] "Our Values (Leave It Better Than You Found It)," Couchsurfing, accessed September 3, 2013, https://www.couchsurfing.org/n/values.

traveller and a place that is to follow is presumed to further reinforce the sense of "insideness."

The experience of developing and reinforcing a feeling of place, however, is not limited to the traveller. The international student who participated in the Couchsurfing community in a capacity of a host reported a radical increase in his knowledge about the city in which he studied, and perceived his engagement in the programme as an expression of his bond with the host area.[43] In the light of this example, a host is not merely a guide; neither is a traveller a passive recipient of the host's spatial knowledge. In fact, they (re-)discover the space together which renders the transformation of space into place their common experience.[44]

Negotiating Space through the Connection to Home

Along with facilitating the development of new social networks in unknown locations, the new information and communication technologies have the potential to assist their users in negotiating foreign space through the connection to the previously existing networks, particularly those located at the country/city of origin. The significance of digital media in sustaining contact with these networks have been confirmed by various researchers.[45] Not surprisingly, in the analysed interviews the digital tools employed to communicate with family and "old" friends were often reported as essential for a satisfactory stay abroad.[46] The respondents focused on the usefulness of ICT in sustaining their position and active engagement within their prior social networks, as well as in reducing the

---

[43] Male participant, aged 24 (interview excerpt: Kraków, 5 January 2013).

[44] What seems particularly interesting, Couchsurfing is, at least to some extent, a gendered space. In the section entitled "Safety" (https://www.couchsurfing.org/n/safety, accessed September 4, 2013) the user can find "Tips for Women Travelers" where women are advised against staying with men (especially single men) and encouraged to educate themselves about the cultural and religious differences between their home countries and travel destinations. The website does not contain analogical advice targeted at men.

[45] See e.g. Zeynap Cemalcilar, Toni Falbo, Laura M. Stapleton, "Cyber Communications: A new opportunity for international students' adaptation?" *International Journal of Intercultural Relations* 29 (2005), 92.

[46] Six out of fourteen respondents could not imagine studying abroad without the Internet as it would deprive them of quick, easy and inexpensive communication means with their networks of home; five further declared that they would find it difficult or even frightening. Eight interviewees stated that their involvement with digital and social media, particularly Facebook and Skype, increased during the period of their study abroad; only three reported reduced participation.

fear of alienation and irrelevance that could be developed between the students and those they (physically) left behind.[47] In many cases the patterns of communication became more frequent and intense in comparison to the period prior to departure.

Several studies have been conducted on the impact of a digitally-facilitated connection to the existing support networks on the general process of international students' adjustment. However, none of them have focused on the experience of space and place. Yet, the analysis of the project interviews has demonstrated that this instant and constant connection strongly affects the students' understanding of space.[48] This impact was particularly conspicuous in the respondents' practices of posting visual materials online. Out of eleven participants who reported sharing photographs on social media sites (mostly Facebook), ten posted images of places they had travelled to, and only two of the latter mentioned other categories of photos. In some cases the experience of space exploration proved to be sufficiently powerful to alter the respondents' previous patterns of online activities regarding visual materials; in such cases travel photographs gained the foremost position, sometimes entirely superseding other types of pictures.[49] Even some of the respondents who generally demonstrated caution against posting photographs online admitted that they considered visual documentations of their travels an important factor in remaining actively involved with their networks of support, particularly those "back home."[50] This is partly explicable through the popularity of such pictures confirmed by the high number of comments and "likes," which could be indirectly translated into the popularity of the person who posted them.[51] Sharing photographs of new spaces and places was also claimed to be a valid evidence of the

---

[47] See e.g. female participant, aged 27 (interview excerpt: Kraków, 17 December 2012); female participant, aged 21 (interview excerpt: Kraków, 25 November, 2012); male participant, aged 32 (interview excerpt: Chicago, 25 March 2013).

[48] For more information, see Timothy B. Smith and David A. Schwalb, "Preliminary Examination of International Students' Adjustment and Loneliness Related to Electronic Communications," *Psychological Reports* 100 (2007): 167; Cemalcilar, Falbo, Stapleton, "Cyber Communications," 103, 105.

[49] See e.g. male participant, aged 21 (interview excerpt: Kraków, 18 December 2012).

[50] Cf. John Urry and Jonas Larsen, *The Tourist Gaze 3.0* (Los Angeles, London, New Delhi, Singapore, Washington DC: Sage, 2011), 186.

[51] "There may be few words written but if the picture follows, you get twice as many likes and comments than just writing without photos. Which is essentially like YouTube views – to rate the popularity of the post"; male participant, aged 21 (interview excerpt: Kraków, 18 December 2012).

respondents' success and wellbeing within the new environment for their families and friends at home:

> [W]hat I usually do when I travel to a new place, I post them there, because my family can see the pictures, and my friends can see the pictures, and they can see that I'm OK and I'm having fun.[52]

An act of taking a photograph is in itself an act of differentiating and conceptualising space; an important moment that shows and shapes the understanding of space of both the photographer and viewer.[53] Taking a photograph of space presents it with certain characteristics of place; a segment of it becomes particular, chosen, and thus — endowed with value.[54] The intention of sharing a photograph online with the members of the networks of home was reported to permit the photographer/the traveller a more careful reflection upon (or, in fact, a more careful *construction* of) their spatial experience. Among the conducted interviews, the most vivid illustration of this tendency was the practice of publishing exclusively those travel pictures which featured the respondent as the central element of the photographed location.[55] Such a construction of a travel image can be interpreted as signifying familiarisation, appropriation or even conquest of the previously unknown space. The real-time interactions stemming from the image publications (other users' queries, comments and expressions of excitement or approval in the form of Facebook "likes") were additionally reported to offer an external reflection upon the negotiated space. According to Tuan, such a perspective is necessary (along with personal experience) for acquiring an intimate knowledge and a sense of place.[56] For some of the respondents the possibility of the immediate sharing of images and the consequent discussions on the places displayed could also, to a certain extent, make the experience of the place transferable and understandable to the family and friends "back home":

---

[52] Male participant, aged 32 (interview excerpt: Chicago, 25 March 2013). Cf. male participant, aged 21 (interview excerpt: Kraków, 18 December 2012).

[53] Here I partly follow Geoffrey C. Bowker, *Memory Practices in the Sciences* (Cambridge, MA: MIT Press, 2005), 15.

[54] See e.g. male participant, aged 21 (interview excerpt: Kraków, 18. December 2012): "I wouldn't put up the photo of me in pub eating kebab because I can do it anywhere. But I will put up the photo of me in front of the Budapest palace [...]."

[55] Male participant, aged 21 (interview excerpt: Kraków, 18 December 2012): "I only put photos of myself taken in spots. [...] I do take pictures only of places but I don't put them up on Facebook, just keep it for myself."

[56] Tuan, *Space and Place*, Loc 299, 303.

> I have put some photos down [from the trip to Auschwitz] and then people were like "Wow, that's amazing. I can't believe that happened." I mean people *know* history [emphasis original]; they just got kind of... that kind of more of realisation that you're actually there where it happened. [...] A lot of people understood, I think, what they need to know about Auschwitz. I think they can make the connection [now].[57]

Tuan claims that the understanding of space, and thus its potential transformation into place, is primarily achieved through movement.[58] Yet, as the project accounts demonstrate, the movement does not need to be corporeal, nor the experience direct, to allow the development of certain ideas of space. As argued by John Urry and Jonas Larsen, the "power of now" enacted by digital photography enables the audience to "gaze upon events unfolding more or less in real time," transforming photographs into "'live postcards' happenings" and removing the aspect of "that has been" from them.[59] Resultantly, to some extent, spaces and their histories can be mediated through the real-time participation in the experiences of friends and acquaintances facilitated by the use of social media. Posting information, stories and photographs of their travels and host locations, the participants believed to be conveying their experience of space to their family and friends which, as reported in several cases, raised awareness and incited curiosity about unknown areas. Occasionally, this resulted in inspiring future migration patterns (friends coming to visit). Furthermore, the significance of visual representations of space and place(s) in the digital interactions with the networks of home was narrated as constituting an additional motivation (or even pressure) for the participants to traverse, familiarise and photograph foreign space.[60] This multiple involvement of the social networks of origin location within the students' experiences of unfamiliar areas, facilitated by the use of digital media, permitted the construction of places that stretched beyond their physical boundaries, corresponding with Massey's understanding of place as dynamic and extraverted.[61]

---

[57] Female participant, aged 21 (interview excerpt: Kraków, 25 November, 2012).
[58] Tuan, *Space and Place*, Loc 199, 211, 812.
[59] Urry and Larsen, *The Tourist Gaze 3.0*, 181.
[60] For instance, a male participant, aged 27 (Interview excerpt: Kraków, 3 December 2012), reported that although he felt more inclined to stay at home during a snowy day, he decided to venture out to take photographs that could be sent "back home."
[61] Massey, *Space, Place, and Gender*, 121, 169.
[61] Massey, *Space, Place, and Gender*, 169.

Conclusions and Further Research

In the contemporary world that is believed to witness "the collapse of spatial barriers,"[62] space becomes increasingly traversable. A growing number of people are able and ready to study and travel abroad, and to explore unfamiliar spaces. In the conducted interviews the experience of space and the ability to transform it into place(s) come across as one of the fundamental conditions of a successful adaptation to a foreign country and culture. The respondents presented the cognition of space as crucial to developing a sense of belonging to a new environment.

As Massey suggests, human perception and understanding of space and place and the participation in social networks are interconnected and mutually influencing. This perspective is clearly reflected within the analysed accounts. The development of a social network located within the unknown space was narrated as an important factor in the process of space familiarisation, just as the maintenance of the connection with the prior networks was to be a means to preserve the sense of belonging to the origin area. The respondents presented the practice of sharing their spatial experiences (through posting photographic documentation of visited places online) as an essential aspect of interacting with family and friends. Moreover, the obstacles in moving through space were communicated as unsettling largely due to the consequent social alienation and/or separation from significant others.[63]

As the instruments and forums of establishing, shaping and sustaining both new and prior social networks at a pace and with an ease inconceivable in the pre-digital times, digital media, and social media in particular, exert a powerful influence over the respondents' experiences of space and place abroad. The new media can, to a large extent, enhance their users' mobility, empower them to appropriate unknown spaces, and provide them with the tools and forums of sharing and reflecting upon their spatial experience, and of facilitating spatial exploration (like Couchsurfing). Young people creatively utilise new technologies in negotiating unfamiliar space and transforming it into homelike place(s).

---

[62] David Harvey, "From Space to Place and Back Again. Reflections on the Condition of Postmodernity," in *Mapping the Futures: Local Cultures, Global* Change, ed. John Bird et al. (London: Routledge, 1993), 4.

[63] See e.g. male participant, aged 27 (Interview excerpt: Kraków, 3 December 2012): "The idea that I could get separated from my girlfriend because some bureaucrat decides that I shouldn't be able to come to [her country], or she shouldn't be able to come to [mine]—I find that offensive. It's a [...] personal relationship; that's a basic human function."

The mediation of digital media in the process permits the construction of place as open and interconnecting with other places and networks.

However, the impact of the ICT usage on the participants' apprehension of foreign space is neither unambiguous nor unproblematic. While the new media empower their users to create social networks in unknown locations, enabling them to explore unfamiliar space through the perspective of local inhabitants, the question of the "authenticity" of such exploration remains to be defined and verified. Such arrangements can certainly result in diminishing the concerns (reducing both the financial costs and the potential "fear of solitude") and enhancing excitement induced by traversing space. However, what was conveyed as the "authentic" and "real" cognition of place, as opposed to the one mediated through a touristy experience, is in fact also mediated through the perspective of a local host.

Secondly, even as the usage of digital technologies can provide a significant support in the process of appropriating foreign space through anchoring their users in the place and networks of home, it can also demotivate young people to seek ties with the host location.[64] As emphasised by one of the respondents, the unremitting connection to the physically distant networks can be detrimental to the capability of dwelling in "here" and "now," and present a risk of becoming "lost" in the space of technology.[65] Following the query of Wendy O'Brien, "How can I truly belong to this place where I am standing, imagining myself in another world? [...] The implications of [such] disengagement cannot be overlooked."[66] The comfort of the digital attachment to home can render the alienation from the space of the host location easier to manage, and a failure in adaptation to it — affordable.

Thirdly, further research is required on the role of photographic representations of space and of the practice of sharing them online in the experience of international students. Paraphrasing Crang's diagnosis of tourism as experienced not "in itself but for its future memory,"[67] the question arises whether new spaces are truly engaged with, or simply gazed upon and recorded for the gratifications it provides in digital social interactions. Particularly, the act of photographing (and thus constructing) space with the predominant intent of consuming the image within the

---

[64] Cf. Cemalcilar, Falbo, Stapleton, "Cyber Communications," 93, 104.
[65] Female participant, aged 27 (interview excerpt: Kraków, 17 December 2012).
[66] O'Brien, "There is No Place Like Home," 7.
[67] Mike Crang, "Picturing practices research through the tourist gaze," *Progress in Human Geography* 21: 366; here I follow Urry and Larsen, *The Tourist Gaze 3.0*, 180.

previously existing networks of home can, in fact, signify alienation and disengagement from the new environment rather than an attempt to seek connection.[68]

Furthermore, there appears to exist a risk of overestimating the role of digital media in the experience of negotiating space through social networking. Although most respondents recognised the digital media role in this process, they also emphasised the predominant importance of non-virtual interactions and physical engagement with places in providing meaning to space. Some respondents expressed doubts about the authenticity of online relations as long as they were not transferred and verified in the non-virtual world:

> [...] I wouldn't want to call it any sort of relationship before we met. [...] It was a *proper* [emphasis mine] relationship with a huge build-up online beforehand.[69]

Similarly, while deeply appreciative of Couchsurfing as a forum of online encounters, the respondents placed its greatest value in its eventual relocation into the non-virtual world:

> [...] you're forced to take it out of the [...] website and actually meet in *real* life. [...] it doesn't take place on that website. [...] The objective is not to replace *reality* but to add to it [all emphasis are mine]. [70]

This perspective resonates in Timothy B. Smith and David A. Shwalb's analysis of the role of electronic communication in the process of students' adjustment to the host country and culture, which has been proven to be less effective than personal socialising.[71]

Last but not least, the limitations of the study presented in David Gunkel's chapter at the beginning of this volume ought to be taken into account. This chapter provides the preliminary examination of the digital media role in the process of negotiating young people's experience of

---

[68] I thank Dr. Małgorzata Zachara for raising this point in our discussion. For more information on the tourist gaze within the analysed interviews, see Ann Gunkel, "Going Native: The Real Problem in Theorizing the Communicative Interaction of Digital Natives," in this volume.

[69] Male participant, aged 27 (interview excerpt: Kraków, 3 December 2012).

[70] Male participant, aged 24 (interview excerpt: Kraków, 5 January 2013). It is worth noting that, while the interviewers spoke about "virtual" and "non-virtual" world/reality, most respondents reserved the notions of "real" and "reality" for the non-virtual world.

[71] Smith and Schwalb, "Preliminary Examination," 170.

foreign space within the context of social networks. Considering the number of respondents and the qualitative character of the assembled data, the generalisation of the results is neither possible, nor intended. Further research is required, including the conduction of follow-up and new interviews with the respondents in different settings, an additional quantitative study, visual analysis of the produced photographs of places, as well as content analysis of the chosen space- and communication-related websites and digital services (particularly Couchsurfing), to further verify and enable the generalisation of the findings.

Bibliography

Bauman, Zygmunt. *Globalization: The Human Consequences*. Polity, 2013. Kindle edition.

Bowker, Geoffrey C. *Memory Practices in the Sciences*. Cambridge, MA: MIT Press, 2005.

Cemalcilar, Zeynap, Falbo, Toni, and Laura M. Stapleton. "Cyber Communications: A new opportunity for international students' adaptation?" *International Journal of Intercultural Relations* 29 (2005): 91-110.

Couchsurfing. "About us." Accessed September 3, 2013. https://www.couchsurfing.org/n/about.

—. "Our Values." Accessed September 3, 2013. https://www.couchsurfing.org/n/values.

Harvey, David. "From Space to Place and Back Again. Reflections on the Condition of Postmodernity." In *Mapping the Futures: Local Cultures, Global* Change, edited by John Bird, Barry Curtis, Time Putnam, and Lisa Tickner, 3-29. London: Routledge, 1993.

Lundberg, Anita, Stasiewicz-Bieńkowska, Agnieszka, and Anna Enhörning Singhateh. "Border Crossing Networks: Virtual Makes It Real." In *Innovative Research in a Changing and Challenging World*, edited by Si Fan, Thao Le, Quynh Le, and Yun Yue, 81–94. Launceston: Australian Multicultural Interaction Institute, 2012.

Massey, Doreen B. "Power-geometry and a Progressive Sense of Place." In *Mapping the Futures: Local Cultures, Global Change*, edited by John Bird, Barry Curtis, Time Putnam, and Lisa Tickner, 59-69. London: Routledge 1993.

—. *Space, Place, and Gender*. Minneapolis, MN, USA: University of Minnesota Press, 1999.

Hubbard, Phil, and Rob Kitchin. "Introduction: Why key thinkers?" In *Key Thinkers of Space and Place*, edited by Phil Hubbard, and Rob Kitchin, 1-17. SAGE, 2010.

Key Thinkers of Space and Place, edited by Phil Hubbard, and Rob Kitchin. Miejsce: SAGE, 2010.

McIntyre, Norman. "Introduction." In *Multiple Dwelling and Tourism: Negotiating Place, Home, and Identity*, edited by Normal McIntyre, Daniel Williams, and Kevin McHugh, 3-14. Wallingford, Oxfordshire, GBR: CABI Publishing, 2006.

O'Brien, Wendy. "There's No Place Like Home." In *Home in Motion: The Shifting Grammars of Self & Stranger*, edited by Pedro E. Marcelino, 3-11. Oxford: Inter-Disciplinary.Net, 2011.

Powell, Mike, and Jürgen Horn. "Żyć jak krab." Interview with Łukasz Długowski. *Wysokie Obcasy* August 24 (2013): 32-36.

Smith, Peter F. *The Dynamics of Urbanism*. London and New York: Routledge, 2013.

Smith Timothy B., and David A. Schwalb. "Preliminary Examination of International Students' Adjustment and Loneliness Related to Electronic Communications". *Psychological Reports* 100 (2007): 167-170.

Tuan, Yi-Fu. *Space and Place: The Perspective of Experience*. London, Minneapolis: University of Minnesota Press, 2011. Kindle edition.

Urry, John, and Jonas Larsen. *The Tourist Gaze 3.0*. Los Angeles, London, New Delhi, Singapore, Washington DC: Sage, 2011.

VK. "About VK." Accessed September 15, 2013. http://vk.com/about.

CHAPTER FIVE

EVERY MINUTE OF EVERY DAY: MOBILITIES, MULTICULTURE AND TIME

YASMIN GUNARATNAM AND LES BACK

Introduction

Human society is both more mobile and connected than at any other moment in its history. Communication technologies are also transforming the experience of movement and the capacity to foster and sustain multiple and simultaneous social connections on a global scale. In cities like London the fabric of everyday life is woven from cultural threads that tie the close at hand to distant places. "Super-diversity" has become the academic buzzword to name this experience, although the notion itself does little to describe the complex and varied ways in which people live with profound forms of bodily connection and division.[1] How to make sense and understand the nature and pace of urban change in this context is an urgent issue not just for sociologists but also for public services.

The tools and devices for research craft are also being extended by digital culture in a hyper-connected world. The mobile phone not only transforms the experience of migration today it is also affording new possibilities to re-imagine observation and the generation, analysis and communication of research. There is a potential to re-think the relationship between not just participants and researchers but also the public circulation of knowledge and the fruits of our sociological curiosity.

This chapter focuses on two questions, namely: how to make sense of multicultural environments undergoing profound social change; and, what are the opportunities afforded by the resources of digital culture to develop novel forms of research craft in the service of this challenge? Here, we discuss one instance where the potential of the new devices of social

---

[1] See Stephen Vertovec, "Super-Diversity and Its Implications," *Ethnic and Racial Studies*, 30, 2007: 1024-1054.

research were used to support a local institution – a children's hospice – in finding out more about how its local communities experience social and economic change. This problem - that appears deceptively simple - formed the basis of the "Every Minute of Everyday" collaborative project with Richard House Children's Hospice in East London (http://everyminuteof everyday.org.uk/).

When we began the project, we had already been using the digital platform Posterous (http://en.wikipedia.org/wiki/Posterous) to conduct group-based multi-media ethnographies, using photography, film and sound recordings.[2] Posterous allowed several researchers to post data simultaneously onto the site in real time, using smartphones. As the data are streamed from the field into the site, the blog is updated in real time, so that the chronology of ethnographic events and reading is reversed – the most recent events appearing first.

For the *Every Minute* project, we were interested in experimenting with the mobility of the senses that digital methods can facilitate, whereby the "static gaze" symbolized by the still photographic image is augmented by sensory "images" taken on the move.[3] We also wanted to explore the relationality of space-time and the possibilities that digital methods offer for the greater "mobile" involvement of research participants.[4] What characterized this research was the different sensory circuits and modes of experience that were fabricated and channelled not only by our devices and platforms (that included the micro blogging platform Twitter) but also between variously able-bodies, namely those of the researchers and our research partners and audiences in the hospice.

What we succeeded in doing was to re-route the circulation of the ethnographic imagination, creating a different constellation of relationships between researchers, participants and readers. In brief, our rapid ethnographic mapping of Newham was "oriented" both spatially and affectively by young people and families at the hospice whose own sense of space and time were continually shifting with illness. Before discussing our emerging findings, we first want to make some critical points about our thinking of the relationships between research knowledge production and temporality in real time ethnography.

---

[2] Les Back, "Live Sociology: Social Research and its Futures," *The Sociological Review*, 60 (2012): 18–39.
[3] John Urry, *Mobilities* (Cambridge: Polity, 2007).
[4] Doreen Massey, *For Space* (London, Thousand Oaks, CA, and New Delhi: Sage Publications Ltd, 2005).

The False Promise of "Real Time"

Until the late twentieth century, ethnographic research was positioned within a field framed by a particular sequence and set of time frames i.e. initial encounter, immersion and fieldwork, note taking, leaving the field and writing up, often from afar. Ethnographies were written within "the ethnographic present" that provided accounts of culture as if captured like timeless snapshots in a hermetically sealed "site."[5] Yet this version of ethnographic representation and authority has always been critically interrogated as ethnographers reflected on the implication of their own presence and writing in the making of ethnographic texts. The unprecedented level of connectivity that exists today poses a further challenge for researchers as any remnants of the illusion of spatio-temporal separation between "the field" and the place of analysis and interpretation no longer holds.[6] The ethnographic present is expanding, resulting in the proliferation of ethnographic accounts that destabilise the relationship between "the field" as the time and place of ethnography and of analysis and "text."

Our particular interest in the temporalities of ethnography is informed by discussions that have sought to displace the hegemony of clock time through the important recognition that "temporality no longer stands outside phenomena…but unfolds *with* phenomena."[7] "Event time" as it has been dubbed, is thought to be a product of contemporary transformations in the social field from a territory to a contingent circulation. If "data" generation, ethnographic attentiveness and understanding *are* a form of time in this way in empirical research, many researchers have also recognised that they are a time when the linear and quantifiable is queered by a qualitative breaching of space/time relationships and not only due to the advent of digital technologies. Such breaches in space-time can occur at a large scale such as in the reach of Empire into the here and now that has led to the advocating of multi-sited, cartographic research methods.[8] They can also include smaller happenings: sensual experiences of

[5] George E. Marcus, G.E, *Ethnography through Thick and Thin* (Princeton: Princeton University Press, 1998).

[6] See also Dhiraj Murthy, "Digital Ethnography: An Examination of the Use of New Technologies for Social Research," *Sociology*, 42, 5 (2008): 837–855

[7] Lisa Adkins, "Feminism after Measure", *Feminist Theory*, 10, 3, (2009): 336.

[8] See Les Back, "Global Attentiveness and the Sociological Ear," *Sociological Research Online*, 14, 4, 2009, accessed May 19, 2011 : http://www.socresonline.org.uk/14/4/14.html; also Marcus *Ethnography Through Thick and Thin.*

fieldwork, smells and sounds, that intrude upon the researcher at her desk or where the shadows of events and people in the researcher's past stretch the spatio-temporal and conceptual boundaries of a research project.[9]

Such combined developments have led to reflections upon the history and social life of methods.[10] Equally, the politics of methodology and the jurisdiction of academic researchers have been keenly debated.[11] The singular promise of using digital tools in collaborative, team-based ethnography is the capacity to re-order the relationship between data generation, analysis and circulation so as to offer the possibility of a near-simultaneity and the multiplication of ethnographic viewpoints. One of the ways in which this can be done in real time is through a pluralization of observers and the "crowd sourcing" of data.

However, technological enchantment should not cloud critical and ethical judgment. New devices cannot fix longstanding epistemological conundrums with regard to the nature of "coeval" relationships (what it is to live with different others in the same time) and how the social world is constituted through the methods and techniques we use to make data and enact social life.[12] Drawing upon the ideas of the feminist activist and poet Gloria Anzaldua, Michelle Bastian has pointed out that a crucial challenge in addressing coevalness is how to recognise the lived simultaneity of different histories by not subsuming them into a commensurable spatial and temporal moment. While real time methods have the potential to show how differences are lived within the same space, they can also risk eliding the simultaneity of time with commensurability. For Bastian the problem of time with relation to social differences is that,

---

[9] See Judith Okely, "Fieldwork Embodied," *The Sociological Review*, 55 (2007): 65–79; Andrea Doucet, " 'From Her Side of the Gossamer Wall(s)': Reflexivity and Relational Knowing," *Qualitative Sociology*, 31, 1 (2007): 73–87; Martha McMahon, "Significant Absences," *Qualitative Inquiry*, 2, 3 (1996): 320 –336.

[10] See Evelyn Ruppert, John Law and Mike Savage, "Reassembling Social Science Methods: the challenge of digital devices," *Theory, Culture & Society*, 30, 4 (2013): 1-24;

Evelyn Ruppert and John Law, "Introduction: The Social Life of Methods – Devices," *Journal of Cultural Economy*, 6, 4 (2013): 1-12.

[11] See Mike Savage, (2011) *Identities and Social Change in Britain since 1940: The Politics of Method* (Oxford, Oxford University Press, 2011);

Mike Savage and Roger Burrows, "The Coming Crisis of Empirical Sociology," *Sociology*, 41, 5(2007): 885-899.

[12] John Law and John Urry, "Enacting the Social," *Economy and Society*, 33 (2004): 390–410.

> ...while time can be thought of as that which divides or separates, insofar as we are thought to share time with others, this shared time has primarily been thought in terms of a homogeneous present or presence...What is important to note, however, is that this commensurability is dependent on ignoring difference and focusing, instead, on what can be made homogenous and uniform.[13]

So although the pencil and notebook might be being replaced by smartphones and tablets these devices produce new kinds of problems as well as opportunities. For example, what might be called spontaneous (or contingent) sociology, seems to be everywhere from My Space to YouTube to Twitter.[14] For us, this adds another dimension to the issue raised by Carolyn Steedman's question as to who is the interlocutor of stories of the self when today self-revelation and self-narrative are uploaded without invitation.[15] Is there any longer a "narrative other" that elicits such tales?[16] Sherry Turkle argues that the ubiquity of "selfie" photographs taken on mobile phones is an indication of an almost insatiable desire to document life. Taking these images, Turkle suggests, inhibits rather than facilitates social communication. We pause silently to be captured by the mobile phone's camera lens held at arm's length.[17]

Upload culture and on-line social networks produce a kind of vulnerability - particularly for the young - that results in varying degrees of self-exposure. Thinking sociologically about real time ethnography also means navigating between the communication possibilities offered by digital culture while remaining attentive to the kinds of time and selves that are being produced through the articulation of on-line experience.[18] In a study of "Identity Construction on Facebook," Shanyang Zhao and

---

[13] Michelle Bastian, "The Contradictory Simultaneity of Being with Others: Exploring Concepts of Time and Community in the Work of Gloria Anzaldúa," *Feminist Review*, 97, 1 (2011): 153.

[14] See Dhiraj Murthy, *Twitter: Social Communication in the Age of Twitter* (Cambridge: Polity Press, 2013).

[15] Carolyn Steedman (2000) "Enforced Narratives" in *Feminism and Autobiography. Texts, Theories, Methods*, ed. Tess Cosslett et al. (London: Routledge, 2000): 25-39.

[16] Following Adria Cavarero, *Relating Narratives: Storytelling and Selfhood* (London and New York: Routledge, 2000).

[17] See Sherry Terkel "The Documented Life," The *New York Times*, 15th December, 2013, accessed December 16th, 2013 http://www.nytimes.com/2013/12/16/opinion/the-documented-life.html?_r=0.

[18] See Rob Kitchin and Martin Dodge, *Code/Space: Software and Everyday Life* (MIT press, Cambridge, Massachusetts, 2011).

colleagues found that on-line identities in the anonymous digital community were shown rather than narrated, expressing ideal-type "hoped-for possible selves" (Yurchisin et al. 2005) or what the philosopher Stanley Cavell has called our "next self."[19] In many ways these different versions of the self, although digitally augmented, restage longstanding dramaturgical themes concerning the "impression management" of public "front stage" selves and the desire to present oneself in the best possible light, particularly when managing/avoiding social stigma and threat or "stigmaphobia."[20] As always, these ethical concerns – regarding the potential damage to an individual and/or group's impression management apply to researchers as much as participants.[21] Nevertheless, the speed of publication of findings and the real time *in situ* personalization of contact with a field, can rearrange risk and exposure, particularly when consent for the making public of audio-visual data is often sought in the moment. For instance, although we provided contact details and the URL for the project's digital platform, none of the individuals who consented to have their images published contacted us and we have little idea of their thoughts and feelings about the public nature of the project.

In taking account of the increasing normalization "publicity" in these "data rich times" we argue that what is required is for social researchers to match innovation with critical reflection upon the ways in which research relationships and vulnerabilities are reconfigured by digital methods throughout the research process.[22] As Annelise Riles points out there is perhaps a warning to be found in the extent to which the notion of real time itself is used in technocratic forms of power to foster market logic.[23]

---

[19] Shanyang Zhao, Sherri Grasmuck, S. & Jason Martin, 2008. "Identity construction on Facebook: Digital empowerment in anchored relationships," *Computers in Human Behavior*, 24, 5, (2008): 1816–1836; Stanley Cavell, *Conditions Handsome and Unhandsome: The Constitution of Emersonian Perfectionism: The Carus Lectures, 1988* (Chicago: University of Chicago Press, 1990).

[20] Erving Goffman, *The Presentation of Self in Everyday Life* (Harmondsworth, Middlesex: Penguin Books Ltd, 1971).

[21] Raymond M. Lee, *Doing Research on Sensitive Topics*, London; Newbury Park, Calif.: Sage Publications, 1993).

[22] Andrew Abbott, "Reflections on the Future of Sociology," *Contemporary Sociology*, 29, 2 (2000): 296-300; David Beer, "Using Social Media Data Aggregators to Do Social Research," *Sociological Research Online*, 17 (3) 10 (2012), accessed June 10th, 2013 http://www.socresonline.org.uk/17/3/10.html.

[23] Annelise Riles, "'Real time': Unwinding technocratic and anthropological knowledge," *American Ethnologist*, 31, 3 (2004): 397

What is being lost and gained when aspects of the generation, coding and analysis of data are not only collapsed but are not fully visible and are dispersed across social spaces and users, leaving certain elements of data/analysis open and unfinished or "de-composed"?[24]

Time: simultaneous but not commensurable

As we have argued, it is a profound mistake to think that digital technology allows privileged access to the unfolding and simultaneous "now" of social life. To clarify: the concept of real time, that is computational in origins, is not so much about immediacy - which is impossible to attain - but concerns the speed, organisation and pacing of time by digital and methodological tools, devices and practices. All research devices have their own temporal apparatus and sensibilities. Each manufactures relationships in the circuits between real time and the archiving of both the content and the process of research relationships. As such, the methods record and confect their own spatio-temporal mobilities and sense of what is in/commensurable.

Mobility in the social sciences is most often discussed as a horizontal movement across space. Our concern here is also to highlight mobility as a vertical displacement, in the sense of being a phenomenological transition - a movement across bodily and affective states and time; in this case profoundly affected by changing experiences of illness, disability and loss.[25] Crip theory – that brings together ideas from disability studies and queer theory – has used analysis of cultural media such as film, novels and television to draw attention to the instabilities and flow of all bodies and to question able-bodied perspectives and containments.[26] In collaborating with the hospice we were interested in how these concerns with debilitated bodies and their shifting constituencies and alliances might also contribute to ideas and concepts of mobility, by unsettling the assumption that mobility is necessarily an externalised and conscious event. The geographers Dikeç, Clark and Barnett explain,

---

[24] Robert McRuer, *Crip Theory: Cultural Signs of Queerness and Disability* (New York and London: NYU Press, 2006).

[25] Yasmin Gunaratnam, *Death and the Migrant: Bodies, Borders, Care* (London: Bloomsbury Academic, 2013).

[26] See McRuer, *Crip Theory* and also Margrit and Janet Price, "Deleuzian Connections and Queer Corporealities: Shrinking Global Disability," R*hizomes*, 11/12, (2006), accessed February 2nd, 2014 http://www.rhizomes.net/issue11/shildrickprice/index.html.

> …amidst all the attention to the negotiation of territorial boundaries which Kant put centre stage and which intensifying globalization has kept on the agenda, what is also always with us are the borders, thresholds, and turning points of ordinary, embodied existence. And these are no less significant than the more concrete figures of mobility and transition…. Illness, destitution, death of loved ones, unexpected pregnancy, love or desire beyond the bounds of communal acceptability, these are all predicaments that 'befall us', exceeding our knowledge and preparedness, carrying with them the risk of a radical de-worlding.[27]

The evolving "deworldings" of disability and loss for those cared for by Richard House are an integral part of the young people's experiences of the city. For instance, degeneration in health can affect movements across and within public space, while also reconfiguring the developmental stages of childhood and differentiating the idea of a homogenous, shared present. As walking becomes supported by or replaced with the rehabilitative aids of sticks, frames or wheelchairs, each transition can mark a change in selfhood, family, peer and institutional relationships. By using the hospice's identified "special places" in the East End as our starting point for our ethnography we were also interested in how our real time methods related to bodily and affective mobilities as they radiated out from the hospice.[28]

Our modest experiment posed some big questions: Do mobile methods provide any different opportunities for participation and reflexivity? How to develop methods that are attentive to the ways in which real time can manage and flatten simultaneous differences? Before exploring the matters raised by this method we first want to take you to Newham and outline some of the issues faced by institutions such as Richard House who offer palliative and end of life care in cities.

This fieldwork post was sent to the *Every Minute of Everyday* website during one of our research trips by Les on Saturday 6th April, 2013.

---

[27] Mustafa Dikeç, Nigel Clark & Clive Barnett, "Extending Hospitality: Giving Space, Taking Time," *Paragraph*, 32, 1 (2009): 11.

[28] See also Yasmin Gunaratnam, "Learning to be affected: social suffering and total pain at life's borders," *The Sociological Review*, 60, (2012): 108–123.

"Green Street Wakes Up": Richard House and its Landscape

9.45am Upton Park. It's striking how few people there are on Green Street on this cold bright Saturday morning. The silver shutters are still down on most of the shops as I walk north from the station. Slowly Green Street starts to wake up. One by one the silver shutters get raised on shop after shop like eyelids. The street is quiet, calm and relatively empty. A shopkeeper advises me if I want a cup of tea I should turn around and head back to the station.

At 10.30am the quiet is shattered by the wail of sirens as four police cars with flashing blue lights speed past followed by a police van. The street is awake now and by 11.00am it is full if people Saturday shopping. Above the Halal Meat Market there is a large flashing red sign. "You buy we deliver... Marinated tandoori... Jerk Peri Peri... Smokey Barbeque... 100% non-stunned." On the opposite side of the street The Queens pub has a sign on the door "Toilets for customers use only."

Sitting in Percy Ingle's Bakery making notes and drinking warm tea to combat an hour spent in the cold. The three young women working behind the counter are comparing London styles of driving. "In my country (Nigeria) people drive on the right hand side. They drive like crazy" she tells her eastern European colleague. Another police siren sounds in the background.

Looking up from the cabinet of illuminated pasties and sausage rolls there is a sign describing the various kinds of bread on sale. One is dedicated to "Cholla - Traditional Jewish bread made with added sugar and eggs, hand moulded and topped with sesame seeds." East End cockney voices hang in the air with the sound of Polish words. The radio announces today is Grand National Day.

Tea is getting cold. On the pages of the annotated A-Z is a quotation from Italo Calvino: "The city does not tell its past, but contains it like the lines of a hand, written in the corners of the streets, the gratings of the windows." I suddenly realise that for the first hour of today's fieldwork on Green Street I have been using the back of my hand like a page from a notebook.

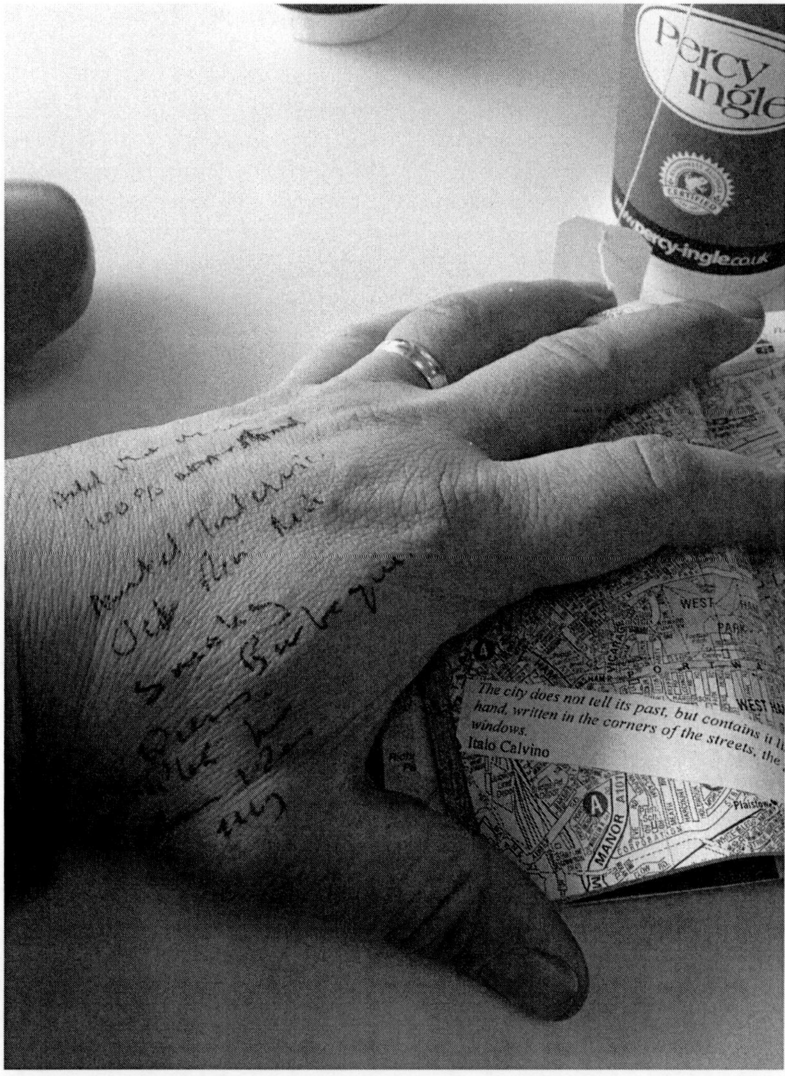

(Figure 1. A Hand Notebook, photograph by Les Back)

Les' description of Green Street shows the diverse cultural traces that are alive within the area, from the residual tastes of Jewish life in the Cholla to the contemporary realities of new settlement from Africa and Eastern Europe. Just 5 miles east of London's financial centre, the London Borough of Newham has a young and diverse population. Composed of the former Essex county boroughs of West Ham and East Ham, Newham's population was 307,984 in 2011.[29] Over one-third of Newham's population was under 25 years of age, compared to the London average of 30.6%.[30]

Newham has the highest proportion of Black and Minority Ethnic (BME) residents of all London Boroughs. It is estimated that by 2026 that these populations will account for 74.7% of all residents. Newham is also characterised by high levels of "population churn" - the turnover of residents moving in and out of the borough. In 2007/2008 19.5% of residents either left or entered the Borough, significantly higher than the London average of 13.6%.[31] Newham has one of the highest population turnover rates in London and a large component of this is international migration.

Poverty in Newham is high and life expectancy is lower than the London average. In 2007, it was ranked as the 6th most deprived area in Britain out of 354 local authorities.[32] As a consequence Newham residents on average live shorter lives than average Londoners by 2-3 years.[33] Sociologist Dick Hobbs commented poignantly that this cluster of neighbourhoods in the shadow of London's commercial centre is "rich only in poverty indicators."[34] The social environment in which Richard House children's hospice offers its services is a profoundly changing one, marked by social divisions and economic hardship.

---

[29] Qpzm LocalStats. *Newham Census Demographics, United Kingdom, 2011*,accessed February 1st, 2014 http://localstats.qpzm.co.uk/stats/england/london/newham.

[30] Newham Regional Planning and Property Directorate, *Newham London Local Economic Assessment 2010-2027* (London: London Borough of Newham, 2010): 4.

[31] Newham Regional Planning and Property Directorate, *Newham London Local Economic Assessment 2010-2027*: 3.

[32] Newham Regional Planning and Property Directorate, *Newham London Local Economic Assessment 2010-2027*: 7.

[33] Newham Regional Planning and Property Directorate, *Newham London Local Economic Assessment 2010-2027*: 7.

[34] Dick Hobbs, *Lush Life: Constructing Organised Crime in the UK* (Oxford: Oxford University Press, 2013): 2.

Richard House was the first children's hospice in London, the vision of nurse Anthea Hare who worked at the Royal London Hospital, Whitechapel. The idea for the hospice was crystallised out of Anthea's experience as a paediatric nurse and through her personal experiences of caring for her autistic brother – Richard – who died as a young man. Richard House is committed to community engagement and has well-developed links with a variety of local institutions from the London Muslim Centre and the East London Mosque to the local football team West Ham United. The hospice is a place of refuge for young people and their families, like many urban hospices it is separated off from the ebb and flow of local life. Paradoxically, it is a place that is both deeply rooted in the area but at the same time remains somewhat spatially disconnected from it.

Our project aimed to take the fascinations of the young people using Richard House out into the local area and to send ethnographic messages back. We began with affects, using the hospice as an epicentre. Richard House displayed posters asking young people and their families to identify their "special places" in Newham. We used this first affective mapping of Newham - that included West Ham football ground, the Royal Albert Docks and Stratford Shopping Centre - to begin identifying coordinates for our ethnography, taking in as many of the hospice's "special places" as we could on a route marked-up on two-pages of an A-Z. We provided a pre-fieldwork training workshop for our 12 volunteer post-graduates, dividing them into pairs and giving each pair an A-Z. The ethnographers could decide what methods and devices to use and what places to go to in the general locality of the route.

Each route on the A-Z was marked randomly with quotations from social theorists from Walter Benjamin to Sara Ahmed. We hoped the quotations would inspire the researchers to (re)visit places with special meaning to our research participants and wander and deviate from these "desire lines" of everyday paths through Newham.[35] One of the methods that Yasmin used in trying to elicit more "desire lines" was a blank map (inspired by http://mapyourmemories.tumblr.com/mappingmanhattan). The map was emailed to students and alumni who lived in Newham and hard copies were also given out on the streets and in cafés. Individuals, like the young people and families at Richard House, were asked to draw in their special places in the borough (stamp addressed envelopes were provided for those who could not fill them in at the time).

[35] After Sara Ahmed, *Queer Phenomenology: Orientations, Objects, Others* (Durham and London: Duke University Press, 2005).

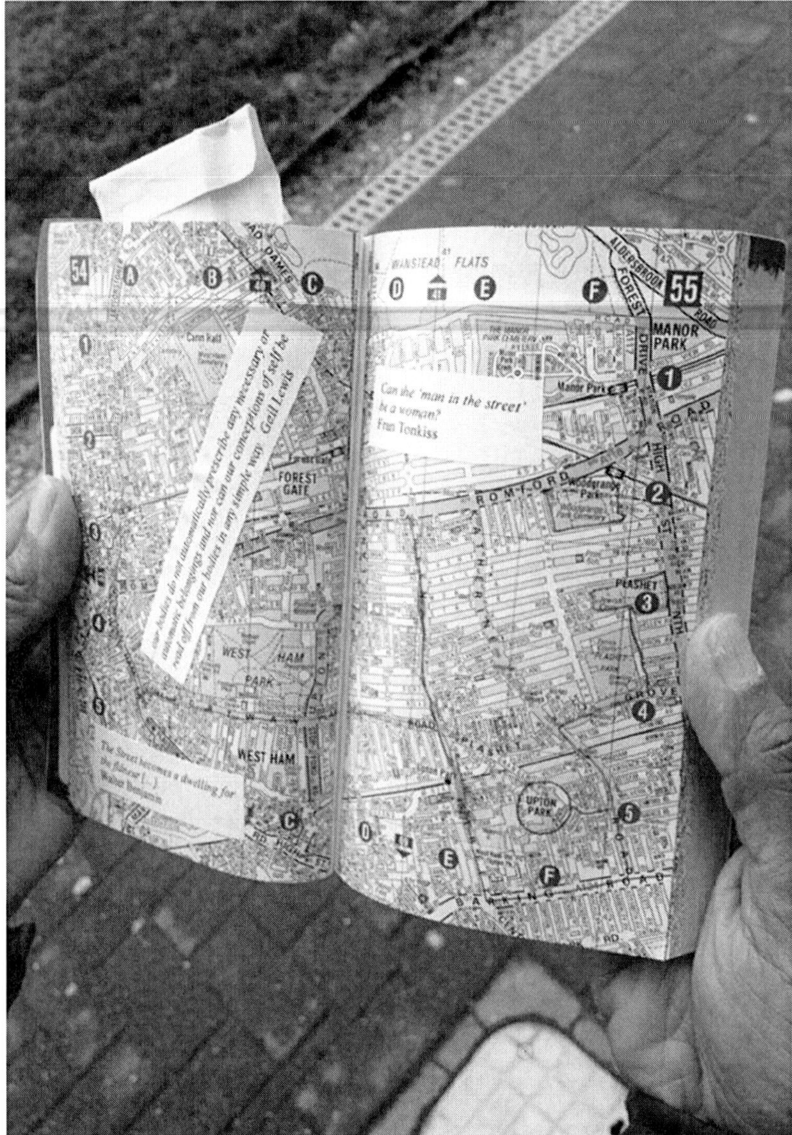

(Figure 2. Yasmin Gunaratnam Holding An Annotated London A-Z photography by Les Back)

The first map of Newham that we received was from Sairah, a former undergraduate student at Goldsmiths. It is a beautifully crafted map, depicting the places that are important to Sairah in her local area and also at different times in her life. At Forest Gate she writes "Priceless Memories of my late Grandma." There is the caption "Story books, Revision and Time Out" to mark the Town Hall and library; "Prayer + reflection = Peace" is how Sairah captions her drawing of her local mosque. At Central Park, we find ourselves some twenty years away at a momentous occasion "My first swing on a swing and ride down a slide - Weee!". Newham College is a place bursting with text "No doubt college days were the best: Amazing teachers; Warren, Kate..., Day dreaming in the 'Link,' Passing notes around the class on (wait for it...) STARBURST wrappers lol"

As well as these maps, the ethnography included photographs, film, audio recorded interviews and multi-sensory maps of the sounds, sights and smells of Newham. Most of the ethnography was done on different days and times within a one-week period. Most importantly for us and despite some glitches with the real time uploading of data onto Posterous, the hospice was able to follow our excursions in real time, with the longest "delays" being days rather than months (these delays were due to the more complex editing and mapping that was being done with some of the data). The identification of "special places" by the hospice gave our data a direction and history, mediating the "presentism" of transactional digital methods and the "streaming" of content back to the hospice.[36]

The live data stream could be ignored, dipped in and out of, and interacted with according to the circumstances and interests of the user. For example, members of staff at the hospice were able to receive Twitter updates of images and short, 3 minute, Audioboo sound files as they went about their daily business. The relatively fast relay of information to the hospice offered a greater capacity for involvement with the research. When asked by Les whether the experience of following the research as it unfolded had been different, Rachel Power, Head of Human Resources responded "Yes, it really was. It made it feel really like live and as it was small amounts I was busy telling people at the meetings what had happened."

[36] For the critique of 'presentism' see Emma Upritchard, 2012. "Being stuck in (live) time: the sticky sociological imagination," *The Sociological Review*, 60, (2012): 124–138.

As we walked through Newham, with our different bodies, biographies and devices, all the time being guided by the hospice's "special places," we generated and collated very different mobilities and real times. Inevitably the ethnography elicited "ordinary affects," seemingly random snapshots of the evolving and improvised life of an area.[37] However, our association with the hospice and our being directed to places with a pre-existing affective value created unpredictable illness and death related collisions and new spatio-temporal coordinates. For instance when distributing our maps in a market, Yasmin and her research partner, Arooj Khan, met a Pakistani shopkeeper whose niece and nephew had both been cared for by Richard House. The woman recounted spontaneously a story about her father who had died three weeks previously. When she had found out that her father had a week or so to live, her family flew with him from East London to Pakistan. He died at eight o'clock in the morning and by three that afternoon they were at his funeral.

Taking imagination for a walk

The results of the *Every Minute* project were quite unexpected. The work of the researchers, under some direction from the hospice, materialized and transported fragments of the life of the local community into the hospice. As vicarious conduits we were also able to take the imaginations and curiosities of young people, families and staff for a walk. In some cases, because of illness and disability, these places were no longer accessible to some of these individuals, so that the "desire lines" that we followed were in some sense belated, removed from the changing experience of impairment and dying, making visible our various abled bodies. For example, a YouTube film by Bill Psarras and Sara Feinstein (http://www.youtube.com/watch?v=i6fRjwROkIg) records images of three hours of "Sensorial Ethnography and Walking" and includes several images of the ground. As kerbs, cracked paving stones and uneven pavements are captured among shots of bunting, chained gates and a curious cat, the camera poses its own questions. Is this somewhere that wheelchairs could move through? How might a sensually impaired ethnographer experience this space, this "walk," this film?

---

[37] Following Kathleen Stewart, *Ordinary Affects* (Durham and London: Duke University Press, 2007).

The content of the posts that we sent were varied. Pluralising the vantage points of observation meant that each observer brought their own ethnographic imagination to what they noticed and noted. Each of the ethnographers made images, audio-visual recordings and wrote ethnographic notes. The subject of the blog posts included observational notes, interview extracts and oral histories. These data included the YouTube film and a multisensory map created by Bill Psarras and Sara Feinstein. One of the iconic local places identified as meaningful to the young people was Upton Park, the West Ham United Football ground. The detail of that material is beyond the terms of the discussion here, but we simply want to illustrate how this process worked.

Technological difficulties did not disappear completely - for example, the arrival of posts to the blog were not quite simultaneous with their sending, but we did manage to make the findings of our ethnography available within a few hours or days. Here are a series of posts by Les on this theme to illustrate the texture of the material and how it was made available to staff and patients at Richard House:

Post: West Ham's Garden of Remembrance

Walking past Upton Park, West Ham United's home ground, on Green Street there is a garden of remembrance near the entrance. Sally, who is having a cigarette break, explains that fans can have their ashes scattered there. "Jeannie Bell ashes were scattered there, she worked for the club. The priest comes and blesses them and everything" Sally says. I explain what I am doing and that we are helping Richard House find out more about the area. Sally is very helpful and says that I am anymore than welcome to take some pictures of the garden.

Post: Blessing True Hammers

The memorial services are conducted by Reverend Alan Boldin who is the club priest. "You can always tell him because he has 'The Reverend' on the back of his West Ham jacket explains a middle-aged man who works for the club. The garden is full of very moving tributes.

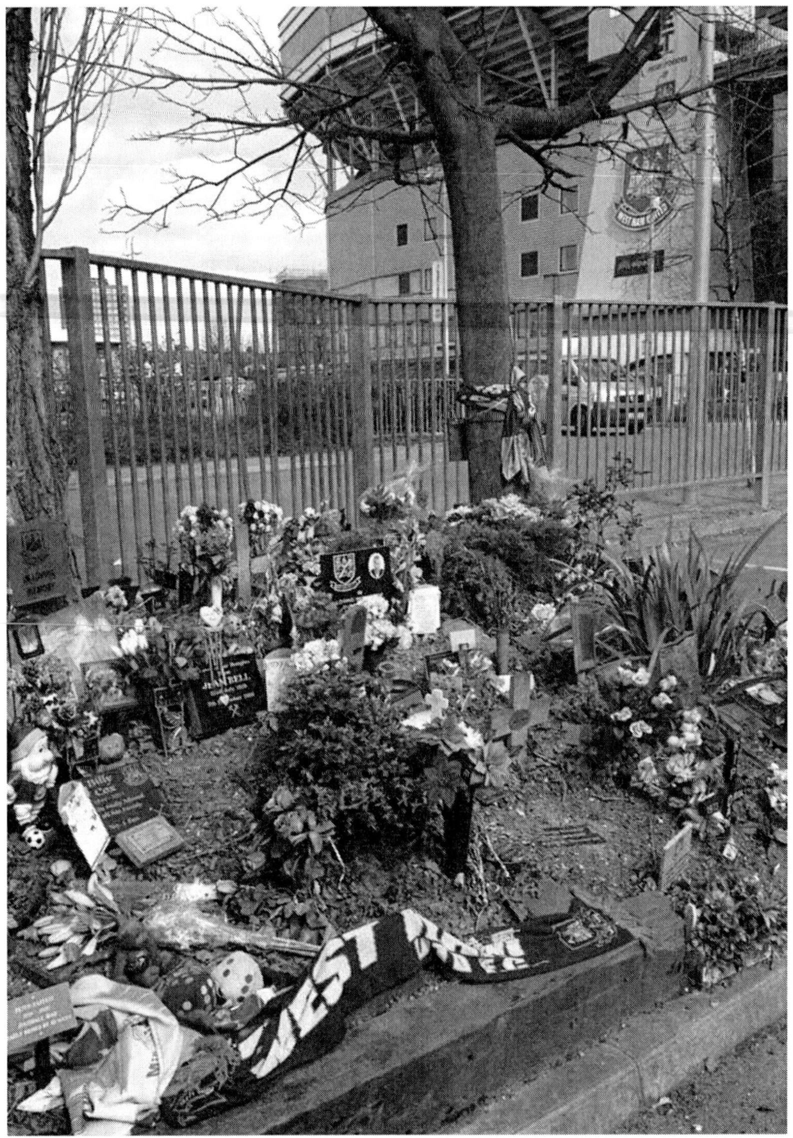

(Figure 3. Garden of Remembrance, Upton Park photograph by Les Back)

(Figure 4. Personal Tributes, Upton Park photograph by Les Back)

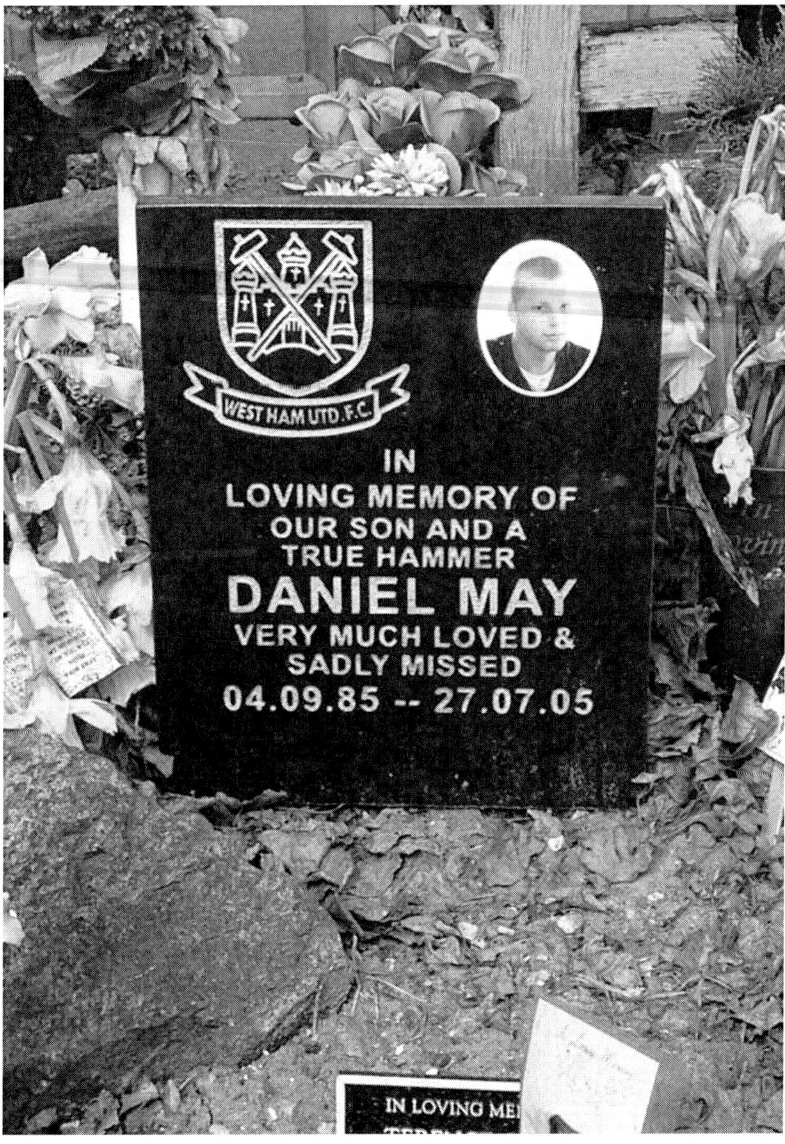

(Figure 5. Tribute to Daniel May, Upton Park photograph by Les Back)

Post: Bringing in a bit of Newham Life: West Ham and Richard House

Inside the foyer Sally is now behind her desk. I explain again that we are working with Richard House and explain that part of what we are trying to do is bring a bit of Newham's life into the children's hospice. She wears her long blonde hair in a ponytail. I can see the fair skin on her neck is reddening as she is fighting tears back. "I just can't bear the thought of it" she says. "The lives of the young people in the hospice carries on and some of them are West Ham fans" I explain. She smiles, regains her poise. Sally looks on the club website and realises that Richard House is one of the club's designated charities along with the Bobby Moore cancer research fund.

Post: Flowers for Bobby Moore

At the southern end of Green Street is a life size sculpture of the famous image of Bobby Moore hoisting the World Cup in 1966.

Moving closer I can see a bunch of flowers and a picture of a young Bobby Moore in a Hammers shirt.

Isn't it strange to use cut flowers as a gesture of remembrance? After just a brief time deprived of water the blooms always wither and quickly fade like this bouquet. Perhaps freshly cut flowers are a symbol of the beautiful and fragile nature of life itself.

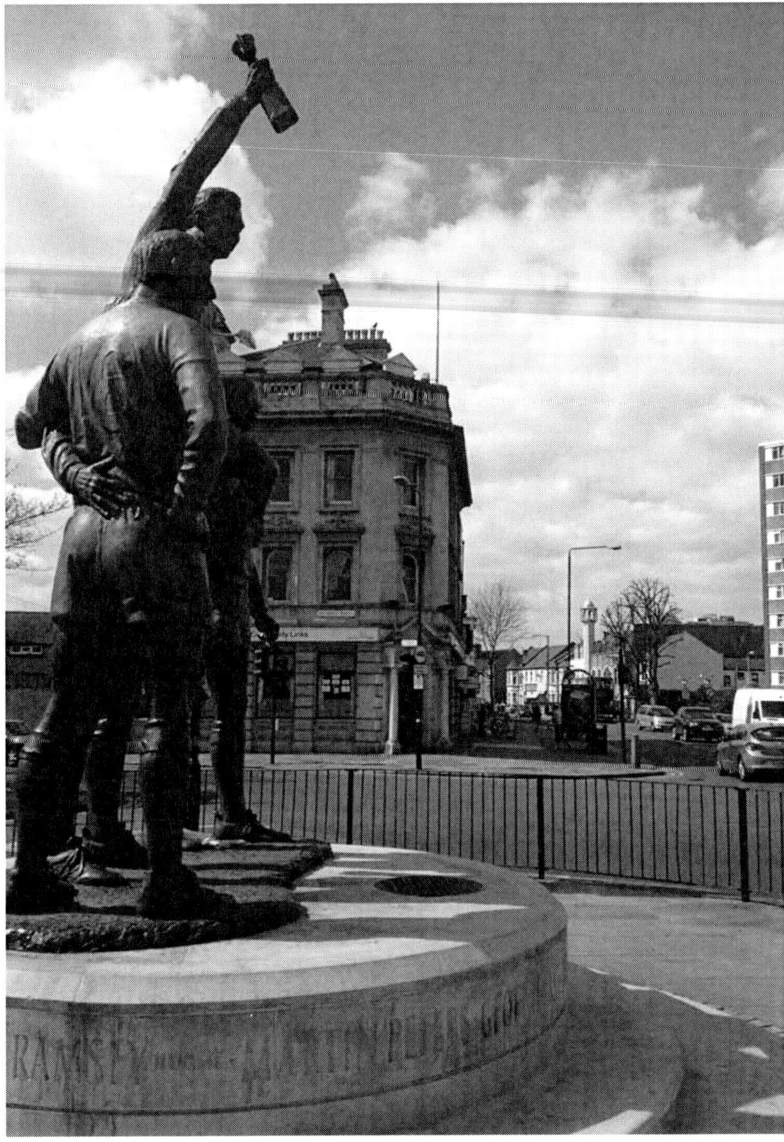

(Figure 6. 1966 World Club Sculpture, Green Street photograph by Les Back)

(Figure 7. Flowers and a Portrait photograph by Les Back)

These posts show how we used the blog format to create and circulate small ethnographic snapshots. For those following the *Every Minute* blog the outcomes of the research unfolded in a series of episodes from different observers. As a result they posed questions of simultaneous differences - for example between those of Christian, Jewish and Muslim heritage – and of how people grieve and remember.

The "real time" dimension of the ethnography meant the research partners could have an on-going relationship with both the research process and what was emerging from the ethnography. The speeding up of the circulation of data and findings was an advantage from the Hospice's point of view, complementing their strategic work. Rachel Power, Director of HR and operations at Richard House, commented that part of the attraction of the approach of the *Every Minute* project is that readers felt they were discovering new things alongside the researchers. "I had no idea that there was a garden of remembrance at West Ham's football ground but also our trustees have been excited by the potential of the project" Rachel told us. The speeding up of the circulation of ethnographic insights produced surprises and a sense of excitement around the project for our research partners. The upload ethnography format also meant that the young people and families – all of them affected by life-limiting illnesses – could engage with the work in their own time, when they felt well enough and only if they wanted to.

The *Every Minute* project provides an example of how using digital platforms enabled us to engage with users and readers differently. However, we were chastened to find out in March 2013 that Posterous - the free multi-media blogging platform that we used to host our findings – had been sold to Twitter who had decided to close down the resource. This posed an immediate problem and revealed some of the challenges in using digital platforms that are not necessarily secure in the long term. This meant migrating the material from the *Every Minute* site and reconstructing them in another blog space (see http://everyminuteof everyday.org.uk/). The insecurity of digital formats makes data storage an ongoing problem and ultimately undermines the longevity of live archiving.

Conclusions

In this final section we want to reflect on what we have learned and also what others may take from this experiment. While the promise of simultaneity in research – i.e. creating and circulating data "immediately" – is a hollow one, our experiment with doing research differently made us think more deeply and critically about the spatio-temporalities created by old and new research devices. The relationship between the field notebook and time (in which the latest entries are last) are reversed in the ethnographic blog. Our experiments with upload ethnography showed that the speeding up of the circulation of ethnographic descriptions and insights can lead to problems of cuing, abundance and data excess. Equally, the dangers of "digital black holes" opening up – illustrated through our example of the winding-down of Posterous as a public platform – adds further difficulties beyond a simple matter of data storage. Put crudely digital formats and platforms may not endure because of the pace of technological change.

We have accentuated the inclusive possibilities of using social media for public engagement.[38] However, as David Beer has pointed out "the message" of the research is also likely to be transformed as a result. He warns: "Research [...] has always had a life of its own. If we are to drop our research into new media's data circulations then this research is likely to take on some vibrancy and unpredictability of these informational swirls. In other words, our research is likely to have a life that is even livelier. We need to be prepared."[39] Conventional modes of academic dissemination have always had an archival quality and stepping outside of them is likely to be risky. Beer suggests this calls for attention to the "politics of circulation."[40] Our experience suggests it is a chance worth taking because in a social world full of screens and lives that are lived oscillating between them, as researchers we can no longer rely on paper formats alone to communicate with an audience.

Our discussion of the possibilities of upload ethnography has also made us reflect upon the creating, giving and taking of time in the craft of thinking, researching and writing sociologically. Speeding up that process can undermine the quality of thought and the importance of recognising diverse historical trajectories that can appear in the same moment. At the same time, social media offer the possibility for the circulation and interaction of multisensory affects and hunches. The uploading of ethnographic insights in the *Every Minute* project offered participants and non-academic partners the opportunity to engage with research *in their*

---

[38] See also Rob Kitchin, Denis Linehan, Cian O'Callaghan, and Philip Lawron, (2013) "Public Geography through Social Media," *Dialogues in Human Geography*, 3, 1 (2013): 56-72.

[39] David Beer, "Public geography and the politics of circulation," *Dialogues in Public Geogra*phy, 3, 1 (2013a): 95.

[40] See David Beer, *Popular Culture and New Media: The Politics of Circulation* (Basingstoke: Palgrave Macmillan, 2013b).

own time.

As a result we managed to foreground within urban multiculture the link between movements through life as well as migrations across space. As a result traces of the past in the present were noticed, noted and circulated. Fragments of Newham's complex cultural history and evolving multiculture became accessible to the staff and patients in Richard House to reflect upon. These produced moments of surprise as well as recognition.

Regardless of the problems, we suggest that the re-ordering of the relationship between space, time and knowledge offers an invitation to cultivate different kinds of research sensibility. This might be described as a commitment to fostering the sociological imagination beyond existing parameters and in ways that explicate and problematise how time can be used to manage diversity.[41] It is the training of an attentiveness not only confined to the predominant lines of sight, the focal points of public concern or attention particularly around issues of migration and "diversity." What lies within the broader depth of field? What we see or hear very often effects what we can imagine. A different attention fosters a wider sense of possibilities.[42] *The Every Minute of Everyday* project was an attempt to embrace the possibilities of re-designing research in a digital age but also to expand the forms and modes that social research can now take, working with and for local institutions rather than simply on them.

Bibliography

Abbott, Andrew. 2000. "Reflections on the Future of Sociology." *Contemporary Sociology* 29, 2 (2000): 296-300.

Adkins, Lisa. 2009. "Feminism after Measure." *Feminist Theory* 10, 3 (2009): 323 –339.

Adkins, Lisa. and Lury, Celia. "What is the Empirical?" *European Journal of Social Theory* 12, 1 (2009): 5-20.

Ahmed, Sara. *Queer Phenomenology: Orientations, Objects, Others.* Durham and London: Duke University Press, 2005.

Back, Les. "Global Attentiveness and the Sociological Ear." *Sociological Research Online* 14,4, 2009. Accessed May 19, 2011 http://www.socresonline.org.uk/14/4/14.html.

---

[41] See Carol J. Greenhouse, *A Moment's Notice: Time Politics Across Cultures* (New York: Cornell University Press, 1996).

[42] See also Noortje Marres, "The Redistribution of Methods: On Intervention in Digital Social Research, Broadly Conceived," *The Sociological Review*, 60 (2012): 139–165.

—. 2012. "Live Sociology: Social Research and its Futures." *The Sociological Review*, 60 (2012): 18–39.

Back, Les. and Puwar, Nirmal. *Live Methods.* Oxford: Wiley Blackwell/ Sociological Review, 2012.

Bastian, Michelle. "The Contradictory Simultaneity of Being with Others: Exploring Concepts of Time and Community in the Work of Gloria Anzaldúa." *Feminist Review*, 97, 1 (2011): 151–167.

Beer, David. "Public geography and the politics of circulation," *Dialogues in Public Geography*, 3, 1(2013a): 92-95.

—. *Popular Culture and New Media: The Politics of Circulation.* Basingstoke: Palgrave Macmillan, 2013b.

—. "Using Social Media Data Aggregators to Do Social Research." *Sociological Research Online*, 17, 3, 10, 2012. Accessed June 10th , 2013 http://www.socresonline.org.uk/17/3/10.html.

Cavarero, Adria. *Relating Narratives: Storytelling and Selfhood.* London and New York: Routledge, 2000.

Cavell, Stanley. *Conditions Handsome and Unhandsome: The Constitution of Emersonian Perfectionism: The Carus Lectures, 1988.* Chicago: University of Chicago Press, 1990.

Dikeç, Mustafa., Clark, Nigel. & Clive Barnett. "Extending Hospitality: Giving Space, Taking Time." *Paragraph*, 32, 1 (2009): 1–14.

Doucet, Andrea. "'From Her Side of the Gossamer Wall(s)': Reflexivity and Relational Knowing." *Qualitative Sociology* 31, 1 (2007): 73–87.

Goffman, Erving. *The Presentation of Self in Everyday Life.* Harmondsworth, Middlesex: Penguin Books Ltd, 1971.

Greenhouse, Carol J. *A Moment's Notice: Time Politics Across Cultures.* New York: Cornell University Press, 1996.

Gunaratnam, Yasmin. "Learning to be Affected: Social Suffering and Total Pain at Life's Borders." *The Sociological Review*, 60, (2012): 108–123.

Gunaratnam, Yasmin. *Death and the Migrant: Bodies, Borders, Care.* London: Bloomsbury Academic, 2013.

Hobbs, Dick. *Lush Life: Constructing Organised Crime in the UK.* Oxford: Oxford University Press, 2013.

Kitchin, Rob and Dodge, Martin. *Code/Space: Software and Everyday Life*. MIT press, Cambridge, Massachusetts, 2011.

Kitchin, Rob., Linehan, Denis., O'Callaghan, Cian. and Lawron, Philip. "Public Geography through Social Media." *Dialogues in Human Geography*. 3, 1 (2013): 56-72.

Law, John. and Urry, John. "Enacting the Social." *Economy and Society*, 33 (2004): 390–410.

Lee, Raymond M. *Doing Research on Sensitive Topics*. London; Newbury Park, Calif.: Sage Publications, 1993.

Marcus, George. E. *Ethnography Through Thick and Thin*. Princeton: Princeton University Press, 1998.

Marres, Noortje., 2012. The Redistribution of Methods: On Intervention in Digital Social Research, Broadly Conceived." *The Sociological Review*, 60, (2012): 139–165.

Massey, Doreen. B. *For Space*. London, Thousand Oaks, CA, and New Delhi: Sage Publications Ltd, 2005.

McMahon, Martha. "Significant Absences." *Qualitative Inquiry*. 2, 3 (1996): 320 –336.

McRuer, Robert. *Crip Theory: Cultural Signs of Queerness and Disability.* New York and London: NYU Press, 2006.

Murthy, Dhiraj. *Twitter: Social Communication in the Age of Twitter*. Cambridge: Polity Press, 2013.

—. "Digital Ethnography: An Examination of the Use of New Technologies for Social Research." *Sociology* 42, 5 (2008): 837–855.

Newham Regional Planning and Property Directorate. *Newham London Local Economic Assessment 2010-2027*. London: London Borough of Newham, 2010.

Okely, Judith. "Fieldwork Embodied." *The Sociological Review*. 55 (2007): 65–79.

Qpzm LocalStats. *Newham Census Demographics, United Kingdom, 2011*. Accessed February 1st, 2014
http://localstats.qpzm.co.uk/stats/england/london/newham.

Riles, Annelise. "'Real time': Unwinding technocratic and anthropological knowledge." *American Ethnologist* 31, 3 (2004): 392-405.

Ruppert, Evelyn., Law, John. and Savage, Mike. "Reassembling Social Science Methods: the challenge of digital devices." *Theory, Culture & Society*,30, 4 (2013): 1-24.

Ruppert, Evelyn. and Law, John. "Introduction: The Social Life of Methods – Devices." *Journal of Cultural Economy* 6, 4 (2013): 1-12.

Savage, Mike. *Identities and Social Change in Britain since 1940: The Politics of Method.* Oxford, Oxford University Press, 2011.

Savage, Mike. and Burrows, Roger. 2007. "The Coming Crisis of Empirical Sociology," *Sociology*, 41, 5 (2007): 885-899.

Shildrick, Margrit. and Price, Janet. "Deleuzian Connections and Queer Corporealities: Shrinking Global Disability." R*hizomes*, 11/12, (2006). Accessed February 2nd, 2014
http://www.rhizomes.net/issue11/shildrickprice/index.html.

Steedman, Carolyn. "Enforced Narratives." In *Feminism and Autobiography: Texts, Theories, Methods*, edited by Tess Cosslett, Celia Lury and Penny Summerfield, 25-39. London: Routledge, 2000.

Stewart, Kathleen. *Ordinary Affects*. Durham and London: Duke University Press, 2007.

Terkel, Sherry. "The Documented Life." *The New York Times*, December 17th, 2013. Accessed December 16th, 2013 http://www.nytimes.com/2013/12/16/opinion/the-documented-life.html?_r=0.

Upritchard, Emma. "Being stuck in (Live) Time: The Sticky Sociological Imagination," *The Sociological Rev*iew 60 (2012): 124–138.

Urry, John. *Mobilities*, Cambridge: Polity, 2007.

Vertovec, Stephen. "Super-Diversity and Its Implications." *Ethnic and Racial Studies* 30, 6 (2007): 1024-1054.

Zhao, Shanyang., Grasmuck, Sherri. and Jason Martin, Jason. "Identity Construction on Facebook: Digital empowerment in anchored relationships." *Computers in Human Behavior* 24, 5 (2008): 1816–1836.

PART III:

'DIGITAL NATIVES' AND COSMOPOLITANISM IN 'REAL' AND 'VIRTUAL' WORLDS

CHAPTER SIX

NEGOTIATING CULTURAL DIFFERENCE IN THE DIGITAL COMMUNICATION ERA: A QUALITATIVE PILOT STUDY OF TECHNOLOGY AND STUDENT EXPERIENCE

DAVID J GUNKEL

1. Introduction

One of the standard assumptions about the Internet and related communication technology is that they facilitate unprecedented opportunities for intercultural exchange and understanding.

> The Internet can appear to be a medium which facilitates communication between cultures and which makes the world a smaller, perhaps even more heterogeneous place to live in. The constant use of terms such as "World Wide Web," "Global Computer Networks," and "Global Village" can give the initiated an impression of people from all over the world working and communicating together in a harmonious environment where cultural background, skin colour, religion and gender mean very little.[1]

Although similar promises were already associated with the technology of telegraphy, radio, and television,[2] it is only recently that the concept appears to have achieved widespread and almost unquestioned acceptance.

---

[1] Robert O'Dowd, "In Search of a Truly Global Network: The Opportunities and Challenges of On-line Intercultural Communication." *Computer Assisted Language Learning—Electronic Journal* (*CALL-EJ*) 3(1) (2001): 1. http://callej.org/journal/3-1/o_dowd.html

[2] James Carey, *Communication as Culture: Essays on Media and Society* (New York: Routledge, 1989). Martin Spinelli, "Radio Lessons for the Internet." *Postmodern Culture* 6(2) (1996). Marshall McLuhan, *Understanding Media: The Extensions of Man* (Cambridge, MA: MIT Press, 1995).

And evidence of this can be seen in the marketing campaigns of equipment manufacturers and service providers (i.e. Apple, Google, Microsoft, Cisco Systems), popular media and entertainment (i.e. *Wired* magazine), and scholarly investigations in numerous disciplines and fields.[3]

The assumption is undeniably powerful and persuasive, particularly because it supplies a technological solution to what many consider to be a social problem. Whether we explicitly recognise it or not, this way of thinking is informed by technological determinism — the theory that technological innovation is a significant contributor to social change. The theory, which comes to us in various forms, is originally attributed to the American sociologist Thorstein Veblen[4] and is clearly part and parcel of much of the literature addressing new media and society. And all of this is persuasive, because it can and has been used to argue for increase investment in technology as a way to develop and enhance international programmes and the experience of students.

As educators interested in international education and involved with international students, we want to know whether this assumption is in fact true. In other words, we want to know whether information and communication technology (ICT) make a difference in bridging cultural difference and negotiating the international experience. In particular, we want to know whether and to what extent recent innovations in digital technology provide assistance to international students in their efforts to live, work, and study abroad. Or to put it in more formal terms, we want to test the technological determinist theory to determine whether and to what extent it is correct in the context of international education. This inquiry is important not only because it challenges an assumption, providing empirical evidence to respond to what has often gone unquestioned, but also because of the way it can help individuals and institutions make sense of the impact of technology, guiding both the planning of international programmes but also strategies for investment, development, and implementation.

---

[3] See for example: Starr Roxanne Hiltz and Murray Turoff, *The Networked Nation: Human Communication via Computer (*Reading, MA: Addison-Wesley Publishing Company, 1978). Pierre Lévy, *Cyberculture* (Paris: Éditions Odile Jacob/Éditions du Conseil de l'Europe, 1997). Sonia Valle de Frutos, *Cibercultura y Civilización Universal: Hacia un Nuevo Orden Cultural* (Barcelona: Erasmus Ediciones, 2011).

[4] Jacques Ellul, *The Technological Society* (New York: Vintage, 1964), xviii. Barry Jones, *Sleepers, Wake! Technology and the Future of Work* (New York: Oxford University Press, 1990), 210.

2. The Study

In order to address these questions, we designed and executed a qualitative study of international students called "Negotiating Cultural Difference in the Digital Communication Era" or "*Negocjowanie różnic kulturowych w erze komunikacji cyfrowej*." The study was funded through the support of the Harmonia2 project of *Narodowe Centrum Nauki*, the Polish National Science Center. The project team consisted of the following five researchers: Garry Robson, Małgorzata Zachara and Agnieszka Stasiewicz of the Jagiellonian University in Kraków, Poland; David J. Gunkel, Northern Illinois University (USA); and Ann Hetzel Gunkel, Columbia College Chicago (USA).

The hypothesis guiding our investigation was that "transformations in the global sphere of communication have a significant impact on the possibilities, perspectives, and character of intercultural encounters." In order to test this hypothesis, we conducted interviews with international students studying at institutions of higher education in both Poland and the United States. The interviews were designed to supply qualitative data concerning the international experience and the impact of technology on student success in dealing with cultural difference and the study abroad experience. The objective of the investigation was to supply data that would not only confirm (or refute) the hypothesis but provide detailed insight into the uses and gratifications of digital technology by international students in the 21st century — what Internet researchers have called "digital natives" (a term that is not without its own set of complications as detailed in several of the other essays included in this collection.)

2.1 Review of Literature

Previous work in this area includes a number of quantitative studies. Among these the most notable are:

- Timothy B. Smith and David A. Shwalb's "Preliminary Examination of International Student's Adjustment and Loneliness Related to Electronic Communications" published in the journal *Psychological Reports*, which used a quantitative survey of 45 students and found that "electronic communication (i.e. email and Internet) may facilitate international students' adjustment through contacts maintained in their native country."[5]

- Two studies undertaken by Jiali Ye. The first — "An Examination of Acculturative Stress, Interpersonal Social Support, and Use of Online Ethnic Social Groups among Chinese International Students" published in the *Howard Journal of Communication* — surveyed Chinese international students attending college in the United States and found that those who used online ethnic social groups experienced lower levels of acculturative stress. The second — "Traditional and Online Support Networks in the Cross-Cultural Adaptation of Chinese International Students in the United States" published in *the Journal of Computer Mediated Communication* — employed an online survey to poll 135 Chinese students attending universities in the United States. It found that perceived support from online ethnic social groups was negatively related to social difficulties and mood disturbance.[6]
- Zeynep Cemalcilar, Toni Falbo, and Laura Stapleton's "Cyber Communication: A New Opportunity for International Students' Adaptation?" published in the *International Journal of Intercultural Relations*, which used a web survey of 280 first-year international students. Findings from this investigation support the hypothesis that "computer mediated communication with the home country affects students' maintenance of home identity, and perceptions of available social support," aiding their "psychological, socio-cultural, and academic adaptations."[7]
- Ying Kong's "Acculturation in the Age of New Media" a paper presented at the 2005 meeting of the International Communication Association. This study also used quantitative methods, specifically a self-administered questionnaire emailed to participants, to investigate whether the use of online television content from the home country had an adverse effect on the acculturation of Chinese students to life in the United States. The findings were determined to be inconclusive.[8]

---

[5] Timothy B. Smith and David A. Shwalb, "Preliminary Examination of International Student's Adjustment and Loneliness Related to Electronic Communications." *Psychological Reports* 100(1) (2007): 167.

[6] Jiali Ye, "An Examination of Acculturative Stress, Interpersonal Social Support, and Use of Online Ethnic Social Groups among Chinese International Students." *Howard Journal of Communication* 17(1) (2006): 1-20.

Jiali Ye, "Traditional and Online Support Networks in the Cross-Cultural Adaptation of Chinese International Students in the United States." *Journal of Computer-Mediated Communication* 11 (2006): 863–876.

[7] Zeynep Cemalcilar, Toni Falbo and Laura Stapleton, "Cyber Communication: A New Opportunity for International Students' Adaptation?" *International Journal of Intercultural Relations*, 29(1) (2005): 91.

[8] Ying Kong, "Acculturation in the Age of New Media." Paper presented at the annual meeting of the International Communication Association. New York, NY. 25 May 2009. http://www.allacademic.com/meta/p13763_index.html

Despite differences in approach, execution, and sample size, these studies all used survey instruments to gather quantitative data from international student populations. And in varying degrees they all offer support for the claim that ICT provides international students with easy access to information and support networks and that these opportunities seem to contribute positively to more effective and successful adaptations to life in the host country.

2.2 Method and Approach

What makes our project distinctive are: 1) The use of qualitative methods, namely in depth interviews with international students. Unlike quantitative survey investigations, interviews are often able to discover not just types of behaviour but the motivations, gratifications, and rationale behind behaviour. Although qualitative studies have their own challenges (which we will get to shortly), they can supply information not able to be captured by the quantitative methods used by previous researchers. 2) The scope of the project. Our concern was not just computer-mediated contact with the students' home country, which was the focus of a number of the previous quantitative studies, but also their use of digital media for interacting with people and organisations in the host country. Consequently our investigation looked at a part of the international experience not addressed by the majority of the earlier investigations.

Although the interviews were guided by a formal questionnaire, we made adequate accommodations for unstructured follow-up questions and comments. Interviews were conducted by Garry Robson and Agnieszka Stasiewicz at the Jagiellonian University in the winter semester 2012/13 and David Gunkel at Northern Illinois University during the spring semester of 2013. The duration of interviews varied, based on the number of follow-up questions and the length of participant responses. The shortest interview lasted 35 minutes and the longest took in excess of 60 minutes. Each interview was audio recorded and transcribed with all identifying information removed to protect the privacy of the participants. Transcribed interviews were archived on password protected computers and were only accessible by the research team. Participants were recruited, following Institutional Review Board (IRB) guidelines, through self-selection, facilitated by posted notifications in offices and facilities frequented by international students and general broadcast email messages to international students currently registered at one of the participating institutions. Qualifications for participation were simple: International undergraduate or graduate students from any country of origin.

2.3 Sample and Demographic Data

We interviewed 14 individuals from 9 different countries and had at least one participant from every continent (Figure 1).

Country of Origin	Number of Participants
Australia	4
Burma	1
China	1
Holland	1
Mauritius	1
Poland	1
South Africa	1
United States	3
Uruguay	1

Figure 1 – Country of Origin

Because participation was voluntary, we did not control for gender. Consequently, our sample was, for better or worse, predominately male with 10 of the 14 participants identifying male and only 4 female. The age of interview subjects ranged from 21 to 36, making the average age 25.6 years of age. Over half of the participants listed English as their native language. But all English-speaking participants were studying in Poland at the time of the interviews, and the only Polish participant was studying in the United States. Consequently all participants were living and working outside their native language (Figure 2).

Time in the host country also varied considerably from one month to eighteen months (Figure 3).

In terms of ICT usage, Facebook and Skype were reported to be the most often used applications, with Facebook utilised by all but one participant and Skype used by 64% of all participants. Other applications reported included email, QQ (a Chinese social media platform), Kontaktor (a Russian language social networking site), and Tumblr, all of which had one reported user per application in the sample group. The main reason reported for ICT usage was maintaining contact with Family and Friends.

The majority of these interactions were with individuals "back home" (a term utilised by participants) but just under half of the participants (5 out of the 14) also said that they used ICT for maintaining contact with friends in the host country (Figure 4).

Native Language	Number of Participants
English	8
Burmese	1
Chinese	1
Creole	1
Dutch	1
Polish	1
Spanish	1

Figure 2 – Reported Native Language

Duration of Stay	Number of Participants
1 to 3 months	3
4 to 7 months	3
8 to 12 months	3
13 to 17 months	2
18 to 22 months	3

Figure 3 – Reported Time in Host Country

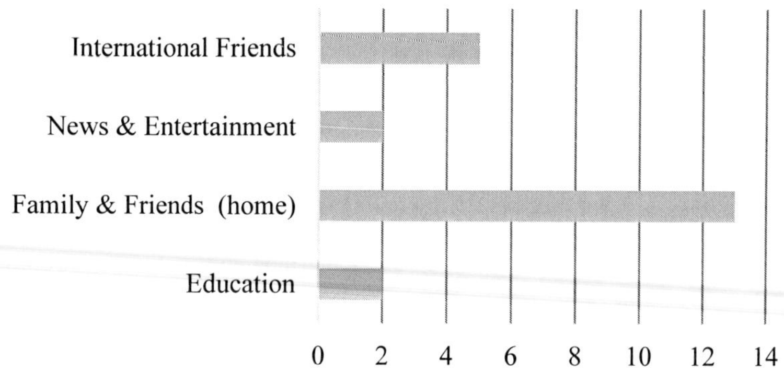

Figure 4 – Main Reason for ICT Usage

Level of usage, defined by actively posting data, adding friends, or sharing images, was rated by most participants as high (Figure 5), and increases in usage while living and studying abroad was reported by more than half of the interview subjects (Figure 6).

Reported Level of Activity with ICT	Number of Participants
High	8
Moderate	2
Low	3
None Reported	1

Figure 5 – Reported Level of Activity

Changes in Level of Activity while Studying Abroad	Number of Participants
More Active	8
Less Active	3
No Change	3

Figure 6 – Reported Changes in Activity

3. Results

Because we collected qualitative information from interviews, the resulting data set is large and complex. Nevertheless a few common elements and trends have emerged related to the main research question and hypothesis.

3.1 Opinions Concerning Technology

Attitudes toward technology cover the spectrum, with neutral accounting for just less than half of the responses and positive and negative equally divided among the remainder. Reasons offered for neutral opinions conform to the instrumental theory of technology, that is, technology understood as a mere tool of human action, the value of which depends upon the use to which it is applied by human users.[9] As one participant characterised it, "I think that the advantages of technology basically depend on the use you want to give to the technology. You can use technology with very good purposes. But you can use technology with bad purposes, or with no purpose, just for the sake of using technology." According to Andrew Feenberg, "the instrumentalist theory offers the most widely accepted view of technology. It is based on the common sense idea that technologies are 'tools' standing ready to serve the purposes of users." And because an instrument "is deemed 'neutral,' without valuative content of its own" a technological device or system is evaluated not in and of itself, but on the basis of the particular employments that have been decided by human users.[10]

Positive and negative comments do not necessarily contest this instrumentalist view point but employ it to focus attention on either the benefits or costs to be derived from using technology. Positive comments, for instance, note easy access to information and entertainment, ease of access to and connection with friends, and opportunities for intercultural communication and dialogue. These responses conform to and support the existing literature, especially early writings on computer networks and cyberspace which predicted rapid and virtually unimpeded access to

---

[9] Martin Heidegger, "Die Frage Nach der Technik." In *Vorträge und Aufsätze* (Pfullingen: Verlag Günther Neske, 1954). English translation by William Lovitt, *The Question Concerning Technology and Other Essays* (New York: Harper Torchbooks, 1977).

[10] Andrew Feenberg, *Critical Theory of Technology* (New York: Oxford University Press, 1991), 5.

information,[11] communities of common interest rather than common geography,[12] and distance shattering interconnections between people, overcoming distance not only in geophysical space but also in culture.[13]

Negative responses, by comparison, were critical of the potentially adverse effect of technology on interpersonal communication and social interaction, especially for young people. According to one participant:

> People no longer have social skills, I think. Personally, I think that people no longer have social skills and we no longer interact in the same way that we used to. If you go to a restaurant you see that. Yes, somebody is talking to you and they're talking… I find it very disturbing. I find it very disturbing that you cannot have a decent conversation with somebody without them going on the social media.

Another participant expresses similar concern that social media is in the process of replacing actual conversation, and s/he targets the "young generation" as particularly vulnerable.

> For younger generations [...] Facebook is their everything. They just live in the world of Facebook. They put different statuses up every second or they constantly...that's just how they communicate with people, how they make friends, and how they talk to their friends. Which is a bad thing for their social skills. Especially younger kids.

This comment follows in a long tradition that is ultimately rooted in Plato's *Phaedrus*, where Socrates faulted the new technology of writing for making its users, and the young in particular, "ignorant and difficult to get along with."[14] There is, therefore, since the time of the *Phaedrus* at least, a significant concern over the potentially corrupting influence of

---

[11] Micheal Benedikt, *Cyberspace: First Steps* (Cambridge, MA: MIT Press, 1991). Nicholas Negroponte, *Being Digital* (New York: Vintage Books, 1995).

[12] J. C. R. Licklider and Robert W. Taylor, "The Computer as Communication Device." *Science and Technology*, April 1968. http://memex.org/licklider.html. Steven G. Jones, ed., *CyberSociety 2.0: Computer-Mediated Communication and Community* (London: Sage, 1994). Hiltz and Turoff, *The Networked Nation.*

[13] William J. Mitchell, *City of Bits: Space, Place, and the Infobahn*. (Cambridge, MA: MIT Press, 1995). Francis Caincross, *The Death of Distance: How the Communications Revolution Will Change our Lives* (Boston, MA: Harvard Business School Press). Wilson Dizard, *Meganet: How the Global Communications Network Will Connect Everyone on Earth* (Boulder, CO: Westview Press, 1997).

[14] Plato, *Phaedrus*, trans. Harold North Fowler (Cambridge, MA: Harvard University Press, 1987), 275b.

technology, which had been, in the context of the Platonic text, characterised as a kind of medicine or poison (the Greek word utilised by Plato is *pharmakon*), depending upon how it is used and who employs it.

Other comments note the way that mediated communication often permit and even facilitate rude behaviour and deception. "People," one respondent pointed out, "are not being real on Facebook" and cites a number of instances where individuals have posted false information online. Another respondent, who uses his/her sister as an example, notes how computer-mediated communication (CMC) removes social inhibitions, allowing individuals to write things they would typically not say.

> I see it all in my younger sister. She writes what she wants in there [social media]. She's a bit naughty. And... she does that as though it doesn't have any consequences. If she said that to somebody in person, it would probably cause a lot more trouble. Like writing something is way different than saying something.

This concern about deception and anti-social behaviour in CMC remains an on-going problem, and it constitutes one of the perennial debates in the literature of Internet studies.[15]

Other respondents took a more technological determinist approach and criticised not just the way the instrument is used (or misused) but found fault in some aspect of the technology itself. In these cases, users criticised CMC, and not just the method of usage and the users of CMC, for being artificial, superficial, and "not real." "I prefer," one participant explained "the relations with people that I have outside of Facebook than the relations I have with people on Facebook. It is very superficial: I am not talking to someone I am talking to their Facebook profile." Another responded:

> I was living in another world that didn't exist; it was very artificial and superficial. It really didn't bring any real substance or meaning into my life, and I have asked myself what am I really doing here on MySpace. [So I] dropped out and never went back.

---

[15] Julian Dibbel, "A Rape In Cyberspace; Or How and Evil Clown, a Haitian Trickster Spirit, Two Wizards, and a Cast of Dozens Turned a Database into a Society," in *Flame Wars: The Discourse of Cyberculture*, ed. Mark Dery (Durham, NC: Duke University Press, 1994), 237-262. Sherry Turkle, *Life on the Screen: Identity in the Age of the Internet*. (New York: Simon and Schuster, 1995). Charles Ess, ed., *Philosophical Perspectives on Computer-Mediated Communication* (Albany, NY: State University of New York Press, 1996).

Like the other opinions, these comments also follow an established precedent, namely, technology produces an artificial and superficial "world" that threatens or even replaces the "real world" of substance. "It creates," as one participant summarised it, "a world that increasingly replaces our reality and real contact." This emphasis on the *real* and the threat to *reality* posed by technological mediation and the "virtual world" is a persistent theme in contemporary research and popular media. It is evident, for example, in Jean Baudrillard's *Simulations*, Michael Heim's *The Metaphysics of Virtual Reality*, and Edward Castronova's *Synthetic Worlds: The Business and Culture of Online Games,* and it has its popular expression in the *Matrix* and the eleven or so books that address the philosophical significance of this cinematic trilogy.[16]

The real problem for all these arguments and opinions, however, is that the concept of the real, despite its discursive importance, is already difficult to define and defend. As one respondent explained:

> I think having a real social life is so much more satisfying that doing it through the Internet. Through the Internet everything is based on image and um spontaneity is gone through the Internet. And it's so much more fun to have a real social life, real people.

Recognising the rhetorical importance and recurrence of the term "real" in this explanation, the interviewer asked for clarification: "You keep saying real. Do you think social life inside media is not real?" To which the participant replied with the following:

> I think it's not real. I mean it's not real. It's another kind of real. But like it's just two different dimensions in a way. There's this Facebook life and real. But there's real life time interaction with people, and then there's Facebook, where....I mean yeah, it's real and stuff. But it's not real in an interactive sort of [way].

This comment indicates how, in leveraging "the real" to make distinctions, the very understanding of what is real begins to breakdown and become incoherent. This is not, it is important to point out, some cognitive failure on the part of the respondent. It is instead a product of the

---

[16] See, for example, William Irwin, ed., *The Matrix and Philosophy* (Chicago: Open Court, 2002). William Irwin, ed., *More Matrix and Philosophy: Revolutions and Reloaded Decoded* (Chicago: Open Court, 2005), and Christopher Grau, ed., *Philosophers Explore the Matrix* (Oxford: Oxford University Press, 2005).

fact that "the real," although a crucial concept in these debates and discourses, is already a complex and not altogether well-defined concept.[17]

What is remarkable in these varied responses is the fact that participants appear to echo or conform to extant theory, giving expression to, for instance, the instrumental theory of technology, technological determinism, Platonic metaphysics, etc. Whether this means that these theories are correct and that the empirical data can be interpreted as lending support to theory, or whether it is the case that the opinions offered by participants draw from and conform to an already established set of possible responses currently in circulation, remains an open but important question.

3.2 Technology and Intercultural Communication

In response to the question, "Does digital media help with intercultural communication?" the majority of participants (9 out of the 14) answered positively, four answered in the negative, and one participant declined to offer an opinion. The most common reasons for positive responses had to do with language. Many of the participants reported that they found online tools — like Google translate and YouTube language tutorials — to be instrumental in helping them prepare for and negotiate the challenges of the international experience.

> When I travel I want to know where I'm going, what's happening there, what's the places to see, what to eat, how the people are and you know, stuff like that. So I need to know. And obviously to learn how to say "hello" and "how are you" [...] And the only way you could know about is through Internet, you know. There is even tutorial lessons on YouTube on how to say this or that in that language or, you know, whether you read it or whether you hear it so... The Internet is always there for you to... There is no excuse, honestly, to say that you don't know anything now. Because everything is just on YouTube, on Facebook, on the Internet.

Another respondent, one who had expressed concern that mediated communication was "superficial," found online translation tools to be surprisingly expedient for resolving linguistic difference.

[17] David J. Gunkel, *Thinking Otherwise: Philosophy, Communication, Technology* (West Lafayette: Purdue University Press, 2007).

> I was with one girl who is Italian, it was like midnight, at her home try to discuss something but her English is quite poor so we couldn't and we spent like 2 hours talking via Google translator. But somehow we had like a really deep, interesting conversation. It was the first time I have this kind of experience.

In this case, the imposition of Google translate actually facilitated that kind of profound interpersonal connection that the respondent cited as being absent from mediated interaction.

Other participants credit social media and photo-sharing applications with helping them understand and deal with cultural diversity. For one participant studying in the United States it helped him/her understand and contend with cultural identity in ways that were previously unthinkable.

> In the States I have met people from different cultures, and when I say different cultures, I say very different cultures. I have met people from all the different continents, from all the different religions, from all the different cultures. That has been very enriching for me, but having them on Facebook or communicating with them has shown me a totally different reality, and it's not the reality I used to have. My country, even though it was established by immigrants, and we are very culturally diverse, it was like a melting pot, and nobody in my country calls themself Italian, or Spanish. […] We don't think of the difference in ethnicity we have. It was not until I came to the States, that I realised how things are here, that you have African Americans, Latinos. I mean, it was the first time I had to think what my ethnicity was. But at the same time, I started meeting people from different countries and from other cultures. They were very remote to me. I didn't even know that those cultures existed. But when I see their pictures on Facebook, I can see what they are doing, for example to celebrate their independence. I can understand many, many more things through media. Definitely, it has changed my mind.

For another respondent, studying in Poland, the Internet in general and social media in particular were seen as essential to gaining access to and understanding the culture of other international students.

> All these media, well, yeah, facilitate intercultural communication. But connecting and being with people, communicating with people you meet. It's obviously easier to keep in contact, to get in contact with them and keep in contact with them. Because they are from far away or things like that. It definitely has an effect on intercultural communication. It's like easiest to communicate with people online. It's easier to understand them. And like knowing about their culture. Like you can go on Facebook and read about their information, you can go see their photos and see the

experiences they have back home. You can get a little bit of idea of what they do for holidays and things like that.

Additional positive responses noted how social media can be used to crowd source problem solving by leverage the knowledge and experience of others.

> I would say more yes than no, because for example there was a new situation in which I know that many of my friends, especially American friends, might have already faced, because they have been living here longer than I have. Then this, I told you, I would be asking a particular group of friends, especially my class friends: how do I go about this thing? And most of the time they would be really helpful and tell me do this, do this and do this. Or they would be, for example, when I told you I was having to go for my driving license and I needed a car to practice because I used to drive on the wrong side of the road. So I needed a car to practice. I have been driving for a while, but it's just like there are so many changes when you are on the other side of the road. And I simply ask someone, the whole group like "is there is anyone who is willing to just give me a couple of hours (for example, a weekend) for me to practice" and as usual they have all been so helpful.

Negative responses to the question came from two participants who thought ICT were only useful for maintaining contact with friends and family back home. Another negative response came from a participant who not only reported that s/he did not use ICT for intercultural communication but expressed preference for direct interpersonal interactions: "I think the most important for me is contact live, face-to-face." The fourth and final negative response was provided by a participant who admitted that s/he was simply not invested in learning about the culture of the host country: "Maybe I am just getting old. I don't see myself living here for a long term so I think I just gave up the emotional investment in Polish culture and language." All four "negative responses," it should be noted, do not so much contest the subject of the inquiry, i.e. "Does digital media help with intercultural communication?" To do so would require that one make the attempt to apply technology to this particular problem. Instead all four respondents reported that they simply do not even try or care to make such an effort. These replies are, therefore, not so much negative responses but an expression of a kind of avoidance of or abstention from what the questions asks about.

3.3 International Experience and the Internet

In response to the question, "Can you imagine living abroad prior to the Internet?" the majority of participants (8 out of the 14) answered affirmatively, five responded "no," and one participant provided a kind of ambivalent response. The majority of those who offered a positive response recognised the difficulty of living without the conveniences of the Internet, but reported that they would have been able to adapt and find other means of coping. For one participant, the main problem would have been time. That is, one would need additional time to access and gather analogue information that is perceived to be instantaneously available in digital form.

> I think I would have done it, but I would have needed more time to look for those things that the Internet brings me immediately like a question that I have about anything. I go to the Internet or Google or something like that. I can just get that information readily. So for example a simple thing of getting a room here to live was relatively very easy, if you have the Internet and you can search for people who live in the apartment or something like that. But had it not been the case, if the Internet did not exist [...] I would have needed so much time just to go, go about and look for people. At least I would need a local newspaper or talk to new people, which would have been more interesting in the sense that you would be meeting new people and networking and all that. But I guess it would take a lot, a lot more time, and it might have been more difficult too.

Echoing this statement, other respondents explicitly recognise the difficulty and expense of life without the conveniences of the Internet but express confidence that they would have been able to cope with such hardships.

> No. I could have still come here. But it would be very, very scary for me, because all my funds are online so I would have to set up a bank account here. I wouldn't be able to book my apartment online here. I would have to do it by phone without seeing pictures. It would be very expensive, because I would have to call my parents. I would probably have to call them on increased frequency, because they wouldn't see that I am all right online.

Other responses affirm this characterisation but do so with important clarifications. One participant, who responded to this question by explicitly noting his/her status as a "digital native," imagines that things would have certainly been more difficult, but carefully notes that this opinion is probably just a result of his/her particular situation.

> I've had digital media in my life forever, so I can't really imagine that without it. I don't know. I think especially for the younger it would be even harder, because they're so prevalent in their lives. But as we get a bit older, I don't know. Somehow people would manage to make things work. We've got them now so it works somehow. But I think having the technology now and knowing how much it makes easier things, and then thinking about not having it, it would be a lot harder, a lot more difficult. But that's because I'm used now to having technology. That's in the first place.

Another individual who responded affirmatively does so by explicitly noting the way the Internet affects language. Prior to the Internet, s/he imagines, one would have needed to know the native language of the host country (in this case, Poland). This would have been necessary, s/he reasons, not only because of the lack of easily accessible information via Google and other online applications but also because of the way the Internet has presumably contributed to the internationalisation of English.

> Everything is on Google. I can find anything on Google. I can just pop in pizza or coffee, and then I have an app that tells me the bus schedules. I don't think it would be impossible. I think people are generally as resourceful as they need to be. Maybe if you all of a sudden took all this away from me, I'd be sort of stranded. But if I were someone who never seen this and I got here, I would do things differently. But I think I would get by. It would be hard. And there is no way I could do it without Polish. And there's probably no way that there would be as many English speakers without the Internet as well.

Implicit in this statement is a curious and potentially contradictory position concerning language acquisition. For the international student, online information sources, like Google, help overcome linguistic difference and make language learning virtually unnecessary. Without a tool like Google, this respondent argues, s/he would be in the rather difficult situation of needing to know Polish, the language of the host country. However, for the people residing in the host country, it is the same technology that, according to the respondent, provides them with an opportunity to learn the English language so that the international student is able to use and get by in his/her native language. Consequently the same technology facilitates the learning of a foreign language in one group and renders such learning unnecessary for another.

The final positive responses come from three participants who answered that they not only could imagine living abroad prior to the Internet but would have preferred such a thing. Two individuals stated a personal preference for social interactions prior to the Internet and the third expressed a neo-luddite desire for a world without the Internet: "Maybe it is my imagination, utopian idea that world without an Internet would be better." These responses are consistent with reported attitudes toward technology and conform to a technological determinist perspective concerning the effect of technology on social interaction that is at least as old as Plato's *Phaedrus*.

Those responding in the negative provided reasons that extended from complete dismay about the possibility of life before the Internet to more practical concerns about the conveniences and speed of digital communications. Indicative of the former are respondents who, for one reason or another, found it difficult to imagine life before the Internet:

> No. I can't imagine how they lived in this situation.

> I read news from back at home and around the world on the Internet. And I can't imagine going a day without.

> No, I don't. No, I don't imagine no contact with my friends and my family, I can't imagine.

In all three cases, respondents reported being unable to imagine access to news and information or family members and friends by any other means. For these individuals, no Internet simply meant no access. Another participant agreed that s/he probably would not have been able to live abroad without the Internet, but then clarifies the response by recognising the existence of other mode of communication — modes that s/he calls "old fashioned":

> I was going through old photos, and my dad sent tons of postcards to my grandma—probably every month, a postcard updating her on everything. I realised I probably would have just be doing that, or I would be more in contact through letters or something. It wouldn't be as instant, but I think I would probably have done that. If digital media wasn't here, I'd probably send some letter, it would be very old fashioned.

The remaining negative comment came from a respondent who also found the prospect of living without the Internet to be virtually impossible but then admits that the concept sounds compelling:

> Well, no. Probably no. I think it would have been great to live here before the age of the Internet. Basically because wouldn't have telephones, smartphones, iPhone. Have you noticed that all the people are not looking at where they are walking, they are looking at their telephones?

This response expresses a kind of nostalgia for a pre-Internet era that is attractive yet nevertheless unrealistic.

Finally, one respondent appeared to have considerable trouble formulating a response to the question and, in the process of "thinking out-loud," provided a kind of ambivalent reply that indicates, among other things, the difficulty of the question itself.

> Yeah, yeah, yeah, that would make it really hard to stay in touch with my friends. It would be hard. But then again, like there is no other option really. 'Cos even going back to my hometown, I don't have a lot of friends there. And I am not gonna move back just for my family. So I think that wouldn't be that enjoyable, but I would stay here. I wouldn't have traded it for somewhere [else] 'cos I don't think that would be really; I mean, even if they cut off the Internet, there are different ways to stay in touch. I'd just have a higher phone bill but, ah, yeah [pause]. Yeah, it's not something I'd be happy with, but yeah, I would stay here. I'd still be — at least, at least, in some way — it would, like, take me away even more from this, well, entirely from this fake reality and force me to live the real life. I have a friend that acted pretty crazy, that had deleted his Facebook account for the summer. Just for the summer. Just to, just to, you know, see what it's like [...] You stop wasting all of your time. So sometimes I feel like doing that. Yeah. I mean I don't really need the Internet — like for my e-mail. But yeah, I mean there are many things like going on in culture that I would not know without the Internet, but still, not like [pause], I could do it. But then again I've never done it. Maybe I can. I don't know. Yeah.

Like Marshall McLuhan's fish, which cannot possibly ascertain or conceptualise the water in which it is already situated and lives, this seemingly confused response demonstrates the difficulty of thinking about life outside that in which one is already immersed and fully enculturated.[18]

4. Conclusions & Future Direction

The generalisable data does lend support to the initial hypothesis. For the majority of participants in the study, ICT is perceived to have a significant

[18] Marshall McLuhan and Quentin Fiore, *War and Peace in the Global Village* (Berkeley: CA: Gingko Press, 2001), 175.

impact on the possibilities, perspectives, and character of intercultural encounters. Nine out of the fourteen participants explicitly stated that the Internet, social media, and web applications assisted with intercultural communication. In particular, participants reported dealing with linguistic difference by leveraging the power of online translation tools and YouTube language tutorials, using Google and other web-based information sources to access data necessary for living and working in an unfamiliar location, and employing social media like Facebook to crowd-source problem solving and to introduce different cultures and experiences. Furthermore this opinion holds despite the fact that a majority of participants report that they either could imagine or might have even preferred living without the Internet and that their general opinions about technology vary significantly and cover the spectrum of available theory. Finally four of the remaining five participants who answered otherwise did not so much reply negatively as they reported not using the technology for the purposes of intercultural transactions.

This conclusion, however, requires two caveats. First, all of the data collected and analysed for this study was based on and derived from self-reporting. Self-reporting has the distinct advantage that it can, unlike any other form of data collection, provide access to participant's thoughts, motivations, emotions, and gratifications. The main disadvantage, of course, has to do with the validity of reported data. This not only involves deception on the part of participants (deliberate or unintentional) but also "leading questions" from the interviewers, which can often shape and influence how participants respond. Furthermore, self-reporting is based on an essentially modernist assumption that subjects are transparent to themselves, know what they do, and can reasonably explain why they do it. I point this out not to undermine our efforts but to caution against reading the results without an informed critical perspective. The data show not that ICT has a positive effect on the study abroad experience but that a majority of users report that they perceive that it does.

Second, the generalisable data certainly provide support for the hypothesis, but they do not offer much more. They do not, for instance, provide any deeper understanding as to why this is the case, how it functions, or what that all means. This is the true value of collecting qualitative data as opposed to just doing a quantitative survey. Consequently what is needed is to drill down into this large and rather complex data set to identify and to analyse the content of individual responses. Although pursuing this effort is something that is beyond the scope of this particular overview, this line of inquiry will be undertaken and developed in the essays provided by other members of the research team: Ann Hetzel Gunkel, Agnieszka Stasiewicz, Garry Robson, and Małgorzata Zachara,

Finally let me end by noting a few items concerning future direction for this research. First, there is clearly a lot to be learned from qualitative investigations of actual users and their behaviours, but the size and composition of the sample could certainly be improved. Fourteen participants is admittedly on the low end even for a detailed qualitative investigation and future efforts should aim to increase the number of interview participants. At the same time, there could be tighter control exercised in the recruitment of participants to ensure adequate representation in the area of gender, previous international experience, duration of residence in the host country, age, etc. Demographic diversity, as we have learned in this study, can be extremely useful for tracking the wide range of opinions and experience, but too much variability in the composition of the sample can, as we have also discovered, hinder efforts at generalising results.

Second, although our study was international, it was, mainly for practical reasons, limited to two institutions in two specific locations (Northern Illinois University in DeKalb, Illinois, USA and the Jagiellonian University in Kraków, Poland). The next step would be to take the experience of this initial study and expand the scope of the investigation. It would for instance be advisable to interview students at more than one institution in each participating region (North America and Europe) and to expand the number of participating regions (i.e. Asia, Africa, South America, etc.). Obviously this effort at expansion has practical limitations and researchers would need to contend with questions of feasibility in both the method of investigation and its funding. But it would, for example, be possible to include at least one other country located in another part of the world. The next iteration of the project, therefore, will seek to include institutions in Brazil in order to open up the scope of the project to a wider international population of students.

For these reasons, the current investigation is probably best situated and understood as a pilot study. As such, it demonstrates the importance, potential insights, and feasibility of using quantitative methods to identify and analyse the influence of ICT on the international student experience. But given the size and composition of the sample and the limited scope of the investigation, it would be imprudent to claim that this one study provides conclusive results or even definitive data. This is not necessarily a deficiency in the method of investigation but an indication of the inherent limitations of the current study that call for and would need to be addressed by extending its efforts and approach. In any event, what is not debated is the fact that understanding how recent innovations in ICT effect the international student experience will be indispensable to students, faculties, and administrators at institutions of higher education involved with and interested in improving opportunities for international student exchange.

Bibliography

Baudrillard, Jean. *Simulacra et Simulation*. Paris: Éditions Galilée, 1981.

Benedikt, Michael. *Cyberspace: First Steps*. Cambridge, MA: MIT Press, 1991.

Caincross, Francis. *The Death of Distance: How the Communications Revolution Will Change our Lives*. Boston, MA: Harvard Business School Press.

Carey, James. *Communication as Culture: Essays on Media and Society*. New York: Routledge, 1989.

Castronova, Edward. *Synthetics Worlds: The Business and Culture of Online Games*. Chicago: University of Chicago Press, 2005.

Cemalcilar, Zeynep, Toni Falbo and Laura Stapleton. "Cyber Communication: A New Opportunity for International Students' Adaptation?" *International Journal of Intercultural Relations*, 29(1) (2005): 91-110.

Dibbell, Julian. "A Rape In Cyberspace; Or How and Evil Clown, a Haitian Trickster Spirit, Two Wizards, and a Cast of Dozens Turned a Database into a Society," In *Flame Wars: The Discourse of Cyberculture*, edited by Mark Dery, 237-262. Durham, NC: Duke University Press, 1994.

Dizard, Wilson. *Meganet: How the Global Communications Network Will Connect Everyone on Earth.* Boulder, CO: Westview Press, 1997.

Ellul, Jacques. *The Technological Society*. New York: Vintage, 1964.

Ess, Charles. *Philosophical Perspectives on Computer-Mediated Communication*. Albany, NY: State University of New York Press, 1996.

Feenberg, Andrew. *Critical Theory of Technology*. New York: Oxford University Press, 1991.

Frutos, Sonia Valle de. *Cibercultura y Civilización Universal: Hacia un Nuevo Orden Cultural*. Barcelona: Erasmus Ediciones, 2011.

Grau, Christopher. *Philosophers Explore the Matrix*. Oxford: Oxford University Press, 2005.

Gunkel, David J. *Thinking Otherwise: Philosophy, Communication, Technology*. West Lafayette: Purdue University Press, 2007.

Heidegger, Martin. *Vorträge und Aufsätze*. Pfullingen: Verlag Günther Neske, 1954.

—. *The Question Concerning Technology and Other Essays*. Translated by William Lovitt. New York: Harper Torchbooks, 1977.

Heim, Michael. *The Metaphysics of Virtual Reality*. New York: Oxford University Press, 1993.

Hiltz, Starr Roxanne and Murray Turoff. *The Networked Nation: Human Communication via Computer*. Reading, MA: Addison-Wesley Publishing Company, 1978.

Irwin, William. *The Matrix and Philosophy*, Chicago: Open Court, 2002.

—. *More Matrix and Philosophy: Revolutions and Reloaded Decoded*. Chicago: Open Court, 2005.

Jones, Barry. *Sleepers, Wake! Technology and the Future of Work*. New York: Oxford University Press, 1990.

Jones, Steven G. *CyberSociety 2.0: Computer-Mediated Communication and Community*. London: Sage, 1994.

Kong, Ying. "Acculturation in the Age of New Media." Paper presented at the annual meeting of the International Communication Association. New York, NY. 25 May 2009. http://www.allacademic.com/meta/p13763_index.html.

Lévy, Pierre. *Cyberculture*. Paris: Éditions Odile Jacob/Éditions du Conseil de l'Europe, 1997.

Licklider, J. C. R. and Robert W. Taylor. "The Computer as Communication Device." *Science and Technology*. April 1968. http://memex.org/licklider.html.

McLuhan, Marshall. *Understanding Media: The Extensions of Man*. Cambridge, MA: MIT Press, 1995.

McLuhan, Marshall and Quentin Fiore. *War and Peace in the Global Village*. Berkeley: CA: Gingko Press, 2001.

Mitchell, William J. *City of Bits: Space, Place, and the Infobahn*. Cambridge, MA: MIT Press, 1995.

Negroponte, Nicholas. *Being Digital*. New York: Vintage Books, 1995.

O'Dowd, Robert. "In Search of a Truly Global Network: The Opportunities and Challenges of On-line Intercultural Communication." *Computer Assisted Language Learning—Electronic Journal* (*CALL-EJ*) 3(1) (2001). http://callej.org/journal/3-1/o_dowd.html.

Plato, *Phaedrus*. Translated by Harold North Fowler. Cambridge, MA: Harvard University Press, 1987.

Smith, Timothy B. and David A. Shwalb. "Preliminary Examination of International Student's Adjustment and Loneliness Related to

Electronic Communications." *Psychological Reports* 100(1) (2007): 167-170.

Spinelli, Martin. "Radio Lessons for the Internet." *Postmodern Culture* 6(2) (1996): Unpaginated.

Turkle, Sherry. *Life on the Screen: Identity in the Age of the Internet*. New York: Simon and Schuster, 1995.

Ye, Jiali. "An Examination of Acculturative Stress, Interpersonal Social Support, and Use of Online Ethnic Social Groups among Chinese International Students." *Howard Journal of Communication* 17(1) (2006): 1-20.

—. "Traditional and Online Support Networks in the Cross-Cultural Adaptation of Chinese International Students in the United States." *Journal of Computer-Mediated Communication* 11 (2006): 863–876.

CHAPTER SEVEN

GOING NATIVE: THE REAL PROBLEM IN THEORISING THE COMMUNICATIVE INTERACTION OF DIGITAL NATIVES

ANN GUNKEL

Reflecting on the purposes, procedures and products of the research carried out by the 2012-14 Harmonia Grant project, "Negotiating Cultural Differences in the Digital Communication Era," this chapter seeks to step back and ask about the nature of our research, the implications of our questions and the concepts being mobilized by the study.[1] My goal in these remarks is less to interpret the data set that has been gathered and presented but rather, to complicate the very premises we deploy in framing research of this type. I want, in the most positive way, to make our work suspect, [from the Latin SUB- + *specere*] to look at it from below, from underneath, from the foundation, as it were, so that in making our work suspect, we can trace in the project its hypotheses, strategies, and formulations, the underlying assumptions that shape and in many ways determine the meaning and significance of our study.

Specifically, I interrogate three areas for questioning; all three are interdependent and implicate each other at a fundamental level. They are: 1) the use of the term digital natives; 2) the limits of qualitative

[1] The research project, "Negotiating Cultural Differences in the Digital Communication Era," was sponsored by the Harmonia Grant of the Polish National Science Center/*Narodowe Centrum Nauki*. The research team consisted of Dr. Garry Robson, Dr. Malgorzata Zachara, Dr. Agnieszka Stasiewicz-Bienkowska (Jagiellonian University, Poland), Dr. David Gunkel (Northern Illinois University, USA), and Dr. Ann Hetzel Gunkel (Columbia College Chicago USA). For a summary of the project data, see David J. Gunkel, "Negotiating Cultural Difference in the Digital Communication Era," in this volume.

methodology in studying digital natives; and 3) the concept of the "real" deployed by digital natives.

1. Considering Digital Natives

The first is the seemingly self-evident terminology describing our subject group: digital natives. What does this term actually mean? We use it effortlessly to indicate some qualities of the interview subjects. But who exactly are digital natives? Who counts as a digital native? Whence this term? And perhaps most importantly, what are the consequences of deploying a marketing term with a distinct colonial and imperial legacy? How does the implicit anthropological formation of the object of study determine and shape that study even before it begins? As a cultural studies scholar, I am deeply suspect of framing a research subject in the language of a marketing scheme. And quite frankly, even more worried about adopting the colonialism of an anthropological gesture toward the "native population" of cyberspace, re-deploying this 19th century term devoid of its political and imperial context.

When positing or deploying a "native identity" formation such as digital natives, it might behove us to consider extant critiques of ethnic identity scholarship. "Images... [of ethnicity]...purveyed by the mass media are neither just the compilation of folk ideas nor the popularization of scholarly findings, but also reflections of the needs of capital and the state. This material link is most easily seen in the advertising media, which not only describe products but also manipulate images of women, men, and children so as to define them as individuals needing those commodities."[2] We see that material link in the ways the term digital natives has been deployed as a marketing category, with the proliferation of hundreds of articles bearing titles such as "Digital Natives: Six Ways Marketers can Engage Millennials."[3] The term digital natives - despite its questionable descriptive capabilities regarding an entire global generation -is fundamentally a marketing category, aimed at selling even more effectively to the consumers who have a personal relationship with Beanie Babies, Tamagochies and Slap bracelets.[4] Conversations in boardrooms

---

[2] Micaela di Leonardo, *The Varieties of Ethnic Experience* (Ithaca: Cornell University Press, 1984), 178.

[3] Kira Sparks, "Digital Natives: Six Ways Marketers can Engage Millennials." (30 July 2013, Shoutlet.com), accessed September 16, 2013, http://www.shoutlet.com/blog/2013/07/digital-natives-six-ways-marketers-can-engage-millennials/.

[4] Sparks, "Digital Natives," 2013.

and blogs resonate with seminars such as “Cracking Today’s Digital Natives: 5 Things to Keep in Mind When Marketing to Millennials” found on the Word of Mouth Marketing Association website which advises, “More than any other generation, millennials value relationships with brands that are authentic and have a one-on-one feel.”[5] We need to be sceptical and wary of mobilising marketing categories representative of what Naomi Klein calls “the triumph of identity marketing” as descriptors for academic research. Digital natives are in fact, the prized target of so-called “cool hunters,” scholars with academic training in the social sciences and humanities, particular anthropology, hired to take on “ethnographic field work” on the demographics of coolness for corporate purposes.[6]

Moving from marketing to the field of higher education, the educational theorist and game designer Marc Prensky claims credit for popularising the term digital native in his 2001 article, “Digital Natives Digital Immigrants.”[7]

> What should we call these “new” students of today? Some refer to them as the N-[for Net]-gen or D-[for digital]-gen. But the most useful designation I have found for them is Digital Natives. Our students today are all “native speakers” of the digital language of computers, video games and the Internet.
>
> So what does that make the rest of us? Those of us who were not born into the digital world but have, at some later point in our lives, become fascinated by and adopted many or most aspects of the new technology are, and always will be compared to them, Digital Immigrants.[8]

---

[5] Allison Jordan, “Cracking Today’s Digital Natives: 5 Things to Keep in Mind When Marketing to Millennials,” WOMMA, The Word of Mouth Marketing Association Blog, June 26, 2013, accessed September 16, 2013, http://www.womma.org/blog/2013/06/cracking-todays-digital-natives-5-things-to-keep-in-mind-when-marketing-to-millennials.

[6] Naomi Klein, *No Logo* (New York: Picador, 2000).

[7] In his blog, Marc Prensky qualifies his claim to originating the term Digital Natives: “Bottom line: I am the person who should get the credit for popularizing – not for being the ‘first to think up,’ – the native/immigrant distinction, and I should get credit as well, until an earlier citation arises, for adding the descriptor ‘digital’.” This is, of course, somewhat like, as Jerry Michalski points out, Marconi getting credit for the radio that Tesla thought up first, or Bell for the telephone thought up first by Elisha Grey and Lars Ericsson.” Accessed 16 September 16, 2013, http://www.marcprensky.com/blog/archives/000045.html.

[8] Marc Prensky, “Digital Natives Digital Immigrants,” In *On the Horizon,* (MCB University Press 9: 5, October 2001), 1.

While asking some crucial questions about the pedagogical methods used to engage students growing up in a different world from many of their teachers, he nonetheless deploys a deeply problematic quasi-anthropological formation to designate generational differences of technological enculturation, using terms such as the "digital immigrant accent." Prensky's tone is earnest because he is addressing the important question of twenty-first century learning styles and the efficacy of outdated pedagogies. However, once again, in service of that serious question he unproblematically deploys an ethnocentric anthropological formulation that — in its wildfire acceptance, especially in popular media — has shaped our assumptions about these "digital natives." Listen to his language as he pleads his case:

> It's very serious, because the single biggest problem facing education today is that our Digital Immigrant instructors, who speak an outdated language (that of the pre-digital age), are struggling to teach a population that speaks an entirely new language. This is obvious to the Digital Natives – school often feels pretty much as if we've brought in a population of heavily accented, unintelligible foreigners to lecture them. They often can't understand what the Immigrants are saying. What does "dial" a number mean, anyway?[9]

While his educational and pedagogical concerns may be quite valid, his plea for the pedagogy of gaming is in fact buried in the baggage of colonial and nativist discourse that shapes claims made about the "new generation."

On the most practical level, critics of the term have noted it suggests a familiarity with technology that not all children have, effectively ignoring the complex political economic contexts within which one has access to technology and the simple facts of unequal access globally.[10] Global

---

[9] Prensky, "Digital Natives, Digital Immigrants," 2.

[10] Doug Holton, EdTechDev, accessed May 12, 2010, http://edtechdev.wordpress.com/2010/03/19/the-digital-natives-digital-immigrants-distinction-is-dead-or-at-least-dying/; Jamie McKenzie, "Digital Nativism, Digital Delusions, and Digital Deprivation," accessed September 16 2013, http://www.fno.org/nov07/nativism.html; George Kennedy, Terry Judd and Barney Dalgarno, "From Now On," *The educational technology journal*, (17: 2, 2010), accessed August 29 2010; Chris Jones, Ruslan Ramanau, Simon Cross, and Graham Healing, "Net generation or digital natives: Is there a distinct new generation entering university?" *Computers & Education* 54:3 (2010): 722-732; and Chris Jones and Binhui Shao, "The net generation and digital natives:

statistics concerning the digital divide estimate that perhaps merely 8 to 10 percent of the world's population have Internet access.

> Writing in the British Journal of Education Technology in 2008, a group of academics led by Sue Bennett of the University of Wollongong set out to debunk the whole idea of digital natives, arguing that there may be "as much variation within the digital native generation as between the generations". They caution that the idea of a new generation that learns in a different way might actually be counterproductive in education, because such sweeping generalisations "fail to recognise cognitive differences in young people of different ages, and variation within age groups."[11]

Although the Harmonia study interviewed international students from all continents and eight languages, one cannot presume that this group is therefore globally representative. In fact, while several of the students in the sample come from developing regions, these young people are not representative of the global population. In fact, "international students comprise a highly populated sojourning group with some specific characteristics that make their experience different from other migrating groups such as guest workers or refugees.[12] As Cemalcilar, Falbo and Stapleton point out, "they are a more homogenous group in that they are typically young and well educated. In general, they arrive in the host country pre-trained in the host language and prepared to adjust to the host culture."[13] Because of their special status, one much more privileged than many migrants, refugees, and guest workers, "keeping in touch with their own culture and society and maintaining existing relationships may be more of a need for student groups, compared to more permanently settled and established groups such as ethnic groups or immigrants."[14] The research data completely supports these earlier studies with all but one student reporting their primary use of computer mediated communication

---

implications for higher education," Higher Education Academy, York (2010), accessed September 16 2013. http://oro.open.ac.uk/30014/.

[11] "Technology and society: Is it really helpful to talk about a new generation of "digital natives" who have grown up with the internet?" *The Economist*, March 4, 2010, accessed April 22, 2012, http://www.economist.com/node/15582279?story_id=15582279.

[12] John W. Berry and David L. Sam. "Acculturation and adaptation," in *Handbook of cross-cultural psychology,* ed. John W. Berry, et al. (Boston: Allyn & Bacon, 1997), 92.

[13] Berry and Sam, "Acculturation," 92.

[14] John W Berry, U. Kim, S. Power, M. Young, and M. Bujaki, "Acculturation studies in plural societies," *Applied Psychology: An International Review* 38 (1989): 135-186.

is contacting friends and family "back home." The survey respondents quite clearly echo the existing research in the field, in that they pointed out not only the primary function of technology for contacting home but also their lack of using that exact same technology (i.e. Facebook) for contacting people in the host country. As a foreign student studying in Poland commented, "I rarely use it to keep in touch with friends here in Cracow." (AG 4)

A second interesting feature of the relative privilege of the group is the almost universal practice in our sample of posting travel photos. While the respondents varied in the level of usage and opinions about digital technologies, almost all of them reported engaging in one practice: posting travel photos. Perhaps the ultimate visual icon of modern cosmopolitan identity, few artefacts measure up - in both ontological weight and sheer surface gloss -to the photograph. Susan Sontag claimed that, "As photographs give people an imaginary possession of a past that is unreal, they also help people to take possession of space in which they are insecure."[15] Rather than assimilating or enculturating, it seems that a predominant digital practice of international students is the reproduction of the tourist gaze and its attendant practices. What Urry and Larson call "the tourist gaze" is a mode of seeing and representation that "regulates the relationship with the tourist environment, demarcating the other and identifying the out-of-the-ordinary. It elucidates the relationship between tourism and embodiment and elaborates on the connections between mobility as a mark of modern and postmodern experience and the attraction of tourism as a lifestyle choice.[16]

The effects of tourism on "natives," particularly the commoditization of culture, are increasingly subject to study. From the early scholarship of Veblen on the leisure class to contemporary analyses of tourism, scholars have asked about the economic and imperialist context of travel extending their analyses to the commodification of "exotic" locales by foreign tourists.[17] We might want to explore how digital natives in their touristic practices construct their participation in modernity and their status as modern subjects on Facebook. "To be a tourist is one of the characteristics

---

[15] Susan Sontag, *On Photography* (New York: Farrer, Strauss and Giroux, 1973), 71.

[16] John Urry and Jonas Larsen, *The Tourist Gaze 3.0* (Thousand Oaks, CA: Sage Publishers, 2011).

[17] See Thorstein Veblen, *The Theory of the Leisure Class*, ed. Matha Banta (New York: Oxford University Press, 2009) and Cynthia Enloe. *Bananas, Beaches and Bases: Making Feminist Sense of International Politics* (Berkeley: University of California Press, 2000).

of 'modern' experience. Not to 'go away'; is like not possessing a car or a nice house. It has become a marker of status on modern societies..."[18] Numerous texts have explored how "the camera and the tourism are two of the uniquely modern ways of defining reality."[19] In fact, the concept of the gaze, as a constitutive part of modernity highlights "that looking is a learned ability and the pure and innocent eye is a myth."[20] The classifications made by the tourist gaze occur within an economy of relations, producing what Said called "imaginative geographies."[21]

Digital photography has expanded the role of the tourist gaze in the space of social media. "Users of Facebook have uploaded more than 10 billion photographs, with the number increasing by an astonishing 700 million each month."[22] Most of the research sample respondents not only post travel photos as a matter of course, but almost all of them mention posting landscape photographs. "The tourist gaze is directed to features of landscape and townscape which separate them off from everyday experience. Such aspects are viewed because they are taken to be in some sense out of the ordinary."[23] The almost universal practice of posting touristic landscape photos in our sample points to not only the privileged status of international students as modern subjects but reinforces the questions raised about mobility, post-modernity, representation and the legacies of colonialism.

We might ask, following Sontag, whether digital natives via their photo posting practices are indeed enacting a "chronic voyeuristic relation" to the world around them. Or perhaps, following Roland Barthes, we might examine photography's tendency to naturalize highly structured meanings.[24] In the texts of *Mythologies*, Barthes explores Myth (including photographic images) as a type of speech; delimiting how the process of mythologisation brings a truth claim to socially constructed notions, narratives, and assumptions.[25] The rhetorical power of photography, made in the now-moment by digital photography and instantaneous posting, is grounded in the ability to naturalise, to make innocent its cultural messages and connotations. "Photographs appear to be not statements

[18] Urry and Larsen, *Tourist Gaze*, 3.
[19] Donald Horne, *The Great Museum* (London: Pluto Press, 1984), 21.
[20] Urry and Larsen, *Tourist Gaze*, 1.
[21] Edward Said, *Orientalism: Western Conceptions of the Orient* (Harmondsworth: Penguin, 1995), 49-73.
[22] Urry and Larsen, *Tourist Gaze*, 185.
[23] Urry and Larsen, *Tourist Gaze*, 3.
[24] Roland Barthes, *Camera Lucida* (New York: Hill and Wang, 1981).
[25] Roland Barthes, *Mythologies*, trans. Annette Lavers (London: Vintage, 2009).

about the world but pieces of it, even miniature slices of reality, without revealing its constructed nature or its ideological content."[26] The claim made upon the real made by photography might prove a most fruitful path for analyses of social media data in that it connects these digital practices directly to the question of the real (to which I will turn shortly.)

While we must remain cautious about the effectiveness of categorization in the term digital native, we need also to consider the epistemological assumptions made about that group. As poster drkhturner notes on the Digital Natives debate site of discusscafe, "If digital natives are people who were immersed in particular digital technologies during their formative years, then yes, they exist. The challenge is that they may see these same technologies as 'natural' -and that they may not be as skilled, self-aware, or critical in their use of the technologies as we might assume they would be."[27] In other words, even if the category of digital natives is valid, it does not follow that the said digital natives have a privileged understanding of technology, the parameters of which have been naturalised. This observation leads to my comments about the relationship of digital natives to the concept of the real, to which I will turn momentarily.

There are a flood of debates, discussions, wikis, and blogs devoted to the argument about digital natives. However, in those numerous sites, what is debated is whether or not the term is valid and whether or not it can be used to describe an entire generation unproblematically. While this is a worthwhile inquiry, it seems to me that the critiques miss something more fundamental: namely, what does it mean to describe an entire generation in terminology derived from colonialism? To redeploy in a supposed post-racial era, the nomenclature of natives and immigrants? Micaela di Leonardo's critique of the anthropological stance of going native notes, "The Other is terminally Orientalized -a proven inferior who must be forced to cooperate in studying his or her own present or past, an exotic individual who, in the aggregate, can provide the *mise-en-scene* for an infinite series of dramas of Western selfhood. Anthropologists participate in this 'colonial chic' or imperialist nostalgia..."[28]

On this point, I would like to cite our previous scholarship on the link between formulations of cyberspace as the new frontier and the colonial project. Following Heidegger, we observe that philosophical terminology

---

[26] Urry and Larsen, *Tourist Gaze*, 168.
[27] Digital Natives Debate, accessed September 16, 2013, http://www.discusscafe.com/drkhturner/digital-natives.
[28] Micaela di Leonardo, *Exotics at Home. Anthropologists, Others, American Modernity.* (Chicago: University of Chicago Press, 1998), 38.

cannot be divorced from the history of the use of that terminology, and thus we cannot avoid confronting questions of language and meaning.

> First, metaphors are always more than mere words. They are mechanisms of real social and political hegemony that have the capacity to determine the current and future shape of what they merely seem to designate. As a result of this, current and future configurations of cyberspace will be determined not only through innovations in hardware and software, but also, and perhaps more so, through the various metaphors that have been circulated and are employed to describe their significance...Because cyberspace has already been submitted to a kind of colonization through the metaphors of the new world and the electronic frontier, its decolonization is a task that, if it ever transpires, must take place in and by engaging the material and legacy of these particular rhetorical configurations.[29]

In the case of the term digital natives, who appear in all research to represent a privileged sample of education and mobility, it is particularly notable that this term appears in the supposedly post-racial era where some commentators have wondered why first world scholars have jettisoned the concept of subjectivity at precisely the moment when third world and native peoples were claiming it. This requires, at the very least, the decolonisation of our categories of research.

2. On Theory & Method: Qualitative Study and Self Reporting

The attendant problem of studying the "native population" of digital culture is the corollary assumption that the natives have a privileged, that is to say unmediated access to their own conditions of existence. This presumption leads us to question the underlying principles embedded in any qualitative methodology, especially those that involve self-reporting. This is not to say that the research is not useful or productive, nor is it to reject that methodology. But I want to take the step back through a consideration of the limitations and complications of certain implicit theoretical moves so as to clarify and qualify what it is we can and cannot claim. As David Gunkel points out, self-reporting has the distinct advantage that it can, unlike any other form of data collection, provide access to participant's thoughts, motivations, emotions, and gratifications.

---

[29] David J. Gunkel, *Hacking Cyberspace* (Boulder, CO: Westview Press, 2001), 51.

The main disadvantage, of course, has to do with the validity of reported data. This not only involves deception on the part of participants (deliberate or otherwise) but also "leading questions" from the interviewers, which can influence how one responds. Furthermore, self-reporting is based on an essentially modernist assumption that subjects are transparent to themselves, know what they do, and can reasonably explain why they do it.[30] This presumed self-transparent subject is further weighted with assumptions about the proximity of digital natives to their native realm. The modernist view of the subject translates directly into/is based upon the modernist, instrumentalist view of the real.

The term digital native seems to presume some more immediate, more automatic, perhaps more intuitive understanding of technology. Our subjects, we presume, are somehow native inhabitants of digital culture. Further, it is generally presumed that this immediacy must mean a more sophisticated understanding of how that technology works in the world and what that means. My analysis will claim that no such superior understanding of the virtual is demonstrated by digital natives, who deploy the very same rhetorical and conceptual frameworks that dominate mainstream commentary, academic studies of communication, and the viewpoints of non-digital natives. Indeed, I want to argue that digital natives express views of the virtual that are closely aligned with commentators and philosophers from ancient through modern times — all of whom predate modern computing. In short, digital natives seem to have no advantage or privileged understanding of the metaphysics underlying the technology with which they have greater familiarity.

That interrogation of the limits of methodology points toward an even more fundamental formulation and the third concept I want to examine: the modernist, instrumentalist view of the technology that animates our interview subjects connects directly to the modernist view of the real underlying their assertions. Our data can tell us about the behaviours and practices of international students in online space, but we cannot — via qualitative interviews, no matter how rich — make claims about the nature of real social interaction as opposed to virtual interaction. Our subjects do, however, make those claims as a matter of course. What we can learn from them is precisely how their rhetoric of the real informs their understanding of their own actions online and offline and furthermore point to the seeming hegemony of that philosophical concept.

[30] Gunkel, "Negotiating Cultural Difference in the Digital Communication Era," in this volume.

3. Concerning the Real

What is clear from our data is that digital natives certainly mobilise the language and rhetoric of the real; in fact, several of them comment on the difference between real and virtual life as though this was a self-evident distinction. This is very informative, not because they are "reporting on" the real/virtual opposition, but because it is an organizing concept deployed by almost everyone in the interviews. We might argue that digital natives have a profound investment in the Platonic metaphysics of reality because while virtually all subjects responded by mobilising the rhetoric of the real at some point in their interview, the interview questions never used that language. Even presuming a caution on the part of our study against leading the subjects to such comments, they emerged seemingly unbidden.

> First, everything depends on how we define and operationalize the concept of the real. Even though online role playing games, social networks, and other forms of avatar-based CMC are often considered to be merely a matter of entertainment, they are involved in serious debates about and meditations on fundamental aspects of metaphysics. And in these situations there appears to be, as there are in many facets of computing, a default setting. This default has been programmed and is controlled by Platonism, which institutes a distinction between the real thing and its phenomenal appearances. In computer-mediated interaction, like online role-playing games and immersive social environments, this Platonic decision is particularly manifest in the discussions and debates surrounding avatar identity and the seemingly indisputable fact that what appears in the space of the virtual world are manipulated representations of real human users, who may themselves be entirely different from how they appear in the computer-generated environment. As long as our research endeavors remain within and proceed according to this Platonic formulation, which as a default setting is often operative without having to select or specify it, we already know what questions matter, what evidence will count as appropriate, and what outcomes will be acceptable.[31]

I want to ask whether digital natives have even begun to problematise the notion of the real –firmly in place since Plato and through Descartes — that animates many of their conclusions and observations. Digital natives — whoever they may be and however tech savvy — don't seem to have

[31] David J. Gunkel, "The Real Problem: Avatars, Metaphysics, and Online Social Interaction," *New Media & Society* 12:1 (February 2010): 127-141, accessed September 16, 2013, http://nms.sagepub.com/cgi/content/abstract/12/1/127.

problematized the underlying metaphysical concepts that the virtual world might have or should have called into question. The students in our sample may be "digital natives" but they have roughly the same theoretical perspective on the virtual world as Descartes, exhibiting and deploying what might be called Descartes 2.0.[32]

I will argue that digital natives have almost no advantage in interrupting or questioning the parameters of reality presumed by rationalist or operationalist concepts of technology. While our survey population is quite young (average age of 25.6), they nonetheless embody varying ancient and medieval notions about technology and metaphysics, with one participant claiming a neo-luddite view that, "A world without an Internet would be better" because computer mediated technologies are "artificial and superficial." In other words, the underlying concept of the real being mobilised by these young people is one straight from Platonic metaphysics where the real is co-extant with an originary entity and all representations are removed to varying degrees from the source. Artifice or superfice is presumed to be derivative, and thus, inauthentic. It is fascinating to see the Platonic schema of appearances and reality mobilised by twenty-first century digital natives, who — following Plato, in a reading straight from Book 10 of *Republic* — worry about the inauthenticity of appearances in the digital realm. As one interviewee noted, "People are not being real on Facebook." As Boellsdorf points out, "There is a gap between virtual and actual self...and a broadly shared cultural assumption that virtual selfhood is not identical to actual selfhood."[33] What our respondent seems to be suggesting by commenting that "people are not being real on Facebook" is that new technologies allow for a performance that should be suspect. What this doesn't take into account, of course, is whether or not subjectivity is always already a performative.

While most of the respondents regularly use Computer Mediated Communication, most of them find it suspicious and possibly lacking in metaphysical authenticity. One student commented that he/she prefers "pre-Internet experience" (G1) and yet another, "I very much prefer my social interactions with people before Facebook. Or even phone." (G4) The dual suspicion of Facebook and the telephone is very telling. A quick glance at the history of technology reminds us that the new invention of

---

[32] See David J. Gunkel and Ann Hetzel Gunkel, "Terra Nova 2.0—The New Worlds of MMORPGs," *Critical Studies in Media Communication* 26(2) (June 2009): 104-127.

[33] Tom Boellstorff, *Coming of Age in Second Life: An Anthropologist Explores the Virtually Human* (Princeton, N.J.: Princeton University Press, 2008), 119.

the telephone was met with precisely the same rhetorical critiques now being levelled at CMCs. In fact, the phone was presumed to create the possibility for deception in social interactions, since you could not see the person you were talking to. An historical perspective on the fear of emergent technologies is very informative for contextualizing digital culture. "With the advent of the telephone and other new media came relatively sudden and largely unanticipated possibilities of mixing heterogeneous social worlds – a useful opportunity for some, a dreadful intrusion for others. New media took social risks by permitting outsiders to cross boundaries of race, gender and class without penalty."[34] In short, the telephone as a new media form proposed the crossing of socially established boundaries of class, race, gender and nation, such that the "wrong" kind of person just might call you on the phone. And this threat is very much the same threat implied in the concern over cyber communication where you might not know exactly whom you're talking to. On one level, technophobia is a fear of miscegenation. "[T]he telephone and other new media introduced a permeable boundary at the vital center of class and family, where innovative experiments could take place in all social relations, from crime to courtship."[35] How strange it is that the social upheaval of the telephone mirrors almost exactly the social upheavals linked to the Internet, in particular, worries about social relations from "crime to courtship," in our time, cybercrime and online dating. The social fears around these new developments produced social policies attempting to limit "illegitimate" access to telephones.[36] Even more immediately, the fear of new technologies is so powerful that our very well-being and even sanity is said to be at stake. Newspaper accounts in the 1880s and 1890s credit the telephone with causing insanity, in one case reporting "that the telephone had driven a Cincinnati citizen insane."[37]

This concern over the "reality" of the interlocutor was applied to telephone conversation and now to Internet avatars using almost the exact same language and metaphysics. This fear of deceptive interaction privileges the face-to-face as the only — or at least, most authentic means of human communication. This, too, is directly reflective of the Platonic schema of the *Phaedrus* which famously poses the new technology of writing (seen as an inferior, and thus, inaccurate representation of speech)

---

[34] Carolyn Marvin, *When Old Technologies Were New* (Oxford: Oxford University Press, 1988), 107.
[35] Marvin, *When Old Technologies Were New*, 108.
[36] Marvin, *When Old Technologies Were New,* 104-5.
[37] Marvin, *When Old Technologies Were New,* 187.

as a threat to the unity and authenticity of the voice.[38] As Walter Ong notes, "Most persons are surprised, and many distressed, to learn that essentially the same objections commonly urged today against computers were urged by Plato in the Phaedrus (274-7) and in the Seventh Letter against writing."[39]

Once again our digital natives seem to have bought into Platonic metaphysics wholesale – at least when it comes to their assessment of technology. This is not particularly odd or unexpected, for as Heidegger certainly reminds, our very understanding of the question concerning technology emerges from the Platonic explication of *techne*. "Plato was thinking of writing as an external, alien technology, as many people today think of the computer. Because we have by today so deeply interiorized writing, made it so much a part of ourselves, as Plato's age had not yet made it fully a part of itself (Havelock 1963), we find it difficult to consider writing to be a technology as we commonly assume printing and the computer to be."[40] The dangers attributed to that technological invention — perhaps one of the most world-changing technological revolutions — are the template by which digital technologies are framed, understood and articulated.

This operationalist view of technology, condemning technology to either the status of a mere tool or in a more morally weighted view, the means of communicative deception, stems from a fundamentally problematic definition of communication itself, one that until only recently had gone uninterrogated even –and perhaps especially –within the field of Communication Studies.[41] There is simply no way that these presumptions of communication can remain undistributed after phenomenology and post-structuralism. The presumption of the dominant sender-receiver model of communication depends on the notion of the self-aware, self-present subject. As Briankl Chang explains, such an understanding of the communicative subject is a theoretical fiction, a Cartesian-based subject "that misses the fact that individuals are constituted as functioning communicators only insofar as they participate in communication, only

---

[38] See Plato, *Phaedrus*, trans. Harold North Fowler (Cambridge, MA: Harvard University Press, 1987).

[39] Walter Ong, *Orality & Literacy. The technologizing of the Word* (New York:Routledge, 1982), 79.

[40] Ong, *Orality & Literacy*, 81.

[41] See James W. Carey, *Communication as Culture. Essays on Media and Society* (New York: Routledge, 1992); Briankle G. Chang, *Deconstructing Communication* (Minnesota: University of Minnesota Press, 1996); and David J. Gunkel, *Hacking Cyberspace* (Boulder, CO: Westview Press, 2001).

insofar as they are positioned as sender or receiver differentially according to the medium and the context of a particular communicative event."[42]

An important consequence factoring in this vital critique of communication theory is that it actually attends, most seriously, to the face-to-face that our interview subjects seem to want to privilege, because it understands the communicative context and the effect of the other — in a Levinasian sense — as the *a priori* foundation for communicative interaction. What the contemporary communicative critique offers is the possibility of restoring the face-to-face to a genuine rather than fictional function. It would be one constitutive event of communication among others instead of *the* constitutive event. This would allow for a kind of Levinasian reading in that it understands the communicative context and the effect of the other as prior to any kind of messaging. There is no *a priori* self-possessed subject totality, pre-given and decontextualized, but rather an addresser who is first addressed by the other. Michel Foucault observes that the image of communication as infinite, free exchange of discourse represents one of the "great myths of European culture."[43] Heidegger's *Being and Time* problematized these assumptions, which were lodged in a prior concept of presence. "Communication is never anything like a conveying of experiences, such as opinions or wishes, from the interior of one subject into the interior of another. *Dasein*-with is already essentially manifest in a co-state-of-mind and co-understanding."[44]

Several of the interview subjects in the Negotiating Cultural Differences study commented that while they use, enjoy, and waste time on Facebook – with some reporting usage "all day", "24/7", and "all the time" – they nonetheless accord it an inferior metaphysical status, commenting that it is "less personal than face-to-face" communication. One interview subject was asked about how digital media helps with intercultural communication and was careful to clarify, "I think the most important for me is contact live, face-to-face…" This fantasy of an unmediated communicative act is just that, fantastic. Our respondents presume that whatever communicative digital practices they embody or especially, avoid are in some way inferior, less direct, and more "mediated" than the face-to-face.

---

[42] Chang, *Deconstructing Communication*, 181.

[43] Michel Foucault, *The Order of Discourse,* trans. Ian McLeod, in *Untying the Text: A Post-Structuralist Reader,* ed. Robert Young (Boston: Routledge, 1981), 48-78.

[44] Martin Heidegger, *Being and Time,* trans. John Macquarrie & Edward Robinson (New York: Harper & Row, 1962), 205.

Within the study data, it was extremely uncommon for respondents to complicate this metaphysics of the real, with only one digital native commenting, "I think our online social life is an important part of daily life. Not a replacement for real life but another dimension of it." This was perhaps the only incursion in the entire sample even remotely problematising the notion of the real. "The real problem [for our respondents as well as our research] is not that investigators of computer-mediated social interaction have used one theory of the real or another. The problem is that researchers have more often than not utilized theory without explicitly recognizing which one or considering why one comes to be employed as opposed to another."[45]

The international students in our study — representing many languages and cultures — seem to indicate that global youth culture is certainly homogenous enough to reproduce a specific metaphysical understanding of the real that is not specific to a native country or native language, but remains firmly lodged in a western, metaphysical conceptual nexus operationalised in our formation and understanding of technology's function. Those same conceptual parameters traced out in Heidegger's "Question Concerning Technology" seem to apply to this global sample.[46] Why would a diverse international group all mobilize a singular conceptual formation? The predominance of a Platonic metaphysical formulation is not surprising in a group of international students who hail from around the globe when one looks at the existing research on international students. That brings us full circle back to the issue of privilege *vis a vis* the relative status of international students with respect to other global peoples on the move, for example migrant workers, refugees, and so on. The digital natives of our sample are relatively well-educated and thus, not representative of global diversity of position and status. They are representative, however, of the ubiquitous naturalisation of this specific formation of the concept of technology.

Unlike recent scholarship on virtuality that complicates this metaphysical inheritance, our sample quite clearly mobilised a single set of assumptions about the nature of the real. For contemporary theorists such as Žižek, "the real is already a virtual construct, and the difference between the real and the virtual turns out to be much more complicated

---

[45] Gunkel, "Negotiating Cultural Differences," Chapter Six, this volume.

[46] Martin Heidegger, *The Question Concerning Technology and Other Essays*, trans. William Lovitt (New York: Harper Torchbooks, 1977).

and interesting."[47] As much of that recent scholarship points out "It is not that virtual worlds borrowed assumptions from real life: virtual worlds show us how, under our very noses, our 'real' lives have been 'virtual' all along."[48]

It is genuinely fascinating to report from our data that so-called digital natives make frequent use of social practices of digital communication which they simultaneously suspect, according those practices less authenticity and even less reality. It is really interesting that in the context of our research, our so-called native informants know just as little about the territory as we do.

Bibliography

Barthes, Roland. *Camera Lucida*. New York: Hill and Wang, 1981.

—. translated by Annette Lavers. *Mythologies*. London: Vintage, 2009.

Baudrillard, Jean. *Simulations*. Translated by Paul Foss, Paul Patton and Philip Beitchman. New York: Semiotext(e), Inc.,1983.

Berry, John W. and David L. Sam. "Acculturation and adaptation." In *Handbook of cross-cultural psychology,* edited by J.W. Berry, M.H. Segall, and C. Kagitcibasi, 292-326. Boston: Allyn & Bacon, 1997.

Berry, John W. U. Kim, S. Power, M. Young, and M. Bujaki. "Acculturation studies in plural societies." *Applied Psychology: An International Review* 38 (1989): 135-186.

"Beyond Natives and Immigrants: Exploring types of net generation students." *Journal of Computer Assisted Learning* 26: 5, 332-343.

Boellstorff, Tom. *Coming of Age in Second Life: An Anthropologist Explores the Virtually Human*. Princeton, N.J.: Princeton University Press, 2008.

Carey, James W. *Communication as Culture. Essays on Media and Society*. New York: Routledge, 1992.

---

[47] David J. Gunkel, "The Real Problem: Avatars, Metaphysics, and Online Social Interaction," *New Media & Society* 12:1 (February 2010): 127-141, accessed September 16, 2013, http://nms.sagepub.com/cgi/content/abstract/12/1/127. P. 46.

[48] Boellstorff, *Coming of Age in Second Life*, 5. See also, David, J. Gunkel, *Thinking Otherwise*: *Philosophy, Communication, Technology* (West Lafayette: Purdue University Press, 2007); Slavoj Žižek, *Interrogating the Real* (New York: Continuum, 2006); Mark Taylor, *Hiding* (Chicago: University of Chicago Press, 1987); and Jean Baudrillard, *Simulations,* trans. Paul Foss, Paul Patton and Philip Beitchman (New York: Semiotext(e), Inc.,1983).

Cemalcilar, Zeynep, Toni Falbo and Laura M. Stapleton. "Cyber communication: A new opportunity for international student adaptation?" *International Journal of Intercultural Relations*, 29 (2005): 91-110.

Chang, Briankle G. *Deconstructing Communication*. Minnesota: University of Minnesota Press, 1996.

di Leonardo, Micaela. *The Varieties of Ethnic Experience*. Ithaca: Cornell University Press, 1984.

—. *Exotics at Home. Anthropologists, Others, American Modernity.* Chicago: University of Chicago Press, 1998.

Digital Natives Debate. Accessed September 16, 2013. http://www.discusscafe.com/drkhturner/digital-natives.

Enloe, Cynthia. *Bananas, Beaches and Bases: Making Feminist Sense of International Politics*. Berkeley: University of California Press, 2000.

Foucault, Michel. *The Order of Discourse*. Translated by Ian McLeod. In *Untying the Text: A Post-Structuralist Reader,* edited by Robert Young, 48-78. Boston: Routledge, 1981.

Gunkel, David J. "Negotiating Cultural Difference in the Digital Communication Era," in this volume.

—. "The Real Problem: Avatars, Metaphysics, and Online Social Interaction." *New Media & Society* 12:1 (February 2010) 127-141. Accessed 16 September 2013. http://nms.sagepub.com/cgi/content/abstract/12/1/127.

—. *Thinking Otherwise*: *Philosophy, Communication, Technology*. West Lafayette: Purdue University Press, 2007.

—. *Hacking Cyberspace*. Boulder, CO: Westview Press, 2001.

Gunkel, David J. and Ann Hetzel Gunkel. "Virtual Geographies: The New Worlds of Cyberspace." *Critical Studies in Mass Communication* 14:2 (June 1997): 123-137.

Gunkel, David J. and Ann Hetzel Gunkel. "Terra Nova 2.0—The New Worlds of MMORPGs." *Critical Studies in Media Communication* 26(2) (June 2009): 104-127.

Heidegger, Martin. *Being and Time*. Translated by John Macquarrie & Edward Robinson. New York: Harper & Row, 1962.

—. *The Question Concerning Technology and Other Essays*. Translated by William Lovitt. New York: Harper Torchbooks, 1977.

Holton, Doug. EdTechDev, Accessed 12 May 2010. http://edtechdev.wordpress.com/2010/03/19/the-digital-natives-digital-immigrants-distinction-is-dead-or-at-least-dying/.

Horne, Donald. *The Great Museum.* London: Pluto Press, 1984.

Jones, Chris, Ruslan Ramanau, Simon Cross, and Graham Healing. (2010). "Net generation or digital natives: Is there a distinct new generation entering university?" *Computers & Education* 54 (3) (2010): 722-732.

Jones, Chris and Binhui Shao. (2011). "The net generation and digital natives: implications for higher education." Higher Education Academy, York: 2010 Accessed 16 September 2013. http://oro.open.ac.uk/30014/.

Jordan, Allison. "Cracking Today's Digital Natives: 5 Things to Keep in Mind When Marketing to Millennials." WOMMA. The Word of Mouth Marketing Association Blog. 26 June 2013. Accessed 16 September 2013. http://www.womma.org/blog/2013/06/cracking-todays-digital-natives-5-things-to-keep-in-mind-when-marketing-to-millennials.

Kennedy, George, Terry Judd and Barney Dalgarno. "From Now On." *The educational technology journal*, 17: 2 (2010).

Klein, Naomi. *No Logo*. New York: Picador, 2000.

Kong, Ying. "Acculturation in the Age of New Media." Paper presented at the annual meeting of the International Communication Association. New York, NY. 25 May 2009. Accessed 10 September 2013. http://www.allacademic.com/meta/p13763_index.html.

Marvin, Carolyn. *When Old Technologies Were New*. Oxford: Oxford University Press, 1988.

McKenzie, Jamie. "Digital Nativism, Digital Delusions, and Digital Deprivation." Accessed 16 September 2013. http://www.fno.org/nov07/nativism.html.

Ong, Walter. *Orality & Literacy. The technologizing of the Word*. New York: Routledge. 1982.

Plato, *Phaedrus*. Translated by Harold North Fowler. Cambridge, MA: Harvard University Press, 1987.

Prensky, Marc. "Digital Natives Digital Immigrants." In *On the Horizon.* MCB University Press 9: 5 (October 2001).

—. "Digital Natives, Digital Immigrants: Origins of Terms." Marc Prensky's Weblog. June 12, 2006. Accessed 16 September 2013. http://www.marcprensky.com/blog/archives/000045.html.

Said, Edward. *Orientalism: Western Conceptions of the Orient.* Harmondsworth: Penguin, 1995.

Sontag, Susan. *On Photography*. New York: Farrer, Strauss and Giroux, 1973.

Sparks, Kira. "Digital Natives: Six Ways Marketers can Engage Millennials." 30 July 2013. Shoutlet. Accessed 16 September 2013. http://www.shoutlet.com/blog/2013/07/digital-natives-six-ways-marketers-can-engage-millennials/.

Taylor, Mark. *Hiding*. Chicago: University of Chicago Press, 1987.

"Technology and society: Is it really helpful to talk about a new generation of 'digital natives' who have grown up with the internet?" *The Economist*. 4 March 2010. Retrieved 22 April 2012. http://www.economist.com/node/15582279?story_id=15582279.

Urry, John and Jonas Larsen. *The Tourist Gaze 3.0*. Thousand Oaks, CA: Sage Publishers, 2011.

Veblen, Thorstein. *The Theory of the Leisure Class*. Edited by Matha Banta. New York: Oxford University Press, 2009.

Žižek, Slavoj. *The Parallax View*. Cambridge, MA: The MIT Press, 2009.

—. *Interrogating the Real*. New York: Continuum, 2006.

CHAPTER EIGHT

DIGITAL NATIVES, FACEBOOK AND BECOMING A GLOBAL CITIZEN: THE POSSIBILITY OF USING FACEBOOK TO HELP STUDENTS BECOME READY FOR A GLOBALIZED WORLD

ANNE L. BIZUB

Due to technology and social media, the world of today has radically changed. Importantly, it has shortened the distance between people and cultures, making it more likely that one will encounter another who is vastly different from one's own self. Thus, in order to be successful in a globalised world individuals need to become aware of, understand and embrace diversity. For the millennial generation currently in college, being able to cultivate such openness and acceptance is crucial; however, achieving it not always easy to accomplish as ethnocentrism, which can limit one's knowledge and experience of the world, can be a powerful force in creating divides. This chapter explores the way academics have been attempting to broaden students' perspectives. More specifically, given how popular technology and social media is with millennials, it investigates the ways academics have employed these potential educational tools in and out of the classroom to facilitate the dual purpose of learning about a subject matter and preparing students for global citizenry.

In *Being and Time,* Martin Heidegger asserted that humans are beings that are in a world with others. Moreover, others are present to us through the objects we encounter. One of the ways he illustrates this point is by describing a scene at the beach where a boat has been anchored. To Heidegger, this boat, while foreign to us nevertheless points to the boat's owner even though the individual might not be present: this individual is nonetheless there in the world with us.[1] Looking more closely at the boat, however, we come to realize that the boat owner is not the only individual implicated as one with whom we share a world. In fact, even a modest skiff can reveal multiple individuals who in one way or another were involved in the boat's construction.

It is doubtful whether many individuals realize that people all over the globe are involved in producing the items that are consumed by individuals on a daily basis, given the international supply chains necessary for any given product. For example, blue jeans that one is likely to wear may have a tag indicating that they were made in Indonesia. However, the cotton from which the jeans were made likely came from the United States that was processed in China and woven into denim fabric in Thailand. The material may then have been shipped to Singapore, where the patterns were cut; they were sewn into jeans or "made" in Indonesia very possibly using Malaysian threads, Taiwanese rivets and zippers from Hong Kong.[2]

What the aforementioned examples demonstrate is that Heidegger's idea of humans fundamentally existing in the world with others has never been more pertinent or apparent. Commerce has indeed been influential in creating a globalized world that has shortened the distance between people. However, other factors are and have been at play (e.g., politics). As such, geographic borders that once separated individuals are no longer an impediment.[3] Rather, many have become easy to cross. Consequently, people from different cultures are interacting with each other with great frequency through the ease and availability of travel and the consumption of a variety of goods produced somewhere other than one's local environment. Additionally, more and more individuals are choosing to live and work in foreign countries, bringing them into contact with those who may be extremely different in terms of linguistic preferences, values,

---

[1] Martin Heidegger, *Being and Time*, trans. John Macquarrie & Edward Robinson, (New York: Harper & Row, Publishers, 1962), 154.

[2] Ethan Zuckerman, *Rewire: Digital Cosmopolitans in the Age of Connection* (New York: W.W. Norton & Company, Inc., 2013), 44-45.

[3] T.S. Chan, Kenny K. Chang and Lai-cheung Leung, "How Consumer Ethnocentrism and Animosity Impair the Economic Recovery of Emerging Markets," *Journal of Global Marketing* 23 (2010): 208; Jörn Rüsen, "How to Overcome Ethnocentrism: Approaches to a Culture of Recognition by History in the Twenty-First Century," *History and Theory, Theme Issue* (December 2004): 118; Joseph Tomkiewicz, Kenneth Bass and Anthony Gribble, "Potential Pitfalls of Ethnocentrism in a Globalizing World," *College Student Journal* 45, no. 2 (2011): 369; and Rakesh Kumar, Bimal Anjum and Ashish Sinha, "Cross-Cultural Interactions and Leadership Behavior," *Researchers World* 2, no. 3 (2011): 151.

norms, etc.[4] Finally, and perhaps most significantly, individuals are using new forms of information technology, especially the Internet.[5] Since its inception the Internet has made the world more available to us. As opposed to the decades before its invention it is now easy to access news from around the world, sometimes more so than it is to learn about local news.[6] Thus, contact between regions of the world is occurring with greater frequency, blending culture, economics and politics in unprecedented ways, metaphorically shrinking our world in the process.[7]

As indicated above, globalism, which connects us to people around the world has had a deep impact on commerce. Thus numerous corporations are going global, and to do so they are hiring executives and CEOs with the ability to appreciate and work with diverse clients, perspectives and ideas. In turn, such individuals are building teams that are diverse as well as ushering in new and at times radical business practices.[8] In short, corporations are placing emphasis on change through global citizenship, or cosmopolitan individuals.

Originally coined by Diogenes, the term "cosmopolitan" refers to being an individual whose citizenship is not limited by a specific geographic place. Rather, the individual considers herself to be connected to others in a significant way. That is, he or she is a universal citizen.[9] A more contemporary understanding of what it means to be cosmopolitan is offered by Appiah,[10] who notes that it is a call to turn toward that which is different, embrace it, and recognize in it that which is truly enriching and productive about it. To that end, the cosmopolitan individuals have a different intentionality than most when it comes to interacting with others. That is, there is a mindful openness, an interest in and curiosity about others such that their ideas, beliefs, values and behaviours are considered, not merely dismissed because they are different. This mindful openness leads the person to work toward understanding differences and perhaps even

---

[4] Amy Montagliani and Robert A. Giacalone, "Impression Management and Cross-Cultural Adaptation," *The Journal of Social Psychology*, 138, no. 5 (1998): 598; and Norhayati Zakaria, "The Effects of Cross-Cultural Training on the Acculturation Process of the Global Workforce," *International Journal of Manpower* 21, no. 6 (2000): 492.

[5] Chan, Chan and Leung, *Emerging Markets,* 209

[6] Zuckerman, *Rewire*, 54.

[7] Kumar, Anjum and Sinha, *Cross-Cultural Interactions*, 152; Tomkiewicz, Bass & Gribble, *Potential Pitfalls*, 369

[8] Zuckerman, *Rewire*, 252-253.

[9] Ibid., 21.

[10] Kwame A. Appiah, *Cosmopolitanism: Ethics in a World of Strangers* (New York: W.W. Norton & Company, Inc., 2006): xv.

choosing these different ways of thinking and being in the world for themselves. The other key element of cosmopolitanism is realizing that because one is inextricably connected to others, one has obligations to treat others not as strangers, but as kin. This is something that resonates deeply and strongly with activists, especially those who are attempting to build bridges between people who have been separated by war and hatred.[11]

From a psychological perspective, an important element of cosmopolitanism is empathy: the ability to put yourself into abeyance and see through another's eyes so as to better understand one's experience, its meaning to the other, and how the other feels about it. The noted American Humanistic Psychologist Carl Rogers asserted that empathy was essential for therapeutic change. He further argued that it was one of the most crucial attitudes and behaviours of therapists as they attempted to accurately understand the world of the client.[12] But beyond psychotherapy, empathy serves as a relationship builder, which is what cosmopolitanism advocates. Thus, as one empathetically gains access to the world of the other, one's interpersonal understanding and appreciation of difference becomes possible.

A lack of empathy and a turning away from cosmopolitanism is not without its consequences. Most importantly, it can create and perpetuate cultural myopia or ethnocentrism. Ethnocentrism is a word derived from two Greek words: "ethnos" or nation and "kentron" or centre. When combined, this term suggests one considers one's culture to be at the universe's centre.[13] The earliest definition of the term by Sumner[14] reflects this blending of terms. According to him, the phenomenon of ethnocentrism involves perceiving one's group as the ultimate reference point from which all else is evaluated. Thus, one who is being ethnocentric is confusing the limits of his or her essentially limited knowledge of culture and experience for general knowledge and experience.[15]

---

[11] Zuckerman, *Rewire*, 192-193.

[12] Carl Ransom Rogers, "The Necessary and Sufficient Conditions of Therapeutic Personality Change," *Journal of Consulting Psychology* 21 (1957): 95-103.

[13] Madelyn Flammia, "Preparing Students for the Ethical Challenges of Global Citizenship," *Systemics, Cybernetics and Informatics* 10, no. 4 (2012): 41.

[14] William G. Sumner, *Folkways: The Sociological Importance of Usages, Manners, Mores, and Morals*, (New York: Ginn and Company, 1906): 13.

[15] Michael Arfken, "Scratching the Surface: Internationalization, Cultural Diversity and the Politics of Recognition," *Social and Personality Psychology Compass* 6, no. 6 (December 2004): 428-437, doi: 10.1111/j.1751-9004.2012.00440.x.

From a sociobiological point of view, ethnocentrism serves the purpose of promoting group survival[16] and therefore has adaptive value.[17] However, in building group solidarity it creates divides. Ethnocentrism functions to boost the pride for members of a given group while regarding outgroups and its members as contemptible. Thus, perspectives that are ethnocentric serve to highlight the differences between different cultural groups.[18] In time such perspectives of the ingroup and outgroups become reified so that the ingroup enjoys positive, permissive attitudes toward it whereas outgroups curry no such favour. By contrast, attitudes toward outgroup members may be openly hostile, and imagery associated with it may be wholly negative.[19] Consequently, the differences between groups that become apparent when looking through an ethnocentric lens are frequently used to rationalize acts of discrimination and violence.[20]

Ethnocentric attitudes can strongly predict avoidance behaviours and come with biases that have numerous adverse consequences, including violence.[21] Thus, ethnocentrism is a worthwhile target for elimination, as it does considerable damage to the global community, flying in the face of cosmopolitanism and making one less empathetic and interpersonally flexible. Unfortunately, it can be a challenge to eradicate due to homophily, or attraction to that which is similar.[22] As a consequence of it, one's perspective of the world is less likely to be globally focused and diverse; what is much more focal is the local environment and like-minded people. Therefore, when ethnocentrism is combined with homophily one's knowledge of the world and others will have many gaps in it, and one's preferences will be biased in favour of that which is familiar and nearby. Thus, ethnocentrism mediated by homophily is a major detriment to the project of being world-ready.

---

[16] Flammia, *Preparing Students,* 41-42.
[17] Chad J. McEvoy, "A Consideration of Human Xenophobia and Ethnocentrism from a Sociobiological Perspective," *Human Rights Review* (April-June 2002): 42.
[18] Flammia, *Preparing Students,* 41.
[19] Jack Block and Jeanne Block, "An Investigation of the Relationship Between Intolerance of Ambiguity and Ethnocentrism," *Journal of Personality* 19 (1951): 303-311.
[20] Flammia, *Preparing Students,* 44.
[21] Yves Dejaeghere and Marc Hooghe, "The Relationship Between Ethnocentric Attitudes and Avoidance Behavior Among Belgian Students," *Social Behavior and Personality* 40 (2010): 15.
[22] Zuckerman, *Rewire,* 70.

Another factor that has an impact on ethnocentrism is human development and those who influence its course. Shimp[23] notes that ethnocentrism tends to begin early in life, and involves parents/caregivers who act as the first agents of socialization. Other adults and one's age peers further influence an individual's developing perspective. Therefore, if one's major influences are those who eschew difference or simply don't show any curiosity about it, one's viewpoint may be considerably narrow and locally oriented by the time one is ready for college. This may be even more the case if one has not been exposed to the world outside his or her immediate geographic region.

The generation pursuing higher education today (i.e., "millennials") truly cannot afford to have a limited worldview as it will be a liability on a personal and professional plane. What may be helpful to combat this potential problem of ethnocentrism is the fact that millennials have had greater exposure to the world at large due to early access to many kinds of communication technologies,[24] hence the reference to members of this group with the somewhat crude moniker, "digital natives." This population has interacted with digital technology from a very early age,[25] perhaps as early as they can remember. Coinciding with their use of computers is the exponential growth of the Internet.[26] As such, they have had access to vast amounts of information about the world through these technologies. The question is: what do millennials gravitate to? Often, it is Facebook.[27]

A social networking site, Facebook is used by over 500,000,000 people worldwide.[28] Today, it is the most popular site of its kind in the world.[29] It

---

[23] Terence A. Shimp, "Consumer Ethnocentrism: The Concept and a Preliminary Empirical Test," *Advances in Computer Research* 11 (1984): 285-290.

[24] Adriana M. Manago, Tamara Taylor and Patricia M. Greenfield, "Me and My 400 Friends: The Anatomy of College Students' Facebook Networks, Their Communication Patterns, and Well-Being," *Developmental Psychology* 48 (2012): 369.

[25] Chris Shaltry, Danah Henriksen, Min Lun Wu and W. Patrick Dickson, "Situated Learning With Online Portfolios, Classroom Websites and Facebook," *TechTrends* 57 (May-June 2013): 20.

[26] Hasrina Mustafa, Hamidah A. Hamid, Jamilah Ahmad and Amaliah Siarap, "Intercultural Relationship, Prejudice and Ethnocentrism in a Computer-Mediated Communication (CMC): A Time-Series Experiment," *Asian Social Science* 8 (March 2012): 34.

[27] Margarita V. DiVall and Jennifer L. Kirwin, "Using Facebook to Facilitate Course-Related Discussion Between Students and Faculty Members," *American Journal of Pharmaceutical Education* 76 (2012): 1-5.

[28] eBizMBA Inc., "Top 15 Most Popular Social Networking Sites," accessed June 13, 2013, http://www.ebizmba.com/articles/social-networking-websites.

is also the most popular social networking site for college and university students in North America and elsewhere.[30] Those who have studied its use with this population have found that Facebook enables today's college students to feel connected[31] and satisfies their desire to belong.[32] The problem is that their friends on this social media site frequently lack diversity. Without friends with different cultural backgrounds from different parts of the world, millennial students are much less likely to learn about divergent worldviews and information about different parts of the world. Consequently, it may be more of a challenge to become globally minded and a globally concerned citizen using Facebook as students informally do.[33]

On their own using Facebook millennials may be even further removed from the larger world and less prepared for becoming a concerned global citizen by the time they reach college because they are highly likely to consult their friends before making decisions.[34] It stands to reason that if their friends are culturally similar and have the same preferences, they are likely to lose out on discovering something new and different from their frame of reference. Complicating things further, Facebook employs an algorithm that filters friends depending on whom you message and how frequently you contact individuals.[35] Thus, even if millennials have a diverse set of friends with divergent beliefs, contacting friends who share their interests and ideas more frequently will lead them to see information such as news posts and opinions from these individuals more frequently, as well. In turn, this material will serve to influence millennial college students more strongly.

Beyond Facebook, there is other evidence to suggest that many millennials are rather limited in view and engage in behaviour that does

---

[29] Yong Gu Ji, Hwan Hwangbo, Ji Soo Yi, P.L. Patrick Rau, Xiaowen Fang and Chen Ling, "The Influence of Cultural Differences on the Use of Social Network Services and the Formation of Social Capital," *International Journal of Human-Computer Interaction* 26 (2010): 1110.

[30] Kathleen Gray, Lucas Annabel and Gregor Kennedy, "Medical Students' Use of Facebook to Support Learning: Insights from Four Case Studies," *Medical Teacher* 32 (2010): 971-976.

[31] Kennon M. Sheldon and Neetu Abad, "Two-Process View of Facebook Use and Relatedness Need-Satisfaction: Disconnection Drives Use, and Connection Rewards It," *Journal of Personality and Social Psychology* 100, no. 4 (2011): 766.

[32] Ashwini Nadkarni and Stefan G. Hoffman, "Why Do People Use Facebook?," *Personality and Individual Differences* 52, no. 3 (2012): 243.

[33] Zuckerman, *Rewire*, 110.

[34] Ibid., 108.

[35] Ibid., 109

not remedy the situation. For example, it has been found that millennials may be much more apt to seek out news that has been suggested by friends through social media, limiting what they might discover about the larger world. Moreover, these individuals may be getting a good deal of their online news from one or only a handful of sources and from individuals who are similar in background and opinion. In accordance with homophily people are far more likely to connect to current events and others that are familiar and personally meaningful. Therefore, one with whom one has little or no direct personal connection is likely to be overlooked or ignored completely.[36] In no way does this facilitate cosmopolitanism.

Taken collectively, the research on today's millennial college students, especially those in North America suggests that these digital natives appear to be woefully unaware of the world. Consequently, they may demonstrate ethnocentrism and be viewed as "ugly Americans," a term that connotes a lack of sensitivity, especially to individuals living overseas.[37] Thus, some colleges and universities in the United States (e.g., Elmira College) have identified the need to help students be globally concerned, cosmopolitan citizens. How they attempt to achieve this important goal varies. One method is to have study abroad programmes that immerse students in a foreign culture or cultures for an extended period of time. However, not all students are comfortable with such a programme, or for a variety of reasons may not be able to partake in such an experience. Another way is to provide students with guest lecturers who present on important subjects and reinforce the need for learning throughout the whole of one's lifespan.[38] This too can be difficult to provide, especially for small schools located in rural areas where a diverse pool of individuals is not readily available.

Without a doubt, direct contact with those from different cultures is preferable in broadening perspectives and stimulating new ideas, but using technology and accessing the Internet to connect to others provides a cost-effective opportunity to reach out to the world beyond that with which the student is immediately familiar.[39] Academics here and abroad have taken advantage of E-mail and videoconferencing to achieve this goal. For

---

[36] Zuckerman, *Rewire*, 70, 73, 106.

[37] Tomkiewicz, Bass and Gribble, *Potential Pitfalls*, 369.

[38] Jeff Cain and Anne Policastri, "Using Facebook as an Informal Learning Environment," *American Journal of Pharmaceutical Education* 75, no. 10 (2011): 1-8.

[39] John V. Rautenbach and Christine Black-Hughes, "Bridging the Hemispheres Through the Use of Technology: International Collaboration in Social Work Training," *Journal of Social Work Education* 48, no. 4 (2012): 797.

example, in an ambitious project, locally placed practicum students in social work from Minnesota State University, Mankato engaged in a practicum seminar with members of their cohort who were completing their practicum at the University of Fort Hare in South Africa via programs such as Skype, Windows Live Messenger and Adobe Connect 6. Through these forms of online technology students in the States were able to learn how dramatically different both the practicum placements and the environments were in South Africa and make comparisons between them. The social work students also became aware of the differences in human rights, equality and racism between these two parts of the world, which one hopes will have a personal and professional impact on the students.

In their article, Rautenbach & Black-Hughes[40] describe another collaboration between students through technology; however, this one connected North American students at the Minnesota State University, Mankato and South African students at the University of Fort Hare in South Africa, making this interaction truly transatlantic. Students at each institution were given E-mail addresses and were required to correspond with each other, answering assigned questions in the correspondences pertaining to their practicum experiences. Eventually, students went beyond the scope of the assignments, addressing topics that foster concerned, global citizenship: self-identity, differences in global environments, and one's aspirations. However, students generally discussed their practicum and what they were learning about the professional practice of social work.

The collaborations between students at Minnesota State University and the University of Fort Hare, South Africa illustrate the value of using technology to help students become more world savvy, which aids the development of globally concerned citizens. However, as illustrated in the first and second study, there were numerous technological snafus that made connection a challenge. Moreover, the amount of technology required beyond computers (e.g., microphones, USB sound cards) as well as the use of an information technology specialist might make having such an interactive experience difficult for those not in larger institutions. Even the E-mail correspondences were initially fraught with difficulties that included mail messages sent to the wrong folder, limited access to computer centres, and servers going offline; some students failed to contact their E-mail partners.[41]

As established above, millennials are digitally savvy; they gravitate toward the Internet. However, more than E-mail, they flock to social

---

[40] Ibid., 805-808.

[41] Ibid., 806

networking sites, especially Facebook,[42] which is used daily. Interestingly, in addition to social purposes, they are using it to discuss topics pertaining to their courses with each other.[43] They are also using it to study and collaborate on homework.[44] This news may come as a surprise to some professors, who at times may wonder if their students think about course content outside of the classroom at all. In fact, many college professors appear to be stymied by the popularity of Facebook. They may perceive Facebook merely as a leisure activity. Even further, they may see such online activity as an impediment to their students' learning.[45]

Despite a certain disdain for social networking and Facebook by some professors, others see the potential power of online social networking sites for teaching and learning.[46] In part, this may be due to the range of functions these sites make available to their users. Specifically, this includes maintaining one's personal profile,[47] building relationships, interpersonal interaction via comments and messages, and information sharing.[48] The latter three functions appear to be particularly valuable. With regard to Facebook, academics in higher education have been finding that its use offers the possibility of collaboration and dialogue with content generated by its users in an informal environment.[49] It therefore enables them to reach their students in new ways.[50] Moreover, students are concurring that Facebook can be a useful tool in the classroom to stimulate dialogue.[51] Therefore, exploring the ways in which Facebook is being used

---

[42] Cain and Policastri, *Using Facebook*, 1.

[43] Gray, Annabell and Kennedy, *Medical Students*, 1

[44] Tim Green and Baynard Bailey, "Academic Uses of Facebook: Endless Possibilities or Endless Perils?," *TechTrends* 54, no. 3 (2010): 20-22.

[45] Jane M. Fife, "Using Facebook to Teach Rhetorical Analysis," *Pedagogy: Critical Approaches to Teaching Literature, Language, Composition, and Culture* 10, no. 3 (2010): 555.

[46] Stuart Boon and Christine Sinclair, "A World I Don't Inhabit: Disquiet and Identity in Second Life and Facebook," *Educational Media International* 46, no 2. (2009): 99-110; Cain and Policastri, *Using Facebook*, 1; and Gray, Annabell and Kennedy, *Medical Students*, 971.

[47] Boon and Sinclair, "*Second Life and Facebook*," 102; Ji et al., *Social Capital*, 1104.

[48] DiVall and Kirwin, *Using Facebook*, 1; Ji et al., *Social Capital*, 1104.

[49] Bahar Baran, "Facebook as a Formal Instructional Environment," *British Journal of Educational Technology* 41, no. 6 (2010): E147; Cain & Policastri, *Using Facebook*, 1; and and Gray, Annabell, & Kennedy, *Medical Students*, 971.

[50] Berhane Teclehaimanot and Torey Hickman, "Student-Teacher Interaction on Facebook: What Students Find Appropriate," *TechTrends* 55, no. 3 (2011): 19.

[51] Baran, *Facebook*, E147.

is merited, and the key question in its use is whether or not it is being used for transcultural education.

Perusing the research on Facebook in college and university teaching through online databases, one finds that the primary use of this social networking site is for facilitating learning in a particular course. For example, DiVall & Kirwin[52] attempted to use FB to encourage students to participate in online discussions about course material and related news events in a course on managing diseases. They further encouraged students to use Facebook as a study aid. Importantly, they wanted to foster engagement with course material outside the classroom, so in keeping with the typical, informal nature of Facebook usage they did not require participation with the Facebook group. Rather, students received reminders about the group's existence on Facebook, and of the 123 students enrolled in the course as many as 117 students followed the group's posts and comments. Students indicated that the most helpful aspects of the integration of Facebook were exam preparation and general learning of the subject matter. However, there was no collaboration with others outside class; the intended purpose of Facebook's use was student learning through increased activity with the material.

In a slightly different vein, Cain and Policastri[53] at the University of Kentucky integrated Facebook into their course to informally expose students to contemporary issues in pharmacy management. Their intent was to use Facebook to share course content and promote dialogues with professionals in the field by creating a Facebook "group" solely for those taking the course. The authors did not require students to interact on the group site, but offered extra credit for their participation in it. Consequently, 78% of the students (N = 128) in this course joined the group. The content of posts focused on the pharmacy business and management, and a wide variety of online resources were used in the Facebook group that was created for the course. However, it appears that the main goals for the course involved domestic pharmacy management. Therefore, it is unclear how much students were exposed to pharmacy practices beyond the United States.

As in the disease management course by DiVall & Kirwin,[54] the students in pharmacy course did not require participation in the Facebook group created by Cain and Policastri.[55] Students indicated that this freedom to participate (or not) reduced their stress while motivating their

---

[52] DiVall and Kirwin, *Using Facebook*, 1-5.
[53] Cain and Policastri, *Using Facebook*, 2-7.
[54] DiVall and Kirwin, *Using Facebook*, 1-5.
[55] Cain and Policastri, *Using Facebook*, 2-7.

desire to read articles posted by others. Even so, the authors note that relatively few students interacted with each other in the group through posts and comments. This finding mirrors Facebook culture by millennial college students; this group tends to make fewer posts and read more content when online.

As reported by Gray, Annabell, & Kennedy,[56] medical students in the United Kingdom have used Facebook to share information. Therefore, they investigated the ways in which medical students in an Australian university were using this social networking site. They found students setting up groups for studying and to offer each other help in doing research. Of their four case study groups, only one was open to anyone within the university; the rest were set up for a discrete set of individuals (i.e., friends in a medical school class) whose dialogues on it were private. A specific focus was on enhancing learning, but solely on medicine, and not necessarily for medicine on an international scale.

Thus far, no studies in which Facebook was used in the classroom had the goal of teaching more to students than course-related content. This may make one wonder if any faculty members are using this social networking site transculturally, to help students expand their cultural/global horizons. As it turns out, a pair of psychologists teaching social psychology at Clarion University in Pennsylvania and the American University of Cairo, have done so. In the fall of 2012, these two individuals created a Facebook page, which their respective students joined as part of the course. Although they do not indicate the reason(s) Facebook was chosen as the primary source of communication between students, one imagines familiarity with the system by students and the features Facebook offers were key.

Students were given three assignments, one of which involved creating a method of diminishing prejudice between Muslims and anti-Muslims. When completed, students posted their work on the page, where they commented on each other's work. In addition, students were encouraged to make posts on the page, noting relevant material. All of their posts and comments were evaluated for a grade.[57] This stands in contrast to the aforementioned examples of courses that employed Facebook. Cain and Policastri[58] indicated that they did not grade students' work on Facebook, nor did they require any participation or specify the kind of participation from them. They believed that placing such strictures on students would

---

[56] Gray, Annabell and Lucas, *Medical Students'*, 971-976.

[57] Judy Chamberlain, "Teaching Cultural Differences Via Facebook," *APA Monitor on Psychology* 44, no. 3 (March 2013): 63.

[58] Cain and Policastri, *Using Facebook*, 2.

negatively impact their opinions of Facebook's use for a course. They further believed this would be all the more so for students that did not already have a Facebook account and who may have been worried about issues of privacy when online.

Even though students' participation was required and graded, the collaboration between students in Egypt and the United States was found to further help students grasp concepts pertaining to culture and group behaviour (e.g., collectivism, social conformity). While this was valuable, what is even more important with regard to global citizenship is that students engaged in fruitful discussions about cultural stereotypes and diversity and had a chance to openly challenge stereotypes about Americans and Egyptians, which they did. Given this experience, students saw the world beyond the limits of their immediate geography and came to appreciate members of each other's culture more deeply. For the students at the American institution, this appears to have diminished their ethnocentric attitudes. As the professor at this institution noted, the ability to use Facebook to connect her students to those in another part of the world was important, as many of her students are not experienced travellers who have seen other parts of the world, let alone their home country. In short, students came away with a great deal more knowledge of self, the world and others through this use of Facebook in the course.[59]

The collaboration between students at Clarion University and the American University in Cairo is unique in a number of ways. Regarding Facebook, it demonstrates how this site may be used in place of E-mail to create a more dynamic and public space for students to engage in critical thought about course material. The organic way in which content and posts flow on it seems to enhance the understanding of a topic and further permit individuals to engage each other in ways that help build bridges between them. While these points matter, the more important idea to glean from this use of Facebook in the classroom is that transcultural learning is in fact a vital part of one's education, which has the ability to diminish ethnocentrism and augment global awareness and concern. Thus, staff need to prioritize both this kind of learning and the possibility of using Facebook to facilitate it. Clearly, the faculty members from the United States and Egypt had a shared vision of making students more aware of the world that gives rise to human thought and action. This point is what seems to be the most salient in their use of Facebook. Therefore, while using Facebook is a very sensible tool for connecting students across the globe to each other so as to enhance learning, it is imperative that the staff

[59] Ibid.

at institutions of higher learning make a conscious choice to internationalize their teaching and work to build their connections with each other worldwide to provide their students with opportunities to make such connections.[60]

To be sure, college and university students the world over would benefit in multiple ways from learning about the world and gaining a sense of themselves in the larger context of it. This is particularly important for anyone who desires to hold a leadership position in the marketplace. [61] More generally, it will help young adults as they find themselves in contact with an increasing number of diverse individuals and their traditions.[62] College/university students also need to become cognizant of the ways in which relationships and communication differ across cultures[63] so as to face the realities of ever increasing intercultural communication and its complexities.[64] As noted above, doing so increases their ability to be successful in the marketplace here and abroad and can enrich their personal lives, enabling them to develop connections with diverse others. Thus, for professional reasons as well as for personal self-enrichment the millennial student needs to be aware of the world's diversity and be able to act in it in a culturally competent fashion. Such knowledge is essential to becoming global citizens who show concern for the larger world of which they are a part.[65] Moreover, it will further help students refine their senses of self as cultural beings among other cultural beings.

Facebook has gained popularity with college students here and abroad.[66] Moreover, millennials, particularly those in the United States desire to be connected to others and show preferences to group-oriented learning.[67] Thus, Facebook, when used wisely in the classroom to collaboratively connect students to others in the world may be a step in the right direction if members of the academy are serious about helping

---

[60] Ibid.

[61] Kumar, Anjum, and Sinha, *Cross-Cultural Interactions*, 152.

[62] Ni Chun-Yan, "Analysis of Ethnocentrism," *US-China Foreign Language* 6, no. 3 (March 2008): 78-81; and Rüsen, *How to Overcome Ethnocentrism*, 118.

[63] Robin M. Kowalski, "Including Gender, Race, and Ethnicity in Psychology Content Courses," *Teaching of Psychology* 27, no. 1 (2000): 18-24.

[64] Jörn Rüsen, *How to Overcome Ethnocentrism*, 118-119; Ethan Zuckerman, *Rewire*, 6.

[65] Kwame Anthony Appiah, *Cosmopolitanism*, xv.

[66] Gray, Lucas and Kennedy, *Medical Students*, 971; Yi et al., *The Influence of Cultural Differences*, 1116.

[67] Trudy L. Hanson, Kristina Drumheller, Jessica Mallard, Connie McKee and Paula Schlegel, "Cell Phones, Text Messaging, and Facebook: Competing Time Demands of Today's College Students," *College Teaching* 59 (2011): 23.

students become globally-minded cosmopolitans. The starting point is having faculty members commit to this vision for students and gain administrative support for it whenever possible. With such a vision, they need to make a concerted effort to build learning opportunities into their courses that allow for international collaborations. The ability of faculty members to do this will vary, and some may need support, but the effort, in time, will be worthwhile.

Bibliography

Arfken, Michael. "Scratching the Surface: Internationalization, Cultural Diversity and the Politics of Recognition." *Social and Personality Psychology Compass* 6, no. 6 (2012): 428-437. doi:10.1111/j.1751-9004.2012.00440.x

Baran, Bahar. "Facebook as a Formal Instructional Environment." *British Journal of Educational Technology,* 41, no. 6 (2010): E 146-E149. doi:10. 1111/j.1467-8535.2010.01115.x.

Block, Jack, and Block, Jeanne. "An Investigation of the Relationship Between Intolerance of Ambiguity and Ethnocentrism." *Journal of Personality,*19, no. 3, (1951): 303-311.

Boon, Stuart, and Sinclair, Christine. "A World I Don't Inhabit: Disquiet and Identity in Second Life and Facebook." *Educational Media International* 46, no. 2 (2009): 99-110. doi:10.1080/09523980902933565.

Cain, Jeff, and Policastri, A. "Using Facebook as an Informal Learning Environment." *American Journal of Pharmaceutical Education* 75, no. 10 (2011): Article 207, 1-7.

Chamberlain, Judy. "Teaching Cultural Differences Via Facebook." *Monitor on Psychology* 44, no. 3 (2013): 63.

Chan, T.S., Chan, Kenny K., and Leung, Lai-cheung. "How Consumer Ethnocentrism and Animosity Impair the Economic Recovery of Emerging Markets." *Journal of Global Marketing,* 23 (2010): 208-225. doi: 10.1080/08911762.2010.487422.

Chun-yan, Ni. "Analysis of Ethnocentrism." *US-China Foreign Language* 6, no. 3 (2008): 78-81.

Dejaeghere, Yves, and Hooghe, Marc. "The Relationship Between Ethnocentric Attitudes and Avoidance Behavior Among Belgian Students." *Social Behavior and Personality* 40, no. 1 (2012): 15-30.

Fife, Jane M. "Using Facebook to Teach Rhetorical Analysis." *Pedagogy: Critical Approaches to Teaching Literature, Language, Composition, & Culture* 10, no. 3 (2010): 555-562.

Flammia, Madelyn, "Preparing Students for the Ethical Challenges of Global Citizenship," *Systematics, Cybernetics, and Informatics,* 10, no. 4 (2012), 41-45.

Gray, Kathleen, Annabell, Lucas, and Kennedy, Gregor, "Medical Students' Use of Facebook to Support Learning: Insights From Four Case Studies. *Medical Teacher* 32 (2010), 971-976, doi:10.3190/0142159X.2010.497826.

Green, Tim, and Bailey, Baynard, "Academic Uses of Facebook: Endless Possibilities or Endless Perils?," *TechTrends,* 54, no. 3 (2010), 20-22.

Hanson, Trudy L., Drumheller, Kristina, Mallard, Jessica, McKee, Connie, and Schlegel, Paula, "Cell Phones, Text Messaging and Facebook: Competing Time Demands of Today's College Students," *College Teaching,* 59 (2011), 23-30, doi:10.1080/87567555.2010.489078.

Heidegger, Martin, *Being and Time,* trans. John Macquarrie and Edward Robinson, New York: Harper and Row, 1962.

Ji, Yong Gu, Hwangbo, Hwan, Yi, Ji Soo, Rau, P. L. Patrick, Fang, Xiaowen, and Ling, Chen, "The Influence of Cultural Differences on the Use of Social Network Services and the Formation of Social Capital," *International Journal of Human-Computer Interaction,* 26 (2010), 1100-1121.

Kowalski, Robin M., "Including Gender, Race, and Ethnicity in Psychology Content Courses," *Teaching of Psychology,* 27, no. 1 (2000), 18-24.

Kumar, Rakesh, Anjum, Bimal, Sinha, Ashish, "Cross-Cultural Interactions and Leadership Behavior," *Researchers World,* 2, no. 3 (2011), 151-160.

Manago, Adriana M., Taylor, Tamara, and Greenfield, Patricia.M. "Me and My 400 Friends: The Anatomy of College Students' Facebook Networks, Their Communication Patterns, and Well-Being." *Developmental Psychology,* 48, no. 2 (2012): 369-380, doi: 10.1037/a0026338.

McEvoy, Chad J. "A Consideration of Human Xenophobia and Ethnocentrism from a Sociobiological Perspective." *Human Rights Review* (April-June 2002): 39-49..

Montagliani, Amy, and Giacalone, Robert A. "Impression Management and Cross-Cultural Adaption." *The Journal of Social Psychology* 138, no. 5 (1998): 598-608.

Mustafa, Hasrina, Hamid, Hamidah A., Ahmad, Jamilah, and Siarap, Amaliah. "Intercultural Relationship, Prejudice and Ethnocentrism in a

Computer-Mediated Communication (CMC): A Time-Series Experiment." *Asian Social Science* 8 (March 2012): 34-48.

Nadkarni, Ashwini, & Hofmann, Stefan G. "Why Do People Use Facebook?" *Personality and Individual Differences* 52, no. 3, (2012): 243-249. doi: 10.1016/j.paid.2011.11.007.

eBizMBA Inc. "Top 15 Most Popular Social Networking Sites." Accessed June 13, 2013. http://www.ebizmba.com/articles/social-networking-websites.

Rautenbach, John Victor, and Black-Hughes, Christine. "Bridging the Hemispheres Through the Use of Technology: International Collaboration in Social Work Training." *Journal of Social Work Education* 48, no. 4 (2012): 797-815. doi:10.5175/JSWE.2012.201100114.

Rogers, Carl Ransom. "The Necessary and Sufficient Conditions of Therapeutic Personality Change." *Journal of Consulting Psychology* 21 (1957): 95-103. doi:10.1037/h0045357.

Rüsen, Jörn. "How to Overcome Ethnocentrism: Approaches to a Culture of Recognition by History in the Twenty-First Century." *History and Theory, Theme Issue* 43 (2004): 118.

Shaltry, Chris, Henriksen, Danah, Wu, Min Lun, and Dickson, W. Patrick. "Situated Learning with Online Portfolios, Classroom Websites and Facebook." *TechTrends* 57, no. 3 (2013): 20-25.

Sheldon, Kennon M., Abad, Neetu, and Hinsch, Christian. "A Two-Process View of Facebook Use and Relatedness Need Satisfaction: Disconnection Drives Use, and Connection Rewards It." *Journal of Personality and Social Psychology* 100, no. 4 (2011): 766-775. doi:10.1037/a0022407.

Shimp, Terence A. "Consumer Ethnocentrism: The Concept and a Preliminary Empirical Test." *Advances in Consumer Research* 11, no. 1 (1984): 285-290.

Sumner, William. G. *Folkways: The Sociological Importance of Usages, Manners, Customs, Mores, and Morals.* New York, NY: Ginn. 1906.

Teclehaimanot, Berhane, and Hickman, Torey. "Student-Teacher Interactions on Facebook: What Students Find Appropriate." *TechTrends* 55, no. 3 (2011): 19-30.

Tomkiewicz, Joseph, Bass, Kenneth, and Gribble, Anthony. "Potential Pitfalls of Ethnocentrism in a Globalizing World." *College Student World* 45, no. 2 (2011): 369-375.

Ji, Yong Gu, Hwangbo, Hwan, Yi, Ji Soo, Rau, P. L. Patrick, Fang, Xiaowen, and Ling, Chen. "The Influence of Cultural Differences on the use of Social Network Services and the Formation of Social

Capital." *International Journal of Human-Computer Interaction* 26, no. 11-12 (2010): 1100-1121. doi:10.1080/10447318.2010.516727.

CHAPTER NINE

COSMOPOLITANISM ONLINE AND OFFLINE: SOCIAL MEDIA AND POLISH STUDENTS IN EUROPE

JOLANTA SZYMKOWSKA-BARTYZEL

> "Not till we are lost, in other words not till we have lost the world, do we begin to find ourselves, and realize where we are and the infinite extent of our relations."
> —Henry David Thoreau, *Walden* [1]

Introduction

New communication technologies have influenced many aspects of higher education including social, cultural and intercultural academic relations. Computer-mediated communication provides new opportunities for constructing new space for intercultural interactions between representatives of different cultures without necessity of actual meeting in a reality. At the same time intensively developing academic mobility gave many students a chance of immersion in a foreign culture and became a significant integrating factor that substantially serves the building of a cosmopolitan society within the European Union. For Ulrich Beck and Edgar Grande, authors of the Cosmopolitan Empire concept, the future of an integrated Europe is dependent upon the building of cosmopolitan attitudes. They posit that transnational ties in the field of education and educational mobility are key factors in horizontal, "from below" cosmopolitanization[2] because they significantly contribute to the development of attitudes

[1] Henry David Thoreau, *Walden; or Life in the Woods* (New York: Dover Publications, 1995), 111.

[2] Ulrich Beck and Edgar Grande, *Cosmopolitan Europe* (Cambridge: Polity Press, 2007), 98-108.

characterized by openness to otherness. Cosmopolitan attitudes may also arise as a result of mediated communication. Networking technologies create new social spaces 'in which people can transcendent cultural boundaries."[3] In the new spaces of intercultural encounters "virtual cosmopolitanism" can be developed.

This chapter examines the concept of cosmopolitanism within the context of political and social changes which have resulted, on the one hand, from Polish accession to the European Union, and, on the other, from the intensive development of communication technologies that have affected patterns of cultural interaction. Qualitative research was conducted among Polish students who participated in the Erasmus Student Exchange Programme in an attempt to gain insight into these changes, and to determine to what extent use of modern communication technologies, especially social media, has influenced the development of virtual cosmopolitanism. The chapter also discusses how the participation in the programme influenced the students' openness to the Other and led to the development of corporeal cosmopolitan attitude.

Cosmopolitanism

Cosmopolitanism is a concept based on the assumption that a person's homeland is the whole world, and that citizenship should extend beyond the borders of states. It implies an understanding of the cultural Self in the context of cultural Others, and an understanding of cultural Others without defining them through the cultural Self.[4] The concept of cosmopolitanism was born in ancient Greece, marking the beginning of the idea of human oneness on the one hand and on the other introducing a kind of problematical contradiction. On the one hand, there is the localness of their place of birth, while on the other there is the universalism and globalness of humanity. Martha C. Nussbaum, in her widely cited article "Patriotism and Cosmopolitanism" published in the Boston Review, explains the dilemma:

---

[3] Bree McEwan, Miriam Sobre-Denton, "Virtual Cosmopolitanism: constructing Third Cultures and Transmitting Social and Cultural Capital Through Social Media" *Journal of International and Intercultural Communication*, Vol.4, No.4, November 2011, p.253.

[4] Schusterman, Richard, *Understanding the Self's Others* in: Chhanda Gupta and D.P. Chattopadhyaya (eds.) *Cultural Otherness and Beyond* (Leiden Boston Koln: Brill, 1998), 110.

> The Stoics who followed his (Diogenes) lead developed his image of the *kosmou politês* or world citizen more fully, arguing that each of us dwells, in effect, in two communities—the local community of our birth, and the community of human argument and aspiration (…)[5]

In the cosmopolitan attitude, negotiating is a basic strategy allowing one to reconcile the familiar and domesticated with the foreign and unknown, the local and individual with the global and universal. It restricts ethnocentric attitudes through thought and action based on relativism. This strategy results from openness and a desire to overcome limitations, to learn and explore. As Gustavo Lins Riberio claims:

> [cosmopolitanism] has become a metaphor for mobility, migrancy, sensitivity and tolerance to otherness, independence from specific authorities, and transcultural and transnational realities and claims.[6]

Cosmopolitanism has become a very important notion in the discussions on the transformation of contemporary Europe where the member states of the European Union have to plan, cooperate and act beyond their national and regional interests. Many scholars have discussed the theoretical concepts of cosmopolitanism which are to bring Europe new forms of political, cultural and social organization. In his "cosmopolitan vision" Ulrich Beck rediscovers the European tradition of openness and tolerance.

Just like the Stoics, he underlines the dual character of cosmopolitanism, and understands it as

> a non-linear dialectical process in which the universal and particular, the similar and dissimilar, the global and the local are to be conceived not as cultural polarities but as interconnected and reciprocally interpenetrating principles.[7]

It is worth noting that understanding cosmopolitanism as a process rather than as a concrete identity is brought about by scholars who see the concept implemented in educational practices. Both David Hansen[8] and

---

[5] Martha C. Nussbaum, "Patriotism and Cosmopolitanism," *Boston Review*, October 01, 1994, Accessed October 25, 2013, http://bostonreview.net/martha-nussbaum-patriotism-and-cosmopolitanism

[6] Ribeiro, "What is Cosmopolitanism?," 20.

[7] Ulrich Beck, *Cosmopolitan Vision* (Cambridge: Polity Press,2006),72-73.

[8] David T. Hansen, *The Teacher and the World: A Study of Cosmopolitanism as Education* (New York: Routladge, 2011)

Gerard Delanty[9] regard cosmopolitanism as a process or a method of orientation in contemporary times, and "as a way of negotiating the world."[10] In the globalized world we are permanently exposed to changes, to facing the new and the strange. It is important that we know how to react to these changes and benefit from them.

For educational philosopher Sharon Todd[11] cosmopolitanism opens new educational space for facing and researching humanity in its plurality and complexity. Beck also tells us to look at cosmopolitanism from a new perspective, different from that of the philosophy derived from Diogenes and the Stoics. It is a societal perspective – "cosmopolitan social science," as Beck calls it – which requires the development of new categories, "new grammar," "new syntax, the syntax of cosmopolitan reality."[12]

In the introduction to "Cosmopolitan Europe," Beck stresses the difference between multiculturalism and cosmopolitanism, which he places in the approach to otherness characterized by openness and a willingness to learn:

> The foreign is not experienced and assessed as dangerous, disintegrating and fragmenting but as enriching. My curiosity about myself and about difference makes others irreplaceable for me. Hence, there is an egoism of cosmopolitan interests. Those who integrate the perspective of others into their own lives learn more about themselves as well as about others.[13]

The egoistic desire to know more and to understand better seems to be a driving force in building a cosmopolitan mind and in forming a young generation of educated Europeans who treat mobility as part of their educational process.

---

[9] Gerard Delanty, *The Cosmopolitan Imagination: The Renewal of Critical Social Theory.* (Cambridge: Cambridge University Press, 2009).

[10] Daniela Camhy, Felix Garcia-Moriyon, Jen Glaser, Maura Striano, "Cosmopolitanism in Education: Theoretical Foundation of the New Peace Curriculum." Accessed, November 8, 2013. http://icpic.cmc-uct.co.za/wp-content/uploads/2013/08/Glaser,%20Moriyon%20and%20Striano%20Cosmopitan%20Engagement%20-Paper.pdf

[11] Sharon Todd, *Toward an Imperfect Education: Facing Humanity, Rethinking Cosmopolitanism* (Boulder: Paradigm Publishers 2010)

[12] Ulrich Beck. *Cosmopolitan Vision,* 18.

[13] Ulrich Beck and Edgar Grande, *Cosmopolitan Europe,* 14.

Poles and cosmopolitan sentiment

In the Polish cultural tradition, the cosmopolitan attitude has very often been negatively evaluated. This resulted from the painful experiences of the nation, which for many years lived in political captivity first under the partitions, then in a totalitarian system in which Polish autonomy existed only in the state propaganda. Consequently, openness to otherness was an unpopular attitude, and a xenophobic approach prevailed. Fear and prejudice from the past influences the present. Although the accession to the EU in 2004 sanctioned Polish ambitions to become a member of the European family, anti-European Union sentiments are very strong in Poland. The vision of the world of the EU's opponents is still built on nationalistic principles, which value everything that is Polish – language, culture, and economy, as well as ethnic, national and racial uniformity, the Catholic religion, etc. – and reject everything that is not Polish. Moreover, the opponents recognize that accepting any difference or diversity becomes a threat to the native norms, values and activities. This is why in contemporary Poland the concept of cosmopolitanism carries many negative connotations. First of all, it is associated with ruling elites who are often accused of having betrayed and sold "Polishness." It is also important that the issues of cosmopolitanism, widely discussed in other European countries, are rarely raised by Polish thinkers and researchers, and cosmopolitan attitudes are not supported in the education process of Polish children and adolescents.

Scholars and students have always been one of the most mobile professional groups, and knowledge exchange and inter-institutional cooperation forms the basis of academic activities. In Poland, however, the situation looks different. A report prepared by the Polish Ministry of Science and Higher Education in 2007 informs:

> In Poland there are no contradictions to mobility, but it is not popular or even appreciated. A career that spans from student to professor at the same university is considered exemplary. Usually a permanent relationship with a university is emphasized during elections for university posts.[14]

[14] "Mobility of Researchers in Poland." Report developed by the Interdisciplinary Team for Mobility Affairs and Research Careers at Polish Ministry of Science and Higher Education. Accessed November 18, 2013.
http://www.nauka.gov.pl/g2/oryginal/2013_05/39accfa94c30481522a0cd1d322b85e3.pdf The Report is published in Polish. The title of the Report and the above quotation are translated by the Author.

Educational Mobility and the Europeanization of Higher Education in United Europe

The phenomenon of educational mobility has a long tradition in Europe. In the fifteenth century it was already widespread, *and European universities were places where representatives of different European cultures met and interacted.* The universities were multicultural and students lived in diverse, international communities. In the seventeenth century, the educational mobility of European students was estimated to be 10 percent, and was much higher than today – nowadays about 3 percent of students study in a EU country other than the one that they are citizens of.[15]Hence, Ulrich Teichler proposes using the term 're-internationalization' for describing the phenomenon of the last several decades of student mobility.[16]

During the processes of unification, the European authorities have decided to return to the original idea of education based on the exchange of experience, learning about the diversity of the world, and building a cosmopolitan attitude. It was presumed that going beyond a national framework and coming into contact with different academic environments would benefit both parties. "Most academics hold cosmopolitan values in high esteem. Cross-border communication and cross-border reputation seem to be viewed as almost identical with 'quality,' the most positive thing in academia."[17]

The largest and best-known mobility program aiming to provide support for European cooperation in higher education is ERASMUS – established in 1987. Poland entered the programme in 1998 and, according to European Union statistics, 119,118 Polish students participated in ERASMUS between 2000 and 2012.[18]

Many scholars and intellectuals consider the programme to be crucial not only for the exchange of academic experiences, but also as an important factor in European integration. Umberto Eco argues:

---

[15] Guy Neave, "Anything Goes: Or, How the Accommodation of Europe's Universities to European Integration Integrates an Inspiring Number of Contradictions", *Tertiary Education and Management*, 8 (2), 2002,1 81.

[16] Ulrich Teichler, *Internationalisation of Higher Education European Experiences,* International Center for Higher Education Research Kassel, 2008, 4. Accessed November 18, 2013.
http://www.utwente.nl/mb/cheps/summer_school/literature/internationalisation.pdf

[17] Ibidem.

[18] http://ec.europa.eu/education/erasmus/statistics_en.htm Accessed, November 28, 2013.

> The university exchange program Erasmus is barely mentioned in the business sections of newspapers, yet Erasmus has created the first generation of young Europeans. I call it a sexual revolution: a young Catalan man meets a Flemish girl – they fall in love, they get married and they become European, as do their children. The Erasmus idea should be compulsory – not just for students, but also for drivers, plumbers and other workers. By this, I mean they need to spend time in other countries within the European Union, they should integrate.[19]

Stefan Wolff, a German political scientist also confirms the significant impact of the programme on creating intercultural relations and building cosmopolitan attitudes among participants:

> (…) a period spent abroad not only enriches students' lives in the academic and professional fields, but can also improve language-learning, intercultural skills, self-reliance and self-awareness. Their experiences give students a better sense of what it means to be a European citizen.[20]

Erasmus is thus perceived by both its creators and observers as a chance to build a new European who, while not rejecting national identity, is open, curious and appreciative of other cultures.

Students studying abroad are exposed on different situations in which they have to react with the respect to otherness, learn and understand different cultural environment and in order to build friendly relationship they need to be open to cultural dissimilarity of the host country citizens. Their real, physical presence in the host country and experiencing local culture, interacting with local people build cosmopolitan attitude.

Social Media in the Process of Building a Cosmopolitan Attitude – online cosmopolitanism

Social media create very special platform for intercultural interconnectivity and they "stimulate transnational awareness and highlight cosmopolitan practices."[21] Yet, the new media neither cause nor determine the development

---

[19] Gianni Riotta, "Umberto Eco: 'It's culture, not war, that cements European identity," *The Guardian*, Thursday 26 January, 2012. Accessed, September, 18 2013.
http://www.theguardian.com/world/2012/jan/26/umberto-eco-culture-war-europa

[20] http://ec.europa.eu/education/lifelong-learning-programme/erasmus_en.htm Accessed, November 28, 2013.

[21] Steven Vertovec, *Fostering Cosmopolitanisms: A Conceptual Survey and Media Experiment in Berlin, 10.*

of cosmopolitanism among young student migrants. What is interesting, though, is understanding the ways in which networking technology has facilitated or enhanced openness to the Other, understanding and learning about other cultures and, in our specific case, how social media help students studying in a foreign countries develop the "egoistic desire" to know more about others, and, through others, about themselves.

Networking technologies have changed the way students interact with their friends, family, and teachers in their homeland, and the way they interact with new friends and teachers in the host country. The technologies have also modified their interaction with both their native and host culture. In the pre-Internet era, when there was no Skype, Facebook or Twitter, and when phone calls were very costly, students studying abroad experienced a natural immersion in the new cultural environment; they encountered and experienced the new culture in an unmediated way. Sometimes the immersion was very painful – the so-called "culture shock" could be a dramatic sensation. Nowadays students use communication technologies before, during and after their study abroad. New media with compressed digital files make cultural products instantly available. But do the technologies assist students in understanding the host culture better, in appreciating the richness and complexity of new places and people, in integrating with the locals, and, finally, in developing a cosmopolitan attitude?

Data for analysis, aimed at showing the impact of new media on learning about new culture and building cosmopolitan attitudes, were provided by in-depth interviews conducted in September 2013 among students of the American Institute and Polish Diaspora, Jagiellonian University, who had taken part in the Erasmus Exchange Programme. The data consisted of interviews with 6 students. Four of them had spent one semester abroad (two in Portugal, two in Spain), and two others had studied abroad for two semesters (one in Germany and the other in Italy). The issues discussed during the interviews can be divided into three theme groups:

All interviewees admitted that they used the Internet, through either the university computers or personal laptops and mobile phones. They justified the intensive use of technology by the necessity to be kept informed. Mobile phones were used for interpersonal contact (calls, texting, and e-mails) and as an information platform (for checking important messages posted by teachers, administration staff or other students on the university website, in university internal information systems or on Facebook). Similarly, laptops were used as study tools (searches for materials needed for classes, researching and writing papers) and as a platform for information (news sites, newspapers, online entertainment including films and TV programmes, and listening to music), but most of all as a platform for communicating with other people. Facebook was the primary cyberspace for meeting people. Interviewees used it to keep track of their current social networks:

> "Through FB I stayed in touch with my friends and family in Poland, and I contacted people I met in Spain."

> "It would have been difficult without Facebook. I was connected to it all the time. My friends from Poland informed me about important events or just gossips. I was in contact with my mum and dad on FB and of course my new Erasmus friends were contacting me that way, although I saw them very often in the real world."

Erasmus students stayed in permanent contact with their native country – friends, family, but also Polish culture – and admitted that they often used Polish information services such as Onet.pl, interia.pl and wp.pl. They also listened to Polish and English music and watched Polish and American films or TV programmes.

The intensity of the media use was very high – all the participants claimed that they entered the mediated world more frequently than they used to while staying at home. In a new, foreign environment they re-located their home into cyberspace. Here they found substitutes for family warmth, and stayed up-to-date with what was going on among their friends in Poland. They developed an e-nearness that helped them to deal with homesickness much better.

The networking technologies were also used to contact teachers and friends the students met abroad: they collaborated on group projects, and organized parties and trips. Surprisingly, very few interviewees used the new media to familiarize themselves with the host country's culture. Their pre-departure contact with the host country was limited to practical matters such as finding an apartment, settling all the administrative issues associated with studying, opening a bank account. They were not very interested in the place where they were about to spend a significant amount of time, and did not care about the country/city/town's history, monuments, local customs, or food. One of the respondents claimed that she learned a lot about Spain because she attended Spanish classes, and Spanish culture was included in the course curriculum.

Two explanations of this phenomenon can be provided. One is that the students were not very interested in experiencing or learning about the new culture; they did not want to, or were not taught how to do it. The second reason we can speculate about is that the place they were to visit was not new for them, and that Europe, whether it is Spain, Portugal or Germany, seems like home. The students did not expect many new things. All of them had travelled within Europe before, and had visited many places during vacations. In their pre-departure time they treated their study abroad more as a business trip than as an educational, enriching experience.

> "I did not look for information about their culture. I knew it is almost like here. Besides I've been there before."

> "I did not search for information about culture. I just looked for information about the university, courses, accommodation and stuff like that."

Learning and Experiencing the Host Culture - Offline cosmopolitanism

The familiarity with Europe, on the one hand, and the intensity of social media use, on the other, resulted in a certain immunity of the respondents to culture shock.

> Culture shock is a phenomenon which occurs when an individual enters into contact with a foreign culture (Hofstede 1994). The concept is based on the assumption that differences between two cultures cause overwhelming difficulties for the newcomers who act on an everyday basis within a host environment (perceived as different, strange or irrational).[22]

Some respondents admitted that although the moment of departure induced fear and uncertainty, the fact that they had the impression that they knew the host culture brought some relief.

> "I was not afraid, maybe a bit at the beginning and more at home than in Spain."

> "Everything in Leipzig is very similar to Poland, but just better. Nothing shocked me."

---

[22] Ewa Krzaklewska and Paulina Skórska, "Culture Shock during ERASMUS Exchange – Determinants, Processes, Prevention," in *The ERASMUS Phenomenon – Symbol of a New European Generation?,* eds. Benjamin Feyen, Ewa Krzaklewska. (Frankfurt am Main: Peter Lang, 2013), 107.

Contrary to appearances, local culture, different and strange, was, in fact, quite difficult for them to encounter. The academic milieu – universities and campuses – are by nature very international and culturally extraterritorial. Immersion in the local culture requires from students a lot of effort and additional activities.

> As the stay of ERASMUS students is relatively short (...), and as they have a specific aim to achieve as far as their educational program is considered, (cultural) integration (…) appears to be a waste of cognitive energies. Students (…) do not invest too extensively in integration, but rather search for the cognitively lightweight experience (…).[23]

A lightweight experience was acquired in the Erasmus student community. The majority of the interviewed students admitted that they lived and spent most of their free time in international groups, primarily with other Erasmus students. They shared similar problems, attended the same courses and took the same exams. Besides, they did not have to know the local language – English was their main language of communication. Students who stayed in Portugal and Spain, where the general level of English competencies is low, benefited much more from their stay abroad because they were forced to use Spanish and Portuguese. Additionally, the students who studied in Coimbra, Portugal, declared that they had established close relations with local people from both the academic and non-academic community. However, even they communicated more often in English or Polish than in the local language.

Living within the international environment of Erasmus students, intensive use of networking technologies and maintaining permanent contact with the home culture created a kind of filter through which the respondents perceived the local culture. They did not experience any real cultural immersion which is necessary for a real and deep participation in the new culture. It seems that both reality and virtuality made the students live in a protective socio-cultural "bubble." The time spent in these special zones of cultural comfort resulted in a very poor cultural output – all of the interviewed students had trouble naming cultural differences, and were not in any way surprised by new things they learned abroad. For them, Europe does not mean diversity, but sameness, and there are three reasons for this. The first one is that their stay is too short and filled with university obligations, which does not leave much time for travelling, sight-seeing, experiencing the local culture, or meeting with local inhabitants. The second reason is the fact that they lived and spent most of their time in an

[23] Krzaklewska and Skórska, "Culture Shock," 106.

academic ghetto of dormitories, classes, student diners, student parties, and the company of other Erasmus students. Finally, the intensive use of communication tools keeps them in touch with their home culture and allows them to lead a comfortable life in a "cocoon community."[24] However, in order to assess properly the impact of the study abroad on building an attitude of cosmopolitan openness, we have to realize that greater benefit than from meeting other cultures derives from the self-knowledge that comes when we extricate ourselves from our own culture.

Influence of the Intercultural Experience on Students' Self-knowledge

All of the interviewed students confirmed that the study abroad and both on-line and off-line intercultural relations significantly influenced their lives, characters and way of thinking.

First of all, they felt that they had become more mature and independent. For some of them it was the first opportunity to live on their own, without the care and control of their parents.

The interviewed students also interpreted their stay abroad as a rite of passage that changed them irrevocably; and from the perspective of these young people it was the most valuable aspect of the experience. A foreign country, and a foreign culture in which they had to manage their everyday life, had increased their self-confidence.

> "The best thing for me was that I could live without my parents. I felt really independent, and it was not only a matter of lack of control, but I really felt that I was totally responsible for myself. When I came back to Poland I decided to move away from home."

A very important aspect of gaining self-knowledge was connected with defining students' place and status in the European community. For Western European students, this issue is not in doubt. However, from the Polish perspective the situation is slightly different – both the geographical location and historical experiences of Poland cause it to be seen as a bulwark of Europe, an Eastern European country which gained democracy and an open market economy only 25 years ago, and many Polish citizens still have the feeling of being inferior to the rest of Europe.

---

[24] For more information about 'cocoon communities,' see Garry Robson's chapter in this volume.

The interviewees were born in the late 1980s or early 1990s, in a free Poland, and do not have any memories of the old system. However, they are still immersed in a catching-up discourse: in the Polish mass media, public debates, and discussions, the concept of "keeping up with Europe" appears very often. When asked about their feelings and opinions concerning their status in the European community, the respondents denied experiencing any sense of inferiority related to their origin. Firstly, nobody gave them the feeling that they were worse in any way. Secondly, their study time abroad and observations of the host country made them realize that Poland, including its culture, infrastructure, and organization of life, represented a similar or sometimes even higher level of development than the country in which they studied.

> What really shocked me was that Poland is really a very comfortable and well-developed country. When I compared our schools, university, or even Polish roads with Italian ones – they are really not bad, and very often better. And we still complain.

> I think our level of education and organization of university is really good, much better than what I observed; the bureaucracy there is just terrible.

Such a discovery leads to the conclusion that, during their stays abroad, Polish students gain confidence as both Polish and European citizens. They feel comfortable in Europe – this is not an alien world for them. But does the stay abroad help them to develop a cosmopolitan attitude? There are many theories suggesting that student mobility enhances cosmopolitan attitudes.[25] However, as Christof Van Mol argues:

> A cosmopolitan feeling would be different from a European identity and would refer to identification with the wider world (…) Existing evidence suggests that a stay abroad mainly influences identification on a supernational scale with Europe, and not cosmopolitanism (…) most students who went abroad stated explicitly that they considered themselves more 'European' than 'citizens of the world'(…).[26]

---

[25] See e.g.: Lynn Jamieson, "Theorising identity, nationality and citizenship. Implications for European citizenship identity," Sociologia, 34/6, 2002, 507-532.

[26] Christof Van Mol, "ERASMUS Student Mobility and Discovery of New European Horizons," in *The ERASMUS Phenomenon – Symbol of a New European Generation?,* eds. Benjamin Feyen, Ewa Krzaklewska. (Frankfurt am Main: Peter Lang, 2013) 167.

The respondents admitted that they felt European, but only in the sense of being connected to the political entity of the European Union, or if they had to define their identity to Americans or Asians. However, within a group of other Europeans they defined their identity on the basis of national criteria, especially when it came to determining a cultural identity. In this aspect, they primarily felt Polish and only then European.

It can be argued that Europe reflects the diversity of the world now – full of people of different colours and religions, inhabited by immigrants from all over the world. It is multiethnic and multicultural, and to be European means to be cosmopolitan. The problem is that Erasmus students have little chance to experience a deep immersion in cultural diversity. The short time of their study period abroad, living in an almost exclusively academic environment, and the intensive use of social media make Polish students fully-fledged members of the European community, who, however function mostly in what Zygmunt Bauman calls "controversy-free zones,"[27] building and enhancing their pro-European attitudes.

On the other hand studies abroad seem to be only the beginning, the breaking point in building students' intercultural relations and creating new attitudes more open to otherness and diversity. Upon their return to the home country students continue their social activities through computer-mediated communication, particularly social media. All interviewed students admitted that their Facebook profiles became more international, they use foreign languages for the communication more often, and they sustain the relations they made while studying abroad. Social media at this stage play crucial role in continuing their relations with foreign friends and in gaining and developing their cultural knowledge.

Conclusion

The Europeanization, not cosmopolitanization, of the academic world was the basic goal of the Erasmus programme when it was created. Having analyzed the experience of Polish participants, it can be confirmed that these objectives were reached in their case. For countries such as Poland, the programme made young Poles actually become true citizens of Europe. For the older generation, such a status is a great achievement, something that Erasmus students' parents could only dream of. In their times Poland was behind the Iron Curtain, which on the one hand made it impossible for

---

[27] The term used by Zygmunt Bauman during the opening lecture at the International Symposium *Negotiating Cultural Differences in the Digital Communication Era,* 2-3 October, 2013, Jagiellonian University, Krakow, Poland.

them to move freely, and on the other meant that if they miraculously got to the other side, they were seen as strange and inferior. In United Europe, also thanks to mobility programmes the differences are compensated for and Polish students feel abroad like home.

This is easier for them to achieve with the social media which help them to organize and familiarize the new environment. Networking technologies play the role of a bulwark in battles over cultural meanings, and make the negotiation process of cultural differences, if they appear, much easier. In this sense, they help to integrate Europe and so-called European values.

However, the research shows that we cannot talk about building truly cosmopolitan attitudes, neither through students' mobility programs nor through networking technologies. David Hansen claims that travelling itself is not a marker of cosmopolitan disposition and is not necessary for it.

> A cosmopolitan –minded education does entail traveling, but with an accent not on physical movement per se but on intellectual, ethical, and aesthetic journeying.[28]

Purely online social activities on the other hand can support intercultural relations, build cultural knowledge but it is doubtful if individuals would be able to build truly cosmopolitan attitude "solely through virtual means."[29]

In order to gain a new cosmopolitan perspective, students should leave their "controversy-free zones," both real and virtual and make an effort to develop the desire of understanding others, and do everything to get, according to Thoreau's advice, "lost in words, and worlds."

Bibliography

Beck, Ulrich. *Cosmopolitan Vision.* Cambridge: Polity Press,2006

Beck, Ulrich and Grande, Edgar. *Cosmopolitan Europe*. Cambridge: Polity Press, 2007.

Benhold, Katrin. "Quietly Sprouting: A European Identity." *The New York Times*, Tuesday, April 26, 2005. http://www.nytimes.com/2005/04/26/world/europe/26iht-enlarge2.html?pagewanted=all&_r=0 Accessed November 14, 2013

[28] David T. Hansen, *The Teacher and the World*, 2.

[29] Bree McEwan, Miriam Sobre-Denton, "Virtual Cosmopolitanism, 256.

Camhy, Daniela, Moriyon, Felix Garcia-, Glaser Jen, Striano, Maura. "Cosmopolitanism in Education: Theoretical Foundation of the New Peace Curriculum." Accessed November 8,2013. http://icpic.cmc-uct.co.za/wp-content/uploads/2013/08/Glaser,%20Moriyon%20and%20Striano%20Cosmopitan%20Engagement%20-Paper.pdf

Delanty, Gerard. *The Cosmopolitan Imagination: The Renewal of Critical Social Theory.* Cambridge: Cambridge University Press, 2009.

Hansen, David T. *The Teacher and the World: A Study of Cosmopolitanism as Education*. New York: Routladge, 2011.

Jamieson, Lynn."Theorising identity, nationality and citizenship. Implications for European citizenship identity," Sociologia, 34/6, 2002, 507-532.

Krzaklewska, Ewa. "ERASMUS Students between Youth and Adulthood: Analysis of the Biographical Experience," in *The ERASMUS Phenomenon – Symbol of a New European Generation?,* eds. Benjamin Feyen, Ewa Krzaklewska. Frankfurt am Main: Peter Lang, 2013. 79-96.

Krzaklewska, Ewa and Skórska, Paulina. "Culture Shock during ERASMUS Exchange – Determinants, Processes, Prevention," in *The ERASMUS Phenomenon – Symbol of a New European Generation?,* eds. Benjamin Feyen, Ewa Krzaklewska. Frankfurt am Main: Peter Lang, 2013, 105-126.

McEwan, Bree and Sobre-Denton, Miriam. "Virtual Cosmopolitanism: constructing Third Cultures and Transmitting Social and Cultural Capital Through Social Media" *Journal of International and Intercultural Communication*, Vol.4, No.4, November 2011, p.252-258.

Neave, Guy. "Anything Goes: Or, How the Accommodation of Europe's Universities to European Integration Integrates an Inspiring Number of Contradictions", *Tertiary Education and Management*, 8 (2), 2002, 181-197.

Nussbaum, Martha C. "Patriotism and Cosmopolitanism," *Boston Review*, October 01, 1994, http://bostonreview.net/martha-nussbaum-patriotism-and-cosmopolitanism Accessed October 25, 2013.

Ribeiro, Gustavo Lins. "What is Cosmopolitanism?" Vibrant–Virtual Brazilian Anthropology, *v. 2, n. 1/2. January to December 2005,* http://www.vibrant.org.br/issues/v2n1/gustavo-lins-ribeiro-what-is-cosmopolitanism/.Accessed October 25, 2013.

Riotta, Gianni. "Umberto Eco: 'It's culture, not war, that cements European identity,'" *The Guardian*, Thursday 26 January, 2012 http://www.theguardian.com/world/2012/jan/26/umberto-eco-culture-war-europa.Accessed November 12, 2013.

Schusterman, Richard. *Understanding the Self's Others* in: Chhanda Gupta and D.P. Chattopadhyaya (eds.) *Cultural Otherness and Beyond*, Leiden Boston Koln: Brill, 1998, pp. 107-114.

Teichler, Ulrich. *Internationalisation of Higher Education European Experiences,* International Center for Higher Education Research Kassel, 2008. http://www.utwente.nl/mb/cheps/summer_school/literature/internationalisation.pdf Accessed November 18, 2013

Thoreau Henry David, *Walden; or Life in the Woods*, (New York: Dover Publications, 1995).

Sharon Todd, *Toward an Imperfect Education: Facing Humanity, Rethinking Cosmopolitanism* (Boulder: Paradigm Publishers 2010).

Van Mol, Christof."ERASMUS Student Mobility and Discovery of New European Horizons," in *The ERASMUS Phenomenon – Symbol of a New European Generation?,* eds. Benjamin Feyen, Ewa Krzaklewska. Frankfurt am Main: Peter Lang, 2013, 163-174.

Vertovec, Steven. *Fostering Cosmopolitanisms: A Conceptual Survey and Media Experiment in Berlin,* Oxford: ERSC Transnational Communities Programme Working Paper WPTC-2K-06.Accessed November 20, 2013 http://www.transcomm.ox.ac.uk/working%20papers/vertovec.pdf10.

CHAPTER TEN

THE DIFFERENCE THAT MAKES NO DIFFERENCE: HOW THE INTERNET EVENS CULTURES BY IGNORING THEM

CIRO MARCONDES FILHO

Introduction

The essay is a study of the influence electronic gadgets have on youngsters who leave to study abroad. The goal is to ascertain the quality of the culture shock, and the hypothesis is that electronic devices soften the shock and help to naturalize students within the life of another country. Though this is not always the case. Brazilian students when they settle in Europe and the United States, do not always have a pleasant experience, being often shut away in ghettos while living abroad; even with the help of electronic devices, and perhaps because of them, living abroad loses its sense of a conscious cultural jump. For it is living with loneliness and its disturbing freedom that promotes a qualitative leap.

I

Brazilian students who participate in international exchange programmes have currently the opportunity to make use, anywhere they go, of all the technological resources available to the companies that manage social networks. For them to carry with them electronic equipment – a notebook, tablet, smartphone or iPhone - almost taking their own country there, including their home, friends, relatives and respective urban spaces. The situation was not the same a few decades ago, when young people, barely knowing the reality and life of the foreign country, arrived at an international airport, asked for help in taking a taxi, in finding the address they were to stay at, and installing themselves. Somehow, the technologies today undo the mystique of the discovery, of the new place, of a different culture, of an urban landscape contrasting with the everyday life of the young student's home.

In the past, a student, upon reaching the new country, suddenly saw himself or herself as someone "thrown into the world," in the words of Heidegger. He was alone, his family was placed far away, and if something happened to him, he would take twelve hours to reconnect with his people and the family environment. The sense of panic would grow in direct proportion to the distance from his country. The city of origin could function as a kind of womb, with arms always opened to protect him from the hardships and difficulties of the world but not now, for he is now face-to-face with the strange and the unknown, often the harsh, with only himself to depend on.

This learning meant, most often, a leap of consciousness: having to get by and survive in a new environment, with another language and other customs, would be a way to achieve faster maturity and distance from the home country itself. It would be a new way of inhabiting the world, yet one now seen as an extension of his national territoriality.

Maturing is built by facing barriers, in which the young experience the need for immersion in the local culture, for mastering the particularities of each language, for adaptation to other food tastes, other ways of dressing, other ways of being and living distinct from their country and traditions.

Having been thrown into the world is the first moment of the life process, in which, suddenly, we find ourselves in an already installed scenario, with its history, its culture and its particular way of life. Existential philosophy speaks of a jump from a first to second significant moment, the hypostasis, passage from mere existing to the existence, from a verb to a noun, in which a being goes out in search of its achievement, it acquires a name and a goal, it surpasses, in short, its mere impersonal existence "as a flock" [as part of a flock]. But in this new stage it is still impregnated by itself, it is an identity and affirmative search. The other has no meaning. This other is only important in the third stage of the search, one where the existing opens itself to the otherness and performs thereby its new qualitative leap, its transformation, namely, its insertion in time, the denial of its self-centeredness and the connection to the otherness. At this time, we say, it *communicates*.

II

A study conducted by us in 2013 about the use of information and communication technologies among 120 exchange students from the University of São Paulo, has revealed that though the first shock still occurs as a result of cultural differences, these are not mandatorily standardized by the processes of globalization. The planet as a "global village" has had as a perverse by-product the increasing of segregation and xenophobia. Something like a differentiating "cultural personality" still survives in this first contact with the other. The Brazilians went to European countries and the United States. The first sensation was of great discomfort because of having to adapt to how others live. Some countries in Europe at the moment make it clear to visitors from emerging countries the anger felt over the current economic crisis. Augusta,[1] for example, reports the coldness of the French environment, inhospitable, even towards their own local students:

> During the presentation of seminars, the tension of the students was such that the majority showed some sign of intense nervousness: tremors, sweating, talking too fast, etc. The presentation was followed by a series of observations of teachers, not only about the content, analysis or linking of ideas, which would be essential, but also on the attitude of the student when he was talking or about an array of topics different from those the teacher had done. Minimum details that sometimes were neither foreseeable by the students (Augusta).

And this was repeated in everyday life, in which, for her, the locals reacted with excessive reserve. Augusta tried to start talking about the weather with a supermarket employee, to talk with the bus driver, a subway passenger, but did not have much success. Bartolo felt a similar feeling, complaining that the French would be "completely distant" without making a point of doing a good service, performing services so bureaucratic and without diverging from regulations. For him, this was not particularly hostile, but only a trace of their culture.

The experience of other students who have settled, for example, in Spain, Italy or Portugal was not different. The latter, in point of fact, should be warmer for it speaks the same language as Brazilians, we being its colony for over three hundred years, and have given us their culture. But no, here, as in Spain, the resentment was common. As Paula says,

---

[1] Fictitious name, as others who appear in this text.

(...) Specifically in Portugal, there is an extremely negative dislike for Brazilians, and vice versa . (...) I found Portugal a country somewhat "evicting," not only with me but with other exchange students with whom I had contact to resolve problems with our residence visa, which was problematic (Paula).

These observations from students abroad reveal more than a mere cultural difference. The feeling was even a resistance to approach one another.

[I realized] intolerance at various levels, and here, was much more explicit. Not that there are no problems in Brazil such as racism, estrangement, machismo, etc., but Europe, throughout mythical about its most "unconcerned" way to live, amazed me in this direction. Portugal is an ultraconservative country, and this was also a shock. On the whole, I think I expected more empathy than I received in Europe, and that coldness just reinforced a particular behaviour of mine, to isolate myself (Paula).

And here we reach the other end of the matter: the hostility ends up in withdrawal behaviour, and even counter- hostility. Being received so coldly by the host Europeans, students approached other foreigners also poorly received, creating ghettos of sociability that fortify themselves before the closing of the local cultures.

Some of the exchange students had spent their childhood in one of these countries. This is the case of Augusta, who had lived in France, had learned the local habits and had immersed herself in their world view. Even so, she found no congruence with our way of being, that, because of the African and Italian influences, perhaps associated with a people's colonized mentality, shows up warmer with those who we do not know. In the streets of Brazil, there are more people talking, smiling, making a noise. The atmosphere always seems to be friendly.

When abroad, the Brazilians, who are already seen by foreigners as an open people, react in a reverse way to the resistance of a Western European – in such a way, facilitating by the said the contrary: the constitution of these survival ghettos. Max Weber calls this "differentiation by closing" (*Ausdifferenzierung*), that is, foreigners and the local population not only differentiate themselves: when they differ from the environment and create a boundary between them and their surroundings , this differentiation occurs in a special way, is the self-fortifying by a differentiation of themselves, by self-confinement.

In these contexts, the use of electronic media transforms old processes of sociability. Before technology, the contact between people and the action of meeting people was more difficult, it took longer, required a greater investment on the part of each party. There was approaching among people, but this occurred only with those people who were seen more frequently. Once in possession of electronic equipment, language barriers disappear, one enters more into the life of others, one knows where the other has been, which journey and trips he has made, which new friends he has. In a way, the particular, the personal, the specific of every one, when they become public, dilutes itself in a kind of overall mix of people and activities.

Virtual sociability, breaking approach barriers, creates a field that resembles the "potential space" of Winnicott. Unlike Freud and classical science, for whom the object appears first, exposing themselves to other subjects in order to construct their representation, in Winnicott what first appears is the potential space, the founder of creation and speech conditions. There is no "original consciousness" endower of sense, but a field of "possibilitations" [conditions which make it possible]. Tentatively, we could say that the field of the Internet would realize that. After all, it facilitates the approximations...

> In student exchange, by adding someone on Facebook , for example , I got to know what trips she had made when she was in town; I talked by messages to arrange to meet, I related to people in my class to talk about work, examinations, practical activities, everything becomes more dynamic, the contents of school are more affordable and one has access to them more easily (Pamela).

However, this will only be the case to a point. The "profanation" that Facebook causes (that remains the desecration by nudity, cited by Levinas), is in no way to be confused with the mystery of the other, with his unfathomable face that cannot bear translatability in a linguistic sense. What matters here is the quality of the relationship that is maintained through the network. The students did report that they can live with people from different countries sharing issues, following their travels, relating with peers in the classroom. But no one is deceived into thinking that those relationships placate differences or discard a face-to-face relationship.

Students think that like with any virtual tool each needs to have the work of making contacts reverberate in the "real world." Vincent reveals that all the friends he made formed emotional bonds but with little interference from the Internet. Paula points out that the richest part is when you feel more comfortable with each other and use fewer forms of technology. Overall, the technologies facilitate but, as Francisco says, the human factor and the pursuit of an interpersonal relationship, of a group, ends up being the strongest bond.

Network connections actually make things easier but lack the body. We would say more, here lacks the face as a mystery. What intrigued the young Marcel, before Albertine, and that kept him in passionate despair, was exactly her impenetrability.

> I could very well hold Albertine on my knees, have her head on my hands, I could caress her, spend my hands on it at length, but, like I've handled a stone that encloses the salt of immemorial oceans or the radius of a star, I felt that I touched only a sealed envelope of a being that through the interior accessed to infinity (La Prisionnière, p. 250, quoted by Tauman, 1949).

The interior of Albertine provided access to infinity. That is the difference between electronic contacts and their disadvantage in relation to presence forms. There is a certain "stripping" of the other on Facebook. Everything a person does, he or she places in a book that the whole world can open. For some people, this stripping is complete. There is nothing else, that person is just this external skin, like the image of the onion, used by Adorno, in which, having taken off all the layers in the end there is nothing left. This is perhaps a trace of certain personalities of our post-technological age. The absolute and empty transparency. Which causes us, in contrast, boredom and muting.

Albertine, in contrast, is in herself the very evidence of instability: the narrator never actually knows who she is or was, nor do we, the readers of Proust. On Facebook, there is profanity, debauchery, usurpation, the act of invading something hidden but the face - not the scanned face that appears smiling on the screen , nor the face photo taken on a trip or a file photo - the face, the "metaphysical" face remains closed, unsearchable, being the "rejection of the expression" spoken of Levinas. It does not lose its mystery when the body is unveiled, it does not reveal itself, is not exposed. Instead, it opens us to our own undetermined journey, to "infinity." The person who we denude gives herself to the other and does not give herself to the other.

Thus, if the virtual network facilitates approximation, it acts on the other side requesting the "real" presence.

III

> (...) The Internet was decisive for that [not missing Brazil] because I could know how my family and friends were, and read news about Brazil daily. (...) In a way , the Internet has allowed me to continue to be "Brazilian" even living in another country. (Vicente)

Electronic devices build worlds in bubbles. You can continue to live in your own country, even abroad. If the tendency of the young is to not actively participate in the life of the new country, the Internet greatly facilitates this proposal. It's what Paula says : "(...) after four months, I am not completely disconnected from Brazil. I realize that my habits have not changed much, and I spent more time talking, being connected with my friends in Brazil than going out and making new friends through face-to-face interaction."

There is a certain paradox in the use of technologies for the integration of young people into new cultures. For Orlando,

> (...) The increased accessibility makes the world somewhat homogeneous in many respects, and makes a difference in experiences like the one I've had. But the cultural traits of each country are very strong, which ends up providing an experience on the one hand familiar, since products, consumption and culture have many traits in common, and different, for historical and cultural reasons (Otavio).

The coexistence in that ambiguity makes the examination of the importance of electronic equipment in situations of negotiations of cultural differences more complicated. In the above case, the Internet contributed to steady the bubble it usually creates between groups, ghettoes and communities that speak for themselves. If the new, strange, different culture has conditions to provoke a "positive shock" in one who only knew the world through his closed universe, in short, if it worked as the otherness that stimulates a breaking of the cocoon and realization of ourselves as a butterfly, then in the case of students, it has hardly worked.

> I believe that the technologies have been a negative factor for this type of experience. If the purpose of an exchange is the "culture shock," the knowledge and understanding of a different culture, and independence and detachment regarding home, technologies dramatically reduce this distance (although clearly not suppressing it). (Beatriz)

The distance remains, and perhaps even worse, since the Internet creates the illusion of the proximity, intimacy, deepening relationships.

Technologies cushion the shock with the new culture. In some cases, they become a kind of survival buoy. Students commented that if they had to stay longer without them, they could not possibly have stayed until the end of the exchange [Augusta]. Tatiana has even said that if it were not for the Internet, it would be very difficult to know something about the culture of a country.

The electronic devices take the place of personal experience, of the sensitive contact with the world, of the ability "to lose oneself in a city." Walter Benjamin commented that "not being able to navigate a city does not mean much, but not to lose oneself like we lose ourselves in the forest, for this is necessary to learn." It is the whole culture of self that is here involved. Learning to get along without maps, guides, previously drawn tours. Innovative experiments only arise from this loss of an overview. In this case, the technologies function as precluding contact with the new.

IV

But the big question, instigated by using technologies in intercultural negotiations, refers undoubtedly to the experience of loneliness.

> The beginning was difficult. Interestingly, at the same time, is that I was "forced" to live simply with myself. Had many hours a day to do "nothing." (...) Living day-to -day alone was an experience of great importance in my life. I could learn to be a long time in silence, thinking. Had more time to read, play sports or do whatever I felt like. We were, most of the time, I and I. It was a big change and intense learning, since I had always been surrounded by friends , I was never alone. This represented not only the positive, (...) I felt loneliness and despair, many times. It's a bit suffocating spending so much time without talking to someone, just exchanging half words and phrases with strangers. (...) In the end, I got used to a certain extent, to live with only a little technology, which was a very important experience for my development (Augusta).

Suddenly, being taken from our natural environment, our "habitat," acts as a strong shock. It is, indeed, an Event, in the philosophical sense of the term, that is, something which causes the crisis, which plots the story. Something unique, exceptional, unpredictable, anonymous and that only occurs once. Nothing that produces myself , but something that "collapses on me," hits me by surprise, alters my experiences, intimates me to be reborn. After experiencing this event, I am no longer the same.

I have been removed from the everyday world, friendships, common places, from the scene that reinforces our everyday existence, it inevitably leads us to the feeling of death. It seems that we have died, and that in any other dimension of the universe we observe, being unable to intervene, life continues to pass yet now without us ... At this point and – for many – for the first time one can palpably feel the weight of the surrounding, the strength of the context in one's existence, as well as the artificiality of taking the water surrounding the fish. We are called by the appeal to survive.

Augusta reports the difficulty of living with nothing. Technological disconnection send us back to the challenge of existence. We did not know to which extent our life was entangled in plots that paralyze us. And how we are unable to confront a framework to be built, with a strange and troublesome freedom. Because we have unlearned how to deal with it, with our own freedom, with the ability to create, produce, perform acts, texts, poetry spontaneously.

Her finding that "we were, most of the time, I and I," testifies to this anxiety and the need to give a new leap to existence. She had not realized that with technology there is a deletion of this fatality, that we are alone, supported only by devices. Now, without them, the confrontation is raw, naked, without mediation. We become aware of the poverty of our insertion in the lives of others, in sharing the ways of living, of the world. We realize that we have become much more distant, light-years distant from our partner or our closest companion...

> The day that I felt more lonely was when I got my university residence and did not have Internet access. At that moment it was clear: I was in another country, without anyone, in a 12 square meters room, and no Internet to speak with anyone known (Bartolo).

Even the weather helps to make it cooler when it was already cold.

> (...) I did not [feel] much [solitude] as a result of the distance from family and friends in Brazil, but because of the weather. The winter was really hard to face (...). The changing seasons were extremely striking. Each "arrival" meant changes in my mood and my relationship with my own city and my everyday life (Maria).

Some people try to overcome this feeling by travelling to other countries, leaving almost journalistically to new realities...

> In the last 15 days of the exchange I visited Copenhagen (Denmark) , Malmö (Sweden), Milan (Italy) and Amsterdam (the Netherlands), and that was when I felt most alone. I had travelled alone to Barcelona, Rome and Paris, but had not felt lonely. However, mainly when I was in Malmö and Copenhagen it was difficult because my family and childhood friends knew that I had always wanted to visit Sweden (nor do I know the reason, but it is something that occurs as a child). And when I had the opportunity to visit Malmö, I talked a lot on the Internet at the hostel with them, but missed a companion while walking the streets of these cities. I missed

> having anyone to share my happiness on having finally done something I had always wanted to (Vicente).

Far beyond the immediate needs of university education, degree extension, obtaining titles, this is maybe the great potential of academic exchanges: to provoke a real and profound change . Living abroad can enable the student to review his/her values , to discard prejudices, to insert him/her within time , denying their electronic self-centeredness and making them back up the otherness.

For some, loneliness served to develop autonomy.

> Some more personal [facts marked my experience abroad], such as the autonomy I developed during my trip and the ability to enjoy my time alone to try new things, to take riskier decisions, to challenge myself and depend less on others (Valdir).

For others, it was, indeed, a life review, "alone and without my pillars of support, I had to work on my weaknesses in my relationship with the outside world. It was a fantastic experience (Vicente)."

The personal relationship with technology is relativized by experiencing this existential shock. Augusta says he returned to Brazil "more introspective, observant, thoughtful, less impulsive and outgoing." Vincent thinks that on returning, São Paulo started to be seen differently and he realized how uncomfortable it is to live in this city, in practical terms. Gilberto says,

> Yes, [I began to see Brazil differently], especially in relation to the notorious lack of my own country and my own city. And I learned to appreciate the small and banal situations of my daily life, such as moments with family and friends (Gilberto).

And Augusta, who proceeded to give more value to our people, our history, our culture, our food, our music. She never imagined she would feel such a lack of it all in six months.

V

Technologies make the difference in the way students establish themselves in another culture and experience one or two semesters of academic life. Gregory Bateson believed that some small differences may provoke major differences in the extent to break old standards and create new ones for organisms to be targeted in their environment. He calls this *information*.

The difference that makes a difference. Technologies, therefore, would be "information" that would enable students to guide their actions in the new reality in which they settle.

But the information in the case would be the very change of environment. This does have the power to bring about substantive changes in the structuring of the existence of these students. Rather, the technology can induce defensive self-centeredness, the students permanence in their "cocoon". A cocoon endowed with a screen, keys and headphones, within which each one's only fantasy is to become a butterfly to others who visit their web site on the Internet.

The experiences are different. We can, like Walter Benjamin, use the new situation as a way to learn to lose ourselves, and in this loss, let the world happen in front of us, let it be itself, to enchant us again. As Michel Serres says, such as a rodeo, "Ulysses demands, wanders, probes, is lurking , scans the space, with the risk of losing or with a chance to find out himself . With the rodeo, one wanders as if he was a thought, one lets the eye shine in all directions, one improvises." Others prefer to remain secure, protected by electronic devices, that will show the best and safest ways.

The issue goes well beyond the technologies themselves. It has to do with the opening up of each, with the ability and willingness of the spirit of surrender to the novelty without masking it with technological shells. One can return to one's country transformed, more mature, less naive and fearful, and one can return the same, without major changes, the difference not having made any difference, having not made the information, even less communication, which, in our way of seeing and thinking, is the only process that actually performs the jump for the butterfly flying.

Bibliography

Bateson, G., *Steps to an Ecology of Mind.* Chicago e Londres, The University of Chicago Press, 2000.

Benjamin, W., *Sens unique, précédé d'une enfance berlinoise*. Paris, 10/18, 2000. [Excerpt translated by me]

Heidegger, M. *Sein und Zeit*. Tübingen, 11. Ed., 1967.

Levinas, E., *Autrement qu'être ou au-delà de l'essence*. Paris: Kluwer Academic, 1974.

Serres, M., *La naissance de la physique dans le texte de Lucrèce.* Minuit. 1977. [excerpt translated by me]

Tauman, Leon. *Marcel Proust: Une vie et une synthèse*. Paris, Colin, 1949 [Excerpt translated by me]

Weber, M. *Die protestantische Ethik unr der Geist des Kapitalismus*. Weinheim, Beltz, 1996.

Winnicott, D. W. 1963: "Distúrbios psiquiátricos e processos de maturação infantile," in *O ambiente e os processos de maturação*. Porto Alegre, Artes Médicas, 1988.

PART IV:

SHAPING POLITICAL IDENTITIES AND NARRATIVES THROUGH SOCIAL MEDIA

CHAPTER ELEVEN

PRIVATE VOICES OF PUBLIC DIPLOMACY: HOW DIGITAL TECHNOLOGY SHAPES THE IMAGE OF STATES AND SOCIETIES

MALGORZATA ZACHARA

The purpose of this chapter is to present relations and dynamics in the formulation and implementation of public diplomacy processes reshaped by the digital media revolution. The information era has transformed international relations and added a new dimension to the sphere of diplomatic dialogue. The practical impact of the explosive growth of telecommunications and information processing capabilities on state sovereignty, democratization, diplomacy, international political economy, international and homeland security and international organization has attracted the attention of scholars from different fields. The main trends, tools and tendencies in this sphere are being observed for the objective of revealing central phenomena, policies and relationships between key actors and factors involved in bringing about changes in the area.

International Policy in a Digital World

The digital revolution has affected every aspect of the social life of industrialized societies. Accelerated globalization has transformed the parameters and contexts of communication on most levels. In areas of the world where digital literacy is a standard of civilization, new Information and Communication Technologies (ITCs) have enabled people to create innovative ways to communicate, cooperate, express their opinion and demonstrate their will. By engaging with social media, anyone active in a public sphere enters a world that is much different than the one known before – shaped by different rules of the game and patterns of behaviour, where multiple kinds of logic determining actions and reactions have been developed.[1] In consequence, the rules of interaction have changed between elected officials and their electors, between governments and societies, between media and its audience, between members of different cultural and national groups. Twitter, Facebook, Youtube, Tumblr, Pinterest, and Vimeo, to list just a few of the most important platforms, have brought deliberation about public issues into the digital age. Digital reality has changed the way people are engaged in politics on a local, regional and global level, whether it is a head of state making a headline-grabbing statement, rebels trying to overthrow a leader, or simply former classmates living continents apart reconnecting. They have become tools of a wider cultural and social phenomenon: networking, new modes of group identification, and reshaped ways of initiating and developing individual interactions.[2]

Digitalization affects nearly all areas of human life and social relations, thus it inevitably also touches the way in which relations with the outside world are carried. While nations have always tried to create and modulate their reputations in order to achieve loyalty at home and influence abroad, today's technological advancements have led to a completely new approach to diplomatic practices. The information age has transformed the challenges of diplomacy, extended its scope and changed its meaning, intensifying the complexity of international interactions and group decision-making. Digital communication empowers hitherto forgotten groups and voices on the international scene. The logic of international communication and dialogue structure has become the logic of the network.[3] It has no centre; the dynamic is generated between the interconnected nods. "The most critical distinction in this organizational

---

[1] Social media in a variety of forms, such as: media sharing; media manipulation and mashups; instant messaging, chat and conversational arenas; online games and virtual worlds; social networking; blogging; social bookmarking; recommendation systems; wikis and collaborative editing tools; syndication. See: Gráinne Conole and Panagiota Alevizou, *A Literature Review of the Use of Web 2.0 Tools in Higher Education.* Report commissioned by the Higher Education Academy, 2010, http://www.heacademy.ac.uk/assets/EvidenceNet/Conole_Alevizou_2010.pdf

[2] See more: Ronald J. Deibert, Parchment, *Printing and Hypermedia: Communication in World Order Transformation*, New York: Columbia University Press, 1997; Andrew Chadwick, *Internet Politics: States, Citizens, and New Communication Technologies*, Oxford University Press, New York and Oxford, 2006.

[3] Danah Boyd, "Social Network Sites as Networked Publics: Affordances, Dynamics, and Implications," in Zizi Papacharissi, *Networked Self: Identity, Community, and Culture on Social Network Sites*, New York: Routledge, 2010, 19-58.

logic is not stability but inclusion or exclusion. Networks change relentlessly: they move along, form and re-form in endless variation. Those who remain inside have the opportunity to share and, over time, to increase their chances. Those who drop out or become switched off will see their chances vanish. In other words, networks – all networks – ultimately come out ahead by reconstructing, whether they change their composition, their membership or even their tasks."[4]

Diplomatic services quickly adapted to technical changes. Arguments about whether public officials should take to digital channels swiftly became not about "whether" but rather "to what extent." This was natural given the fact that at the centre of the very idea of diplomacy stands the objective of effective communication – communication that is obliged to use each available tool in order to achieve a better understanding. Wilson P. Dizard, in his book on the new era of American diplomacy, presents the view that digitalization "…is the most important innovation affecting diplomatic practices since the fifteenth century, when permanent ambassadors were first exchanged among the royal courts of Europe."[5] Widely available technologies are used by government members, diplomacy staff and politicians to reach out to international relations actors. They are employed in the fight aimed at "power over opinion." In E. H. Carr's view, this kind of power is not less essential for political purposes than military or economic power, and has always been closely associated with them.[6] "Twiplomacy," an annual global study of world leaders on Twitter, shows that in 2013 more than three-quarters (77.7%) of world leaders had a Twitter account, and two-thirds (68%) had made mutual connections with their peers.[7] US President Barack Obama is still the most followed world leader on Twitter, with more than 33 million followers, while the Pope is the most influential, with an average ratio of

---

[4] Manuel Castells, "Information, Technology, Globalization and Social Development," UNRISD *Discussion Paper No. 114*, 09.1999, p. 4; Nicholas A. Christakis and James H. Fowler, *Connected: The Surprising Power of Our Social Networks and How They Shape Our Lives – How Your Friends 'Friends' Friends Affect Everything You Feel, Think, and Do*, New York: Little, Brown and Co., 2009.

[5] Wilson P. Dizard, *Digital Diplomacy: U.S. Foreign Policy in the Information Age*, Westport, CT: Praeger, 2001, 1.

[6] Edward Hallett Carr, *Propaganda in International Politics*, Oxford: Clarendon Press, 1939.

[7] Data was taken in July 2013 from the accounts of 505 heads of state and government, foreign ministers and their institutions in 153 countries worldwide, looking at over 50 variables using Twitonomy (http://twitonomy.com).

11,000 re-tweeted communicates. The British Embassy in the USA has close to 20,000 followers on Twitter and over 5,400 "likes" on its official Facebook page, while Israel's combined reach with both popular services exceeds 100,000. The Polish Embassy is on YouTube, while the United Arab Emirates also created its own iPhone and iPad app.[8] Even members of the Iranian government – known for their efforts in Internet censorship – have used Twitter on several occasions to manage its external affairs: to comment on the crisis in Syria and to establish closer ties with the global Jewish community.[9] However, virtual media is not only the sphere of governors. In the world of diplomacy that has found a place for itself in digital space, everyone is invited, and digital technologies highlight the cultural and participatory features of civil activism.

International events are debated on Twitter and Facebook private channels, the communication traffic between officials and members of the public has grown substantially, and the comments of popular bloggers are quoted in the main information services. Innovative technologies are used to build bridges between people and ideas, between peripheries and centres. The US State Department has supported efforts aimed at helping Africans to use mobile phones for banking, and has set up online networks to fight crime in Mexico. Although it is impossible to draw any coherent picture of international relations in cyberspace, digital tools and processes have definitely transformed the features of political and power influence. Digital platforms have given birth to new networks and interest groups actively disseminating opinions and information, whose areas of interest and boundaries of engagement are unlimited. Many traditional mechanisms of power stayed untouched by the cyberspace development, however digitalization in politics is not limited to discourse formation, consultation or information sharing but often effects in involvement in decision-making process. The use of social media increases social capital and may result in strengthening countries' ability to benefit from an active presence in the global network of power. According to the concept introduced by Ann Marie Slaugther in today's globalised world much more important than traditional "power over" is "power with." The first refers to the political and legal means enabling hierarchical institutions to

---

[8] Martin Austermuhle, "Tweet This: Embassies Embrace Digital Diplomacy," *The Washington Diplomat*, 01.04.2013.
http://www.washdiplomat.com/index.php?option=com_content&view=article&id=9049:tweet-this-embassies-embrace-digital-diplomacy&catid=1501&Itemid=428

[9] David Stout, "Tweet on Tehran? Iran Unblocks Twitter, Facebook," *Time* 17.09.2013, http://world.time.com/2013/09/17/tweet-on-tehran-iran-unblocks-twitter-facebook/

govern societies, while the latter is the power to mobilize actors connected in a network.[10] In the future the connectivity factor, reflecting the level of diffusion of technology, ideas, and norms, would be one of the most important in estimating the potential of the country and any other political entity.[11]

In the pre-digital world, the diplomacy sphere was static and formal; Alec Ross of the US State Department used to define it as "men in black suits, white shirts and red ties, talking to other men in black suits, white shirts and red ties."[12] Now it seems this sphere, like many other previously specialized fields, is becoming less and less elite. Digitalization has strongly weakened the notion that an official is an expert whose role is to share his/her expertise with the public. This part of authority is now challenged by informal experts who, despite not having been officially appointed by any government, are highly respected and constantly pass the tests of public credibility. It is recognized that habitual international dialogue with foreign officials is not enough in the complex condition of the global power game. The real challenges are posed by communication with foreign audiences, possibly with the involvement of talented and skilled private actors who influence the public by bringing together narrative, technology, and community building. As Joseph Nye suggests, "postmodern publics are generally skeptical of authority, and governments are often mistrusted. Thus it often behooves governments to keep in the background and to work with private actors."[13] Under the circumstances of the global media environment it is becoming increasingly more difficult for governments to undertake public diplomacy successfully on their own. Therefore, "private voices," opinions and content generated by individuals, have become important as a tool for creating an image, attracting interest, and generating reactions. As the international communication sphere becomes more competitive and global publics gain greater access to streams of information, diplomatic strategies of representation and image management are constructed with the involvement of private actors. Power

---

[10] Ann Marie Slaughter, "Filling Power Vacuums in the New Global Legal Order", *Boston College Law Review*, vol. 54, no. 3, 2013, http://lawdigitalcommonsbc.edu/bclr/vol54/iss3/4

[11] Ann Marie Slaughter, "America's Edge. Power in the Networked Century," *Foreign Affairs*, 88, 1, 2009, 94-113.

[12] Jimmy Leach, *Digital Diplomacy: Facing a Future without Borders*, http://www.independent.co.uk/voices/comment/digital-diplomacy-facing-a-future-without-borders-8714293.html

[13] Joseph S. Nye, *Soft Power. The Means to Success in World Politics*, New York, 2004, 106.

has been shifted to the people engaged in facilitating and contributing to networks of social exchange and discourse.[14] And public events across the period of the digital era have proven that the impact of non-state actors or non-state representatives in the international debate is growing. The tendency is reflected in a number of events where communication platforms have played a central role for mobilizing public opinion and creating international networks of common interests, rearranging the rules of political activity and patterns of mobility within the physical, real world. Examples vary from protests against the World Bank coordinated by mobile phone, through the Arab Spring to the digital base of the protests in Turkey and revolution in Syria.

Digital platforms serve as a gateway that connects people with events, enabling them to make their stories heard in the world. The ability of effectively communicating to global public audiences has become an important feature of image-building and undertaking successful public diplomacy campaigns. Diplomacy has become more "public" than ever before; it is no longer planned according to a scenario created in the offices of the foreign service. Changing realities have created new rules, new geographies and new maps of interests that cannot be contained in formal rules or official ranks. Several types of issues have emerged:

Access to information has empowered individuals and groups, causing a situation in which non-state actors are playing an increasingly prominent and autonomous role in the ways that governments interact with their citizens and with external publics. The social conditions of determining a course of events or formal decision-making process have altered profoundly, leading to new conflicts and chaos. The digital revolution has changed the role of individuals in public communication processes, giving them a fair opportunity to participate in the forms of meaning-making that constitute them as citizens and activists. Cyberspace communication – free and uncontrolled – has also become open for a wide variety of criminal networks, militant groups, extremists and terrorists. Utilization of new technology offers groups and individuals a scope for direct action in international affairs that was not hitherto available.

Digital tools have expanded the operating modes of traditional diplomacy, providing new ways and opportunities for making an impact. Diplomacy has always used distinctive, unique personalities to strengthen its effect. This can be clearly seen in the history of cultural diplomacy or propaganda efforts. Digital technology has started a new era of

---

[14]Andrew Keen, *The Cult of the Amateur: How Today's Internet is Killing our Culture and Assaulting our Economy*, New York: Doubleday/Currency, 2007.

"storytellers" – not necessarily artists, scientists or celebrities, but individuals with the ability to attract interest and create a fresh, interesting and captivating narrative. Narratives of citizens, professionals, students, and travellers sharing their experiences and thoughts have become important components of the communication strategies created by governments in order to tell the world about themselves. Storytelling can lead to emotional involvement, strengthening relationships, and building power. "Private voices" in diplomacy have become the condition of the credibility of the message. In the pre-digital era, the message was created on behalf of the public, but now the public speaks for itself and is part of the official narrative. All of the voices build a multi-layered story that reflects the intentions, emotions and worldviews of nations or groups of people. Their influence under the conditions of the global era is increasing, in which, as Joseph Nye claims, "success depends not only on whose army wins, but also on whose story wins."[15]

The "digital divide" has become an important descriptive category of the global state of affairs. It refers to the different levels of access to information and educational, economic and social opportunities provided by the Internet. The "digital divide" separates wealthy from poor countries in terms of Internet cost and connectivity, but also highlights competences important in making cyberspace a tool for approaching individual and common goals: effective use of information, the ability of the user to be part of technological trends and advancements, and the availability of relevant, useful, appropriate, and affordable content. Cyberspace has been heralded as the "Great Equalizer," but technical access to the global net does not bring about an automatic effect. All examples of social movements developed with the help of digital tools confirm the crucial role of active creators and distributors of information.

The impact of digitalization on social change and communication patterns has been widely analyzed since the Internet became the first and foremost tool for managing human affairs. The depth, direction, and civic nature of the political impact made through digital communication is the subject of intensive debate.[16] Yet many areas still remain undiscovered.

---

[15] Joseph S. Nye, "The Rise of China's Soft Power," *Wall Street Journal Asia*, 29. 12. 2005.

[16] Michael Best and Keegan W. Wade, "The Internet and Democracy: Global Catalyst or Democratic Dud?" Berkman Center for Internet and Democracy, Harvard University, 30.12. 2005.
http://cyber.law.harvard.edu/publications/2005/Internet_and_Democracy_Global_Catalyst_or_Democratic_Dud; Rebecca MacKinnon, "Blogging, Journalism, and

The influence of digital reality on political behaviour, political mobilization and intercultural interactions has not yet been matched by substantive theoretical discussions. It is not known to what extend the Internet and communication networks are directly impacting the democratic process by influencing participation in political processes such as voting. Does ITC really offer a *technological fix* for basic problems of political activity and the trust of citizens in government? On the one hand research indicates that the Internet availability does not influence substantially public political participation.[17] On the other hand after the 2008 presidential campaign Barack Obama was called the King of Social Networking by the Washington Post, since the Clinton-Levinsky scandal *Drudge Report* created by a citizen journalist has been transforming American daily news cycle and transnational Internet-based advocacy networks have impact on global public policy making in many areas (landmines, child soldiers, human rights). Some spectacular successes of bringing social media tools to political debate suggest that organizations and politically oriented groups can benefit from this realm in achieving their aims. Those contradictions indicate that there are urgent demands for more complex research in order to understand and analyze the behavioural characteristics of computer-mediated and intercultural communication.

Virtual Worlds of Public Diplomacy

While an important shift driven by digital reality can be noted in the area of traditional "government to government" diplomacy, a real revolution occurred in the field of public diplomacy. The term, coined originally by Edmund A. Gullion in 1965, was further defined as a form of diplomacy that focuses on the influence of public attitudes in foreign policy by reaching out to public opinion in other countries, building support, and creating long-term positive associations and emotions using tools beyond traditional diplomacy.[18] The term received increased attention after the Cold

---

Credibility: Battleground and Common Ground," Berkman Center for Internet and Democracy, Harvard University, 01.02.2005.
http://cyber.law.harvard.edu/publications/2005/Blogging_Journalism_Credibility

[17] Robin Effing, Jos Van Hillegersberg and Theo Huibers, "Social Media and Political Participation: Are Facebook, Twitter and YouTube Democratizing Our Political Systems?" in: Efthimios Tambouris, Ann Macintosh and Hans De Bruijn, (eds.) *Electronic Participation* Springer Berlin / Heidelberg 2011.

[18] *The Public Diplomacy and Public Affairs Missions*, The Public Diplomacy and Public Affairs Missions Reorganization Plan and Report Submitted by President Clinton to Congress on December 30, 1998, Pursuant to Section 1601 of the

War, when the challenges of political transformation on the global scene, the role of ideas in political change, and a revolution in communication affairs had made it evident that the creation of images and information had a new relevance in international relations. The transnational flow of information and ideas, creating a fundamental base for global integration, constitutes the central feature of this sphere. Global communication simply redefines power in the world's power game in ways that traditional theories of international relations have not yet seriously considered, bringing about significant changes in major arenas of hard and soft power. "New media" has profoundly transformed the operational principles of the exercising of "soft power" in international relations. Apart from the internal communication/propaganda aimed at influencing the views of domestic societies, the focus of attention of the government's public relations activities has shifted towards the international public. "Soft power" is perceived as the ability to achieve political ends through attraction, shape preferences and create persuasive meanings that translate into political support, economic gains (i.e. foreign investments), and a strong position on the international scene and in the global decision-making processes.[19] In this strategy, the value of culture, lifestyle, and ideas in shaping events – often downplayed in the past – is taken into account and treated as an important asset. It is an important part of the concept of "smart power" – a dynamic combination of hard power and soft power that is now elaborated as the best way to achieve political ends on the international scene.

The winning of hearts and minds has become a necessity not only during times of war and occupation, but as part of everyday political processes.[20] There is a growing belief that productive intercultural dialogue can serve as an effective tool for overcoming conflicts and avoiding misunderstandings. Public diplomacy, which is also conducted in cyberspace, is regarded as part of a newly emerging paradigm of collaborative diplomacy which requires an approach that is fundamentally

---

Foreign Affairs Reform and Restructuring Act of 1998, as Contained in Public Law 105-277, www.fas.org/irp/offdocs/pdd/pdd-68-docs.htm, http:// ieie.nsc.ru:8101/nisnews/let5/easa.htm.

[19] Joseph S. Nye, *Bound to Lead: The Changing Nature of American Power*, New York: Basic Books, 1990; Jan Melissen (ed.), *The New Public Diplomacy. Soft Power in International Relations*, New York: Palgrave Macmillan, 2007; Matthew Kroenig, Melissa McAdam, and Steven Weber, "Taking Soft Power Seriously," *Comparative Strategy*, 29, 5, 2010, 412-431.

[20] The "winning hearts and minds" strategy has been a key to recent U.S. wars ranging from Vietnam to Iraq and Afghanistan.

dialogue-based. Its value was recognized in diplomatic practice long before the contemporary debate on new forms of public diplomacy emerged. Technology created a new level of interaction, adding interactivity to the static diplomatic monologue, and the pervasiveness of new media changed the extent and framework of public dialogue. The nature of the "public" to which public diplomacy is directed has changed. Today's audience is well-informed, autonomous in communication management and less inhibited about challenging the information they are given. Political authorities are not the only people entitled to disseminate visions of the world and interpretations of current affairs, although many governments use social media to present political viewpoints, and to promote culture, tourism and elements of public diplomacy that expose their audiences to messages that support a certain image of the country. Public diplomacy in the digital era is a result of social interaction often taking place in cyberspace. Such a process can be inspired or guided by governments, but cannot be controlled by them or any other single political power. It involves a variety of social agents: public institutions, non-governmental organizations, private corporations, private individuals, and social networks. Several new trends in the area have emerged in the aftermath of digitalization:

> Public diplomacy has become one of the main mechanisms for deploying soft power;
>
> Although the ultimate end of a country's public diplomacy is to achieve its strategic priorities through engagement with the public overseas, this engagement is no longer mere propaganda – it is not limited to formulating and sending a message. Rather, part of the role played by its apparatus now consists of listening, being open to others, and receiving feedback. The monologue formula in the era of interactivity is considered outdated, and intercultural dialogue has been followed by cultural and psychological change.

Many influential interpretations of reality are created by the private members of the "public" affecting a common view, group memory or social expectations, hopes or fears. Nowadays, the nature of these processes is more like a conversation – listeners in the digital platforms become speakers themselves, and the continuous circulation of messages, ideas and comments cannot be controlled. Digitalization has expanded the tools of traditional statecraft, incorporating the new technologies and strategies of the modern era. Technology does not substitute traditional foreign policy, but creates another important level of interactions that influence international and intercultural relations. Social media is not only increasingly bringing citizens into contact with their governments, but enables the creation of a platform for communication between representatives of different nations and interest groups. They all become actors in the field, and their activities in cyberspace attract the attention of others – often unknown, undefined others, who come across information and create independent channels for exchanging it. Messages created by individuals have the potential of reaching numerous, diverse and strategic – from the point of view of diplomatic affairs – audiences. Successful, persuasive digital communication is inextricably linked to the way individuals collaborate and build relationships.

Today's impact of communication channels developed by private citizens to transmit cultural content has to be estimated according to long-term criteria, but cannot be neglected. As Clay Shirky sustains, "…social media's real potential lies in supporting civil society and the public sphere – which will produce change over years and decades, not weeks or months."[21]

Quiet and Loud Diplomacy – Changing the Message in International Communication

The appearance of social media and communication technologies transformed many forms of human interaction, providing new structures and code systems that affect even actors who are not directly involved in the particular interactions. McLuhan's "Media is the message" is also appropriate in the case of the new information infrastructure. The Internet is another form of technology that has come after the wheel and the alphabet, telegraph, airplane, typewriter and television that changed social relations and mental attitudes.[22] The effect of digitalization – also in the context of creating intercultural dialogue – is independent from the information, symbolic meanings and cultural signs transmitted every second through the channels of the global web. Digital technology affects human behaviour very profoundly, changing the patterns of perception and persuasion. In order to create dialogue on a different scale, communication must adapt to the new circumstances as well as to the new dynamics of constantly changing rules and mechanisms. In the era of infotainment,

---

[21] Clay Shirky, "Technology, the Public Sphere, and Political Change," *Foreign Affairs*, January/February 2011; Melissa A. Wall, "Social Movements and Email: Expressions of Online Identity in the Globalization Protests," *New Media & Society*, vol. 9, no 2, 2007, 258-277.

[22] Marshall McLuhan, *Understanding Media: the Extensions of Man,* Abingdon: Routledge, 1964, 8-10.

unstoppable flows of information provide data, but no interpretations, and fail to explain the world. People often refrain from even trying to understand processes or relevant topics. Image-creating strategies of countries and institutions have to adapt to the realities of this information chaos, and build a coherent picture of ideas and messages. Given the nature of this task, classic diplomacy in its "quiet," formal interaction style needs to be widened while orienting the goals of public diplomacy. Traditional forms are reserved for the government-to-government level of relation-building. The evolution in public diplomacy strategies that has taken place for the last thirty years indicates that to the realm of politics, especially within its area of symbolic and identity components, marketing and brand-building perspectives have been successfully implemented. Network communication has enabled the development of digital diplomacy concepts explicitly derived from marketing – especially place and nation branding.

Interrelations and linkages are as hard to find in cyberspace as in traditional media coverage, but the first area offers the advantage of personalized views. User-generated content (UGC) poses the question of credibility to a greater extent than the intellectual products of news services and professional journalists, but is valued for its *authenticity* and the fact that it is provided for no explicit financial gain, but rather out of interest or passion. Communication in the digital sphere can cause powerful effects, especially given the fact that the technical possibility and social function of digital activities give users space for creative engagement. Those who create meaningful digital content influence and transform not only cyberspace. Visions, hopes, and metaphors are created and convey ideas and experiences.[23] In the past, many areas besides politics that involve human emotions and vivid reactions have been a powerful force for reaching individuals in every corner of the globe. Cultural diplomacy or sport diplomacy were used to ease tensions and build understanding between nations, and educational exchanges could be seen as a similar tool.[24]

While rock and roll music or the Hollywood industry were strong points of cultural reference during the Cold War era, today cultural heritage is still seen as a platform for promotion of national/political contexts. However, digital realities have profoundly changed the rules of

---

[23] George Lakoff and Marc Johnson, *Metaphors We Live By*, Chicago: University of Chicago Press, 1980, 150-156.

[24] See: Margaret J. Wyszomirski, Christopher Burgess and Catherine Peila, *International Cultural Relations: A Multi-Country Comparison*, Washington DC: Arts International and Center for Arts and Culture, 2003, 24.

the persuasion game, providing potential target groups with sophisticated and need-oriented communicates. The Swedish embassy in the USA established in 2012 a website presenting thc country through the lens of crime fiction, which has recently become a Swedish trademark amongst the millions of international fans of Stieg Larsson, Henning Mankell and Camilla Läckberg.[25] Japan has built its national brand by using mange and anime, and has attempted, with the use of digital tools, to strengthen associations with high-tech products and a futuristic orientation. These projects are at times purely public in nature; in many cases they also constitute hybrid structures between public and private efforts aimed at image building.

It has become evident while studying text-based virtual realities, as well as Internet games ("massive multiplayer online games"), that building a society of players who are present simultaneously in one of the digital worlds of games, forums, blogs and social media has created a parallel space for social interactions. In order to attract attention or stimulate interest, new codes are invented. Visual tools such as memes circulate the web, generating emotions and gaining attention. Political activities reach beyond the "real" world and take place in virtual town halls or forums (for example, the live stream of Barack Obama's speech to the Muslim world, available in a forum for players of the popular MMOP "Second Life" to watch and discuss).

New media has also democratized political relations to a great extent, and restricted Internet access has become one of the synonyms of oppression. An alternative to official versions of reality in countries governed by authoritarian or totalitarian rulers has always been seen as an important sign of the condition of the society – its spirit and political orientation.

The power of communication technology is an important point in Yoanni Sanchez's blogging activity. The author of the "Generación Y" blog, which presents the realities of Cuban society, opposes and fills in the incomplete, inaccurate, and indifferent news coverage by the official media. By creating an alternative vision of Cuban life, dissident bloggers not only advocate for change, but also provide powerful visions and influential communicates that oppose political efforts and influence popular views, making a deep emotional impact. The dissident and opposition media have always played this role, even in their traditional forms, but the impact and range of digital narratives seem to be much greater.

---

[25] See: www.swedenbeyond.com

> "They forget that in cyberspace my voice can travel without limits, leaving and returning without asking for permission... It doesn't matter that they have taken my passport. As of a year ago I have another, on which, in the section for nationality, appears a short word: 'blogger.'"[26]

"Guerrilla blogging," digital activities aimed at presenting personal views of the members of oppressed societies, not only challenges what the regime-sanctioned media presents as the only possible interpretation of reality, but also mobilizes society for change and furthering dialogue. It is not difficult to understand the potency of the "guerrilla" messages. What can be more persuasive than personal views that express individuality and freedom?

Conclusion

Cyberspace is widely used to help the image-building of societies and to disseminate a variety of information aimed at receiving international, positive attention, but there are limitations connected to the use of this tool. Certainly, digital contact cannot replace direct interaction. This can be derived from observation of the real-life diplomatic scene. High-quality video-conferencing and other increasingly sophisticated communication tools help to initiate and develop relations, but personal contact still stands at the centre of it. High-ranking diplomats travel a lot, as if promoting the conviction that communication carried out face-to-face carries more weight in terms of trust-building and common understanding than contact enabled by electronics.[27]

Private individuals have become, undoubtedly, agents of states in their international dealings, but their role in actual diplomatic processes and developments is very hard to evaluate. "Private voices" create an important part of public diplomacy but it cannot be measured how or to what extent they translate into the realization of foreign policy objectives. The ability of the digital networks of private individuals to enable effective performance usually depends on the existence of shared principles, interests, and goals. In the case of image-building activities, such as digital content produced by international students or tourists, it is hard to generate shared ideas or points of interest which could span the

---

[26] Henry Luis Gómez, *The Role of Blogs in Breaking the Media's Embargo and Telling the Truth about Cuba: Comment*, 2008, http://www.ascecuba.org/publications/proceedings/volume20/pdfs/henken.pdf

[27] Marcus Holmes, "The Force of Face-to-Face Diplomacy: Mirror Neurons and the Problem of Intentions," *International Organization*, 4(67), 2013, 829-861.

nodes of the network and to which the members would subscribe in a deep way. In the case of subject-oriented groups, the involvement of the members may be as temporary and superficial as the nature of the structures they form. But the persistence of their activity may not be the main negative factor, putting it in the context of the nature of cyberspace – dynamically evolving and fragmented. It is rather the question of whether they manage to attract the interest of the public abroad. Image-building agents are effective if they are able to construct the world for people, and involve them in intercultural, meaningful dialogue. Cultural norms form a foundation for political organizations and policy-making processes, which – again – is not measurable, but hard to question. Change in the social norms and processes brought about by digitalization underlines the importance of culture in human relations, especially on the broader ground of transnationalisation, multilateralism, and integration. Participation in many virtual "third places" may be seen as a form of bridging social capital – social relationships, which at least expose the individual to a diversity of worldviews.[28] Multiple global systems are shaping the course of events today; some of them are still works in progress. Participation and the ability to create trends and initiate processes within these systems provides real gains for the actors involved. Globalization has dynamized international communication and established the framework within which successful strategies involve cross-cultural interactions. The gravity of democracy, ideas and attractiveness has to be re-evaluated. Digital spheres and social media stand at the centre of this phenomenon. In the opinion of Megan Kenna, the effects of social media are "changing the landscape of diplomacy, governance and international relations. Social media has become an important limitless resource to connect and inform people, transcending borders and impacting all demographics. It presents a real-time stream of information in which one source can instantaneously broadcast to many sources and stimulate debate on a personal level. These developing communication methods have dramatically changed politics: democratising the flow of information, exponentially increasing awareness and quickly globalising ideas and concepts."[29] Digital communication is hyperpluralistic. Cyberspace definitely creates a space for creativity, self-expression, and relation-building, with the potential to intensify public relations and give a voice to citizens – whether they be international

---

[28] James S. Coleman, "Social Capital in the Creation of Human Capital," *American Journal of Sociology*, no 94, 1988, 95-121.

[29] Megan Kenna, *Social Media: Following EU Public Diplomacy, and Friending MENA*, European Policy Centre Policy Brief, July 2011, http://www.epc.eu/documents/uploads/pub_1320_social_media.pdf

students, members of the Palestinian diaspora or Cuban bloggers. It lays a solid foundation for the "battle of ideas," increasing the participation of individuals in actively shaping their political and cultural reality.

Bibliography

Austermuhle, Martin "Tweet This: Embassies Embrace Digital Diplomacy," *The Washington Diplomat*, 01.04.2013, http://www.washdiplomat.com/index.php?option=com_content&view=article&id=9049:tweet-this-embassies-embrace-digital-diplomacy&catid=1501&Itemid=428

Best, Michael and Keegan W. Wade, "The Internet and Democracy: Global Catalyst or Democratic Dud?" Berkman Center for Internet and Democracy, Harvard University, 30.12. 2005, http://cyber.law.harvard.edu/publications/2005/Internet_and_Democracy_Global_Catalyst_or_Democratic_Dud

Boyd, Danah "Social Network Sites as Networked Publics: Affordances, Dynamics, and Implications," in Zizi Papacharissi, *Networked Self: Identity, Community, and Culture on Social Network Sites*, New York: Routledge, 2010, 19-58.

Coleman, James S. "Social Capital in the Creation of Human Capital," *American Journal of Sociology*, no 94, 1988.

Conole, Gráinne and Panagiota Alevizou, *A Literature Review of the Use of Web 2.0 Tools in Higher Education*. Report commissioned by the Higher Education Academy, 2010, http://www.heacademy.ac.uk/assets/EvidenceNet/Conole_Alevizou_2010.pdf

Carr, Edward Hallett, *Propaganda in International Politics*, Oxford: Clarendon Press, 1939.

Castells, Manuel "Information, Technology, Globalization and Social Development," UNRISD Discussion Paper No. 114, 09.1999.

Chadwick, Andrew, *Internet Politics: States, Citizens, and New Communication Technologies*, Oxford University Press, New York and Oxford, 2006.

Christakis, Nicholas A. and James H. Fowler, *Connected: The Surprising Power of Our Social Networks and How They Shape Our Lives – How Your Friends' Friends' Friends Affect Everything You Feel, Think, and Do*, New York: Little, Brown and Co., 2009.

Deibert, Ronald J. *Parchment, Printing and Hypermedia: Communication in World Order Transformation*, New York: Columbia University Press, 1997.

Dizard, Wilson P. *Digital Diplomacy: U.S. Foreign Policy in the Information Age*, Westport, CT: Praeger, 2001.

Effing, Robin, Jos Van Hillegersberg and Theo Huibers, "Social Media and Political Participation: Are Facebook, Twitter and YouTube Democratizing Our Political Systems?" in: Efthimios Tambouris, Ann Macintosh and Hans De Bruijn, (eds.) *Electronic Participation* Springer Berlin / Heidelberg 2011.

Gómez, Henry Luis, *The Role of Blogs in Breaking the Media's Embargo and Telling the Truth about Cuba: Comment*, 2008, http://www.ascecuba.org/publications/proceedings/volume20/pdfs/henken.pdf

Holmes, Marcus "The Force of Face-to-Face Diplomacy: Mirror Neurons and the Problem of Intentions," *International Organization*, 4(67), 2013.

Keen, Andrew *The Cult of the Amateur: How Today's Internet is Killing our Culture and Assaulting our Economy*, New York: Doubleday/ Currency, 2007.

Kenna, Megan *Social Media: Following EU Public Diplomacy, and Friending MENA*, European Policy Centre Policy Brief, July 2011, http://www.epc.eu/documents/uploads/pub_1320_social_media.pdf

Kroenig, Matthew, Melissa McAdam, and Steven Weber, "Taking Soft Power Seriously," *Comparative Strategy*, 29, 5, 2010.

Lakoff, George and Marc Johnson, *Metaphors We Live By*, Chicago: University of Chicago Press, 1980.

Leach, Jimmy *Digital Diplomacy: Facing a Future without Borders*, http://www.independent.co.uk/voices/comment/digital-diplomacy-facing-a-future-without-borders-8714293.html

MacKinnon, Rebecca "Blogging, Journalism, and Credibility: Battleground and Common Ground," Berkman Center for Internet and Democracy, Harvard University, 01.02.2005, http://cyber.law.harvard.edu/publications/2005/Blogging_Journalism_Credibility

McLuhan, Marshall, *Understanding Media: the Extensions of Man*, Abingdon: Routledge, 1964.

Melissen, Jan (ed.), *The New Public Diplomacy. Soft Power in International Relations*, New York: Palgrave Macmillan, 2007.

Nye, Joseph S. *Bound to Lead: The Changing Nature of American Power*, New York: Basic Books, 1990.

—. *Soft Power. The Means to Success in World Politics*, New York, 2004.

—. "The Rise of China's Soft Power," *Wall Street Journal Asia*, 29. 12. 2005.

Shirky, Clay "Technology, the Public Sphere, and Political Change," *Foreign Affairs*, January/February 2011.

Slaughter, Ann Marie "America's Edge. Power in the Networked Century", *Foreign Affairs*, 88, 1, 2009, 94-113.

—. "Filling Power Vacuums in the New Global Legal Order", *Boston College Law Review*, vol. 54, no. 3, 2013, http://lawdigitalcommonsbc.edu/bclr/vol54/iss3/4

Stout, David "Tweet on Tehran? Iran Unblocks Twitter, Facebook," *Time* 17.09.2013, http://world.time.com/2013/09/17/tweet-on-tehran-iran-unblocks-twitter-facebook/

The Public Diplomacy and Public Affairs Missions, The Public Diplomacy and Public Affairs Missions Reorganization Plan and Report Submitted by President Clinton to Congress on December 30, 1998, Pursuant to Section 1601 of the Foreign Affairs Reform and Restructuring Act of 1998, as Contained in Public Law 105-277, www.fas.org/irp/offdocs/pdd/pdd-68-docs.htm, http://ieie.nsc.ru:8101/nisnews/let5/easa.htm.

Wall, Melissa A. "Social Movements and Email: Expressions of Online Identity in the Globalization Protests," *New Media & Society*, vol. 9, no 2, 2007, 258-277.

Wyszomirski, Margaret J., Christopher Burgess and Catherine Peila, *International Cultural Relations: A Multi-Country Comparison*, Washington DC: Arts International and Center for Arts and Culture, 2003.

CHAPTER TWELVE

DISCURSIVE CROSSINGS AND THE EMERGENCE OF A MULTIPLE POLITICAL SELF IN SOCIAL MEDIA

JASMIN SIRI

1. Introduction and Epistemological Interest: Observing the Politics of Social Media

How is cultural difference negotiated in the digital communication era?[1] The question points towards the need for a deeper understanding of emergent forms of interaction between media and users. It strives for a deeper understanding of the influence, tools, and interfaces that social media exercise on intercultural contacts and relationships. In the following I want to examine the influence of social media on political communication. How do social media shape the political as a social field? What kind of political subjects emerge in social media? Do social media change the way we discuss and argue about political issues? Are social media apolitical or do they even produce new forms of solidarity?

Since the disorganization of traditional patterns and individualization shape the politics of modernity, the fabrication of political identities has been revealed as a laborious and precarious act.[2] But the membership in political parties or movements is transformed not only by the loss of

---

[1] This article builds on a speech given at the international symposium "Negotiating cultural differences in the digital communications era," October 3rd, 2013. I would like to express my thanks to the anonymous reviewers and to the editor Garry Robson for their helpful comments.

[2] Cf. Rose, Nikolas and Peter Miller, "Political power beyond the State: problematics of government." *British Journal of Sociology*, Vol. 61 (2010) (s1): 271-303 and Bauman, Zygmunt, *Life in Fragments. Essays in Postmodern Morality* (Cambridge, MA: Basil Blackwell, 1995).

traditional embedding or class consciousness,[3] but also by the emergence of new media and new forms of political communications that strongly shape and influence the culture of the political.

Theoretically, my argumentation follows a (de-)constructivist tradition. I will refer to discourse analytical, systems-theoretical and postmodern sociological approaches as well as to constructivist media theory. This is because I am interested in understanding the emergent processes of media use in political communication. I am interested in how interfaces create a political self that is very much dependent on the rules and structures of every single social medium.[4] The process of "becoming/being a political self" I define as a process of interpellation. The interpellation of subjects is created by specific cultural, organizational and social normativities.[5] I will try to separate this process of interpellation from the political as a systematic field of modern society. Political communication I define with Niklas Luhmann as any communication that longs for a decision that is legitimately binding and obligatory for a certain collective. The medium of political communication is power.[6] Politics is a functional system of modern society, which follows the code of having power/having no power. In democracy that code is redoubled in the distinction of government and opposition.[7] These are the most important influences and the ideas I am going to use and explicate further in the following argumentation.

Empirically, I draw on data from three studies and follow-up observations and interpretations to those studies: The first study analyzed with a qualitative approach the change of party membership in the established German parties. The empirical data consists of a discourse analysis of German academic literature and medial communication about parties since 1910, campaign material from 1920-2009 and 23 narrative interviews with party-members of different functions (to range from

---

[3] Giddens, Anthony, *The consequences of modernity* (Cambridge: Polity Press/ Blackwell, 1990).

[4] Here I follow Marshall McLuhan's dictum that the medium is the message/massage. C.f. McLuhan, Marshall, *Understanding Media: The Extensions of Man* (Berkley: Ginko Press, 2002).

[5] Cf. Foucault, Michel, *Dispositive der Macht. Über Sexualität, Wissen und Wahrheit* (Berlin: Merve, 1978) and Butler, Judith, *The Psychic Life of Power. Theories in Subjection* (Stanford: Stanford University Press, 1997).

[6] Luhmann, Niklas, *Die Politik der Gesellschaft* (Frankfurt/M.: Suhrkamp, 2002), 32.

[7] Luhmann, *Die Politik der Gesellschaft*, 100.

members of government to base-members) and their political advisors.[8] The second study undertook a quantitative and qualitative inquiry into the political communication of parties and their members on Facebook.[9] The third study analyzed political communications on Twitter with a qualitative approach.[10] The studies presume that every user interface promotes specific connectivities and thereby forms the communications of the users. The questions of the research can thus be summarized as follows: How do politicians and parties use social media, how do they interact with other politicians and with the public, what public do they envision, in which way is the communication of actors formed by the medium, which restrictions and connectivities can be observed, how does the political self appear in the medium, and: which performances are succeeding and how does thc medium operationalise a successful performance? Since the collected empirical material originates from German studies I will just translate a very few examples and generally draw on re-narrations and interpretations of this data.

So why is it interesting to observe the web-practices of political protagonists with a (de-)constructivist agenda? By taking a closer look to the web communication of politicians and citizens the fragility and processuality of political self-descriptions and performances comes to the fore. We can observe that every social medium constructs a unique idea of success and successful communication – and therefore a unique political performance. It seems, that the political and the political self multiplies corresponding to the variety of political contexts. There are crossings between the political and politics of life-style that seem to work without political objectives or an idea of long-term solidarity with a special group or defined ideologies.

Referring to empirical examples I am going to ask in the first step how political identities are shaped and influenced by media practices (2.). By contrasting the different empirical findings I demonstrate how different

---

[8] Cf. Siri, Jasmin, *Parteien. Zur Soziologie einer politischen Form* (Wiesbaden: Springer VS, 2012).

[9] Cf. Siri, Jasmin, Melchner, Miriam and Anna Wolff, 2012, "The Political Network - Parteien und politische Kommunikation auf Facebook", in: *Kommunikation @ Gesellschaft – „Phänomen Facebook*, eds. Christian Stegbauer, Jan-Hinrik Schmidt, Klaus Schönberger und Nils Zurawski, 2012, accessed September, 13, 2013, http://www.ssoar.info/ssoar/View/?resid=28273.

[10] Cf. Siri, Jasmin and Katharina Seßler, *Twitterpolitik. Politische Inszenierungen in einem neuen Medium. Mit einem Vorwort von Lutz Hachmeister* (Berlin/Köln: IfM. Gefördert von der Stiftung Mercator, 2013), accessed September, 13. 2013, http://medienpolitik.eu/cms/media/pdf/Twitterpolitik.pdf.

social media create different forms of the political, the politician or the political movement. I will argue that every medium produces a specific aesthetic and narration of politics, political collectives and a political self. Secondly, I am going to ask if there is a significant shift in the politics of social media; such as in practices of solidarity and engagement (3.).

2. The Multiplicity of the Political Self in Social Media

What are the terms and exclusions which are shaping the process of being an addressable political identity (a citizen, a politician, a critical observant, a subversive or member of an opposition group, etc.) in media practices? I will argue that the interface forms a political self that would not be existent without the medium's autopoietic logics. This quality of the media leads to the multiplication of the political persona as well as the political public in medial practices. The difference between TV or printed media and the dynamics of social media is decisive. The public on Twitter is not the same as on Facebook and what we see depends on how we use the medium's structures. While every reader of a newspaper consumes the same articles, the users of social media observe different images that are heavily dependent on real-time-processes. At first, I will be taking a look at some selected empirical findings on how the medium forms the political communication and performance on Facebook (2.1) and Twitter (2.2). Subsequently, I am going to discuss the empirical findings theoretically (2.3).

2.1 Politics and Politicians in the Medium of Friendship

Following Marshall McLuhan's guideline that the medium is both the massage and the message (1994) the empirical observation of Facebook asks for the medium's structuring effects and demands on the users. In the mixed-method-designed study conducted by Miriam Melchner, Anna Wolff and myself we undertook a qualitative and quantitative inquiry of political communication on Facebook. By observing the Facebook-communications of selected politicians and parties over a six-week-period we concluded that political communication on Facebook follows a code of like and dislike resp. and in the slightly "Schmittian" language of the medium: the distinction between friend and fiend is reactualized as the distinction of friend and the invisible, disregarded non-friend.[11] Facebook promotes a politics of friendship. By its very structure Facebook prefers

[11] Siri, Melchner and Wolff, *The Political Network*, 22-26.

consensus. The code of friendship and the medium's questions "What are you doing?" or "How do you feel?" displayed on the cover page of Facebook as well promotes personal and intimate communications. This is why a lot of politicians communicate not only in their political role but display their private lives like average users. While one parliamentarian writes about cutting her lawn, another one posts numerous pictures of his dog. Besides those private communications we found a lot of party-related content which is only interesting for other party members and those who already agree with a political position. This is, because conflict is somehow hidden and hard to articulate in a medium that is constantly promoting semantics of friendship and agreement. Since friendship and membership are usually overlapping in the politics of Facebook, Social Democrats befriend other Social Democrats, Christian Democrats other Christian Democrats etc. Nonetheless, most German parliamentarians feel attracted towards the medium or if not attracted, forced to participate. In this context it might be interesting to remember that more and more reports on Facebook's "overaging" have been published recently. While young people are leaving the network, more and more older people subscribe to it.

But what is the effect of Facebook usage on parties and organizing? The following passage from an interview with an advisor of the German liberal party, FDP, shows that engaging in social media is connected to the myth of the Internet as a space of boundless possibilities:

> "The point is, well, many tried to copy the Obama-Campaign And said: 'He did that thing with that Internet and he raised millions in funding. So let's make a website and be millionaires.' That is what some people were saying, you know? 'If Obama can do it, why can't we do it?' And I had to bring those guys back to earth by saying: Yeah, very nice that Obama had such a super campaign but this is not the USA. This is not the Obama-Campaign. This is Germany."[12]

The myth of the Internet as a space of unimaginable possibilities for political campaigning irritates organizations, which must now hold off the phantasmatic idealizations of their members, journalists and advisors at the same time. While politics on Facebook works with an affirmation of party-related content and a strong displaying of a private politician in public (politicians talk about cutting the lawn, sick children and the love for their partners) the performance of politicians on Twitter works differently.

[12] Translated by the author.

2.2 Politics and Politicians on Twitter

> "Twitter is like a tragically hip New York night club. It is a cool, easy way for companies to engage customers in social media. But the experience can be loud and crowded." (Bob Warfield)

We observed the twitterwalls of thirteen German politicians for four weeks, counting their followers and observing their behaviour aiming at a typology of political language on Twitter (Siri & Seßler 2013). What is interesting about Twitter is that politicians of different parties interact strongly with each other in an *ironic* way. For example, the German minister of the environment, a Christian Democrat, often jokes and argues with a prominent member of the Green Party. Both are strong users of Twitter and therefore perform nicely on the stage of their followers' interest. The performance follows the idea of Twitter that the self can only be visible by giving up the agency over the distribution of messages – and communicate anyway. If both were interested in what their communities may think about their behaviour, they could not perform this stage play. There is no professionalized use of Twitter in German election campaigns, yet. German political Twitter is not ruled by politicians but rather by journalists, trolls and political bloggers.

> "It was choosing people for the team who not only were creative – and knew their social media shit – but were really kind of fanatical about fact checking and accuracy. It was getting people that understood there had to be serious fear of God before posting anything."

This is how Laura Olin, a strategist in the 2011 Obama campaign, described the process of picking her staff.[13] While professionalized campaigns in the US are all about the distinction of channels and professional accuracy in the handling of diverse publics, the use of social media in Germany still is "handicraft work" for and by a small group of web-affine politicians. There is yet no conversion of social media strategy for electoral campaigns that operate with the same theoretical or empirical background. This makes the "Obama myth" even more powerful semantics.

---

[13] Ries, Brian, "Meet the Mind Behind Barack Obama's Online Persona", *Storyboard*, November 19, 2012, accessed September 13, 2013, http://storyboard.tumblr.com/post/36063978132/meet-the-mind-behind-barack-obamas-online.

As for the use of Twitter by activist there was one prominent campaign that received the attention of the established media. Using the Hashtag *#aufschrei* ("outcry") feminists started a discussion about sexual harassment and gender discrimination. The vast majority of posts did not discuss theoretical questions or questions of political power but reported the personal stories of users in 140 characters. In September 2013 efforts have been made to repeat the campaign with the Hashtag *#schauhin* ("look closely"). *#schauhin* aims to call the users attention to *"Alltagsrassismus"* ("everyday racism"). Both Hashtags were still in use in January 2014. A characteristic of political communication on Twitter seems to be the expression of anger or revulsion about a societal state without the deduction of political programmes to abolish it. "In this combination of focusing on a single task of demolition with leaving vague the image of the world the day after the demolition, lies the strength of people in the streets – as well as their weakness."[14] This quote of Zygmunt Bauman applies well to Twitter activism as in *#aufschrei* or *#schauhin*. The majority of contributions to both campaigns express a strong urge for change, without elaborating on concrete policies. They prefer moral communication to solution-orientation. It would seem that web activism on the one hand is a great possibility to negotiate political identities without the need to "come out" in the public sphere. On the other hand, this missing link to other political contexts leads to the inefficacy of those campaigns, to hubris and disillusionment.

As for the concrete interaction the hardest thing for those campaigns seems to deal with the personal harassment by (in this cases: antifeminist or neo-Nazi) trolls. The trolls operate out of anonymity and multiple user accounts. They use the hashtags to attack the activists – or to say it in a less normative way – to hold a different view against the feminist or antiracist activists. This exhausting and appalling side-effect of web activism often leads to the sadness, anger and exhaustion of web-activists. While activism on Facebook can be very easily protected by blocking or reporting offensive user accounts, this is not as easy on Twitter (since Twitter is not a medium that prefers consensus). Communication on Twitter therefore is more dangerous and risky what may be the reason for career politicians to use it rather warily and carefully. Since a tweet cannot be deleted once it is re-tweeted, the potential for a scandal is high. Giving up the agency over one's tweet and the chance of being re-tweeted by

[14] Bauman, Zygmunt, "The 'Why's' and 'What for's' of People taking to the Streets." *Social Europe Journal,* October 19, 2011, accessed September 13, 2013, http://www.social-europe.eu/2011/10/the-whys-and-what-fors-of-people-taking-to-the-streets/.

anyone who reads the tweet allows for political enemies to reiterate a tweet cynically, critically or to make fun of the politician. To tweet always means to give up the agency over one's statement, to surrender to *mimesis*, to include the possibility of ironic, unpleasant or even rude memes. Since Twitters' public is infinitely big the potential for misunderstanding and denunciation is unlimited. While Facebook allows for a narcissistic self-portrayal and suggests the users' control, Twitter is much crueller – and therefore at the same time possibly more honest – by exposing the users' tweets to an unimaginably large and at best neutral, but potentially sarcastic and hateful public.

By comparing the data with the outlined socio-theoretical interest, the ambiguity and diversity of political media performances comes to the fore. While on Facebook politicians fabricate private representations of their political and non-political self for an audience of supporters, Twitter produces isolated political individuals who (due to the function of the retweet) perform for an unimaginably numerous public. At the same time, this publicity is neglected by the mediums real-time stream in which a message seems to perish in a stream of information. This is what makes Twitter so dangerous for politicians, since the repression of the unimaginable large audience can result in fatalism and unwariness. An example for this would be a highly-ranked diplomat twittering offensive opinions about a politician of another country. Or a politician provoking a "shitstorm" by using authoritative language towards a critical citizen. Last but not least, the potential for scandals results from the speed at which interesting tweets are spread through diverse social media. In all the empirical data we can observe multiple performers who experience, that their own idea of publics is a precarious one. Must this empirical impressions lead to a postmodern diagnosis of disorganization or disintegration in theory? I am not sure about this. On the one hand, the simultaneity of medial contexts seems to be a characteristic of contemporary politics. On the other hand, there are still the "old" political organizations and institutions. Those organizations – still linked to the nation state – reproduce contexts that completely ignore media evolution like the diplomatic protocol, the confidential counsel, rounds of ministers and many more. I will take up these thoughts on the change of the social field of politics at the end of my argumentation in the third part. Before, I would like to discuss more precisely how the process of being a political self is shaped by media use.

2.3 Theoretical Recapitulation: Political Self and Medial Interpellation

> "Every discourse, even a poetic or oracular sentence, carries with it a system of rules for producing analogous things and thus an outline of methodology."[15]

This brief discussion of empirical findings should have shown that the presentation of a political self differs from medium to medium. Political identities are not stable, but emergent and processual. They are shaped and influenced by media practices. To gain a better understanding of the social effects of media, the question, how the code and idea of *politics* as the struggle for a collectively binding decision is changed by social media, should be separated from the emergence of a multiple political self in those media. I have pointed out before, that I am referring to a (de-)constructivist perspective on modern society and its political organizations[16] and political performances[17] and to a discourse analytical empirical approach[18] that emphasizes the historical dimension of the construction of the social. As different as they are, Butler, Luhmann and Foucault all emphasize the contingency and the constructedness of the social world through communication (esp. Luhmann), language (esp. Butler) and constructions of truth and knowledge (esp. Foucault). All of them see mass media as an influential factor for the construction and observation of modern society. Also, they all conceptualize social practice as an operative real-time practice which is highly processual and instable and therefore in need of historical and semantic structures that stabilize the chaos of contingency and infinite eventualities of communication. This is why modern society, organizations and, of course, individuals form out narrations and self-*descriptions* in the first way.

The sociologist Hannelore Bublitz, who is following a Foucaultian tradition of interpreting media communication, has shown that a linguistic and visual performing subject presents itself in a "*Beichtstuhl der Medien*" (English: medial confessional).[19] The subject actually only comes into

---

[15] Derrida, Jacques, *Points…:Interviews 1974-1994* (Stanford: University Press, 1995), 200.

[16] Luhmann, *Die Politik der Gesellschaft.*

[17] Butler, *The Psychic Life of Power.*

[18] Foucault, *Dispositive der Macht.*

[19] Bublitz, Hannelore, *Im Beichtstuhl der Medien. Die Produktion des Selbst im öffentlichen Bekenntnis* (Bielefeld: transcript, 2010).

existence in the mirror of the media. The "medial confessional" becomes a place of real time self-revelation. Zygmunt Bauman argues as well, that

> "We live in a confessional society, promoting public self-exposure to the rank of the prime and easiest available, as well as arguably the most potent and the sole truth proficient, proof of social existence. Millions of Facebook users vie with each other to disclose and put on public record the most intimate and otherwise inaccessible aspects of their identity, social connections, thoughts, feelings and activity."[20]

Bauman and Bublitz both draw a convincing picture of confessional practices in the mass media and social media of modern society. Observing the social media as a structure of communication we could add, that the aesthetic form of the confessional follows the structure and logics of the medium, as in Facebook the logics of friendship or the comment on actual happenings and the dangerous communication towards an anonymous public on Twitter. To say it with Butler, different social media perform different interpellations of a desired political self, welcomed and rewarded with success and attention. The gain of the deconstructivist perspective on an emergent political self that is defined as an effect of media use, is not to allow oneself to be tempted to describe this processes as a *political* process of defragmentation. Defragmentation and disembedding from traditional contexts can be observed in the field. But they are rather an effect of media evolution than of a change in social structure or politics. Then, we would underestimate the possibility of users in knowing that their confession is only possible as a substrate of the medial practice and therefore not as "intimate" as an observing social scientist may think. Moreover, there is an aspect of playful (not strategic!) use of the medium and its possibilities. What I have discussed up to now is the question of how the performance of political persona changes through different media. What I would like to reflect in a last part is the question as to whether there are substantial changes in the form of the political as well.

---

[20] Bauman, Zygmunt, "Do Facebook and Twitter help spread Democracy and Human Rights?" *Social Europe Journal,* May, 8, 2012, accessed September, 13, 2013, http://www.social-europe.eu/2012/05/do-facebook-and-twitter-help-spread-democracy-and-human-rights/.

3. Discursive Crossings: Are Social Media changing (more than) the aesthetics of the political?

> "Were Marx and Engels, two youngsters from the Rhineland, setting today to pen down their almost two-centuries old Manifesto, they could have well started it from the observation that 'a spectre hovers over the planet; the spectre of indignation'... Wherefrom this spectre rises, is a moot and contentious question."[21]

By contrasting the results of the case studies in social media with the research into traditional party organizations, which I conducted in an observation over 6 years it is possible to observe how the organizations deal with the uncertainty introduced by practiccs of the Web 2.0. The digital medium produces new narrations of a political self that affect organizational self-descriptions of the old political organization and irritate their traditional patterns of decision-making. The emergence of the digital medium and especially of social media challenges political organizations by introducing new logics of decision. For instance the organizations and the different media apprehension of time differ radically. Social media politics is a job of 24-hours and does not tolerate the slowness of decision-making in traditional patterns. So there are in fact changes and challenges for the so-called traditional political organizations.

3.1 Social Media and the Organization

There is a huge discussion going on in both media and social science about the risks and odds of the Internet medium. I do not participate in this controversy and rather conceptualize all media as "neutral" respectively ambivalent. As Stefan Münker has brightly argued, a letter can be used to declare both war or deep love.[22] All media – starting with the classic novel of the 18th century – have been declared to be a danger for publica (so the novel was said to be hurtful for the female constitution) or, like the radio and the television as a gateway for propaganda and individuals' dullness. Those narratives are actualized in the observation of the digital medium as well. But even though social media are as ambivalent and neutral as all other media with regard to the democratic or undemocratic effects, there may still be a "revolutionary" aspect about them: they are radicalized real-time media and therefore elude the demands of a bourgeois public

---

[21] Bauman, *The 'Why's' and 'What for's' of People taking to the Streets.*

[22] Münker, Stefan, *Emergenz digitaler Öffentlichkeiten. Die Sozialen Medien im Web 2.0* (Frankfurt/M.: Suhrkamp, 2009), 30.

sphere.[23] Social media evolve from user practices and decompose radically if there is no usage. They promote a real-time read/write-culture[24] that rules out anyone who is not online. It is this very quality that makes them so interesting for an observation of modern political logics. Logics that transcend the boundaries of the traditional organizations – without denying those organizations' functionality and usefulness. Therefore more research on the question of how organizational decisions and programs and the communication and self-descriptions of political actors in social media interact and irritate each other is badly needed. Social media challenge – but certainly do not abolish – the form of the traditional political organization by introducing a new idea of the political public as a diverse and multiple non-place. This is of course what Jürgen Habermas already had in mind when he wrote about the structural changes of the public sphere in 1962. At that time, Habermas critically commented on the decline of the bourgeois public sphere by the mass society of the welfare state.[25] What is new about social media is that the idea of mass society and mass media becomes precarious. Since social media are operative real-time-media, they make the idea of simultaneity and synchronicity – the ideas mass media and mass society are based on – completely obsolete. Social medias' idea of the collective is one of radical presence.[26] This is what the observation of political twitterers has shown. The medium Twitter is fast and usually the half-life-period of messages is extremely slight.

In my opinion the most important modification of the political field through social media is one of the perception of political performances. Every medium defines its own connectivities and an idea of success in communication and therefore a distinct way to form the political self. The performances of political personae become fragmented and they can be observed as what they are: performances of a political actor who approaches diverse publica with a diverse set of self-descriptions, with a multiplicity of political selves that are constructed in specific channels of communication. For organizations this has paradox effects: on the one hand, there is no observation point from which they can locate the importance of social media and therefore they are insignificant for the

[23] Habermas, Jürgen, *The Structural Transformation of the Public Sphere. An Inquiry into a Category of Bourgeois Society* (Boston: MIT Press Edition, 1991 [1962]).

[24] Lessig, Lawrence, *Remix* (London: Penguin Books, 2008).

[25] Habermas, *The Structural Transformation of the Public Sphere.*

[26] Benkler, Yochai, *The Wealth of Networks. How Social Production Transforms Markets and Freedom* (New Haven: Yale University Press, 2007).

organizational decisions; on the other hand, parts of party elites and journalists are "strong users" of social media and therefore social media are a topic of organizational talk and hypocrisy.[27]

3.2 Discursive Crossings, the Future of Propaganda and the Need for Intersectional Research

The invention and use of social media as a part of mass culture changes the perception of the political in two ways: *Firstly*, the processuality and performativity of political language becomes totally obvious. *Secondly*, the perception of political performance changes since the medium to some extent treats all users equally. Average citizens experience how it feels to present themselves with a profile on Facebook whereas before only a few citizens knew how it felt to take part in a panel discussion, a radio interview or a talk show. Unlike the "average" user of social media one always expects political actors to use these media strategically and to be aware of their rules and codes. Surprisingly, however, the politicians' self-descriptions in social media do not differ so much from those of other users. Politicians on Facebook talk about their favourite quotes or books or show pictures of their pets. This shows that the presentation of the political self is very much dependent on the rules and structures of every single social medium. Social media strongly demonstrate that there is no such thing as a given unity of the political self before it is set in the context of the particular medium. Citizens are becoming used to the staging of politicians. Since citizens who use social media experience themselves as inventors of a biography, illustrated with pictures and statements the practical construction of the political performance becomes observable more easily. This leads to the pressing question, whether the politics of social media lead to *the individualization of the political cause*. Zygmunt Bauman is sceptical towards social medias' capacity to create lasting solidarity.

> "Rehearsed verbally on Facebook and Twitter, now finally experienced in flesh. And without losing the traits that made it so endearing when practiced on the web: the ability to enjoy the present without mortgaging the future, rights without obligations. [...] Solidarity on demand, and as long lasting (and no minute longer) as the demand endures. Solidarity not that much in sharing the chosen cause, as solidarity in having a cause; I

---

[27] Cf. Brunsson, Nils, *The Organization of Hypocrisy: Talk, Decisions and Actions in Organizations* (Chichester: John Wileyand Sons, 1989).

and you and all the rest of us ('us', that is people in the square) having purposes, and life having a meaning."[28]

In this text Bauman asks what is taking the people in the Arab Spring and the Blockupy movement to the streets. But do his observations correspond well to the empirical observations on Twitter in the previous chapter? What happens to politics when protest becomes a lifestyle? What happens when policy making is excluded from protest movements' agenda?

"Our fathers could quarrel about what needs to be done, but they all agreed that once the task has been defined the agency will be there, waiting to perform it – namely the states armed simultaneously with the power (ability to have things done) and politics (ability to see to it that the right things are done). Our times, however, are prominent for the gathering evidence that such kind of agencies are no longer in existence, and most certainly not to be found in their heretofore usual places. Power and politics live and move in separation from each other and their divorce lurks behind the corner."[29]

To Bauman, solidarity without a collective perspective is empty and erratic. Of course, his critique does not apply to all the different manifestations of the political in social media, but probably to a great number of them, especially on Twitter. In a discussion with David Lyon, Bauman argues that the fear of being unseen and ignored is the most important fear of modern citizens.[30] To present a political self in an arbitrary social room seems to be the answer to such fears. The structure of this performance then is similar to other techniques of the self[31] such as confessionals in talk shows, body modification or dieting. Is this in the end political action if we keep defining politics with Luhmann as a communication that longs for a collectively binding decision?[32] Indeed it seems, that some of the protests movements of our time lack a political cause. Is this an expression of the hipsteresque lifestyle of western middle- and upper-class members? Or are we entering a new age of politics without a cause? It is too early to say. But since the politics of social media are an exclusive space, research must be aware that social media

[28] Bauman, *The 'Why's' and 'What for's' of People taking to the Streets.*
[29] Bauman, *The 'Why's' and 'What for's' of People taking to the Streets.*
[30] Bauman, Zygmunt and David Lyon, *Liquid Surveillance: A Conversation* (Boston, Mass.: PCVS-Polity Conversations Series).
[31] (Foucault, Michel, The Government of Self and Others: Lectures at the College de France, 1982-1983 (New York: Palgrave Mcmillan, 2011).
[32] Luhmann, *Die Politik der Gesellschaft.*

politics are neither representative for the people nor do all social groups take part in social media discourses. This leads to the challenge of thoughtful intersectional research in social media that takes into account factors such as gender, class, ethnical and regional background, health and age.[33] Based on the empirical observation of the fragility and processuality of political self-descriptions, it will be more and more important to ask for terms and exclusions which are shaping the process of being an addressable and valued political citizen.

Bibliography

Anderson, Margaret L. and Patricia Hill Collins. Eds. *Race, Class and Gender: An Anthology*. Boston: Cengage Learning, 2012.

Edelman, Murray. *Political Language: Words that succeed and Policies that fail*. New York: Academic Press, 1977.

Bauman, Zygmunt, *Life in Fragments. Essays in Postmodern Morality.* Cambridge, MA: Basil Blackwell, 1995.

—. "The 'Why's' and 'What for's' of People taking to the Streets." Blogpost. *Social Europe Journal, October* 19. 2011. Accessed September, 13. 2013. http://www.social-europe.eu/2011/10/the-whys-and-what-fors-of-people-taking-to-the-streets/.

—. "Do Facebook and Twitter help spread Democracy and Human Rights?" Blogpost. *Social Europe Journal,* May, 8. 2012. Accessed September, 13. 2013. http://www.social-europe.eu/2012/05/do-facebook-and-twitter-help-spread-democracy-and-human-rights/

Bauman, Zygmunt and David Lyon. *Liquid Surveillance: A Conversation.* Boston, Mass.: PCVS-Polity Conversations Series.

Benkler, Yochai. *The Wealth of Networks. How Social Production Transforms Markets and Freedom.* New Haven: Yale University Press, 2007.

Brunsson, Nils. *The Organization of Hypocrisy: Talk, Decisions and Actions in Organizations*. Chichester: John Wileyand Sons, 1989.

Bublitz, Hannelore. *Im Beichtstuhl der Medien. Die Produktion des Selbst im öffentlichen Bekenntnis*. Bielefeld: transcript, 2010.

Butler, Judith. *The Psychic Life of Power. Theories in Subjection.* Stanford: Stanford University Press, 1997.

---

[33] Anderson, Margaret L. and Patricia Hill Collins, Eds. *Race, Class and Gender: An Anthology* (Boston: Cengage Learning, 2012).

Derrida, Jacques. *Points…: Interviews 1974-1994.* Stanford: University Press. 1995.

Foucault, Michel. *Dispositive der Macht. Über Sexualität, Wissen und Wahrheit.* Berlin: Merve, 1978.

—. *The Government of Self and Others: Lectures at the College de France, 1982-1983*. New York: Palgrave Macmillan, 2011.

Giddens, Anthony. *The consequences of modernity.* Cambridge: Polity Press/ Blackwell, 1990.

Habermas, Jürgen. *The Structural Transformation of the Public Sphere. An Inquiry into a Category of Bourgeois Society.* Boston: MIT Press Edition, 1991 [1962].

Lessig, Lawrence. *Remix.* London: Penguin Books, 2008.

Luhmann, Niklas. *Die Politik der Gesellschaft.* Frankfurt/M.: Suhrkamp, 2002.

McLuhan, Marshall. *Understanding Media: The Extensions of Man.* Berkley: Ginko Press, 2002 (1964).

Münker, Stefan. *Emergenz digitaler Öffentlichkeiten. Die Sozialen Medien im Web 2.0.* Frankfurt/M.: Suhrkamp, 2009.

Ries, Brian. "Meet the Mind Behind Barack Obama's Online Persona". Blogpost. *Storyboard*, November 19. 2012. Accessed September, 13. 2013. http://storyboard.tumblr.com/post/36063978132/meet-the-mind-behind-barack-obamas-online

Rose, Nikolas and Peter Miller. Political power beyond the State: problematics of government. *British Journal of Sociology*, Vol 61 (2010) (s1): 271-303.

Siri, Jasmin. *Parteien. Zur Soziologie einer politischen Form.* Wiesbaden: Springer VS, 2012.

Siri, Jasmin, Miriam Melchner and Anna Wolff. The Political Network - Parteien und politische Kommunikation auf Facebook. In: Kommunikation @ Gesellschaft – „Phänomen Facebook", eds. Christian Stegbauer, Jan-Hinrik Schmidt, Klaus Schönberger und Nils Zurawski, 2012. Accessed September, 13. 2013. http://www.ssoar.info/ssoar/View/?resid=28273.

Siri, Jasmin and Katharina Seßler. *Twitterpolitik. Politische Inszenierungen in einem neuen Medium.* Mit einem Vorwort von Lutz Hachmeister. Berlin/Köln: Institut für Medien- und Kommunikationspolitik. Gefördert von der Stiftung Mercator, 2013. Accessed September, 13. 2013. http://medienpolitik.eu/cms/media/pdf/Twitterpolitik.pdf.

CHAPTER THIRTEEN

UNIFICATION OF DISCOURSES OF SOCIAL MEDIA DURING THE *GEZI* RESISTANCE

IREM INCEOGLU

Introduction

What we had seen by the end of May 2013 in Turkey was a social movement arising over a local park in Istanbul that spread around the country within a few days. Since 31 May 2013, hundreds of thousands have taken over the streets on a continuous basis. During this process of mobilisation, social media not only proved to be the main source of information but also the space of articulating the discourses of the resistance movement. Social media has been a popular site for analysis in relation to contemporary uprisings as the social media sites are utilised widely by activists around the world in a variety of political systems. In many of the scholarly contributions social media as a concept is considered as being the tool for activist communication and dissemination of information in a relatively liberal way especially in rather authoritarian systems. In my analysis I regard social media as a radical democratic public space within which constant negotiations and dislocation occur in relation to constructing the discourses of social movements at play. In other words, social media platforms provide a space for the visibility of various identity positions and enhance diversity. Meanwhile they allow temporary coalitions and collaborations against the hegemonic discourse.

Now known as the Gezi Resistance, this rather recent mobilisation in Turkey quickly moved beyond a struggle to protect a particular park and instead became a larger scale collective reaction to the existing and ongoing urban modelling projects as well as the increasing authoritarianism in relation to policies of everyday life in Turkey. Significantly, the Gezi Resistance that reclaims public spaces has started to mobilise multiple identity groups who entered into political arena in the radical democratic sense.

It is difficult to come up with an absolute answer to the questions why now and why with all these people, as the movement seems to move to different phases within a short time-span. I would like to suggest that the waves of resistance on the streets in Turkey starting from the last days of May 2013 have been the result of a preceding struggle for representation and the voicing of dissent for a longer period. In Turkey, the dominant discourse of the government is mainly focusing on the level of representation they claim due to the percentage of votes AKP[1] received in the 2011 General elections. The Prime Minister Recep Tayyip Erdoğan is over-reliant on the 50 per cent backing he gained in elections. The government has been proposing or issuing legislation that disturbed many people for different reasons but mainly for the reason that they have not been included in the decision making process although the legislative meddling would affect their life directly. In that context, the resistance that peaked at the end of May 2013 has been triggered by the passive resistance of some people to protect a "few trees" at Gezi Park, but could be traced back to the dissent vocalised within the last few years. That is to say, it would not be wrong to link this recent outburst to a few previous occasions and the accumulated feelings of fear of repression and distrust.

In fact, the reaction against the use of police force to evacuate the peaceful occupiers of Gezi Park was the culmination of a series of incursions into basic liberties such as the restrictions on women's reproductive rights; the recent limitations on alcohol sale; the demolition of cultural landmarks for the sake of neo-liberal gentrification; the unfair trial process following the assassination of Hrant Dink - an Armenian-Turkish journalist; naming the third bridge on the Bosporus after the Ottoman Sultan known for the massacre of the Alevis; the bombings of civilians in Roboski - a border village with a Kurdish population - by Turkish military forces in December 2011; the major crackdown on 1 May demonstrations in 2013; have all contributed to the widespread discontent on display. Meanwhile the people of Turkey witnessed a major media censorship/self-censorship while these incursions were taking place. The mainstream media were quiet for about 14 hours about this the Roboski bombing and the main source of information for many has been social media; similar to that the government officially banned the media

[1] Adalet ve Kalkınma Partisi (Justice and Development Party), the ruling party in Turkey since 2002.

coverage in relation to the bomb attack in Reyhanlı.[2] Therefore, people from different walks of life and identity positions and ideological stands were linked to one another around this recent authoritarian path the government took.

Regarding the multifarious feature of the constituents and the scattered political positioning of the Resistance I aim to provide a conceptual analysis of discourses of dissent that have been articulated via social media in Turkey. In that context I espouse the approach arguing that any social space is discursive, and resistance(s) that have a political character are discursively constructed. Focusing on dissident struggles formulated around identity positions, I suggest reading the social media as a radical democratic public space where constant negotiations and dislocations occur on identity construction. That is to say, social media enhance the diversity of discourses as well as opening up a space for the visibility of each of these particularistic positions to construct a sense of coalition and collaboration against the defined oppressing discourses. Yet, instead of fixing the definition, there is a continuous process of deconstruction and re-identification taking place. Therefore, the following sections of this article provide examples of these collaborative discourses of the "marginalised" subjectivities through a selection of specific examples.

Social Movements and Repertoire of Action

Historically, social movements have been influencing one another, not only within a specific cultural and/or national context but also on a global level. In fact, in the era of networked societies and globalisation, social movements and mobilisations have proved their broad influence as agents of social and political change.

Charles Tilly[3] uses the concept of "protest repertoire" to highlight the fact that most protesters are inspired by the examples utilised by previous protest events. In that sense, repertoire refers to a shared understanding of methods of protests, as well as the shared values and ethos in which the movement evolves.

What we have seen in the recent past was the influence of 1960s new social movements having an influence on the (anti)globalisation movements that peaked at the end of 1990s. Despite the fact that there was a new

---

[2] Burçe Çelik. "The Diverse Revolt of Turkish Youth and the Production of the Political," Opendemocracy, June 6, 2013, accessed September 10, 2013. http://www.opendemocracy.net/burce-celik/diverse-revolt-of-turkish-youth-and-production-of-political.

[3] Charles Tilly, Social Movements, 1768-2004 , (London: Paradigm, 2004).

technology around to facilitate a global mobilisation, many of the tactics could be considered as a continuation of a previous action repertoire or, as Electrohippies[4] mentioned (cited in Dominguez) in their statement, extensions of "the philosophy of activism and direct action into the 'virtual' world of electronic information exchange and communications."[5]

Having a look at the Gezi Resistance's repertoire of action to date we can observe that it is fed by the repertoire of other globally effective social movements, going back to the 1968 student movements to the more recent Occupy movement. Briefly, it is a mobilisation gathered around the idea of protecting the trees of a public park, and following the police violence against the masses, the building up of barricades on the streets and the occupation of the Square as well as the Park are tactics that are not novel to this particular era. Gezi Resistance also appropriated a distinctive tactic of global justice movements during forums. The uses of hand gestures to facilitate the discussions where individuals exercise a radical democratic platform is adopted during the forums established in the parks as an extension of the resistance movement.[6]

However, the Gezi Resistance is also different from these preceding movements. First of all this is not a movement organised by a certain identity group. It is not a labour movement, neither is it a student movement. This makes it different than the 1960s movements and similar to the twenty-first century's social movements (Occupy, *Indignados*, etc.) but the claim is not around fiscal policies and the protests are not explicitly about financial crisis. Despite the fact that the Gezi Resistance occurred in the same era as the Occupy Movement, it also differs from that movement in terms of context and message. As opposed to *Indignados* or the Occupy Movement, Gezi Resistance flared-up during a relatively stable economic condition. Another specific feature of this movement is that, as far as we could observe and despite the fact that the Prime Minister Erdoğan argues the opposite - compatible with some of the common conspiracy theories - it is not a pre-organised movement. That is to say, NGOs, political parties,

---

[4] Electrohippies was an international collective of Internet activists (hacktivists) that expressed their dissent against the use of the Internet as a tool for corporate communications. The group also challenged the governmental control over the Internet that would provide a safe environment for the corporations mainly.

[5] Ricardo Dominguez. "Electronic Disturbance: an Interview," in Cultural Resistance Reader, edited by Stephen Duncombe, 379-396. (London: Verso, 2002), 390.

[6] İrem İnceoglu. " The Gezi Spirit and the Forums ," Opendemocracy, July 17, 2013, accessed September 10, 2013. http://www.opendemocracy.net/%C4%B0rem-%C4%B0nceo%C4%9Flu/gezi-spirit-and-forums.

interest groups etc. were not involved as leading constituents at the beginning of the protests, but they gathered at the park and the square to represent their positions following the occupation. According to surveys and my personal observations, the protesters are coming from all walks of life and there is a wide range of middle and upper middle class participation.[7] Hence, the success of the movement and the occupation of the park and the square could be considered the result of horizontal networking of independent individuals, most of whom have not been involved in institutionalised politics. In that context social media plays an important role, of course, as the social media networks provide the platform just suitable for that kind of spontaneous, individualistic but networked resistance.

In that context, the means of communication and organisation differs from the earlier examples of social movement activism but also makes it similar to the ones in the near future. For example, the use of a powerful hashtag to disseminate the discourses of the uprising to a global audience is one similar repertoire of action the Gezi Resistance appropriated from the tactics of the Occupy Movement.

Social Media and Political Mobilisation

Before examining the ways social media is being used in general in Turkey, in order to establish a discursive space, we should consider the possibilities and the limitations that are offered by the social media platforms used by activists within the last few years in general. In his recent book *Why It's Kicking off Everywhere: The Global Revolutions*, BBC Journalist Paul Mason writes:

> If you look at the full suite of information tools that were employed to spread the revolutions of 2009–11, it goes like this: Facebook is used to form groups, covert and overt – in order to establish those strong but flexible connections. Twitter is used for real-time organisation and news dissemination, bypassing the cumbersome newsgathering operations of the mainstream media. YouTube and the Twitter-linked photographic sites – Yfrog, Flickr and Twitpic – are used to provide instant evidence of the claims being made. Link-shorteners such as bit.ly are used to disseminate key articles via Twitter.[8]

---

[7] Esra Ercan Bilgiç and Zehra Kafkaslı, Gencim, Özgürlükçüyüm, Ne İstiyorum? (Istanbul: Bilgi Üniversitesi Yayınları, 2013).

[8] Paul Mason. Why It's Kicking off Everywhere: The Global Revolutions, (London: Verso, 2012), 75.

Again in a recent book based on ethnographic research and analysis in Egypt, Spain and the US Paolo Gerbaudo writes that social media usage by activists is diverse but there are two major ways: one that they are used as a "means of representation, a tool of 'citizen journalism' employed to elicit 'external attention', for example in the use of web live-stream services like Bambuser, or YouTube videos documenting episodes of police brutality." And the other and more interesting is the way the social media were used for the activists "internal" or "local" use "as *means of organisation* of collective action, and more specifically as *means of mobilisation* in the crucial task of 'getting people on the streets'."[9]

Using social media platforms in mobilising both digital and physical protests proved to be successful in various occasions in Turkey. In May 2011, we witnessed a massive nationwide protest organized mostly through social media networks (namely Facebook and Twitter) against the proposal to control and censor Internet access. "Don't Touch My Internet" campaign managed to mobilise more than 630 thousand people who protested against the proposed legislation, taking to the streets. The protests were somehow successful, despite some control over Internet usage, the legislation offered packages that would allow more flexible Internet access upon request. One of the points researchers paid attention to was the mobilisation during this particular campaign of young generations that were considered apolitical and indifferent towards social and political issues.

One other protest that was mainly social media based was the more recent "My Body My Decision" campaign in May 2012, which was designed to protest against the legislation on the reproductive rights of women. Women all around the country provided photos of themselves/ their bodies written on "my body my decision," the campaign was also supported by demonstrations. One of the latest examples of a digital campaign was in relation to protesting against the Ministry of Health decision to remove the initial T.C. (abbreviation for Republic of Turkey) from outdoor signs of some of the health institutions. The campaign went viral via Facebook and within two days 9 million Facebook users out of 32 million in Turkey changed their profile names to include TC in front of their names. This mass protests resulted in one top bureaucrat resigning and the Minister taking a step back and cancelling the notice that requested the change to outdoor signs.

[9] Paolo Gerbaudo. Tweets and the Streets, (London: PlutoPress, 2012), 3.

(Hash)tagging Resistance

Regarding this rather short but effective history of using social media platforms for purposes of political protest and mobilisation, the Gezi Resistance proved to be a unique case though. In the process of the Gezi Park occupation and the demonstrations that took over the streets around the country Twitter not only served as a useful source of information, despite the risks of disinformation, and a space for defining the name of the movement in the process of its becoming. The choice of certain hashtags to facilitate the uprising's viral diffusion also created the movement's discourse. In other words, the hashtags commonly used and even the sign of the hashtag itself (#) became associated with the Gezi Resistance Movement and provided a visual symbol for solidarity.

As an example of praising the influence and power of social media networks in the process of causing social mobilisation, Berkowitz in his Reuters report writes:

> It all started innocuously enough with a July 13 blog post urging people to #OccupyWallStreet, as though such a thing (Twitter hashtag and all) were possible. It turns out, with enough momentum and a keen sense of how to use social media, it actually is.[10]

However, Gerbaudo disagrees with the argument that the OccupyWallStreet movement was the success of Twitter and other social media networks and emphasises that the hashtag #Occupy WallStreet mostly became useful after the physical occupation of a public space:

> …social media only acquired importance during the phase of sustainment of the movement, being used to create a sense of attraction to the occupations, and to invoke a sense of solidarity between 'physical occupiers' and 'internet occupiers', activists on the ground and people following events from a distance.[11]

In regards to the use of social media networks during (and especially at the initial stages of) the Gezi Resistance, I could argue that the hashtag sign (#) became part of the repertoire of this particular movement.

---

[10] Ben Berkowitz. "From a Single Hashtag, a Protest Circled the World," Reuters, October 17, 2011, accessed September 12, 2013. http://uk.reuters.com/article/2011/10/17/us-wallstreet-protests-social-idUSTRE79G6E420111017.

[11] Gerbaudo, Tweets and the Streets, 103.

This little sign started to make the protesters recognise outputs in relation to the protests. The first instance of the use of #direngeziparki (resist gezi park) was on 30 May at around 1 a.m. which came from more than one users at almost the same time. It then became the global trending topic (TT) on 30 May-1 June throughout the day with about 1.7M tweets. The total number of #direngeziparki tweets reaches 5.7M in total between 30 May–15 September 2013, 5M of which were actually produced in Turkish. In addition to this particular hashtag, there seems to be an attempt to globalise the discourse of the resistance movement during the initial days. Users started to use #occupygezi even before #direngeziparki to disseminate information about the ongoing resistance in the park. The initial use of #occupygezi, linking the Gezi Resistance to the global Occupy Movement goes back to 28 May 8.50 a.m. The number of tweets including #occupygezi (both original and RTs) since 28 May 2013 is about 3M in all languages; 1.3M being in Turkish.

Following the success of the particular hashtag (#direngeziparki) the discourse of the movement seems to be defined by the use of this hashtag both within social media networks (primarily Twitter but also Facebook) and as a part of many other resistance related publications. Starting with Twitter, millions showed solidarity with the issues they were not necessarily aware of or bothered about before the Gezi Resistance. Many publications produced following the resistance used the hashtag sign (#) to indicate their coverage of the resistance process as well as their position as being sympathetic to the movement.[12] Even a resistance humour developed via the use of popular hashtags. The hashtag started to be a sign of street writing and graffiti. Especially #diren (translates as "resist") became the unifying ground for various protests around the country. Through the use of #diren, the dissenting masses showed solidarity with various other protests in various other locations and/or contexts. For example, when an ethnically Kurdish, Turkish citizen was killed by the police in Lice (a town in Diyarbakir, in the south east of Turkey) masses started to chant "*Diren Lice*" (resist Lice) during demonstrations, and in fact #direnlice became a popular hashtag on 28-29 June, on the day and the day following the event, with 142K tweets in total. Similar to this but on an entirely different matter, appropriation of resistance to the LGBT context in a humorous way, #direnayol (*ayol* is an interjection associated with gays and transgender individuals in Turkish) became another popular

[12] For example, the bimonthly magazine *Express* issue 136, the monthly magazine *Tempo* July 2013 issue, the monthly *Tarih* magazine issue 54, the monthly cultural journal *Birikim* issue 291, the bimonthly magazine *Altüst* July-August 2013 issue etc.

hashtag with 147.5K tweets, especially during the LGBTI Parade on 30 June.

Conclusion

As one of the most frequent chants of the resistance announces "this is just the beginning, the struggle will continue." As I tried to outline in the introduction, the AKP government with a very strong parliamentary group has been moving along an authoritarian path relying on the popular support they perpetuated by the latest general elections. The fact that the governing party enjoyed a popular support that amounted to 50 per cent of the valid votes in the 2011 elections which resulted in 3/5 of the seats in the parliament being held, meant that they were able to make any legal arrangement they intended to. This power also meant for the rest of society that their demands and oppositions were unregistered. The fear of moving towards a majoritarian tyranny alerted many individuals, even those without apparent political affiliations as they started to feel that the legislative power was extensively interfering in their everyday life practices. Therefore, people from different identity positions and ideological stands have linked up with one another to resist the authoritarian tone of the government: cutting down trees in a public park was the last straw and the ensuing occupation has turned into a once-in-a-lifetime uprising in Turkey. This outburst reached many parts of the country and in different cities uprisings began to articulate to the Istanbul-centred movement, along with a diversity of claims and identity positions. This article aimed to scrutinise the uses of "hashtags" as a method of defining the character of the most recent movement that we have been witnessing in Turkey. The character of the movement, which is identified with occupation of the park as a public space, is branded with the word "Diren" (Resist) on social media, which then has been the tag of all other related uprisings. Although I refrain from arguing that the social media platforms have been the only triggering element of this recent uprising, I argue that social media, and especially Twitter, helped to shape the hegemonic discourse of the movement, which functions as cement for the radical democratic struggle. The popularised hashtag with the word "*diren*" that is collectively produced, has set the common ground for diverse motivations and facilitated the production of the political discourse that is rapidly disseminated.

The common hashtags also help to outline the grassroots uprising as a resistance movement. It indeed becomes a resistance movement as the constituents are resisting against a totalitarianising discourse which presents itself as a majoritarian democracy, whereas in fact it resembles more of a tyranny of the majority, where the alleged 50 per cent is argued to vote for AKP is represented by the government. In the case of the Gezi Resistance though, non-majority identity groups and so-called marginal subjectivities claimed the hegemonic position to oppose this stand, as they constitute a recognisable mass. That is to say, with the unification of discourses, even temporarily, various components of the opposition articulated themselves to the hegemonic block of resistance.

Bibliography

Berkowitz, B. "From a Single Hashtag, a Protest Circled the World," *Reuters*, 17 October 2011, accessed September 12, 2013. http://uk.reuters.com/article/2011/10/17/us-wallstreet-protests-social-idUSTRE79G6E420111017.

Bilgiç E.E. and Kafkaslı, Z. *Gencim, Özgürlükçüyüm, Ne İstiyorum?* Istanbul: Bilgi Üniversitesi Yayınları, 2013.

Çelik, B. "The Diverse Revolt of Turkish Youth and the Production of the Political," *Opendemocracy,* 6 June 2013, accessed September 10, 2013. http://www.opendemocracy.net/burce-celik/diverse-revolt-of-turkish-youth-and-production-of-political.

Dominguez, R. "Electronic Disturbance: an Interview," in *Cultural Resistance Reader*, edited by Stephen Duncombe, 379-396. London: Verso, 2002.

Gerbaudo, P. *Tweets and the Streets*. London: PlutoPress, 2012.

İnceoglu, İ. "The Gezi Spirit and the Forums," *Opendemocracy,* 17 July 2013. accessed September 10, 2013. http://www.opendemocracy.net/%C4%B0rem-%C4%B0nceo%C4%9Flu/gezi-spirit-and-forums.

Mason, P. *Why It's Kicking off Everywhere: The Global Revolutions*, London: Verso, 2012.

Tilly, C. *Social Movements, 1768-2004*, London: Paradigm, 2004.

CHAPTER FOURTEEN

NEGOTIATING DIGITAL SHOAH MEMORY ON YOUTUBE

ALINA BOTHE

Introduction

> "Thank you so much for sharing your story."[1]

> "what nonsense are you stating? there is so much evidence out there that unfortunately these atrocities towards 6 million people did happen. how weird, if not to say obnoxious from you not to grant people their memories ….. go away pls, don't waste this space."[2]

In this article, I will discuss digital Shoah memory, the fast evolving new form of Shoah memory and remembrance culture. Digital Shoah has a lot of different facets, like an interactive exhibition, YomHaShoah on Second Life, apps providing guided memorial tours, web pages, digital archives of survivors testimonies or thematic clips on YouTube.[3] One facet are

---

[1] User Novarhynes, Comment to Shoah Survivor Ursula Levy's USC Shoah Foundation testimony on YouTube, USC Shoah Foundation. "Jewish Survivor Ursula Levy Testimony." YouTube. YouTube, January 30, 2009, accessed October 8, 2013.

[2] User Cassandra 1821, reply to a comment by other user to the Shoah Survivor Esther Stern's USC Shoah Foundation testimony on YouTube, USC Shoah Foundation. "Jewish Survivor Esther Stern Testimony." YouTube. YouTube, October 4, 2011, accessed October 8, 2013.

[3] See for example the app Erinnerungsorte für die Opfer des Nationalsozialismus (memorials for the victims of National Socialism) by the German Federal Agency for Civic Education, http://www.bpb.de/shop/multimedia/mobil/146941/app-erinnerungsorte. C. Giacobini, "YomHaShoah. Remembering the Holocaust," in *2Life*, No. 2, May 2007, 9. The magazine was available on:

survivors' testimonies of the USC Shoah Foundation on YouTube. More than 1,000 testimonies from the USC Shoah Foundation's Visual History Archive (VHA) are available on YouTube. YouTube – a virtual community of short clips, known for its harsh comment culture – assembles very private narrations of the victims of the destruction of the European Jews. Many questions arise from this. The USC Shoah Foundation uses YouTube to reach out to those without access to their education on human rights and genocide prevention. I see these testimonies differently and understand them as narratives of Shoah memory. In this article, I will focus on the liquid fabric of digital Shoah memory as it is evolving in the comments to the above mentioned testimonies on YouTube. Liquidity first describes that this kind of memory is rebound to a certain modernity and second it is a depiction of the instable substance of the digital Shoah memory. Therefore, I analyse the commentary culture that develops beneath the 15 most requested USC Shoah Foundations digital survivors' testimonies on YouTube. The testimonies are full-length videographed interviews with the survivors from the mid-1990s, which were digitized and are now accessible on YouTube. I conceptualize these testimonies as forming the core of an accessible online survivors' testimonies network, a virtual in-between of memory where digital Shoah memory is formed. Based on the chosen YouTube sample, I will link theory and practical analyses and work out how first of all a new tablet of agents emerges, whose interaction is the base for digital Shoah memory The method used therefore is a combination of discourse analysis as well as a close reading of the comments. Then I will show how digital Shoah memory is constituted and communicated in a liquid, in-between existing remembrance community or maybe even culture. Excluded from my analysis here is the urgent problem of the ethics of remembrance, which are, as my findings indicate,

---

www.2lifemagazine.com, the Website has now been removed, the magazine was retrieved on March 6, 2009. One example is Loretta Walz's digital archive with interviews with Ravensbrück concentration camp survivors (http://www.videoarchiv-ravensbrueck.de). Another one would be the collection of the United States Holocaust Memorial Museum (http://www.ushmm.org/research/research-in-collections/overview/oral-history. Rachel Baum (University of Wisconsin) in her paper on "A Second Life for the Jews of Europe: Rethinking Holocaust Memory in the Digital Age" at the Southampton conference on "The Future of Holocaust Studies," July 2013, analysed the USHMM's virtual exhibition on the so called "Kristallnacht." A screencast of the exhibition can be found here: https://www.youtube.com/watch?v=ib0NnFktRqQ, accessed November 5, 2013.

necessary to discuss. First, I will briefly describe the archive from which the testimonies are taken , in the second part USC's usage of YouTube is analyzed, in the third the case study will be discussed and my conclusions will be drawn.

The Visual History Archive as a virtual in-between of memory

The USC Shoah Foundation - founded by Steven Spielberg - established the world's largest digital archive with survivors testimonies in the mid-1990s. After directing *Schindler's List*, he donated the profit from the successful movie to the Survivors of the Shoah Visual History Foundation, which was later transformed into the USC Institute for Visual History, but is commonly referred to as the Shoah Foundation. Based on the work of many volunteers, the foundation was able to interview nearly 52,000 people. The vast majority of them were survivors of the Shoah, of the Porajmos, those who were persecuted in accordance with paragraph 175 b or surviving victims of the so-called T4-Aktion but the Foundation also conducted interviews with liberators, aid-givers and participants of war crime trials. The interviews were usually taped within the homes of the interviewee and the videographed interview was on average between two and three hours long. These interviews were later digitized and digitally archived in the Visual History Archive (VHA).[4] Most of the interviews can only be viewed in one of the few institutions with full access, but up to 3,000 testimonies are available through different online platforms: this is the 2012 launched VHA online, different educational platforms like IWitness, a platform mostly for high school students[5] in use to date in 52 countries,[6] the German-based platform "Zeugen der Shoah,"[7] maintained

---

[4] For an overview on the archive see for example Verena Lucia Nägel, "Das Visual History Archive des Shoah Foundation Institute in Forschung, Lehre und Schulunterricht," in *Ich bin die Stimme der sechs Millionen. Das Videoarchiv im Ort der Information,* ed. Daniel Baranowski (Berlin, 2009), 185-191. More information on the VHA can be obtained from the following web pages: http://www.vha.fu-berlin.de and http://sfi.usc.edu/what_is_the_vha.

[5] Andrea Petö and Helga Dorner at the Central European University of Budapest gained remarkable results in using Iwitness for teaching Masterstudents. (See Petö and Dorner in *Geschlecht und Erinnerung im digitalenZeitalter - neue Perspektiven auf ZeitzeugInnenarchive*, ed. Alina Bothe and Christina Brüning (Berlin: LIT Verlag, Reihe "Historische Geschlechterforschung und Didaktik," 2014 [forthcoming])

[6] USC Shoah Foundation: Statistical report, Web. November 4, 2013,

at Freie Universität Berlin and the already mentioned YouTube. Most of the archival features of the digital testimonies are missing on YouTube, they are not segmented, one cannot search them or search through them, etc. But the main difference is that only on YouTube, can users comment and rank[8] the testimonies.

The virtual in-between describes the technologically given infrastructure of a new layer of reality that has its own quality in respect to the analogue world.[9] The virtual sphere is a space in which the dualism of the activity of time and the passivity of space is, different than in the modern era, as Zygmunt Bauman reminds us, no longer valid. Both have become more and more fluid. But not only time and space, but also the subject itself becomes more fugitive. The former physical boundaries and natural limitations of the living subject diminish. New network agents are established in digital Shoah memory. Figure 1 shows the network of agents that is involved in the creation of digital Shoah memory. The first main agent is the USC Shoah Foundation that collected the interviews, digitized them and made them available on YouTube. Second, there are the survivors, whose testimonies are central to the archive. Third, there is a bundle of agents, the digital media meaning devices, networks, software, optical fibre cables and so on. For the creation of the interview, the interviewer and the videographer are not to be neglected as they enabled the interview to be a stand-in for future users as well as saved the interview first hand.[10] The last agent is YouTube, the platform that allows us to display the testimonies as well as to comment on them.

In their interaction with the testimonies, users realize at least four of the above mentioned agents as relevant. Small-scale studies[11] show that

http://sfi.usc.edu/news/2013/11/first-quarter-2013-shows-increases-usc-shoah-foundation%E2%80%99s-academic-media-and, accessed November 5, 2013.

[7] http://www.zeugendershoah.de/

[8] Ranking testimonies as well as ranking comments to testimonies is ethically difficult on many levels.

[9] Alina Bothe, "Im Zwischen der Erinnerung. Virtuelle Zeugnisse der Shoah," in *kunsttexte.de*, No. 1, 2012, 11 pages, accessed November 8, 2013, http://edoc.hu-berlin.de/kunsttexte/2012-1/bothe-alina-6/PDF/bothe.pdf.

[10] See figure Christina Brüning, "Unterricht mit videografierten Interviews aus dem Archiv 'Zwangsarbeit 1919-1945'. Die Lehrer_innen-Perspektive," in *Erinnern an Zwangsarbeit. Zeitzeugen-Interviews in der digitalen Welt,* ed. Nicolas Apostolopoulos and Cord Pagenstecher, 273-286, 279.

[11] Juliane Brauer and Aleida Assmann, "Bilder, Gefühle, Erwartungen. Über die emotionale Dimension von Gedenkstätten und den Umgang von Jugendlichen mit dem Holocaust," *Geschichte und Gesellschaft* 37, 1, (2011): 72-103. Juliane Brauer and Dorothee Wein, "Historisches Lernen mit lebensgeschichtlichen

users of the VHA (1) have the impression of a real meeting with the survivors, (2) try to engage in dialogue while some of them (3) use YouTube to be able to ask their questions or (4) continue the dialogue from their side. They often bond very emotionally with the survivor. Users address the USC Shoah Foundation directly, thanking them, offering advice on how to better display the testimonies or ask personal questions. They hardly ever address YouTube, and if mostly then to reply to other users. Or they use the ranking opportunities of each comment. Interestingly enough, users pay attention to the importance of the interviewer for example by discussing the style of interviewing.

USC Shoah Foundations testimonies on YouTubc

In 2005, YouTube was founded by two former Stanford students and quickly became the fastest growing website ever. In autumn 2006, Google bought up the former rival and is still running it today. Even though a high number of other video sharing platforms have evolved, YouTube is the model and benchmark for each subsequent project. Economically, it works as a platform for specialized advertisements, therein following the Google business model. On YouTube, every user can upload his or her own video clips. That's why its slogan is "Broadcast yourself!" Successful clips are clicked on millions of times and are vastly commented on and answered with other clicks. This way, YouTube produces web 2.0 celebrities, gaining their 15 minutes of fame. It is important to note, that YouTube itself offers no options to download clips, but this can be easily done by a browser add. It is assumed by most YouTube experts that its users, especially those active users who upload clips or comment on others, are young and male.[12] Clips are rated by the users and clips clicked on more often are ranked higher in the clip hierarchy. When opening YouTube, a user is offered a wide range of clips from different topics. While searching the site, the user is not only offered a choice of different clips concerning

---

Videointerviews - Beobachtungen aus der schulischen Praxis mit dem Visual History Archive" *Gedenkstättenrundbrief* 153: 9-22, Alina Bothe and Martin Lücke, "Im Dialog mit den Opfern. Shoah und historisches Lernen mit virtuellen Zeugnissen," in *Shoa und Schule. Lehren und Lernen im 21. Jahrhundert*, ed. Peter Gautschi, Meik Zülsdorf-Kersting, and Béatrice Ziegler (Zürich: Chronos, 2013), 55-74, Kay Andrews, "A damned good cry," *PastForward* 1 (2013): 14. That the USC Shoah Foundation started to develop Survivors holograms is proof of this observation.

[12] Roman Marek, *Understanding YouTube. Faszination und Plastizität eines Mediums (*Bielefeld: transcript, 2013), 47.

the search word, but other often watched clips or clips the YouTube algorithm assumes the user might be interested in judging by his/ her further searches and clicks. These are linked and a small standstill of ten to twenty clips appears on the right hand side of the clip just watched. Even though a lot of legal problems occur around YouTube, e.g. copyright problems, only very few clips are taken down, normally when other users have marked them as inappropriate and have reported them to the company. Roman Marek explains this as follows: "Censorship and paternalism are seen more sceptical than so called 'harmful content'." (Marek 2013: 17)[13]

It is not easy to describe YouTube and to explain its on-going fascination from a historical or sociological point of view. Three main sociological or cultural studies publications can be listed. In 2008, Geert Lovink edited *The Video Vortex Reader*, a year later Pelle Snickers and Patrick Vonderau composed *The YouTube Reader* and very recently Roman Marek's *Understanding YouTube* was published.

YouTube is not simply a video sharing platform, but a digital symbol. "YouTube has become the very epitome of digital culture […] by allowing "you" to post a video which might incidentally change the course of history."[14] For their analysis of YouTube, Snickers and Vonderau offer three different categories, it is understood as "an industry, an archive and a cultural form."[15] As will be shown, all three categories are working interwoven in the case of the USC Shoah Foundation's usage of YouTube. In his convincing *Understanding YouTube*, Roman Marek offers two main interpretations of YouTube as a still fascinating media. The first one is, that clips on YouTube are getting into a process of circulation, "circulation does not aim at reciprocity or just simple dissemination but circulation does have an impact on the circulating material itself."[16] He secondly states that on YouTube a fluent "*virtual community*"(Herv. i.O) which is a "Kommunikationsgemeinschaft" a community formed through communication.

---

[13] My translation of: "Zensur und Bevormundung werden innerhalb der Community kritischer gesehen als sogenannte >>schädliche Inhalte<<." Roman Marek, *Understanding YouTube. Faszination und Plastizität eines Mediums* (Bielefeld: transcipt, 2013), 17.

[14] Pelle Snickars and Patrick Vonderau, ed., *The YouTube Reader*, (Stockholm: KB, 2009), 11.

[15] Snickars, Vonderau, *The YouTube Reader,* 11.

[16] My translation of: "bei der Zirkulation geht es nicht unbedingt um Reziprozität, und schon gar nicht um bloße Weitergabe, sondern die Zirkulation wirkt sich auf das zirkulierende Material selbst aus." Marek *Understanding YouTube, #.*

In trying to describe the meaning of YouTube, Snickers and Vonderau refer to its subversive potential.

> "In our globalized, corporate-controlled mediascape, it is also liberating to see a madly laughing toddler attracting more viewers than *Harry Potter* and *Pirates of the Caribbean* together".[17]

To sum up this overview on recent YouTube research: it is a fluent virtual community, where mostly banal video clips are shared, commented, copied and sometimes even satirized.

The two quotations at the beginning of the introduction are taken from the comments beneath two VHA testimonies on YouTube. The comments of users are highly interesting to interpret, as they show how subjects adapt to and interact with the new layer of memory that is evolving. They indicate some of the challenges and changes of digital Shoah memory. The first user quoted, Novarhynes, addresses the survivor directly, showing her gratitude for telling her memories. This is not an unusual response which seems to enable the users to at least respond to a testimony, a personal intimate recollection of traumatic experiences in the past during the Shoah that seems appropriate to them. The novelty of digital Shoah memory is here a certain option of response, not given to any saved oral testimony[18] before. The second quotation points to one of the challenges of digital Shoah memory: the testimonies are vulnerable, open to negotiation and even to attack. In the comments to each testimony I have included in the sample for this article at least one, but often many more highly aggressive anti-Semitic or Shoah denying messages can be found. Users reply to many of these posts as can be seen in the comment of User Cassandra 1821, but a lot goes by unchallenged.

The USC Shoah Foundation began to use YouTube in 2009 with an own channel. It started with some 100 testimonies, in 2012 they added another nine hundred. Concerning the copyright, the survivors transferred all rights to the Foundation.

---

[17] Snickars, Vonderau, *The YouTube Reader,* 11.

[18] Audio taped testimonies from Shoah survivors were collected as early as 1946 from David Boder. Since then a growing collection of audio and later video testimonies were collected in many countries, from small initiatives to "big players" like the USC Shoah Foundation. For an overview see Stefanie Schüler-Springorum, "Welche Quellen für welches Wissen? Zum Umgang mit jüdischen Selbstzeugnissen und Täterdokumenten," in *Wer zeugt für den Zeugen? Positionen jüdischen Erinnerns im 20. Jahrhundert*, ed. Dorothee Gelhard and Irmela von der Lühe (Frankfurt am Main: Peter Lang, 2012), 175-192.

> "Consistent with these purposes, we may use the interview edited or unedited, by itself or combined with other interviews or with other materials, in any medium including literary, print, audio, audio-visual, computer-based or any other medium now known or created in the future." (USC Shoah Foundation Institute 2007: 1)

In the first quarter of 2013 45,065 testimonies were viewed on the Foundation's YouTube channel, this is an increase of more than 5,000 views.[19]

The data used for this article was collected on May 7th and 8th 2013. As more than 1,000 survivor testimonies of the USC Shoah Foundation are available on YouTube, I decided to save the comments for the 15 most watched testimonies of Jewish survivors by this date.[20] Today, the sample would look like different. These 15 testimonies and especially the commentary beneath these form my sample here. This is a simple

---

[19] USC Shoah Foundation: Statistical report, Web November 4, 2013, http://sfi.usc.edu/news/2013/11/first-quarter-2013-shows-increases-usc-shoah-foundation%E2%80%99s-academic-media-and, accessed November 5, 2013.

[20] USC Shoah Foundation. "Jewish Survivor Renée Firestone Testimony." YouTube. YouTube, July 10, 2009. accessed October 8, 2013; USC Shoah Foundation. "Jewish Survivor Paula Lebovics Testimony." YouTube. YouTube, December 3, 2009. accessed October 8, 2013; USC Shoah Foundation. "Jewish Survivor Esther Stern Testimony." YouTube. YouTube, October 4, 2011. accessed October 8, 2013; USC Shoah Foundation. "Jewish Survivor Abraham Bomba Testimony." YouTube. YouTube, January 29, 2009. accessed October 8, 2013; USC Shoah Foundation. "Jewish Survivor Kristine Keren Testimony." YouTube. YouTube, January 30, 2009. accessed October 8, 2013; USC Shoah Foundation. "Jewish Survivor Sally Roisman Testimony." YouTube. YouTube, July 13, 2009. accessed October 8, 2013; USC Shoah Foundation. "Jewish Survivor Ellen Brandt Testimony." YouTube. YouTube, January 30, 2009. accessed October 8, 2013; USC Shoah Foundation. "Jewish Survivor Ernest Lobet Testimony." YouTube. YouTube, November 9, 2009. accessed October 8, 2013; USC Shoah Foundation. "Jewish Survivor Ester Fiszgop Testimony." YouTube. YouTube, January 30, 2009. accessed October 8, 2013; USC Shoah Foundation. "Jewish Survivor Itka Zygmuntowicz Testimony." YouTube. YouTube, February 11, 2009. accessed October 8, 2013; USC Shoah Foundation. "Jewish Survivor Sonia Berson Testimony." YouTube. YouTube, July 11, 2009. accessed October 8, 2013; USC Shoah Foundation. "Jewish Survivor Ursula Levy Testimony." YouTube. YouTube, January 30, 2009. accessed October 8, 2013; USC Shoah Foundation. "Jewish Survivor Leopold Page Testimony." YouTube. YouTube, May 12, 2009. accessed October 8, 2013; USC Shoah Foundation. "Jewish Survivor David Abrams Testimony." YouTube. YouTube, January 30, 2009. accessed October 8, 2013; USC Shoah Foundation. "Jewish Survivor Henry H. Sinason Testimony." YouTube. YouTube, January 30, 2009. accessed October 8, 2013.

numerical decision, which goes along with the principle of the YouTube-algorithm, that a clip with a lot of clicks is recommended to other users more often and therefore watched more often. So the results discussed here are to be looked at with some limitations, they might have been different with another sample. But with this sample, my guidelines were pragmatic as well as media specific. The number of comments to each testimony was quite different. The number of clicks to each testimony and the number of comments can be seen in Figure 2.[21]

Survivor	Clicks	Comments	Survivor	Clicks	Comments
Renée Firestone	64642	484	Ellen Brandt	8981	80
Paula Lebovics	27893	113	Ernest Lobet	8550	31
Abraham Bomba	19384	147	Ester Fiszgop	8450	75
Esther Stern	17472	86	Itka Zygmuntowicz	8154	12
Kristine Keren	11688	37	Sonia Berson	8001	16
Sally Roisman	11008	21	Ursula Levy	7089	25
Leopold Page	10570	25	Henry H. Sinason	6351	83
David Abrams	10102	32			

I analysed the comments systematically, looking for regularities, similarities, the exceptional as well as for voids. As there is still no convincing historical approach to analyse YouTube pages, my approach here did partly consist of discourse analysis as well as of a critical reading of sources. The difficulties in deciding on a fitting methodology reflect in my opinion the unique newness of the media, as I have already described.

The data used is the first data of a longer term sample that I am going to collect until November 2014. This is the first evaluation of the material, the whole research design is part of my current research project on the impact of digitality for Shoah remembrance While writing this article, I rechecked the YouTube-Pages on October 8th 2013 to see if major changes had happened. For many testimonies this did not occur, but for three testimonies major changes have to be noted. There was a further intense debate or poster battle in the commentary beneath Renée Firestone's testimony, adding more than 120 new comments. The tone of the commentary culture of this testimony changed, it became rougher, more

[21] As all survivors are to be found on YouTube with their full name, I decided to use their full names in this article as well.

unfriendly and a lot more anti-Semitic. The comments to Esther Stern's testimony, which nearly doubled and an anti-anti-Semitic and anti-Semitic posting battle or discourse, had taken place here for about two months. Sad news was spread by the daughter of the survivor, Judith Becker, who announced her mother's death on Succot 2013. For all testimonies the number of clicks and comments had increased in general, between more than 10,000 new clicks and 120 comments plus to Renée Firestone's testimony and around 500 new clicks and one new comment to Judith Becker's testimony. From this data it is to be assumed that views and comments will increase steadily. As Figure 1 shows, there seems to be no direct relation between the number of times the testimonies were clicked on and the number of comments. For the testimonies with a comparable high number of comments it seems the offline prominence or education work of the survivor is highly relevant. Renée Firestone, Itka Zygmuntowicz and Paula Lebovics were/are highly active in meeting high school and university students, Abraham Bomba is well known from Claude Lanzmann's Shoah, Kristine Keren donated a green sweater, which was relevant during her persecution, to the United States Holocaust Memorial Museum,[22] Leopold Page was a well-known figure in the US and the survivor who inspired Thomas Keneally to write *Schindler's List* and Ernest Lobet features in Denis Avey 2011 memoirs "The Man who broke into Auschwitz." But this is just one part of the explanation, a second explanation might be the inner dynamics of YouTube commentators' communications, sometimes posting an on topic dialogue or an anti-Semitic rant and thereby increasing the number of comments unintentionally and very quickly. The statistics about clicks on each clip are highly unreliable, as a click does not mean the user who clicked upon the clip watched it longer than for a few seconds. Only in combination with the comments, of which some show that users watched more than a few seconds, but even the whole lengthy testimony, do the clips give some insights into the creation of digital Shoah memory.

The USC Shoah Foundation's usage of YouTube is atypical in many ways: 1. The clips are several hours long, which is unusually lengthy. 2. Some viewers spend an unusually long time on one clip, as we can conclude from the comments where specific statements or parts of the narration are commented on or questions asked. 3. The content of the clips is very serious, but many serious clips can be found nowadays on

[22] There is even a YouTube clip by USHMM about this green sweater. YouTube. "United States Holocaust Memorial Museum on a cherished object: Kristine Keren's Green Sweater. Curators Corner 3," accessed November 7, 2013, http://www.youtube.com/watch?v=adwU_M1rdTA.

YouTube. 4. The number of views is very low for YouTube. 5. Users' reactions are in a different style than usual, there is only one video clip answer, fewer hater comments, if one may say so, and I have not found any parody so far. Although a lot of Shoah parody exists on YouTube, like the clip "Hitler hates Beckham."[23]

From the statistical evaluation, some general observations can be drawn: 1. Most commentators post one comment only. 2. They have a wide background in terms of age and education. 3. Different to most assumptions about active YouTube users a large number of women write posts. 4. From 2009 to 2011, nearly no comments were posted, most comments were posted between 2012 and the collection date of the sample. 5. Only a few comments were deleted or marked as spam, therefore supporting Marek's claim, that the YouTube community is not willing to accept censorship. 6. And with a few exceptions all comments were made in English. The other languages were Spanish, Polish and German. 7. It is only a minority of users who leave a comment, which constitutes a limitation for this study.

With regard to contents, very different kinds of comments can be noted. The following list of categories were assembled from all the examined commentaries. Most types of comments are completely acceptable, even if they sometimes seem to be a little bit strange or funny, when reading the dialogue between two school students, who try to explain to each other, what communism was and when and where it was invented (maybe in the 1950s in Russia?). The following 17 types are the main types of comments and they can be structured into 11 more or less appropriate and 6 non-appropriate types of comments. The distribution between both main categories depends on each testimony. For example, for Ursula Levy's testimony and for Leopold Page's testimony the distribution is: 60 percent acceptable to 40 percent unacceptable, and 96 percent to 4 percent.

1- thanks to the survivor for sharing his or her story
2- thanks to the USC Shoah Foundation and advises how to better display the testimonies
3- general messages of shock and horror and declaring the will to pass on the memory

[23] In his paper on "Auschwitz is made of Lego and Hitler hates Beckham: Youtube and the Future of Holocaust Remembrance" at the Future Holocaust Studies conference in Southampton July 2013 Jason Hansen raised my attention to this special parody.

4- references that one worked in school or college with the testimonies
5- discourses of historical culture
6- general or specific questions about the Shoah or the testimonies
7- messages discussing the testimonies as historical sources
8- messages (sometimes highly aggressive) against Shoah denial and fascism
9- messages defending the survivor against personal attacks
10- notes from users, who met the survivor "in real life"
11- (mostly very positive) comments on the witnesses' personality or outer appearance.
- comments which challenge the personal integrity of the survivor
- comments that insult the survivor
- Shoah denials or relativisations
- anti-Semitic comments
- insults against other users
- Anti-Semitic comments were made and reposted in different versions from just a few commentators, from which some commented openly under different nicknames and beneath different testimonies.

After this broad overview, I would like to discuss four aspects of digital Shoah memory in the form of virtual community memory in more detail: a) Crossing boundaries of time in communication, b) anonymity, c) different commentary cultures and d) connections between online and offline world

a.) Crossing boundaries of time in communication

First I would like to highlight that this form of a community is extremely fluid, users attach mostly just one at most, others do come back for a longer period of time, which normally does not exceed four weeks. But users are reading through other users' comments, sometimes answering them a year or two years later than the original entry was made. This shows to me that they recognize the absent other not as a person they are in direct dialogue with but as someone to whom they nevertheless feel entitled to respond. Also users do recognize other users as agents in the formation of digital memory, addressing them directly, even if they are not very kind towards each other. We can see that most of them recognize the survivors telling their stories as agents, addressing them directly, responding to the testimony or as already mentioned, attacking them. Users as agents of digital Shoah memory are crossing the boundaries of time at least twice, making it thereby very visible, that time lost its ligation to physical space, as it was the case in the modern era. They are engaging in a certain kind of dialogue with the survivors, feeling a connection, which they are acting out in their comments, that seems to make the time gap between the taping of the testimonies and the moment of reception irrelevant.

b) Anonymity

Most users act anonymously, especially hater posters or anti-Semitic posters. Nevertheless, some users are open about their identity. Some openly post under their real names, sometimes even with accounts proved by YouTube, others use a nickname but combine this with a picture that is most likely showing themselves and some dismantle their identity in their posts, mostly when they are close relatives of the survivor. And there are even some users who are survivors themselves. It is often to be found that users integrate into their comments further information about themselves and the identity they have chosen to display. So we learn about users whose relatives have been murdered, users who are connected to the topic being German or Jewish, their sexual orientation, and sometimes information about their profession is revealed, them being film makers, teachers, students and so on. But it is up to the user to decide the scale of openness or anonymity he or she prefers, different to the survivors and to a smaller extent to the interviewer and the camera(wo)man. They have to act openly under their full name. Their non-anonymity makes their testimonies even more compelling, if this is at all possible, as a verified real person is telling her or his story. This is even more relevant, as the web tends to be under the suspicion of the easy manipulation of content.

c) Different commentary cultures

An interesting result of my research is (as Figure 2 shows) that beneath each testimony a quite distinct communication culture develops. In regard to the topics discussed, the way the witness is addressed, as well as the dominating tone of discussion. Itka Zygmuntowicz is, for example, very often addressed by her pet name, Itkala. These different communication cultures might be explained by the different strain of each testimony from hater or troll posts. Another explanation is that users perceive the survivors on YouTube as individuals to whom they develop a certain degree of connection and for whose testimonies they have searched for different reasons. For Renée Firestone or Paula Lebovics an often articulated reason is that the user met the survivor offline, for Ernest Lobet it is his role in

Denis Avey's memoirs. The degree of connections seems to be dependent on sympathy and the survivor's personality.

d) Connections between the offline and online world

As mentioned above, users often relate directly to offline meetings, films, books or other things related to the individual survivor in their posts. I interpret this observation as it is relevant to connect both spheres of remembrance for most users or as they are trying to get both layers of memory overlapping. In this way they transfer offline meaning to the online world and establish new meaning in the online world. And it might also be connected to the still occurring suspicion of online data being more easily manipulated. If online testimonies can be backed up with offline world knowledge it makes it more stable, more credible. This seems a fortiori important, as the testimonies on YouTube are open to negotiation.

Summary

Digital Shoah memory in the form I have analysed for this article is highly ambivalent. In general it can be understood as a new layer to Shoah remembrance culture. This new layer contains emotional bonding to the survivor in a way that can only be acted out in digital surroundings. And it contains personal attacks towards survivors, hate speech and insults that seem impossible offline. A few traits of digital Shoah memory are to be highlighted: first of all, one has to acknowledge the new network of agents in whose interactions digital Shoah memory is created. Secondly, YouTube users are forming small and unstable communities, negotiating Shoah memory with the survivors, the USC Shoah Foundation and with other survivors openly. In this process different aspects of digital Shoah memory can be worked out: a) users cross offline time barriers in the communication culture they are developing and b) they act with different layers of their identity, concealing their offline identify online or overlapping both to different extends. Third, they use their knowledge and their communicative skills to stabilize Shoah memory online. Fourth, and this has to be paid attention to, Shoah memory online is vulnerable to anti-Semitic or denying attacks, a situation that needs an appropriate response. If one decides to place testimonies on YouTube as the USC Shoah Foundation does, one needs to develop a response to hate speech. One possible response could be moderating the comments.

Bibliography

A. Books

Marek, Roman. *Understanding YouTube. Faszination und Plastizität eines Mediums (*Bielefeld: transcript, 2013).

Snickars, Pelle, and Patrick Vonderau, ed., *The YouTube Reader*, (Stockholm: KB, 2009).

B. Articles

Bothe, Alina. "Im Zwischen der Erinnerung. Virtuelle Zeugnisse der Shoah," in *kunsttexte.de*, No. 1, 2012, 11 pages, accessed November 8, 2013, http://edoc.hu-berlin.de/kunsttexte/2012-1/bothe-alina-6/PDF/bothe.pdf.

Bothe, Alina. and Martin Lücke, "Im Dialog mit den Opfern. Shoah und historisches Lernen mit virtuellen Zeugnissen," in *Shoa und Schule. Lehren und Lernen im 21. Jahrhundert*, ed. Peter Gautschi, Meik Zülsdorf-Kersting, and Béatrice Ziegler (Zürich: Chronos, 2013), 55-74.

Brauer, Juliane, and Aleida Assmann, "Bilder, Gefühle, Erwartungen. Über die emotionale Dimension von Gedenkstätten und den Umgang von Jugendlichen mit dem Holocaust," *Geschichte und Gesellschaft* 37, 1, (2011): 72-103.

Brauer, Juliane, and Dorothee Wein, "Historisches Lernen mit lebensgeschichtlichen Videointerviews - Beobachtungen aus der schulischen Praxis mit dem Visual History Archive" *Gedenkstättenrundbrief* 153: 9-22.

Brüning, Christina. "Unterricht mit videografierten Interviews aus dem Archiv 'Zwangsarbeit 1919-1945.' Die Lehrer_innen-Perspektive," in *Erinnern an Zwangsarbeit. Zeitzeugen-Interviews in der digitalen Welt,* ed. Nicolas Apostolopoulos and Cord Pagenstecher, 273-286.

Giacobini, C. "YomHaShoah. Rembering the Holocaust," in *2Life*, No. 2, May 2007, 9. The magazine was available on: www.2lifemagazine.com, the Website has now been removed.

Nägel, Veresa Lucia. "Das Visual History Archive des Shoah Foundation Institute in Forschung, Lehre und Schulunterricht," in *Ich bin die Stimme der sechs Millionen. Das Videoarchiv im Ort der Information,* ed. Daniel Baranowski (Berlin, 2009), 185-191.

Stefanie Schüler-Springorum, "Welche Quellen für welches Wissen? Zum Umgang mit jüdischen Selbstzeugnissen und Täterdokumenten," in

Wer zeugt für den Zeugen? Positionen jüdischen Erinnerns im 20. Jahrhundert, ed. Dorothee Gelhard and Irmela von der Lühe (Frankfurt am Main: Peter Lang, 2012), 175-192.

C. Accessed Online

Andrews, Kay."A damned good cry," *PastForward* 1 (2013): 14.

Giacobini, C. "YomHaShoah. Rembering the Holocaust," in *2Life*, No. 2, May 2007, 9. The magazine was available on: www.2lifemagazine.com, the Website has now been removed.

USC Shoah Foundation: Statistical report, Web. November 4, 2013, http://sfi.usc.edu/news/2013/11/first-quarter-2013-shows-increases-usc-shoah-foundation%E2%80%99s-academic-media-and, accessed November 5, 2013.

—. "Jewish Survivor Renée Firestone Testimony." YouTube. YouTube, July 10, 2009, accessed October 8, 2013.

—. "Jewish Survivor Paula Lebovics Testimony." YouTube. YouTube, December 3, 2009, accessed October 8, 2013

—. "Jewish Survivor Esther Stern Testimony." YouTube. YouTube, October 4, 2011, accessed October 8, 2013

—. "Jewish Survivor Abraham Bomba Testimony." YouTube. YouTube, January 29, 2009, accessed October 8, 2013

—. "Jewish Survivor Kristine Keren Testimony." YouTube. YouTube, January 30, 2009, accessed October 8, 2013

—. "Jewish Survivor Sally Roisman Testimony." YouTube. YouTube, July 13, 2009, accessed October 8, 2013

—. "Jewish Survivor Ellen Brandt Testimony." YouTube. YouTube, January 30, 2009, accessed October 8, 2013

—. "Jewish Survivor Ernest Lobet Testimony." YouTube. YouTube, November 9, 2009, accessed October 8, 2013

—. "Jewish Survivor Ester Fiszgop Testimony." YouTube. YouTube, January 30, 2009, accessed October 8, 2013.

—. "Jewish Survivor Itka Zygmuntowicz Testimony." YouTube. YouTube, February 11, 2009, accessed October 8, 2013.

—. "Jewish Survivor Sonia Berson Testimony." YouTube. YouTube, July 11, 2009, accessed October 8, 2013.

—. "Jewish Survivor Ursula Levy Testimony." YouTube. YouTube, January 30, 2009, accessed October 8, 2013.

—. "Jewish Survivor Leopold Page Testimony." YouTube. YouTube, May 12, 2009, accessed October 8, 2013.

—. “Jewish Survivor David Abrams Testimony.” YouTube. YouTube, January 30, 2009, accessed October 8, 2013.

—. “Jewish Survivor Henry H. Sinason Testimony.” YouTube. YouTube, January 30, 2009, accessed October 8, 2013.

YouTube. “United States Holocaust Memorial Museum on A cherished object: Kristine Keren’s Green Sweater. Curators Corner 3,” accessed November 7, 2013, http://www.youtube.com/watch?v=adwU_M1rdTA.

PART V:

DIGITALISING HUMAN FUNDAMENTALS ACROSS CULTURES

CHAPTER FIFTEEN

FRIENDSHIP IN A DIGITAL AGE: ARISTOTELIAN AND NARRATIVE PERSPECTIVES

DOUGLAS PONTON

Introduction (i)

Social network sites such as Facebook propose a relation of digital friendship, which can be obtained by a simple click on the mouse. Friendship, like love, is a human relationship which most find congenial. Has the digital revolution, then, made it easier for us to find friends? Problems such as loneliness and social isolation would have been overcome, if this is true, by the kind of relations found in virtual communities. Some players of computer games do indeed claim that the online relationships they form are more important and satisfying than those they find in real life.[1] Some commentators have suggested that such online intimacy is a technological version of "shipboard syndrome," in which friendships are fostered because contact after the voyage is impossible.[2] Of this, Reid observes that there is little danger of subsequent interference in participants' everyday lives, so they are not inhibited by the demands of "social self-preservation."[3] While some participants in online friendships claim to re-evaluate their real-world relationships in the light of the intimacy they find in an online context,[4] others say that their

---

[1] Harris 2005: 71, Parker 2008: 6.
[2] e.g. Curtis 1992, in Reid 2005: 114.
[3] Reid 2005: 114.
[4] Roberts et al 2006: 45.

> very best and closest friends are members of their electronic group, whom they seldom or never see. [5]

Claims like these, however, raise fundamental questions about ontology that apply to every kind of web-based experience. To call reality "virtual," in the first place, implies that it is at best only a substitute for the "real." The question of identities created in an online environment can also be problematic, as these can bear little or no relation to the real-world identity of the user. While "selective self-presentation" occurs in real-world friendships too, there are few clues in online contexts to enable users to check the authenticity of identity claims.[6]

Against such positive testimonies of online friendship are other voices which see such relationships as superficial:

> The superficial emptiness clouded the excitement I had once felt..It seems that we have lost, to some degree, that special depth that true friendship entails. [In quitting MySpace and Facebook] I'm not sacrificing friends, because if a picture, some basic information about their life and a web page is all my friendship has become, then there was nothing to sacrifice to begin with.[7]

How far virtual friendships can provide what is normally found in the social webs of real communities is an important question. This paper cannot provide an answer, for the question lies more in the area of sociology than linguistics. There are, however, questions of interest whose answer can be sought in the language people use to describe their experiences. Firstly, how far narratives of virtual friendship appeal to traditional descriptions of real-world friendships. A perspective on narrative based on that of Labov[8] will sound whether online relationships respond to the same human needs as traditional friendships. In Georgakopoulou's words, narrative analysis has generally dealt with autobiographical content about "non-shared, personal experience and single past events"[9] which, as will be seen below, is a fair description of much web discourse on friendship.

Secondly, the analysis will be interesting in terms of the ontological

[5] Hiltz, S.R. and M. Turoff. *The network nation: human communication via computer.* (New York: Addison-Wesley 1978), 101.

[6] Varis et al 2011: 269.

[7] Baron, Naomi, S. *Always on. Language in an online and mobile world.* (Oxford: OUP, 2008), 230.

[8] Labov 1972.

[9] Georgakopoulou 2007: 1.

question just raised. Considering the central role the computer has acquired in societies worldwide, and the continuous increase in time spent online for reasons of work and leisure, the question of how "real" online experiences can be is a fundamental one. In the case of the relationship of love, online services seem to expedite real-world relationships, acting as improved versions of traditional dating agencies. Online users are able to exchange information, find like-minded people with whom they become friendly, eventually meet up with and either find that their "virtual" feelings correspond and form the basis of a lasting relationship, or else find that these are dispelled by real contact. In the case of friendship, however, it is not unusual to find that these are carried on wholly in a virtual environment, without any expectation of real contact.

The study explores the state of friendship generally, in the digital age, and whether, as some have claimed, it is in terminal decline as an institution. It also asks how far accounts of online relationships square with narratives of the more traditional form of friendship, with a view to responding to some of the questions raised above. It therefore involves a consideration of what friendship is, in a traditional perspective, as well as an analysis of current, web-based narratives.

Introduction (ii) Traditional, Aristotelian friendship

In 1960, C.S. Lewis gave a well-known description of the state of friendship in British society:

> To the Ancients, Friendship seemed the happiest and most fully human of all loves; the crown of life and the school of virtue. The modern world, in comparison, ignores it. We admit of course that besides a wife and family a man needs a few 'friends'. But the very tone of the admission, and the sort of acquaintanceships which those who make it would describe as 'friendships', show clearly that what they are talking about has very little to do with that *Philía* which Aristotle classified among the virtues.[10]

Such remarks relate to what Hyatt terms the "epoch" features of the social context, how a society understands and legitimates itself.[11] The decline of the institution of friendship in modern times has been noted by other social commentators than Lewis.[12] However, his claim that the modern world

---

[10] Lewis, C.S. *The four loves*. (New York: Harcourt Brace Jovanovich 1991), 57-58.

[11] Hyatt 2005: 522.

[12] e.g. Miller 1991.

"ignores" friendship cannot be accepted at face value. If this were so, sites like Facebook would have no need to propose their instant friendships, nor would there be sites which aim to build communities based on friendly relationships. On the contrary, research suggests that at least some modern people *do* place a value on friendship, but they seem to find it in an online context rather than in the real world.[13]

Lewis's contention relates to the quality of modern friendships, which he suggests has been eroded to the level of mere acquaintance. A friend, in this sense, is hardly more significant than a number on Facebook, amounting to little more than someone to play a round of golf with, or go out for a drink.

Here are three accounts from the web of people's experiences of modern friendship that seem to support Lewis' claims:

> **Carrob** I am great at socializing and true friendship of all kinds...but most are paired up in their 30's and have very little time for true friendship. Many prefer the superficiality of Facebook and Twitter. Yes, I have my cats, my plants, my television, my computer, my acquaintances, my mother...but oh, how I would long for one or two platonic friends.[14]
>
> **Rick** Maybe it's California. Maybe it's me. Despite my best efforts, living in the same community for decades, I have no friends here. None. I make all the effort, I listen. I have friends from years ago 3,000 miles away in upstate New York, and some in Colorado, where I lived for a few years, but none in California. I lived for a couple of years in New York City, and found it very similar. Relationships never developed beyond a veneer of at best, polite chatter. Many times it was a game of one-upmanship, name dropping, comparing toys. I learned to live in the moment, no expectations, happy to have a glimpse of intimacy from time to time. Loneliness is the human condition.
>
> **Giesela** I'd love to have friends...but everyone is too busy with family. Family has replaced friendship.

Rick laments the superficiality of his real world relationships, while virtual friendships, according to Carrob, are also "superficial". By inference, "true" friendship, for which Carrob also uses the word "Platonic," is something deeper, summed up by Rick with the word "intimacy." Carrob and Giesela underline Lewis's assertion that the most basic human relational needs are to have a "wife and family" Indeed, Giesela explicitly

[13] Thelwall 2009: 25.

[14] http://www.wilsonquarterly.com/essays/america-land-loners

identifies the family as the cause of the decline of the institution of friendship. When Carrob says that most of her acquaintances are "paired up in their 30's," the inference is that they are too busy with family matters to have time for other relationships. As for acquaintances, it is significant that Carrob lists them after her cats, plants, television and computer.

The web is an inexhaustible source of discursive data, and these extracts, found by a Google search for the keyword "friendship," are not intended as evidence that Lewis' assertions are correct. It would perhaps be possible to find other samples from blogs in which people swap stories about their rich social lives and their many true friendships. What is of interest in these narratives is the implicit appeal to a common notion of what "true friendship" might bc, and a shared sense that they lack this desirable thing.

In a discussion of friendship in the western tradition, an obligatory starting point is the work of Aristotle, and his well-known accounts of the subject in the Rhetoric and the Nichomachean Ethics. Friendship for Aristotle was of three kinds; of utility and of pleasure[15], and of perfect friendship.[16] The first term is self-explanatory, and relates to the kind of friendly relations people carry on with acquaintances in their everyday lives, for practical reasons. Such friendships are weak and easily change with changing circumstances, when one or the other partner no longer finds it useful to carry them on. Friendship of pleasure, meanwhile, is typified by passionate attraction, and is especially found among the young. Again, such friendships, though they may be intense, are easily dissolved. Aristotle gives an example of two whose friendship is dissolved when one loves the other for reasons of pleasure, the other for utility. If this is the case, says Aristotle,

> the friendship is dissolved when they do not get the things that formed the motive of their love; for each did not love the other person himself but the qualities he had, and these were not enduring; that is why the friendships also are transient.[17]

What Aristotle calls perfect friendship is the relationship between two virtuous people who, being good themselves, love the good that they see in the other:

---

[15] Ross 1999: 129.
[16] ibid: 130.
[17] Aristotle. *The Nicomachean Ethics.* Translated by W.D. Ross. (Kitchener, Ontario: Batoche Books 1999),130.

> Perfect friendship is the friendship of men who are good, and alike in virtue; for these wish well alike to each other qua good, and they are good themselves. Now those who wish well to their friends for their own sake are most truly friends; for they do this by reason of their own nature and not incidentally; therefore their friendship lasts as long as they are good - and goodness is an enduring thing. [18]

Aristotle's discussion at times reaches idealistic heights, suggesting that for a person to have such a friend is to have "another self"[19], infusing the relation with an essentially virtuous, philosophical character. Since such elevated souls are, by their nature, rare, so will true friendship be extremely uncommon. However, his discussion has historically formed the basis of thoughts on the subject of human friendship in a general sense. The essential point is that perfect friendship - in Carrob's modern idiom, "true" friendship - is a relation based on wishing someone well "for their own sake", in contrast with the utilitarian or pleasure-seeking relationships, that can only exist as long as the partners find in the other something they need. Aristotle puts this more plainly, in the Rhetoric:

> We may describe friendly feeling towards any one as wishing for him what you believe to be good things, not for your own sake but for his, and being inclined, so far as you can, to bring these things about. [20]

The following exploration of Internet data assesses the relevance of Aristotle's three-fold classification of types of friendship to the modern world.

Data (i) Triratna. Aristotelian friendship?

The Internet is a massive source of data for testing linguistic hypotheses[21]; though, as Leech (2007: 144) points out, there are questions over whether data collected via a search engine like Google can be truly called representative. This study advances no claims in this sense, however; as I have said above, there are web pages for every shade of opinion on friendship, and no way to make generalised, sociological conclusions about them. What I have done is collect some web data which deals with

---

[18] Aristotle. *Ethics*, 130.

[19] Stern-Gillet 1996.

[20] Aristotle. *Rhetoric.* Translated by W. Rhys-Roberts. (New York: the Modern Library, 1954), 100.

[21] Rohdenburg 2007.

the topic and used it to explore nuances in its current use, relating these to the Aristotelian concepts, alluded to by C.S. Lewis, as touchstones for understanding the modern variety.

From initial Google searches for "friend/s/friendship," it was apparent that two strands of research among the wealth of material available would be fruitful. Firstly, to explore narratives of real-world friendship which are available online. Such material may challenge Lewis's claim that Aristotelian "philia" is not to be found in modern friendships. Secondly, blogs and websites in which people discuss the merits of virtual friendship. This may shed light on the ontological questions outlined above about the value of virtual friendship, as well as showing the extent to which such relationships are conceived of in terms of their real-world counterparts.

In the real world context, one finding was an organization called "Triratna," formerly known as the Friends of the Western Buddhist Order. The role of friendship in this organization is apparent from a first glance at the material on its site. Using the site's search motor to find the word "friendship" produces the following:

> Ananda, the Buddha's long-time attendant, asks the Buddha if friendship is half of the spiritual life. The Buddha's reply, that spiritual friendship is the whole of the spiritual life is something to come back to again and again.[22]

Such a remark recalls the important role the institution of friendship has traditionally played in religious orders; certainly the social context of religious institutions appears to be one worth exploring further.

The following analysis of attempts to sort corpus references[23] for the keywords "friend" and "friendship" into two groups; those Aristotle would classify as friendship for utility or pleasure (and Lewis as "mere acquaintances"), and those involving a form of what he would call "perfect friendship."

1. Perhaps they introduce that new	**friend**	to other friends of theirs, and in
2. rows up. You introduce your new	**friend**	to your old friends. Perhaps they
3. like normally to introduce that	**friend**	to your old friends. So in that

[22] See web references.

[23] The FWBO corpus consists of all downloadable articles on the Triratna site (see web references).

4. our friend, or for the sake of your	**friend**	, what you would not perhaps
5. , you learn perhaps to do for your	**friend**	, or for the sake of your friend,
6. snatches away the king's close	**friend**	and favourite advisor and then
7. that and I thought if you make a	**friend**	, if you make a new friend, you
8. in life. In that sense it is a	**friend**	, a counselor to be welcomed. It
9. to listen to my answer. Recently a	**friend**	of mine died of AIDS . I was not
10. blaze. From being outsiders, my	**friend**	and I gradually became guests of
11. below the monastery. I and a	**friend**	decided to attend the cremation.
12. at the birth of the daughter of a	**friend**	. I saw for myself how giving
13. he shouted, and he hurried my	**friend**	Amogabhadra and I out of the hot
14. Team'. Last summer I met a	**friend**	whose first child was then just on
15. to hear of the death of an old	**friend**	from AIDS. Although I had not
16. In 1988, Henry, a college	**friend**	, told me that he too had 'full

Table 1: "Friend" in the FWBO corpus

As Stubbs states, the characteristic collocations of words tell us much about their associations and connotations.[24] The verbs "introduce" (1-3) and "meet" (14), occurring close to the keyword, imply a conventional sense of friendship, as does its use in familiar phrases like "a close friend," (6) "to make a friend,"(7) "my friend and I,"(10) "an old friend,"(15) "a college friend." (16)

An interesting finding was the collocation "spiritual friend/s" (Table 2). Of such "strong collocates"[25], Baker says:

[24] Stubbs 1996: 172.

[25] Sinclair 1991: 112.

> the discourses surrounding them are particularly powerful - the strength of collocation implies that these are two concepts which have been linked in the minds of people and have been used again and again.[26]

41. a recognition, by our spiritual	**friends**	, that we are effectively going
42. be a practising Buddhist. Spiritual	**friends**	help us to make spiritual
43. in spiritual discussion with	**friends**	or listening to a lecture on
44. human, and without spiritual	**friends**	one can hardly be a practising
45. good spiritual teachers, spiritual	**friends**	. And I've had the opportunity
46. when they become spiritual	**friends**	, well what happens? They have
47. founded. So the friends, spiritual	**friends**	especially, are helping each

Table 2: "Spiritual Friends" in the FWBO corpus

These references all come from talks by Sangharakshita, the movement's founder. Reference (46) in full shows that something close to Aristotle's philia is intended:

> When two people become friends, and especially when they become spiritual friends, well what happens? They have an influence on each other. They produce something between them. They produce between them a relationship, an experience, a mental state which we call that of friendship, metta.

In the final part of this text Sangharakshita's description of friendship is reminiscent of Christ's "greater love hath no man than this":

> [...] you learn perhaps to do for your friend, or for the sake of your friend, what you would not perhaps hardly even do for yourself. And in this way friendship becomes what I've called somewhere in the past a sort of mutual transcendence of egoism.

---

[26] Baker, Paul. *Using corpora in discourse analysis*. (London and New York: Continuum, 2006), 114.

"Spiritual friendship," then connotes an intensity of communication, of interaction; a sincerity, a depth, and a final goal of "mutual transcendence of egoism." Such friendships have a clear connection with the Aristotelian tradition of perfect friendship.

Expanding one of the references produced the following narrative of friendship within the FWBO. An Order Member, Amritavajra, who has HIV, speaks of the importance of friendship to him:

> Another important factor which enables me to cope with my diagnosis is my friendships. AIDS and HIV infection can be a very isolating disease. Many people in the modern world are lonely and are starved of deep and effective communication with others, but when you are diagnosed with a disease like HIV you are forced to become aware of exactly how isolated you actually are. Because the disease is still a very taboo subject in large areas of society, it is very easy to feel ostracized and alienated from the community. To some extent I have managed to deal with these feelings of isolation and intense aloneness by forming deep and satisfying friendships. And it is my experience that these friendships can only form to the extent that you share the same vision and are committed to that vision. This is the case in the Sangha, where friendship, especially spiritual friendship, is presented as the guiding principle of spiritual development. I don't think it is possible ever to over-estimate the importance of friendship. Without it I feel I would have given up a long time ago. Real friendship is both nourishing and healing. Happiness is impossible without it. My friends help me on all sorts of levels, from asking me how I am, to taking an active interest in my health, and coming down to the hospital with me when I go for a check-up. Perhaps the most important way in which my friends help is simply by asking me how I am - and having the care and attention to listen to my answer.

In terms of Labov's narrative structure theory, this narrative gives a prominent place to Evaluation. Evaluations of the importance of friendship are inserted in a personal narrative of *illness* (Labov's complication) and how this is dealt with (resolution). Long sections of evaluation (lines 2-7 and 9-16) help place this text as an example of a didactic genre, attempting to persuade readers of the importance of friendship, understandable in the light of what has been said about the importance of friendship to the FWBO. Of interest are the correspondences with Aristotle's notions of friendship, especially that perfect friendship is a moral matter, only possible between two "good" people:

> Perfect friendship is the friendship of men who are good, and alike in virtue (Aristotle)[27]

> these friendships can only form to the extent that you share the same vision and are committed to that vision. (Amritavajra)

Again, the writer's contention that happiness is impossible without friends (12-13) is also found in Aristotle.[28] As for the details of the narrative, the writer says that it is the conversation and company of his friends that mean most to him. Aristotle tends to theorize about friendship, rather than provide details of how perfect friends behave towards each other. He does, however, recognize their importance in times of trouble, of which Amritavajra's sickness would be an instance:

> In poverty and in other misfortunes men think friends are the only refuge.[29]

The most telling detail of the story is Amritavajra's repeated phrase "asking me how I am." (14, 16) Such a phrase is part of the conventional conversational routine on greeting acquaintances. The depth of true friendship, however, is revealed by his conclusion: "having the care and attention to listen to my answer." In other words, his friends, like Aristotle's perfect friends, are interested in his well-being, *for his own sake* (Ross 1999: 130). From Sangharakshita's idealizing rhetoric, to the details of this narrative of friendship, it is plain that Aristotelian ideals of friendship are still to be found today in the context of the FWBO.

Data (ii) Online friendship sites

From among the many sites dealing with friendship issues I selected three to include in a corpus and for close reading: the Friendship Blog, Mike Arauz's blog, specifically the page "Spectrum of online friendship," and Chris Pirillo's blog, specifically the page "Is a virtual friend a real friend?"[30] All three sites have in common the desire to exchange views on friendship, both real-world and virtual, and to foster virtual environments

---

[27] Aristotle. *Ethics*, 130.
[28] Ross 1999: 127, also 157-8.
[29] Aristotle. Ethics, 127.
[30] See web references.

in which participants can have friendly contact which may lead to the development of friendship. Such sites are one step back from providing data about actual online friendships. There are sites of this kind, but there are practical and ethical difficulties that make it impossible to obtain data records of such private exchanges.

From a glance at the results for "friends" (Table three) it is apparent that exploring the nature of virtual as opposed to real friendship is a constant of these sites. As well as highlighting difficulties with both real and virtual friendship (2, 3, 8, 9, 12, 13),[31] contrasts are drawn between real-world contexts and virtual (10, 11, 15):

1. was $600, while the brides'	**friends**	and my husband's friends all did…
2. 13 at 8:11 am. Seems most my	**friends**	were fair weathered birds. I was
3. to have a lot of former best	**friends**	that are now burnt bridges. This is
4. have a hard time making local	**friends**	…over lunch one day she asked why
5. have a career and many other	**friends**	from college and her community, so
6. about quality, not quantity of	**friends**	for sure. Debbie :) reply Debbie says
7. based on age. I'm 50 and my	**friends**	, about my age or younger, respond
8. he has lost all of her one-time	**friends**	after being sick. After many years
9. doing – when my old friends	**friends**	can't. Long story short I stopped
10. myself and I love those new	**friends**	dearly but I also love my old friends
11. meeting my longtime (real)	**friends**	face to face. reply Jane Boursaw say
12. , and didn't see that your	**friends**	did not reciprocate the loyalty that
13. sting and the feeling that our	**friends**	only want to hang out with us if we
14. and the adult children were	**friends**	now, so it was awkward for them. I

[31] For reasons of space, the paper only includes the first fifteen instances of both "friends" and "friendship" (tables three and four).

15. as cut and dried as are virtual	**friends**	real friends. I'm sure we've all

Table 3: "friends" in web corpus

Some of these references come in the context of explicit comparison between real-world and virtual friendship. For example, expanding (11) leads to:

> Social media tends to make friendships happen overnight, which feels a tad superficial to me. For that reason, I limit my time online and make a point of getting out and meeting my longtime (real) friends face to face.

The superficiality of online friendships is denied by (15), in which the user emphasises the real-world benefits of online support:

> I don't think it's as cut and dried as are virtual friends real friends. I'm sure we've all experienced great moral support from online communities when things get tough. Case in point, my wife's online pregnancy community. This group has been amazingly supportive for her during very challenging pre- and post-natal experiences.

The same pattern is found in results for "friendship" (Table Four):

1. Try to improve the	**friendship**	by being a better friend, or 2)
2. thinking of breaking the	**friendship**	off. I've had enough.Truly, online
3. chat all day via text, the	**friendship**	isn't going work long term. Reply.
4. as a spectrum), but online	**friendship**	also differs in kind in radical ways.
5. promise even a very close	**friendship**	While a friend may appreciate your
6. please do not give up on	**friendship**	life and love. I'm proof that it's
7. the real power of	**friendship**	through a virtual friend? How has so
8. to feel the warm glow of	**friendship**	Now that I am older, I don't put up
9. forget his selfless act of	**friendship**	and compassion.
10. a good person. I had a	**friendship**	like this once, years ago – your

11. to decide whether the	**friendship**	was worth the frustration of
12. to preserve an important	**friendship**	even though it can be so difficult to
13. may very well end this	**friendship**	but it sounds like you've had enough.
14. me that a long-standing	**friendship**	ended when her friend made a
15. a nonprofit organization.	**friendship**	is about reciprocity for me. Not

Table 4: "friendship" in web corpus

(2) is a narrative of a failing online friendship. While the poster's comments are negative about online friendships, the comparison she makes is of interest because it shows that, for her, there is no essential difference in kind between virtual and real friendships:

> I'm actually thinking of breaking the friendship off. I've had enough. Truly, online friendships can cause as much pain or joy as offline friendships. Like offline relationships, online friends also have certain expectations of each other, and when those expectations aren't met, the friendship begins to fall apart.

Her comments exactly parallel Aristotle's analysis of friendships, mentioned above, that fall apart because one of the parties has a utilitarian perspective.

Against this is a testimonial like (9), where the writer tells of an act of financial help from an online friend who he had never met.

From a brief look at this corpus data it is apparent that, to these users, friendship and friends are of great importance. Users of these online discussion groups and virtual communities seek help with personal issues in their everyday lives, and some of them at least find that they are able to form meaningful friendships online.

Close reading of the online material confirms these impressions, as users exchange narratives and offer comments on each others' experiences. The Friendship Blog centres on the personality of Irene S. Levine, a self-styled "friendship doctor," who provides agony aunt style comments on user's friendship problems, which are then the focus for discussion among the sites' users. Users also post their problems for comment, and in this way an online community develops. In the following extract, a user responds to a girl's entry:

> I had a friend that was a bit of a shady user like this girl, who only called me up to hang out when she really wanted a ride somewhere, like a far away restaurant or store, much like this girl.

This post implies that the Aristotelian model still forms part of what discourse analysis refers to as "shared speaker knowledge"[32] or "cognitive context"[33], meaning the relevant mental structures of assumptions, cultural attitudes and belief systems that guide pragmatic interpretations during interaction. The poster confirms the first girl's assumption that to be exploited by a so-called "friend" is evidence that what is offered by the third person is a form of utilitarian friendship. Both seem to have in mind the notion that friendly relations ought to consist in Aristotle's pattern, of wishing someone well "for their own sake", not for whatever one can get out of the other, either in the form of pleasure or some other practical good, such as a lift to a faraway place. The following extract, from the same source, provides more evidence of this girl's exploitative approach to friendship:

> We weren't really talking for awhile. Then suddenly, she texted me:
>
> Her: Heyyy can I have your old homework?
> Me: Is school starting for you in a few days?
> Her: Ha yep.
> Me: No.
> Her: WHY?! D:
> Me: Because you had more than a month to do this including the winter break. You're smarter than me, and I find this assignment easy. Don't expect me to just give it to you.

The page as a whole confirms that norms of "true" friendship are based on a version of the Aristotelian position, i.e. that there can be conflict between "perfect friendship" and "utilitarian," and people on this site at least evaluate the former positively over the latter.

The other two sites included in the corpus are personal sites of professional individuals with an interest in the subject of online friendship. Mike Aruaz has a business background, and created a business-style presentation of what he calls a "spectrum" of online friendships. The

[32] Coulthard 1992: 42.
[33] Archer et al 2008: 619.

model he presents (Figure One) is of interest as it charts the progress of virtual friendships through the stages of idle curiosity about a blog, to more consistent forms of online contact such as repeated postings on a blog or webpage, through to direct contact and exchange of private emails.

As contact deepens, the prospective friend becomes part of a virtual web, an online community. Just as in the real world, s/he is introduced to the friend's other friends, via posts, re-tweets, the sharing of links, and so on. Of this process, Aruaz comments "I also have made myself more valuable, because I am now partly responsible for the spread of your ideas." Such friendships could remain at this utilitarian level, in which both parties enjoy benefits from a fairly superficial contact. The final stages, however, of deepening trust, which occur in private dialogue through email and other forms of direct messaging can lead to what Aruaz sees as a true friendship. In Advocacy, one of the friends can risk his reputation by publicly supporting the other's ideas, while in the final stage, he is willing to actually do something on his friend's behalf.

One comment on this post is the following:

> A while ago, I had created my own version of a "spectrum", which I did as a tweet:
> How Friends are Born: Stranger > follow > @ > DM > FB > Phone > Meet > Friend

The significant difference, however, is in the final stages. Whereas this user sees real-world meeting as an essential preliminary to friendship, it seems that Aruaz's model is intended to relate entirely to the virtual world.

Chris Pirillo, finally, is a young entrepreneur in the field of technology and media, who oversees online communities which have both virtual and real-world elements. In the page selected for the corpus, he gives an instance of how virtual and real-world contexts intersect through friendship:

> One of our long-time community members unexpectedly lost his mom two days ago. The poster talks about how he lives several hundred miles from his family. While waiting to travel home, he turned to his friends in our community for support. The support was instant and unconditional. This reinforces the fact that you don't have to necessarily meet someone face-to-face in order to form a true and lasting bond. Many deep friendships are made online, only to have the involved persons never lay eyes on each other (beyond webcams and photos). I see it happen every day. I witness the bonds that many of our regular community members share.

Passive Interest	Active Interest	Sharing	Public Dialogue	Private Dialogue	Advocacy	Invest-ment
Starting point. -Curiosity -Repeat visits -Blog readers -Fans -Followers	Let you know I'm listening. - Blog Comments -FB wall -@replies on Twitter	You become part of my identity - I talk to my friends about you - I spread your ideas. -social bookmarking, -retweeting, -post links and content in my sites	Public indication of friendship -Other friends know about us - I join your group -referrals in their blog posts	Mutual interest becomes mutual trust. -private sharing of thoughts, ideas, experiences -trust each other with direct access -exchange email -TXT messages, -direct messages on Twitter, Facebook, YouTube	Explicitly recommend you to my friends. -"This is important. It's worth my friends' time". - risk my reputation to convince my friends to check it out.	Real online friendship. -virtual friends will take action on your behalf.

Figure 1: the spectrum of online friendship (Aruaz)

A poster confirms that such things do indeed occur. Several years ago, he says, the same thing happened to him, and he didn't have the money to pay for a flight home:

> One of my oldest and best on-line friends read what I wrote and sent me an email telling me to check my PayPal account. He had deposited enough to cover the flight there and back, a fairly substantial sum. I've known this wonderful person for over 7 years though we have never met face-to-face and have only spoken on the phone once. I consider him one of my closest friends, on-line or off. I will never forget his selfless act of friendship and compassion.

Pirillo and Aruaz clearly believe in a modern version of the Aristotelian ideal. What is more, it is some such form of friendship that posters seem to be in search of. As cited above[1], the willingness to wish good things for a friend, and to act in order to bring them about, is one component of perfect friendship, and some posters at least testify that they find it in a virtual context.

Discussion

One of the narratives cited above is worth looking at in full because it encapsulates many of the issues explored in this study. A participant in a virtual friendship complains that she is thinking of breaking off the relationship:

> I've had what I thought was a close online friendship for 5 years - this friend has a similar competitive online business to mine. We've exchanged several emails daily, sharing everything that's going on in our lives, the good and bad. But lately, she has become increasingly "competitive," imitating my work. And sometimes her actions are hurtful - like the time I sent her some photos of my beloved dog and she didn't bother to comment, or the time I emailed her about a painful medical procedure that I was having complications with, and she didn't reply. And she was rude after I sent her a gift in the mail, never thanking me for it; even worse, the gift was something that was personally meaningful to me and something I wanted to share with her.
>
> I'm actually thinking of breaking the friendship off.
>
> I've had enough.

[1] Rhys-Roberts 1954: 100.

15 Truly, online friendships can cause as much pain or joy as offline
16 friendships. Like offline relationships, online friends also have
17 certain expectations of each other, and when those expectations
aren't met, the friendship begins to fall apart.

In Aristotle's terms, the virtual relationship began as a utilitarian one. The poster relates (1-3) that the friends had similar professional interests, and therefore the exchange of information about "everything that's going on in our lives" would include details of business procedures, initially of benefit to both. However, the fact that both had similar jobs made it possible for the user's friend to overstep the mark and begin to exploit the friendship to steal a march on her professionally. As we have seen, such a situation, in Aristotle's view, is likely to strain the friendship. The poster, meanwhile, demonstrates that she was in search of not utilitarian but perfect friendship. She shares details of her intimate, affective life (5-6), seeks help, advice and comfort in troubled circumstances (7), and treats her friend with generosity and kindness (8-10). In all of these actions she is disappointed by her friend's indifference. The suspicion is that, as in other friendship narratives we have explored, "perfect" friendship from one partner is met with "utilitarian" behaviour from the other. Once again, the relevant perspective is that of Aristotle, who the user paraphrases in her Evaluation of the story (13-17):

> the friendship is dissolved when they do not get the things that formed the motive of their love [2]

This narrative illustrates, finally, an important aspect of the discourse of online friendships. For this user, at least, it would seem that there is no essential difference between virtual and real friendship. Some posters talk of the "superficiality" of online contact. However, as virtual friends become more and more familiar with one another they can exchange more intimate details, and deepen their friendships until, in the terms of Aruaz's spectrum, they are willing to do things for each other in exactly the same way as real-world friends. When the poster talks of the pain and joy associated with real and virtual friendships being identical, she is making an ontological statement. There is no such thing as "virtual" pain.

[2] Aristotle. *Ethics*, 146.

Conclusion

Virtual friendships did not begin with the Internet. Joinson describes the formation of such friendships between telegraph operators in an earlier technological age, who developed shorthand forms of communication analogous to today's online forms.[3] Nevertheless, the computer revolution has had an impact on the interpersonal relationships of humanity in a general sense, and the issues discussed in this paper have global relevance.

From the starting point of the study, which was Lewis's scepticism about the state of friendship in the modern world, we have found a wealth of online data that suggests the contrary. People seem to turn to Internet friendship sites precisely because the relationship of friendship is important to them. We have seen that some seek to explore issues with real-world friendship, difficulties with making friends, and problems with keeping them. We have seen, too, that in certain sectors, for example, in the religious context explored in the discourse of the FWBO, the Aristotelian concept of perfect friendship represents a spiritual ideal to be striven towards. Not only that, but an Aristotelian analysis of the different types of friendship seems as relevant today as ever. A constant of posts providing narratives of tensions in friendship is that, while the poster feels that his/her own feeling towards the friend is that of perfect friendship, that of the other partner tends to be exploitative, or utilitarian. Many seem to have, at the back of their minds, an implicit notion of philia which guides their behaviour towards their friend/s, and which is constantly disappointed.

It is, of course, impossible to generalise, from such a limited study, and suggest that C.S. Lewis was wrong, that the modern world cares about friendship as much as the ancient. For every user of friendship sites there could be as many more indifferent to the whole question. Nevertheless, the intensity with which some posters on these sites pursue the matter, and the circumstance that virtual friendships can arise which seem to be as intense, long-lived, and mutually beneficial as their real world counterparts, is suggestive that the relationship is still an important one. What is more, analysis of the implicit and, at times, explicit comparison of virtual and real-world friendship carried on in these forums has shown that Aristotle's insights about friendship are as relevant today as they were in his own time.

[3] Joinson 2003, in Harris 2005: 63.

Bibliography

Archer, Dawn, Jonathan Culpeper and Matthew Davies. Pragmatic annotation. In *Corpus Linguistics: an international handbook (volume 1)*, edited by Anke Lüdeling and Merja Kytö. Berlin and New York: Walter de Gruyter, 2008.

Aristotle. *Rhetoric.* Translated by W. Rhys-Roberts. New York: the Modern Library, 1954.

—. *The Nicomachean Ethics.* Translated by W.D. Ross. Kitchener, Ontario: Batoche Books, 1999.

Baker, Paul. *Using corpora in discourse analysis*. London and New York: Continuum, 2006.

Baron, Naomi, S. *Always on. Language in an online and mobile world.* Oxford: OUP, 2008.

Coulthard, Malcolm. The significance of intonation in discourse. In *Advances in spoken discourse analysis*, edited by Malcolm Coulthard. London and New York: Routledge, 1992.

Georgakopoulou, Alexandra. *Small Stories, Interaction and Identities*. Amsterdam: John Benjamins, 2007.

Harris, Jacobson Frances. *I found it on the internet: coming of age online*. Chicago: American Library Association, 2005.

Hiltz, S.R. and M. Turoff. *The network nation: human communication via computer.* New York: Addison-Wesley, 1978.

Hyatt, David. "Time for a change: a critical discoursal analysis of synchronic context with diachronic relevance." *Discourse and Society* Vol. 16(4): 515–534. London, Thousand Oaks, CA and New Delhi: Sage, 2005.

Joinson, Adam, N. *Understanding the psychology of internet behaviour. Virtual worlds, real lives.* Basingstoke, UK: Palgrave Macmillan, 2003.

Labov, William. *Language in the Inner City*. Philadelphia: University of Pennsylvania Press, 1972.

Leech, Geoffrey. New resources, or just better old ones? The Holy Grail of representativeness. In *Corpus linguistics and the web,* edited by Marianne Hundt, Nadja Nesselhauf and Carolin Biewer. Amsterdam and New York: Rodolpi, 2007.

Lewis, C.S. *The four loves*. New York Harcourt Brace Jovanovich, 1991.

Miller, Stuart. *Men and friendship*. New York: Penguin Books, 1991.

Parker, Jim.Where Is the Shaman? In *Electronic tribes: the virtual worlds of geeks, gamers, shamans, and scammers*, edited by Tyrone, L.

Adams, and Stephen, A. Smith. Austin: University of Texas Press, 2008.

Reid, Elizabeth. Hierarchy and power: social control in cyberspace. In *Communities in cyberspace,* edited by Marc, A. Smith and Peter Kollock. London: Routledge, 2005.

Rohdenburg, Günter. Determinants of grammatical variation in English and the formation/confirmation of linguistic hypotheses by means of internet data. In *Corpus linguistics and the web.* Edited by Marianne Hundt, Nadja Nesselhauf and Carolin Biewer. Amsterdam and New York, Rodopi, 2007.

Roberts, Lynne, D., Leigh M. Smith, and Clare, M. Pollock. Communicating in synchronous text-based virtual communities. In *Encyclopedia of virtual communities and technologies*, edited by Subhasish Dasgupta. Hershey, London, Melbourne and Singapore: Idea Group Reference, 2006.

Sinclair, John, McHardy. *Corpus, concordance, collocation.* Oxford: OUP, 1991.

Stern-Gillet, Susan. *Aristotle's philosophy of friendship*. New York: State University of New York Press, 1996.

Stubbs, Michael. *Text and Corpus Analysis*. Oxford: Blackwell, 1996.

Thelwall, Mike. Social networking and the web. In *Advances in computers vol. 76*, edited by Marvin, V. Zelkowitz. Burlington, London and Amsterdam: Elsevier, 2009.

Varis, Piia, Wang, Xuan and Du, Caixia. Identity repertoires on the internet: opportunities and constraints. In *Applied linguistics review 2,* edited by Wei, Li. Berlin and New York: De Gruyter Mouton, 2011.

Web references

Curtis, Pavel. Mudding: social phenomena in text-based virtual realities, 1992. Accessed 27/09/2013. http://w2.eff.org/Net_culture/MOO_MUD_IRC/curtis_mudding.article

Chris Pirillo's Blog. Accessed 27/09/2013. http://chris.pirillo.com/is-a-virtual-friend-a-real-friend/

Mike Aruaz's Blog. Accessed 27/09/2013

The Buddhist Centre. Accessed 27/09/2013 http://thebuddhistcentre.com/search/node/friendship

The Friendship Blog. Accessed 27/09/2013 http://www.thefriendshipblog.com/category/making-friends/

CHAPTER SIXTEEN

E-OBITUARY AND *E-NEKROLOG* AS EMERGENT ONLINE GENRES: A CONTRASTIVE STUDY

MAGDALENA SCZCZYRBAK

Introduction

Originating from the Middle Latin *obituārius* denoting a record of the death of a person, the term "obituary," according to the *New Oxford Dictionary of English*, refers to "a notice of a death, especially in a newspaper, typically including a brief biography of the deceased person." However, as observed by Kściuczyk, the present-day obituary increasingly departs from its standard format of a brief newspaper insert informing of a person's death and it is becoming more of a "culture text," revealing the beliefs and status of the deceased and being a story about the living.[1] It is even more visible in the case of online obituaries, which, thanks to the use of multimedia and interactive components, offer new functionalities, contributing to what Martin terms the "obituary experience."[2]

Accordingly, the aim of the current study is twofold: on the one hand, to show how traditional genres such as obituaries evolve to accommodate changes in the socio-rhetorical setting in which they are produced, and, on the other, to demonstrate that, whether paper-based or electronic, obituaries not only mirror the way societies approach death and end-of-life

---

[1] Kściuczyk Joanna, "Wartościowanie we współczesnych nekrologach," in *Antynomie wartości. Problematyka aksjologiczna w językoznawstwie*, ed. Agnieszka Oskiera (Łódź: Wydawnictwo Wyższej Szkoły Humanistyczno-Ekonomicznej w Łodzi, 2007), 315.

[2] Martin John, "The Obituary – A Genre Analysis, " North Carolina State University, accessed June 30, 2013, http://www.nematome.info/RevisedGenreAnalysisJohnMartin.pdf.

issues, but also operate as vehicles for conveying social values, attitudes and emotions. What is more, though not of intuitive importance, obituary research, as I believe, can provide insights into how obituaries contribute to grief support community forming, both offline and online. Finally, it might also be added that I chose to compare data from American and Polish websites, that is Legacy.com and wspomnijbliskich.pl, respectively, in order to determine how the culturally-conditioned "obituary experience" is being created by different Internet users, namely Poles, considered to be rather conservative and reserved, and Americans, believed to be more open and straightforward, for which purpose contrastive genre analysis, frequently applied in discourse studies, appears to be a suitable analytical tool.

Obituary genres in American and Polish cultures

Organisation and content of traditional obituaries

Approached from a broad perspective, obituaries can be situated alongside other funeral and consolatory genres such as *eulogies*, *memorials*, *testimonials*, *tributes* or *epitaphs*. In a more local context, i.e. in North American culture, *obituaries* are free, newsroom-produced articles reporting a person's death and informing of the upcoming funeral, whereas *death notices* and *memorial advertisements* are paid advertisements written by the family or the funeral home. However, while paid death notices are "formulaic announcements of a person's death," published obituaries are "concise factual accounts of a person's life meant to contribute to the historical record" and as such they are "one of the most-often utilized archival materials for historians, genealogists, scholars and the general public."[3] Historically, brief announcements of death were published in America already in the 16th century, yet it was only in the 18th century, following the British tradition, that more detailed accounts of death gained currency in the American press.[4]

In the Polish context, in turn, the recent death of a person is traditionally reported in *nekrolog.* Other related genres include: *klepsydra,*

[3] "Writing Tips for New Obituarists," Funeral Consumers Information Society, accessed June 4, 2013, http://www.funeralinformationsociety.org/yourlastwrites/history.html.

[4] Gilbert Holly S., "A Brief History of the Obituary," Funeral Consumers Information Society, accessed June 4, 2013, http://www.funeralinformationsociety.org/yourlastwrites/history.html.

epitafium, *biogram*, *anons wspomnieniowy* and *wspomnienie* or *ogłoszenie pośmiertne*. Interestingly, the Polish *nekrolog*, unlike the English *obituary* (or *obit*) which is of Latin origin, is derived from the Greek words *necrós* (corpse) and *logos* (word). For the sake of clarity it should be noted, though, that while the plural *nekrologi* denotes both obituaries and medieval or contemporary records with names of the deceased (held by cathedrals and monasteries), the singular *nekrolog* refers, like its English counterpart, chiefly to a notice of somebody's death which is made publicly available (usually in the press), containing information about the funeral as well as concise data about the deceased's life and activity. Alternatively, it may refer to an article or a note related to a person's death. At this point it is also worth mentioning that contemporary Polish obituaries were preceded by press articles providing detailed accounts of funeral celebrations which had already taken place.[5] Today, conversely, *nekrolog* is a form of invitation to the upcoming funeral; therefore, it is vital that it be placed in the most up-to-date medium with the broadest reach possible. Finally, the familiar genre of *klepsydra* (formely *kartka pogrzebowa*) refers to a black-edged poster containing an obituary and it is usually found in public places, e.g. on notice boards, house walls or in churches. Originally, these funeral cards were hand-written texts, but they were later replaced by woodcut, lithography or even copperplate engraving.[6]

Contentwise, both American and Polish obituaries share a number of properties. To start with, American obits typically include the following details:

12- Name, age, occupation and address of the deceased
13- Time, place and cause of the deceased's death
14- Date and place of birth of the deceased
15- Survivors (usually immediate family)
16- Details of funeral arrangements
17- Disposition/memorial donation wishes of the deceased/family
18- Life history, the deceased's outstanding activities/achievements
19- Memberships of organisations/service in the armed forces.

[5] "Na marginesie tematyki cmentarnej. Nekrolog," Cmentarium, accessed May 16, 2013, www.cmentarium.sowa.website.pl.

[6] "Na marginesie tematyki cmentarnej. Klepsydry albo kartki pogrzebowe," Cmentarium, accessed May 16, 2013, www.cmentarium.sowa.website.pl.

Alternatively, information about the deceased's pets as well as anecdotes or recollections from their friends or relatives are also included.[7]

Predictably, the composition of the Polish *nekrolog,* though evidently less detailed, roughly corresponds to the organisation of its American counterpart. As observed by Bzdoń, the thematic progression of text usually follows the pattern outlined below (with some elements being optional):

20- Date of the deceased's death (less frequently the cause of the death)
21- Occupation of the deceased
22- Achievements of the deceased
23- Character traits of the deceased
24- Details of funeral arrangements
25- Signature.[8]

As regards the signature, it should be noted that in the case of private obituaries the text is signed by a family member, relative or friend,[9] whereas in the case of institutional obituaries by a representative of the institution. It is also in institutional obituaries that more elaborate information on the deceased's professional life and achievements is provided, with private obituaries focusing more on the loved one's character traits, beliefs or ideals. As for the visual components, a striking feature of traditional Polish obituaries is the black edge accompanied by Christian symbols such as palm leaves, the cross and the abbreviation *Ś.P.* (late) preceding the deceased's name. Thanks to these elements, readers instantly recognise the type of genre they are dealing with, despite the fact that customarily it has no headline. Worth mentioning is also the fact that obituaries can be written not only in the third person, but also in the first person. Furthermore, as stressed by Kolbuszewski (2009), the genre entails the presence of the themes of war and Polish martyrdom or the deceased's eminent professional or cultural achievements.[10]

---

[7] It might also be added that writing pet obits is not uncommon in North America, a practice I have not encountered in Poland.

[8] Bzdoń Jadwiga, "Nekrolog jako gatunek tekstu. Uwagi o pokrewieństwie stylistycznym z biogramem," in *Język – Styl – Gatunek*, ed. Małgorzata Kita et al. (Katowice: Wydawnictwo Uniwersytetu Śląskiego, 2009), 55.

[9] It should also be stated that no specific names are provided; instead, the signature contains information about the family connection (e.g. grandchildren, brother, son).

[10] It is interesting to note that, depending on their predominant function, Polish obituaries can be divided, as proposed by Kolbuszewski, into the following sub-

It might also be added after Corona Marzol analysing British and American realisations of the genre, that one of the constant organisational elements of obituaries is what she calls the "Family stage," which usually "comprises two pieces of information: the trajectory of the deceased in family terms (marriages, divorces, offspring and deceased members) and the surviving members."[11] In fact, the researcher concludes that the Family stage is a "regular, highly formulaic, genre-specific and multipurpose-driven element"[12] of obituaries.[13] It can be easily noted, however, that in the case of Polish *nekrologi* this stage is missing, with the family members customarily marking their presence in what might be called the "Signature stage." Finally, apart from the constant elements of obituaries, textual silences or meaningful omissions of certain facts are also vital in the discoursal interpretation of the genre, a view followed in this study. Evidently, in agreement with the Latin *de mortuis nihil nisi bonum* (Of the dead, nothing unless good) principle, obituaries mention only the outstanding activities and achievements of the deceased and, what follows, certain details about the person's life are left out. The most striking "silences" are, unsurprisingly, those related to the deceased's family life and sexual orientation, which can be best detected when compared with competing obituaries.[14]

Pragmatic functions and the social role of obituaries

As is apparent from the preceding sections of this chapter, obituaries are primarily linked to the informative function, since their traditional role is to provide details of a person's death and the upcoming funeral. Yet, with the ongoing transformation of the genre, resulting in less rigidly structured texts incorporating novel and more individualised elements, it has come to perform a number of related functions. What follows, as proposed by Martin,[15] obits also serve to: educate the readers, honour and commemorate

---

genres: *nekrolog informacyjny* (informational obit), *nekrolog kondolencyjny* (condolence obit), *nekrolog pożegnalny* (farewell obit), *nekrolog podziękowanie* (thank-you obit) and *nekrolog rocznicowy* (anniversary obit) alongside mixed formats (Kolbuszewski 1997, 42).

[11] Corona Marzol Isabel, "Coming out of the Closet 'Six Feet Under': Textual Silences and the Social Construction of the Family Stage in the Obituary Genres," *Revista Alicantina de Estudios Ingleses* 19 (2006): 70.

[12] Corona Marzol, "Coming out," 78.

[13] Typically, the phrases "is survived by" and "was preceded in death by" are used.

[14] For a fuller discussion see Corona Marzol "Coming out."

[15] Martin, "The Obituary."

the deceased, thank the family and carers, provide psychological closure of the deceased's life, to create a public or historical record and, finally, to create a community. Worth highlighting at this point is also the expressive function of obituaries, which is directly related to the use of emotive and evaluative lexis and which is frequently realised with the help of linguistic devices such as metaphors, hyperboles or euphemisms. Not infrequently, obituary writers also rely on poetry or Latin maxims, thus enhancing the artistic value of the message conveyed. It may then be posited that obituaries are multifunctional goal-oriented texts which operate as part of a social practice.

Obviously, the social role of obituaries should not be underestimated. As observed by Crespo Fernández, in the Victorian period the genre was a medium which reflected the social status, wealth and position of the deceased, with more eminent members of local communities having longer and linguistically more elaborate tributes written for them.[16] Seen from a current perspective, obituaries continue to serve social purposes. On the one hand, they perform the role of public announcements in small communities; on the other, they allow the bereaved to connect to the people that their loved ones knew and, ultimately, to find grief support and consolation. Therefore, obituaries can be perceived as covert dialogues intended to provoke a response from the deceased's friends or relatives. In addition, emotionally loaded words and the informative function attest to the dialogicality of the genre, too.[17]

Unsurprisingly, like human interest stories, obituaries attract a large number of readers, some of whom regularly rely on information about the funeral services held for local community members. In fact, as revealed by the Readership Institute's Impact Study,[18] improving obituaries is one of the most effective ways in which newspapers can increase readership. The practices recommended by the Institute include: provision of complete lists of area deaths; publishing obits by region (and not just in alphabetical order); leading every obituary page with a longer "story obituary" about an ordinary person, followed by shorter obituaries; tombstone-like practice of including birth and death dates immediately under the name of the deceased; publishing a daily list of funerals in addition to obituaries. It is also noted that obituaries are "ordinary people" stories in disguise and

[16] Crespo Fernández Eliecer,"Linguistic Devices Coping with Death in Victorian Obituaries," *Revista Alicantina de Estudios Ingleses* 20 (2007): 18.

[17] Wierzbicka Anna, "Genry mowy," in *Tekst i zdanie*, ed. Teresa Dobrzyńska and Elżbieta Janus (Wrocław: Ossolineum, 1983), 135.

[18] "Obituary Best Practices Gallery," Readership Institute, accessed June 10, 2013, http://www.readership.org/content/obit_gallery.asp.

therefore are often worth displaying on the first page. Finally, it is argued, paying great attention to detail in the formatting and typography can enhance the overall visual impact and add an air of dignity and respect. What matters most, however, is the creation of an emotional connection with the reader.

In light of the foregoing discussion, it can be justifiably concluded that obituaries are texts which convey "private intentions within the socially recognized communicative purposes."[19] As such, they are amenable to change in response to changing socio-rhetorical situations and contexts, especially given the fact that they serve "to negotiate individual responses to recurring and novel rhetorical situations."[20] Naturally, the flexibility of generic forms, including the genre of *obituary*, can be easily exploited in the online environment creating new ways of interaction and becoming a home to hybrid e-genres.

American and Polish online obituary sites

Form, content and purpose of online obituary sites

As follows from the above, the genre of *obituary* has been evolving to address the users' needs and reflect changes in extra-linguistic reality. Thought of in this way, *e-obituaries* – seen as a hybrid genre subsuming death notices, traditional obituaries, tributes, epitaphs or even books of condolences – are clearly a step towards the sensory and interactive "obituary experience" referred to earlier in this chapter and made possible thanks to the existence of dedicated sites (including new generic forms such as e.g. *obit blogs*, *obit fora* or *video obits*). The motto "Expanding the way in which we remember," visible at the top of the Legacy.com website, encapsulates the very essence of online obituary sites and succinctly defines the role they perform. One of the ways is the inclusion, apart from the conventional elements described in Section 2, of interactive components, multimedia and related services. Below, I will include the most common "expansions" or "enhancements" of the traditional genre, focusing on their form, content and purpose, especially as exemplified by two memorial portals: the American Legacy.com and the Polish wspomnijbliskich.pl.

[19] Bhatia Vijay K., *Analysing Genre – Language Use in Professional Settings* (London: Longman, 1993).
[20] Bhatia, Vijay K., *Worlds of Written Discourse: A Genre-Based View* (London: Continuum, 2004), 23.

Collaborating with more than 900 newspapers, Legacy.com aims "to provide ways for readers to express condolences and share remembrances of loved ones."[21] Being "the leader in the online memorial and obituary market," the site hosts more than 10 million obituaries and provides access to more than 78 million records from the Social Security Death Index dating back to 1937.[22] The site contains four main sections:

26- Obituaries & Guest Books
27- Memorial Sites (for sharing legacies, with special groups like: WWII veterans, Iraq and Afghanistan or the 9/11 attacks)
28- LegacyConnect (offering non-stop grief support and advice)
29- ObitMessenger™ (with free obituary alerts).

As can be easily noticed, even though the primary communicative purpose remains the same, the online realisation of the genre expands the ways in which it is addressed. What may strike the reader who is used to the traditional format are the interactive tools that Legacy.com offers. Among these additions in the "Obituaries and Guest Books" section, users can see, for instance:

30- Search tools (search by newspaper, by name or keyword)
31- Featured obituaries with photos, including Facebook, bookmark, e-mail and print options
32- Guest books in which readers can leave a message, add a photo or light a candle.

The very same obituaries and guest books can be accessed via the "Memorial Sites" section, in which they are divided into thematic groups such as, for instance:

2013 – Remembering famous figures lost in 2013
Remember 9/11/2001 – Honoring those we lost on September 11, 2001
Teachers – Honoring and remembering teachers

Information about grief support groups as well as condolence and funeral etiquette advice can, in turn, be found in the "LegacyConnect" section. Thematically arranged communities include discussion fora dealing with specific types of loss: "loss of a parent," "bereaved spouses," "loss of a

[21] "About Legacy.com, Inc.," Legacy.com, accessed June 4, 2013, www.Legacy.com/NS/about.
[22] "About Legacy."

child" or "suicide survivors," to name but the first few options,[23] all of which can be followed on Facebook, Pinterest, Twitter or Google+.[24] Finally, ObitMessenger™, with its free obituary alerts, offers "timely, customized obituary news delivered directly to your email inbox."

While the potential of interactive tools to create lasting tributes cannot be denied, worthy of note are also other ways of remembering, as offered by the Gift Shop featured by Legacy.com. Apart from traditional flower arrangements, the available options include:

-sympathy baskets (with plant and fruit) to be offered as an expression of sympathy
-plantable cards from which wildflowers will grow in memory of your loved one
-Walking Beside Me Reflections Frames featuring a photo and a laser-engraved name of your loved one
-personalised memorial photo wall canvas
-memorial tree seedlings
-custom heritage albums which can be created with the use of free and easy-to-use software.

Alternatively, users may opt for one of the featured charities and make a donation.

Clearly, it is thanks to the interactive content that Internet users can both share their memories and offer bereavement support.[25] Thus, the discourse community includes not only obituary writers and editors, funeral directors, families, relatives and friends of the deceased, but also, to use Martin's words, "emphatic passers-by"[26] ready to offer consolation. It can be argued then that grief support groups like the ones hosted by Legacy.com are what marks the greatest contrast between traditional, static obituaries and obituary sites incorporating dynamic and interactive content. Among the elements enhancing the "obituary experience," elements such as music or videos featuring the deceased should not go unnoticed, either.

---

[23] Similar discussion topics can be seen in the "Our Community" section on GoneTooSoon.com.

[24] It might also be added that Facebook, with its MyMemorials™ application, also enables its users to create memorial pages on which they can pay tribute to family members, friends and celebrities by sharing memories and adding photos.

[25] By analogy, sites like FondPetMemories.com, on which users can post their pet's memorial or obit, offer pet loss support.

[26] Martin, "The Obituary."

As for interaction patterns, obituary sites in general exemplify asynchronous online communication, involving the reciprocity of the roles of sender and receiver. In addition, they are hierarchically organised, contain hypertext links and rely on multimedia. As such, they represent a hybrid type of discourse in Crystal's words,[27] combining spoken and written language characteristics, some of which are especially prominent. For instance, while e-obituaries themselves are space-bound, elaborately structured, factually communicative and generally not repeatedly revisable, related interactive content (condolences or consolatory messages posted in response to obituaries) is spontaneous, less loosely structured and more socially interactive.

Some of the features highlighted above can also be found on the Polish site wspomnijbliskich.pl. It is evident, however, that its American counterpart incorporates more tools and offers more advanced solutions.[28] When compared with Legacy.com, the Polish service seems to be in its nascent stage. The types of announcements offered to the site users include: *in memoriam* announcements, condolences, obituaries as well as thank-you announcements. On average, as revealed by this study, these are much shorter messages than those found on Legacy.com. Also, it can be noticed that obituaries hosted by the American site are frequently quite lengthy narratives or "life stories" about the deceased (whose photographs typically accompany text) including detailed information about the survivors too, whereas their Polish counterparts tend to stick to the traditional pattern of a rather short informative text with elements of poetry and praising or consolatory language. What is more, users of wspomnijbliskich.pl are invited to offer their sympathy by leaving a message or tribute, which, in turn, can be enhanced by one of the following options:

33- Lighting a candle
34- Posting a message or image
35- Animating the message
36- Inviting others to share their family videos
37- Adding an event

[27] Crystal David, Language and the Internet (Cambridge: Cambridge University Press, 2004), 42–43.

[28] What is more, it also appears that online obituary sites are less popular with Polish Internet users than they are in the US and therefore that they are less firmly established in Polish culture, as indicated by the fact that two of the Polish obituary sites which I selected for analysis had already disappered before I started my investigation.

38- Sharing slideshows.

By analogy to Legacy.com, all messages posted on wspomnijbliskich.pl can be sent to a friend, followed, added to the timeline on Facebook or shared on Twitter and Google+. In addition to ordinary e-obituaries, Polish Internet users can also place *Anons Premium* enriched by additional elements. Once upgraded to the premium status, a paid online obituary may include videos, slideshows as well as personalised graphics. As part of this option, a star showing the way to the related obituary appears on what is called *Wirtualne Nocne Niebo* (Virtual Night Sky), a feature not offered by Legacy.com.[29]

Yet, even though the tools listed above clearly invite dialogue with other users, there is no single option (or forum) dedicated to the creation of an online community centred around one type of loss or involving continuous grief support and consolation, which, as has been shown, is the case with Legacy.com.[30] Interestingly, though, the site has different language versions apart from Polish, including e.g. English, German or French, which indicates that its content is aimed at an international audience, too. Yet, it may be speculated that since death is still a bit of a taboo subject in Polish culture, it will take some time before Polish Internet users take to new services like the ones offered by American sites. What is more, given the Polish mentality and attitude to end-of-life issues, unusual ways of remembering loved ones (such as e.g. "consolation baskets" offered to families of the deceased or jewellery with cremated remains) may take a while before they find followers, if at all. Nevertheless, it may be concluded that despite these differences and American Internet users' greater openness and willingness to share their grief and to talk about the loss of their dear ones, both American and Polish obituary sites are inescapably linked to a direct and indirect evaluation of the deceased, which is a feature they share with traditional obituaries.

[29] However, Wirtualne Nocne Niebo bears resemblance to the Celestial Sky option, one of the Remembrance Gardens made available on MuchLoved.com.

[30] It may be added, however, that there are other websites or online fora which offer grief support. A case in point is pomocpostracie.pl, a private site set up by a psychologist sharing her painful experience and offering consolation and advice to others. However, I have not found a single portal which would offer many such fora in one place.

Emotive and evaluative language

It might again be reiterated that the deceased are often assessed and identified by reference to the events and values of which they were part. It may then be claimed that information about the deceased is invariably axiologically marked and that it is always a subjective account resulting from the obituarist's personal attitude to them.[31] Further, as noted by Kolbuszewski, an obituary is "a confirmation of somebody's existence," in which we can look for "values, facts, events, but, above all, values related to the deceased: a diligent worker, a good mother, an educator of many generations, a soldier awarded medals […]."[32] To this end, as revealed by Kaptur, obituarists either rely on evaluative or descriptive-evaluative lexemes (direct evaluation) or exploit stereotypes evoking certain connotations and rely, though less frequently, on presupposition (indirect evaluation).[33] Further, the scholar observes that evaluation of the deceased in Polish obituaries follows certain schemata and conventions, including, for instance, references to the deceased's military history, positions and titles held as well as their achievements and memberships in various organisations.[34] Adopting Kściuczyk's evaluative categories as a framework for my study (Table 1), I will now try to compare their respective realisations on the two obituary sites under analysis.[35]

---

[31] Kaptur Ewa, "Wartościowanie osób zmarłych w poznańskich nekrologach prasowych," in *Antynomie wartości. Problematyka aksjologiczna w językoznawstwie,* ed. Agnieszka Oskiera (Łódź: Wydawnictwo Wyższej Szkoły Humanistyczno-Ekonomicznej w Łodzi, 2007), 337.

[32] Kolbuszewski Jacek, "Z głebokim żalem, czyli nekrolog życia," *Dziennik Zachodni,* October 29, 2009, accessed August 8, 2013, http://www.dziennikzachodni.pl/artykul/179166,z-glebokim-zalem-czyli-nekrolog-zycia,id,t.html?cookie=1 [The translation is mine].

[33] Kaptur, "Wartościowanie osób," 337.

[34] Kaptur, "Wartościowanie osób," 338.

[35] Kściuczyk, "Wartościowanie," 315–328.

CATEGORY	REALISATION
Naming strategies	First and last name, nicknames, diminutives
Place	Place of birth, life, death
Image of the deceased	Professional: occupation, achievements, awards, publications etc. Private: personal qualities
Conceptualisation of death	Positive: 'good' death, death of natural causes, death as sleep Negative: sudden/tragic death, death after a long illness

Table 1. Categories of evaluation in obituaries

Undoubtedly, evaluation of the deceased against the background of the values and events related to them or in which they were involved can be felt in the address forms used. Accordingly, Figure 1 shows examples extracted from the two sites analysed to show similar naming strategies. As can be noted both in American and Polish obits, family terms, e.g. *mother*, *sister* or *husband*, are used alongside nouns such as *friend* or *matriarch* and references like *szef* (boss) or nicknames ("Bev," "Ania").

Legacy.com	***wspomnijbliskich.pl***
Beverly L. "Bev" [...] (*TC Palm,* Feb. 21, 2010)	*ŚP Stanisława [...] „Ania"* (*Gazeta Wrocławska*, July 25, 2013)
the devoted matriarch of a family who adored her (*The Columbian*, March 20, 2012)	*ŚP Ewa [...] Najukochańsza Siostra, Szwagierka i Ciocia* (*Dziennik Polski*, July 31, 2013)
Our dear friend and beloved Scott (*Daily Record*, May 11-18, 2012)	*śp. Wojciech [...] nasz kochany Mąż, Ojciec, Teść, Dziadek i Zięć* (*Głos Wielkopolski*, July 25, 2013)
Kitty was a beloved mother to [...] Loving grandmother of 16 and great grandmother of 10. (*The Seattle Times*, Oct. 12, 2011)	*żegnamy naszego Szefa ś+p Wojciecha [...]* (*Głos Wielkopolski*, July 25, 2013)

Figure 1. Naming strategies

Secondly, as argued by Grzesiak,[36] a place can shape one's personality and, what follows, it can be rightly perceived as an evaluative category. Accordingly, Figure 2 shows a sample of references to places connected with the deceased which are believed to have affected their character. For instance, in the Polish context, references are made to Siberian prisons and the Polish Home Army community, whereas their American counterparts include references to American states or the US House of Representatives.

Legacy.com	***wspomnijbliskich.pl***
Norm was born in Seattle, Washington and lived for periods of time in Kansas, California, and Idaho (*San Jose Mercury News/San Mateo County Times*, Jan. 8, 2012) *She pursued her career in Washington, D.C., retiring in 2005 as the Director of Financial Counseling for the United State House of Representatives.* (Skagit Valley Herald Publishing Company, Oct. 1, 2010)	*Żołnierz Armii Krajowej walczący na Kresach Wschodnich, [...] więzień Workuty, sybirak* (*Głos Wielkopolski*, July 31, 2012) *seniorka małopolskiego środowiska żołnierzy AK* (*Dziennik Polski*, Aug. 6, 2013)

Figure 2. Place as an evaluative category

Next comes affective language with a plethora of emotionally loaded adjectives like *dear*, *great*, *beloved, loving*, *wonderful* in English and *kochany/a, najdroższy/a, najukochańszy/a, wspaniały/a, niezastąpiony/a* in Polish as well as other qualifiers (see Figure 3). All of them evoke positive connotations and are meant to add to a positive image of the deceased. Clearly, a distinction is made between the deceased's "professional image" and "private image," resulting in descriptions of their professional qualifications and skills, on the one hand, and personal qualities, on the other.

[36] Grzesiak Romuald, "O sposobach wyrażania wartości w tekstach nekrologów," in *Język a kultura: Wartości w języku i tekście, vol. 3,* ed. Jadwiga Puzynina and Janusz Anusiewicz (Wrocław: Wiedza o Kulturze, 1991), 82.

Legacy.com	***wspomnijbliskich.pl***
Professional image:	*Professional image:*
He served our country as a Naval Aviator during World War II. He then served the Jackson community as a dentist for many years (*Jackson Citizen Patriot*, April 27–28, 2013)	*śp. Adam [...], Inżynier budownictwa, Były Dyrektor Biura Studiów i Projektów Przemysłu Mleczarskiego oraz wieloletni pracownik przedsiębiorstw: PRK-9 i KRAKBUD* (*Dziennik Polski* Aug. 20, 2013)
Bill served in the U.S. Army Air Force during WWII. (*Dignity Memorial*, Nov. 26, 2012)	*Ś+P Daniela [...] wieloletnia księgowa ŁZR „Fonica"* (*Dziennik Łódzki*, Aug. 6, 2013)
Lillian worked as an auditor for Hanford government contractors (Harvey Family Funeral Home - Seattle, Oct. 10. 2011)	*Private image:*
Private image:	*Pozostanie w naszej pamięci nie tylko jako wybitny fachowiec, ale pełen ciepła i życzliwości dla chorych i współpracowników Człowiek* (*Głos Wielkopolski*, July 22, 2013)
He will be remembered for the unwavering loyalty and love he showed his family and friends. He was the epitome of a gentleman who was committed to serving others (*Orange County Register*, July 31, 2013)	*Wychowawca i trener wielu pokoleń sportowców, wspaniały Kolega i życzliwy wszystkim Człowiek* (*Głos Wielkopolski*, July 20, 2013)
Mary was a wonderful, loving wife, mother and grandmother who could put a smile on any one of our faces. She was an amazing lady and will be greatly missed by all. (Palmer Bush & Jensen Family Funeral Homes Lansing Chapel, April 22, 2013)	*Mój życiowy towarzysz, niezawodny i niezastąpiony Przyjaciel. Prawy Człowiek* (*Dziennik Polski*, Aug. 20, 2013)
	ś+p Anna [...] Żołnierz AK (*Głos Wielkopolski*, July 25, 2013)

Figure 3. Image of the deceased

Unsurprisingly, the last category is that related to both positive and negative conceptualisations of death (Figure 4). More often than not, death is described as a journey, loss, sleep, eternal guard or the ultimate end of all earthly things. A striking difference between Polish and American obituaries is that the latter contain relatively few negative references to death, illnesses or tragic causes of death, unlike their Polish counterparts, in the case of which this practice is more common. On the other hand, unlike American realisations of the genre, Polish obits often start with a poem containing vivid death-related metaphors and imagery.

Legacy.com	***wspomnijbliskich.pl***
Positive conceptualisation:	*Positive conceptualisation:*
passed peacefully surrounded by her family on July 30, 2013 to become a forever heavenly angel (*San Jose Mercury News/San Mateo County Times,* Aug. 4, 2013)	*Opuścił dzieci, by połączyć się z ukochaną Żoną Urszulą* (*Dziennik Bałtycki*, July 22, 2013)
entered her heavenly reward (Palmer Bush & Jensen Family Funeral Homes Delta Chapel - Lansing Delta Chapel, Dec. 9, 2012)	*przeżywszy lat 80, zasnęła w Panu* (*Dziennik Polski*, July 8, 2013)
walked into the arms of the Lord (*Flint Journal*, Feb. 16-19, 2012)	*odeszła na Wieczną Wartę* (*Dziennik Polski*, Aug. 6, 2013)
She joyfully stepped into the presence of Jesus Christ between the third and fourth verses of Amazing Grace (*The Columbian,* March 20, 2012)	
Negative conceptualisation:	*Negative conceptualisation:*
was received into the hands of her Lord Jesus on September 18, 2010 after a short battle with cancer (Skagit Valley Herald Publishing Company, Sept. 22, 2010)	*po długiej i ciężkiej chorobie odeszła do wieczności* (*Dziennik Łódzki*, Aug. 6, 2013)
lost a courageous and intense battle with cancer (Skagit Valley Herald Publishing Company, Oct. 1, 2010)	*po ciężkiej, nieuleczalnej chorobie, przeżywszy 48 lat odszedł w otchłań świata* (*Dziennik Łódzki*, July 22, 2013)
	opuściła nas na zawsze (*Dziennik Polski*, July 30, 2013)

Figure 4. Conceptualisation of death

Final remarks

I hope to have shown in the foregoing discussion that the genre of *obituary* has the potential to develop, especially in a virtual reality. As with other genres, conventional formats co-exist with (or are being gradually phased out by) their dynamic and interactive successors. And even though, as it seems, the basic communicative function remains the same, online "enhancements" of traditional obituaries or death notices can serve new purposes. More specifically, the study has revealed that although the very idea of integrating interactive and multimedia content in American and Polish e-obituaries is the same, Legacy.com by far exceeds its Polish counterpart in as far as the number of users and the number of tools are compared. Needless to say, crossing the boundaries of the traditional 'static' obituaries and moving towards their flexible realisations is possible thanks to new interaction patterns and non-linguistic elements which, as it appears, are becoming an inseparable part of the genre.

It may also be observed that unlike the predominant informative function of paper-based obituaries, the expressive and consolatory functions take over in their online realisations, with a marked shift towards greater interactivity and dialogicality afforded by tools promoting online bereavement support communities, including not only immediate family and friends, but also any online "passers-by" willing to offer consolation. Still, it remains to be seen how American and Polish realisations of the genre evolve and how the traditional format is exploited to address the needs of obituary users in American and Polish online environments, respectively. Notwithstanding the above, however, it may be speculated that – despite the technological progress and the consequent digitalisation of life – death notices or obituaries, in whatever shape and form, will continue to exist as long as people attach much importance to death and feel the need to share their grief and relate to other human beings.

Bibliography

Bhatia, Vijay K. *Analysing Genre – Language Use in Professional Settings*. London: Longman, 1993.

—. *Worlds of Written Discourse: A Genre-Based View*. London: Continuum, 2004.

Bzdoń, Jadwiga. "Nekrolog jako gatunek tekstu. Uwagi o pokrewieństwie stylistycznym z biogramem." In *Język – Styl – Gatunek,* edited by Małgorzata Kita, Maria Czempka-Wiewióra, Magdalena Ślawska, and Maria Wacławek, 48–58. Katowice: Wydawnictwo Uniwersytetu Śląskiego, 2009.

Cmentarium. "Na marginesie tematyki cmentarnej. Klepsydry albo kartki pogrzebowe." Accessed May 16, 2013. www.cmentarium.sowa.website.pl.

—. "Na marginesie tematyki cmentarnej. Nekrolog." Accessed May 16, 2013. www.cmentarium.sowa.website.pl.

Corona Marzol, Isabel. "Coming out of the Closet 'Six Feet Under': Textual Silences and the Social Construction of the Family Stage in the Obituary Genres." *Revista Alicantina de Estudios Ingleses* 19 (2006): 67–82.

Crespo Fernández, Eliecer. "Linguistic Devices Coping with Death in Victorian Obituaries." *Revista Alicantina de Estudios Ingleses* 20 (2007): 7–21.

Crystal, David. *Language and the Internet.* Cambridge: Cambridge University Press, 2004.

Funeral Consumers Information Society. "Writing Tips for New Obituarists." Accessed June 4, 2013. http://www.funeralinformationsociety.org/yourlastwrites/history.html.

Gilbert Holly S. "A Brief History of the Obituary." Funeral Consumers Information Society. Accessed June 4, 2013. http://www.funeralinformationsociety.org/yourlastwrites/history.html.

Grzesiak, Romuald. "O sposobach wyrażania wartości w tekstach nekrologów." In *Język a kultura: Wartości w języku i tekście, vol. 3,* edited by Jadwiga Puzynina and Janusz Anusiewicz, 76–93. Wrocław: Wiedza o Kulturze, 1991.

Kaptur, Ewa. "Wartościowanie osób zmarłych w poznańskich nekrologach prasowych." In *Antynomie wartości. Problematyka aksjologiczna w językoznawstwie,* edited by Agnieszka Oskiera, 329–339. Łódź: Wydawnictwo Wyższej Szkoły Humanistyczno-Ekonomicznej w Łodzi, 2007.

Kolbuszewski, Jacek. "Z głebokim żalem, czyli nekrolog życia." *Dziennik Zachodni,* October 29, 2009. Accessed August 8, 2013. http://www.dziennikzachodni.pl/artykul/179166,z-glebokim-zalem-czyli-nekrolog-zycia,id,t.html?cookie=1.

Kolbuszewski, Jacek. *Z głębokim żalem... O współczesnej nekrologii.* Wrocław: Wydawnictwo Uniwersytetu Wrocławskiego, 1997.

Kściuczyk, Joanna. "Wartościowanie we współczesnych nekrologach." In *Antynomie wartości. Problematyka aksjologiczna w językoznawstwie,* edited by Agnieszka Oskiera, 315–328. Łódź: Wydawnictwo Wyższej Szkoły Humanistyczno-Ekonomicznej w Łodzi, 2007.

Legacy.com. "About Legacy.com, Inc." Accessed June 4, 2013. www.Legacy.com/NS/about.

Martin, John. *The Obituary – A Genre Analysis*. North Carolina State University. Accessed July 30, 2013. http://www.nematome.info/RevisedGenreAnalysisJohnMartin.pdf.

Readership Institute. "Obituary Best Practices Gallery." Accessed June 10, 2013. http://www.readership.org/content/obit_gallery.asp.

Wierzbicka, Anna. "Genry mowy." In *Tekst i zdanie*, edited by Teresa Dobrzyńska and Elżbieta Janus, 125–137. Wrocław: Ossolineum, 1983.

Contributors

Les Back, Professor of Sociology, Goldsmiths College, University of London (l.back@gold.ac.uk)

Jolanta Bartyzel-Szymkowska, Assistant Professor, Jagiellonian University Institute of American Studies and Polish Diaspora (jolanta bartyzel-szymkowska@uj.edu.pl)

Anne Bizub, Associate Professor of Psychology, Elmira College, NY (a.bizub@elmira.edu)

Alina Bothe, Research Fellow, Centre for Jewish Studies, University of Berlin-Brandenberg (a.bothe@zentrum-juedische-studien.de)

Ciro Marcondes Filho, Professor of Communication and Journalism, University of Sao Paolo (ciromarcondesfilho@gmail.com)

Ann Gunkel, Associate Professor of Cultural Studies and Humanities, Columbia College Chicago (gunkelweb@gmail.com)

David Gunkel, Presidential Teaching Professor, Department of Communication, North Illinois University (dgunkel@niu.edu)

Yasmin Gunaratnam is a Senior Lecturer in the Department of Sociology, Goldsmiths College University of London (y.gunaratnam@gold.ac.uk)

Irem Inceoglu, Assistant Professor, Faculty of Communication, Kadir Has University (irem.inceoglu@khas.edu.tr)

CM Olavarria, Independent Scholar, digitalself@gmx.fr

Douglas Ponton, Researcher in English Language, Department of Political and Social Sciences, University of Catania (dmponton @hotmail.co.uk)

Garry Robson, Associate Professor of Sociology, Jagiellonian University Institute of American Studies and Polish Diaspora (garry.robson@uj.edu.pl)

Jasmin Siri, Associate Professor, Institute of Sociology, Ludwig-Maximilians University Munich (*jasmin.siri*@soziologie.uni-*muenchen*.de)

Agnisezka Stasiewicz-Beinkowska, Assistant Professor, Jagiellonian University Institute of American Studies and Polish Diaspora (a.stasiewicz-bienkowska@uj.edu.pl)

Magdalena Szczyrbak, Assistant Professor, Jagiellonian University Institute of English Philology (Magdalena.szczyrbak@uj.edu.pl)

Marek Wojtaszek, Assistant Professor in the Humanities, Department of Transatlantic and Media Studies & Women's Studies Center, University of Lodz (marek_wojtaszek@uni.lodz.pl)

Malgorzata Zachara, Assistant Professor, Jagiellonian University Institute of American Studies and Polish Diaspora (malgorzata.zachara@uj.edu.pl)

INDEX

A

Aboujaoude, Elias 47
Ahmed, Sara...............................102
Althusser, Louis 19
'anchoring' 14, 87
Annabel, Lucas...........................175
Appiah, Kwame Anthony...........166
Aristotle.....................................278
autonomy.................37, 58, 61, 208
Avey, Denis................................266

B

Barnett, Clive 98
Barthes, Roland 150
Bastian, Michelle..........................94
Bateson, Gregory........................208
Baudrillard, Jean 60, 131
Bauman, Zygmunt..... 195, 236, 240, 243, 244, 260
Beck, Ulrich 184, 185
Beer, David 114
Benjamin, Walter 102
Berger, Peter..........................12, 21
Berkowitz, Ben 253
Black-Hughes, Christine 172
body, the..................20, 30, 64, 204
Bourdieu, Pierre 21
Brooks, David 62
Bublitz, Hannelore 239
Butler, Judith..............................240
Bzdoń, Jadwiga 302

C

Cain, Jeff....................................174
Carr, E.H. 214
Carr, Nicholas 37
Cartesian 20, 22, 25, 157
Castronova, Edward 131
Cemalcilar, Zeynep 123
Chang, Brankl 157
Clark, Nigel 98
cocoon, social 5, 12, 29, 193, 205, 209
cognitive reformatting 64
Cohen, Jared 59
Cooley, Charles Horton 20, 26
Corona Marzol, Isabel 303
cosmopolitanism 167, 183, 186
couchsurfing 86
Crang, Mike 87
Crespo Fernández, Eliecer......... 304
Crystal, David............................ 308
Csordas, Thomas 21
cyberspace ..128, 145, 151, 218, 220
'cyberspace citizens'.................... 74

D

Delanty, Gerard 185
Deleuze, Gilles 65, 68
Dervin, Fred............................ 2, 14
Descartes, Rene 24, 154, 155
Dickinson, Emily 70
digital detox 35, 39
digital natives ..5, 17, 122, 144, 149, 152, 169
Digital Natives........................... 145
'digital natives' 5
Dikeç, Mustafa 116
DiVall, Margarita 174
Dizard, Wilson P 214
DSM-5, the 41

E

Eco, Umberto............................. 187
Ellul, Jacques..........2, 19, 29, 40, 48
embodiment........................... 20, 21
empathy 26, 167, 202
empowerment 30, 96
ethnocentrism 167, 176
ethnography 92, 94, 113

European Union, the 184, 195
Evens, Aden 66
and existential philosophy 200
and existential shock 208

F

Facebook 3
  and face-to-face interaction 14
  and homophily 5, 18
  and managing vulnerability 3
  and narcissism 237
  and political communication .232
  and public diplomacy 213
  and self-centeredness 16
  and the individualization
    of politics 243
face-to-face communication 5, 8, 12, 134, 156, 200, 205, 225, 291
Falbo, Toni 123
Fanshawe, Simon 1
Foucault, Michel 158, 239
friendship 9, 25, 41, 206, 234, 240, 276

G

Georgakopoulou, Alexandra 277
Gilroy, Paul 1
globalism 166
globalization. 1, 4, 98, 201, 212, 226
Google 62, 121, 139, 261, 280
  and posthuman ideology 23
  and the internationalization
    of English 136
  as 'hive' 23
  as replacement for memory 46
  business model of 261
  Translate 79, 132, 133
Grande, Edgar 182
Gray, Kathleen 175
Grzesiak,Romauld 312
Gullion, Edmund A 219

H

Habermas, Jurgen 242
Hansen, David 196
Havelock, Eric A 157
Hayles, Katherine 25
Heidegger, Martin....... 3, 19, 21, 29, 36, 151, 157, 158, 159, 164, 165, 200
Heim, Michael 131
heterophily 7
homesickness 6, 190
Horn, Jurgen 74
Hubbard, Phil 75

I

immersion
  in cultural environment 189, 195, 200
  in culural environment 192
  in digital technology 2, 17
  in the virtual 65
Immersion
  in cultural environment 192
intercultural 1, 219, 220, 221

K

Kant, Immanuel 67, 98
Kaptur, Ewa 310
Keen, Andrew 18
Keneally, Thomas 266
Kennedy, Gregor 175
Kirwin, JL 174
Kitchin, Rob 75
Klein, Naomi 146
Kogler, Christian 22
Kolbuszewski, Jacek 302, 310
Kong, Ying 123
Korpela, Mari 2, 14
Kściuczyk, Joanna 299, 310
Kurzweil, Ray 23, 30

L

Labov, William 277, 285
Lanier, Jaron 18
Lanzmann, Claude 266
Larsen, Jonas 85
Leonardo, Micaela di 151
Levinas, Emmanuel 158, 203, 204
Lewis, C.S. 278, 295
Lewis, Norman 28

loneliness...........41, 56, 61, 79, 122, 199, 208, 276
looking glass self, the...................20
Luckmann, Thomas................12, 21
Luhman, Niklas.................231, 239

M

Mani, Mono...................................40
Marek, Roman............................262
Mason, Paul................................251
Massey, Doreen............................85
Massumi, Brian............................64
McLuhan, Marshall.....37, 138, 222, 234
Mead, George Herbert............20, 21
mediation......16, 60, 80, 87, 131, 207
mobility.......1, 4, 56, 64, 74, 75, 86, 97, 150, 152, 182, 187, 194, 217
Mobility.......................................97
Montaigne, Michel de 26
Morozov, Evgeny.........................18
multiculturalism 1, 185
Murthy, Suhir Rama.....................40

N

Nancy, Jean-Luc...........................54
narcissism...............................46, 61
neuroscience................................26
Newham, London Borough of......92
Nussbaum, Martha C..................183
Nye, Joseph........................216, 218

O

Obama myth, the.........................236
Obama, Barack...........................214
off/online merged 4, 5, 8, 12, 47, 88, 159, 270, 277
Ong, Walter...............................157
Other, the.....5, 6, 12, 55, 56, 58, 81, 149, 158, 167, 183, 189, 200, 203, 280
Other. the.....................................22

P

Phaedrus, the 129, 137, 156
Plato 129, 137, 154
Platonic.......................130, 154, 157
Poland................122, 133, 186, 190
Poles
    and cosmopolitan sentiment.. 186
Policastri, Anne 174
Polish Ministry of Science
    and Higher Education, the 186
posthuman, the......................... 2, 54
Postman, Neil 19, 36
Prensky, Marc...................... 17, 146
Proust, Marcel 204

R

Rautenbach, John B 172
Reid, Elizabeth 276
Riberio, Gustavo Lins............... 184
Riles, Annalise............................ 96
risk.............................13, 16, 47, 96
Rousseau, Jean-Jacques.............. 36

S

Schindler's List.......................... 266
Schmidt, Eric.............................. 58
Scruton, Roger............................ 25
self, the ...7, 15, 18, 20, 25, 29, 39, 47
Serres, Michael 209
Shoah the 257
Shwalb, David A 88, 122
simulacra 57
Simulated Partial Connectedness (SPC) 45
Smith, Timothy B 88, 122
social media
    and 'anchoring' 12
    and European identity 195
    and self-reduction 15
    and self-centeredness 30
    and the 'real' 5
    as public sphere 212
    'bubble'.................................. 14
    and classroom practice............. 6
    and cosmopolitanism 5
    and diplomacy...................... 226
    and employment recruitment .. 50
    and 'enframing'......................... 2
    Gezi resistance..................... 247

and immunuty to culture shock 191
and intercultural communication 4
and intercultural experience...1, 7
and millenials 164
and narcissism 27
negotiating unfamiliar space with 76
as political platforms 233
and reflexivity 1
replacing actual conversation . 129
and research methodology 4
and social capital 215
sojourning with 7
and virtual cosmopolitanism..183
and political participation 219
Socrates 129
solitude 49, 55, 62, 207
Sontag, Susan 149
Sriskandarajah, Danny 1
Stapleton, Laura 82, 123, 141
Steedman, Carolyn 95
Stoics, the 184, 185
surveillance 48

T

Taylor, Charles 21
techne 2, 29, 56, 157
Teichler, Ulrich 187
Thoreau, Henry David ... 19, 182, 196
Tilly, Charles 249
Todd, Sharon 185
Trilling, Lionel 61
Tuan, Yi-Fu 75
tumblr 102
Tumblr 125, 213
Turkle, Sherry 18, 95
Twitter
political communication on .. 232
public diplomacy 213
world leaders' use of 214

U

United States, the 122, 199, 266
Urry, John 85
USC Shoah Foundation, the 259

V

Van Moll, Christof 194
Veblen, Thorstein 121, 149
Vertovec, Stephen 2

W

West Ham United Football Club 102
Wolff, Stefan 188

Z

Zhao, Shanyang 96
Zuckerman, Nathan 18, 165